The Complete Book of American Muscle Supercars

Quarto is the authority on a wide range of topics.
Quarto educates, entertains and enriches the lives of our readers—enthusiasts and lovers of hands-on living.
www.quartoknows.com

© 2016 Quarto Publishing Group USA Inc.
Text © 2016 Tom Glatch
Photography © David Newhardt except where noted otherwise.

First published in 2016 by Motorbooks, an imprint of Quarto Publishing Group USA Inc., 400 First Avenue North, Suite 400, Minneapolis, MN 55401 USA. Telephone: (612) 344-8100 Fax: (612) 344-8692

quartoknows.com

Visit our blogs at quartoknows.com

All rights reserved. No part of this book may be reproduced in any form without written permission of the copyright owners.

All images in this book have been reproduced with the knowledge and prior consent of the artists concerned, and no responsibility is accepted by producer, publisher, or printer for any infringement of copyright or otherwise, arising from the contents of this publication. Every effort has been made to ensure that credits accurately comply with information supplied. We apologize for any inaccuracies that may have occurred and will resolve inaccurate or missing information in a subsequent reprinting of the book.

Motorbooks titles are also available at discounts in bulk quantity for industrial or sales-promotional use. For details contact the Special Sales Manager at Quarto Publishing Group USA Inc., 400 First Avenue North, Suite 400, Minneapolis, MN 55401 USA.

10 9 8 7 6 5 4 3 2 1

ISBN: 978-0-7603-5006-5

Library of Congress Cataloging-in-Publication Data

Names: Glatch, Tom, 1956- author.
Title: The complete book of American muscle supercars : Yenko, Shelby, Baldwin Motion, Grand Spaulding, and more / Tom Glatch.
Description: Minneapolis, Minnesota : Quarto Publishing Group Inc., Motorbooks, [2016]
Identifiers: LCCN 2016014511 | ISBN 9780760350065 (hardcover)
Subjects: LCSH: Muscle cars--United States. | Antique and classic cars--United States.
Classification: LCC TL23 .G645 2016 | DDC 629.2220973--dc23
LC record available at https://lccn.loc.gov/2016014511

Acquiring Editor: Darwin Holmstrom
Project Manager: Jordan Wiklund
Art Director: James Kegley
Layout: Becky Pagel

Cover: TOP: 1969 Yenko Camaro. BOTTOM: 1965 Shelby GT350. *Paul Markert*
Endpapers: The engine of a 1969 Yenko Camaro. *Paul Markert*
Title page: Front end of a 1969 Yenko Camaro. *Paul Markert*

Printed in China

Contents

Dedication 6
Acknowledgments 6
Introduction 7

Section One—The Dealers

Chapter 1	Royal Pontiac: Superstar Pioneer 11
Chapter 2	Yenko Chevrolet: Pure Genius 22
Chapter 3	Mr. Norm's Grand Spaulding Dodge: The High-Performance King 36
Chapter 4	Baldwin Motion: New York Minute Muscle . . . 47
Chapter 5	Nickey Chevrolet: Quick (With a Backward "K") . 58

Section Two—The Specialists

Chapter 6	Shelby American: The Legend, The Legacy 70
Chapter 7	Hurst Performance: Detroit's Image Maker . . . 96
Chapter 8	Saleen Automotive: The Mustang Reborn 109
Chapter 9	Callaway Cars: Automotive Artistry 122
Chapter 10	PAS, Inc.: Performance DNA 137
Chapter 11	Street-Legal Performance: Power Play 145

Section Three—The Manufacturers

Chapter 12	SVO/SVT: Unconventional Wisdom 165
Chapter 13	Chevrolet: Conquering the Green Hell 185
Chapter 14	SRT: Right-Brain Thinking 199

Conclusion 222
Index 222

Dedication

To my wife, Kelly. On a summer night in 1992, I hired her to help me photograph a 1958 Corvette with a very special story. Three months later we were engaged. It's been an incredible journey ever since.

To our children, Keara and Sean. They endured years of being dragged to car shows—and they survived.

And to my late brother, Ray. He bought the most gorgeous 1960 Oldsmobile 98 convertible imaginable when I was at an impressionable age. That car planted the seed of my fascination with automotive history. Thank you.

Acknowledgments

This book would have been impossible without the following people: David Newhardt, whose images grace this book—it's an honor, David; Scott Kelly and Terry "Zeke" Maxwell, who took time away from caring for loved ones to answer my questions; Reeves Callaway, a very successful businessman who always has time for my projects; Gary Patterson from Shelby American and Maxwell Matthewson from Saleen; Greg Rager, my former editor at *Mopar Muscle* magazine; Gary "The Local Brush" Kupfer and Phil Frank, both tremendous artists; and, last, to the Royal Pontiac Club of America, the Automotive History Preservation Society, Hurst/Olds Club of America, Saleen Club of America, Saleen Owners and Enthusiasts Club, Nickey Chicago, and SLP Registry—these organizations define the word "enthusiast."

Introduction

The story of the American muscle supercar has been told many times. My challenge was to take all those stories, wrap them together, and do it in a way that hasn't been done before. So many books focus on the Golden Age of performance, the 1960s and early 1970s. I understand that: I grew up in that era, and my first car was a used and speedy 1970 Plymouth Duster 340.

Because so many great automobiles have been created since then—despite the challenges of crushing government regulation, inflated fuel costs, and a roller coaster economy—this book is divided into three sections.

Section One: The Dealers

These speed merchants took great cars and made them supercars. Sometimes it was mild-to-wild upgrades, sometimes it was showing the Big Three how to do it—but the results were always spectacular.

Section Two: The Specialists

Like the dealers, these companies took the manufacturers' vehicles and turned them into their eras' supercars (and supertrucks). Their work with the manufacturers distinguishes them from dealers, as does the way they sold their cars and truck through the manufacturers' dealer networks with factory warranties. Some of these companies have survived but mostly with a different aftermarket-style business model.

Section Three: The Manufacturers

In reality, only giants like General Motors, Ford, and Fiat-Chrysler have the resources to engineer and build today's supercars. By necessity, they've triumphed over the regulators and special interests and are building the best vehicles on the planet.

The past half century has seen the creation of amazing automobiles at the hands of many brilliant, passionate people. This book is really about American exceptionalism, a reality that some people want to ignore or even suppress. That's why this is a story that must be told.

Tom Glatch
Elm Grove, Wisconsin
November 2015

SECTION ONE

The Dealers

Chapter 1
Royal Pontiac
Superstar Pioneer

Saturday night. It could be any town in 1960s America. Dozens of cars driven by young men cruise from drive-in restaurants to burger joints to coffee shops, meeting with other friends, looking for girls, or showing off their rides.

But this is no ordinary town. This is Detroit, Michigan, the Motor City. And the kids driving these hot muscle machines weren't always kids. That green '66 Coronet with the '57 Fury wheel covers? That was Tom Hoover, lead engineer on Chrysler's 426 Hemi. That white AMX? That might have been American Motor's vice president of design, Dick Teague. And that white Firebird you sometimes saw late at night? John Z. DeLorean, general manager of Pontiac Motor Division.

Today, anthropologists would call these young people "baby boomers," the generation born in the two decades following World War II. The first of these postwar babies came of age in the early 1960s, while the great majority reached adulthood by the end of the decade. Where their parents had lived through the Great Depression and World War II—and were forever influenced by the austerity, sacrifice, and shared hardship of that era—the boomers themselves saw things differently. Jobs were plentiful in the 1950s and 1960s, and these kids spent money freely. They were also highly mobile and could be downright rebellious. Few adults "got" this new generation, this "youth market."

Over at Pontiac Motor Division, General Manager Semon "Bunkie" Knudsen was one leader who *got* it. So did his chief engineer, Elliot M.

LEFT: The Super Duty Catalinas went on a serious diet, with aluminum front fenders, hood, and bumpers. Most dealers knew nothing about the Super Duty program, but Royal Pontiac did.

PREVIOUS PAGES: The 1970 Baldwin Motion Phase III Camaro was a sublime beauty of automotive engineering.

11

Asa "Ace" Wilson Jr. wanted nothing to do with his family's dairy business. Wilson's Dairy Store, one of the big names in the Detroit area, was located on Mack Avenue and Lenox Street. It appeared briefly in the 2002 movie *Eight Mile*.

"Pete" Estes, an up-and-coming engineer named John Zachery DeLorean, and Jim Wangers, the young account manager for Pontiac's advertising agency, MacManus, John & Adam. They all understood what the kids wanted: it was the start of a convergence of talent and events that led to historic vehicle design.

In 1959, a new Pontiac dealership opened on Main Street in the Detroit suburb of Royal Oak. The proprietor, Asa "Ace" Wilson Jr., was a baby boomer himself. He was a member of the family that ran Ira Wilson & Sons Dairy, a popular hangout for Motor City kids, famous for the giant fiberglass cow's head that looked down on Wilson's main plant and at least one of their stores. The Wilson's Dairy Store on Mack Avenue and Lenox Street was even seen briefly in the 2002 movie *Eight Mile* in a scene where Eminem aims at it with a pink paintball. But Ace Wilson Jr. wanted nothing to do with the milk and ice cream business—cars were more his taste, and his father bought the dealership in Royal Oak.

Bunkie Knudsen had gotten Pontiac engineering involved in high-performance vehicles after taking over the division in 1956. The new Super Duty Group consisted of engineers Malcolm "Mac" McKeller and Russ Gee in engine development, with Bill Collins in chassis engineering. Stock car racing, both in NASCAR in the South and USAC in the Midwest, was their first focus, and it got to the point where the joke in the pits was, "It will be a good race if the Pontiacs don't show up."

Then the Super Duty Group turned their attention to the nationwide phenomenon of drag racing. Unlike racing on an oval track, drag racing was truly a participant sport. Anyone with a running car could find a class to compete in, and the stars of the big events were not the fast nitro-fueled rails or wild gasser coupes, but the Super Stock class and the Sunday "Top Eliminator" racers.

At the time, bad press due to the deaths of several competitors and fans in recent years had driven General Motors away from official involvement in auto racing, an agreement all US automakers signed in 1957. While Ford blatantly bypassed the agreement when it worked with contractors like Holman & Moody and Bill Stroppe, the high visibility of General Motors' position on the issue remained a roadblock for others. Only Pontiac chose to follow Ford's lead, encouraging the Super Duty Group to work behind these scenes with teams like Smokey Yunick and Ray Nichols to develop their dominant stock cars—now they were looking for a partner to front their drag race operations.

In his autobiography, *Glory Days*, Jim Wangers recalled this conversation with Bunkie Knudson in 1959. "Go out and find a dealer who would like to become a performance specialist, like a guinea pig," Knudson said. "I can't guarantee him any money, but you can tell him that the factory is interested. Tell him that if there is ever an opportunity for us to do him a favor, he can count on it." Packer Pontiac, a hugely successful dealership with stores in Detroit, Flint, and in Florida, wasn't interested. Ace Wilson, however, had different ideas.

Royal Bobcat Catalina 1961

Royal's first race car was a 1959 Coronado Red Catalina Hardtop Coupe with 389-cubic-inch "tri-power" engine and three-on-the-tree manual transmission. Pontiac was yet to offer floor-mounted shifters, and aftermarket conversions weren't allowed, so Royal's drivers had to use the column shift. Wangers remembers a best time of about 13.93 seconds, but shifting—and, ultimately, the car's times—were inconsistent.

Things improved in 1960, when Royal was able to get a stripped Catalina that included some of the first over-the-counter Super Duty parts and the first factory-installed, floor-shifted four-speed. Drag racing's biggest event, the National Hot Rod Association (NHRA) Nationals on Labor Day weekend, returned to Detroit Dragway the same year. Wangers was driving Royal's '60 Super Duty Catalina, tuned by their brilliant mechanic, Frank Rediker. It was time to make a statement, and Wangers did just that.

Wangers beat a field of fifty-five cars in Saturday night's Super Stock Eliminator event. Then, in the big Top Stock Eliminator on Labor Day, Wangers worked his way through the field, racing another Pontiac sponsored by Royal in the final. It was Pontiac versus Pontiac on the biggest stage in drag racing, and Wangers prevailed. Super Duty had scored its first win, and the first victory of a Pontiac in a national drag race event.

Though Royal Pontiac couldn't sell the ultra-rare Super Duty racers for street use, performance Pontiacs were available at the dealership. To bring the Royal touch to the street, a version was packaged in the special '61 Catalina called the Royal Bobcat. Most Royal Bobcats were powered by the Tri-Power 389 "A" engine

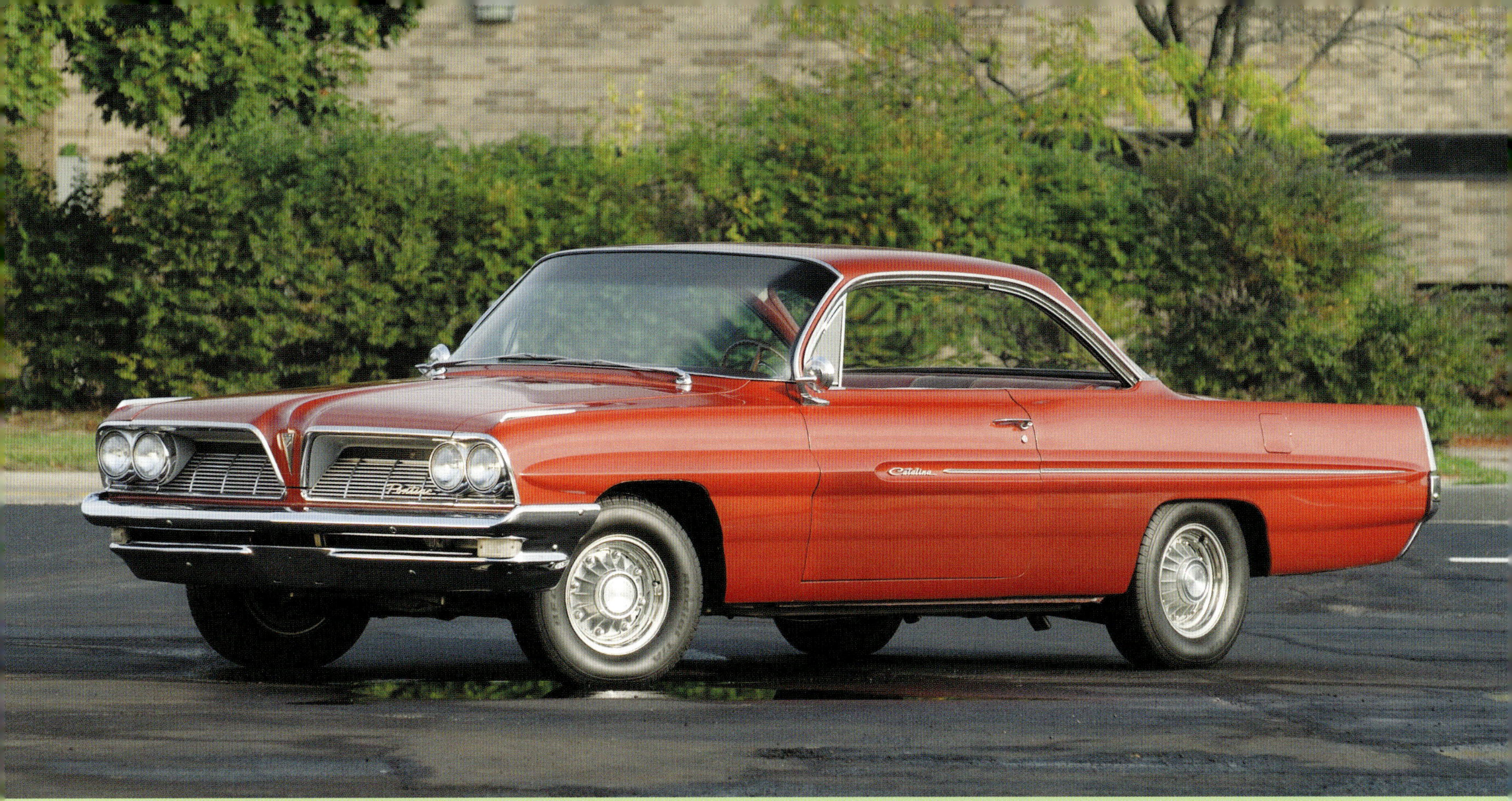

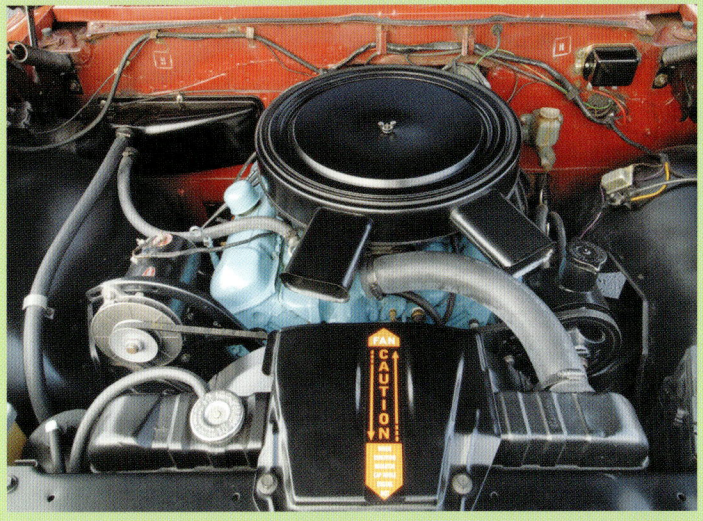

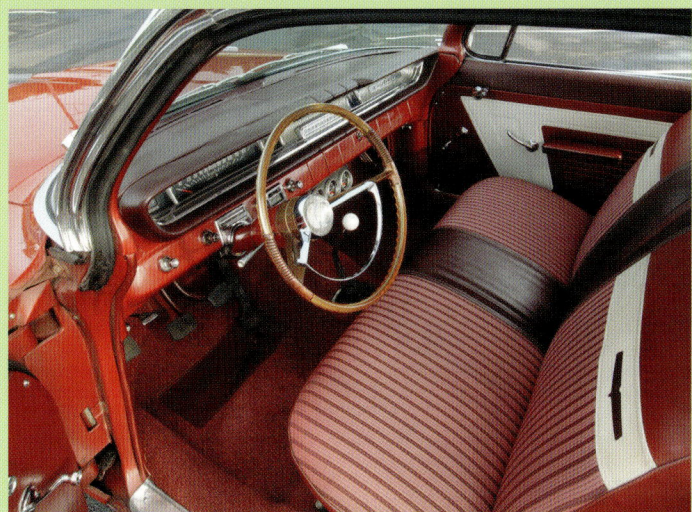

TOP: The Pontiac Catalina was the cream of the performance crop in 1961. Add a Royal Pontiac tune, and nothing could top it. The most expensive option was the Tri-Power 389, going for $168.40. This Catalina was purchased new from Royal Pontiac.

ABOVE, LEFT: Keep it simple, and the hot '61 Catalina could be yours for just over $3,100. Hiding under the giant air cleaner is the Tri-Power 389 "A" engine, good for about 348 horsepower.

ABOVE, RIGHT: Four-on-the-floor was still a rare sight in 1961, but Pontiac paved the way for the future.

RIGHT: What could a Royal Pontiac tune give you? The quarter mile in 13.02 seconds at 116 miles per hour—a shocking number for 1961.

AN OFFICIAL TIMED RUN AT THE

DETROIT DRAGWAY

THE WORLD FAMOUS
DETROIT DRAGWAY
DIX AT SIBLEY ROAD • 1 MILE OFF TELEGRAPH

CAR NO. ________ MAKE AND YEAR ________

ELAPSED TIME ________ MILES PER HOUR ________

NHRA approved Chrondek Electronic Timing
for accuracy and dependability

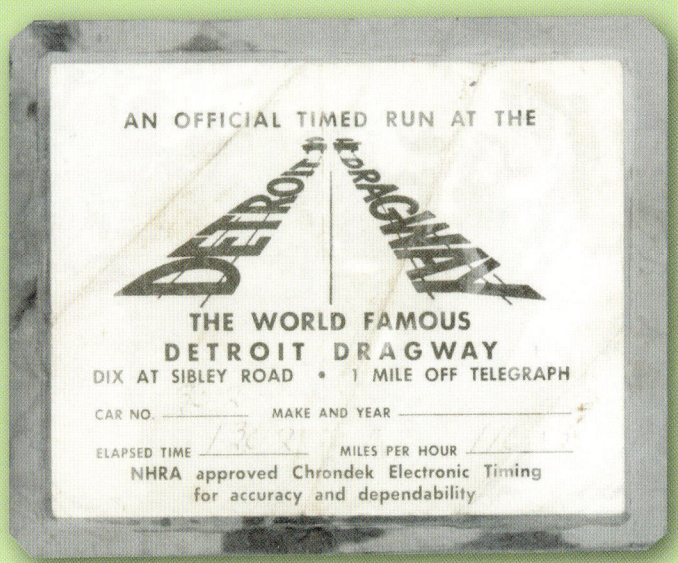

TOP: Pontiacs dominated drag racing in 1962, and the Royal Pontiac Super Duty was one of the best.

ABOVE, LEFT: The Super Duty 421 Catalinas used dual Carter AFB four-barrels, not the Tri-Power setups from the street. The Super Duty was rated at 405 horsepower.

ABOVE, RIGHT: Only the tach mounted on the steering column indicates that this is more than just another '62 Catalina. Note the column shift.

and four-speed manual, though an automatic was available. The vehicles were equipped with heavy-duty suspension, a performance rear-axle ratio, a tachometer, and Pontiac's famed eight-bolt wheels painted to match the body. Royal also added their tune-up package, with thin head gaskets, recurved distributor, progressive carb linkage, and other performance touches.

And the name? That came from a little automotive Scrabble: Pontiacs of that era had their names spelled out in identically sized, individually cast letters along the trunk lid, and Wangers "played around with the letters in 'Catalina' and 'Bonneville' to see if I could come up with a catchy name. It didn't take long to come up with the word 'Bobcat' . . . and it looked like it came right out of the factory."

The first real performance car for the street was born.

Royal Bobcat Catalina & Grand Prix 1962

The culmination of the Super Duty Group's work was evident on the cover of the May 1962 issue of *Motor Trend*. Coverage included the Daytona 500, which had been won decisively by Glenn "Fireball" Roberts in Smokey Yunick's Pontiac, and the NHRA Winternationals from Pomona, which was dominated by three Mickey Thompson Pontiacs tuned by Hayden Proffitt. Inside, the issue tested the first 421 Super Duty Catalina off the assembly line, driven by Wangers.

"A new factory hot rod that makes fantastic power a buyer's option," gushed reporter Roger Huntington. "The scene was anything but suggestive of the big blast to come—a cold, gray January day, timing tower all locked up, puddles of ice and water down the center of the strip . . . and BOOM. Wangers got into that big Poncho, and we

14 CHAPTER 1

TOP: The 1962 Royal Bobcat Grand Prix has a striking pose, thanks to the added gold paint and Pontiac's "Wide-Track" look.

ABOVE, LEFT: The 1962 Pontiac Grand Prix's emblem was the inspiration for the embossed aluminum emblem used by Royal Pontiac.

ABOVE, RIGHT: The Royal Bobcat Grand Prix was mostly stock, except for the Hurst shifter and optional Pontiac tach.

RIGHT: In 1962, Royal Pontiac could build a Bobcat for you, or you could order the parts from Royal's new catalog.

Royal Bobcat Catalina & Grand Prix 1962

 # PRODUCED: unknown
ENGINE: 421-cubic-inch V-8
HORSEPOWER: 405
TORQUE: 425 lb-ft
¼-MILE TIME: 13.9 at 107 mph

The May 1962 edition of *Motor Trend* reported on what might have been Pontiac's finest hour—the victories at the Daytona 500 and the Winternationals. A Royal Bobcat Catalina was also road-tested in the issue. *Author's Collection*

The May 1962 issue of *Motor Trend* featured a full-page ad illustrating all the performance parts available from Pontiac. *Author's Collection*

went." With nothing more than a spark advance check and valve lash adjustment, Wangers went 13.9 at 107 miles per hour. "In its fresh-off-the-assembly-line form, the big Pontiac stands a good chance of taking Stock Eliminator at any drag strip," Huntington continued. Proof of that came at Pomona a month later.

Most significantly, the Super Duty package was now offered as a factory-installed option. Until 1962, fewer than a dozen in-the-trunk Super Duty cars had been built, sold only to insiders like Royal Pontiac, Mickey Thompson, and Arnie "The Farmer" Beswick. Also significant: a Hurst four-speed shifter was installed at the factory with the Super Duty package. While the $1,342.85 Super Duty option was much too expensive for anyone other than serious racers, Royal Pontiac could still deliver street performance that was close to the Super Duties

in any Catalina. With the new Catalina-based Grand Prix, speed enthusiasts had an even more stylish Pontiac, with no compromise in performance, thanks to the Bobcat package. Royal could build a Bobcat for you, or you could order the parts from Royal's new catalog. The Bobcat phenomenon was breaking out nationwide.

The First GTO 1964

The following year was tough for Pontiac and the Super Duty Group: the new Pontiacs were larger and heavier. Even with the most drastic of diets (the infamous "Swiss Cheese" Super Duties), the cars were losing ground to the competition. A further blow to the line came on January 24, 1963, when General Motors renewed its rejection of auto racing. With the US government concerned about monopolies (GM held nearly 60 percent of the US automobile market) and threatening to force the division of Chevrolet from its parent company, GM was determined to be the best corporate citizen possible.

This meant no more Super Duty cars, no more factory support, and little "backdoor" covert engineering coming through places like Royal Pontiac. The division's chief engineer, DeLorean, understood there was no getting around the anti-racing mandate. A month later, a Ford won the Daytona 500.

Throughout this period, DeLorean visited the engineering buildings at the Milford Proving Grounds on Saturday mornings to keep up with his team's latest work. The original Tempest was a front-engine/rear-drive compact that shared the Corvair's platform, transaxle, and independent rear suspension. For 1964, the Tempest was slated to be a new "Intermediate" class car, with a full frame and regular rear suspension. The original plans called for the 326 V-8 as a top engine option for the Tempest, but, in the early spring of 1963, Chassis Engineer Jim Collins had an idea.

That Saturday morning, a '64 Tempest prototype was up on a lift. "You know, John, with the engine mounts being the same, it would take us about twenty minutes to slip a 389 into this thing. We'll probably need some heavier springs in the front end, but the engine will fit right in." Engine Man Russ Gee agreed. The next Saturday, DeLorean was driving the same car, now powered by a 389 Tri-Power.

Spend any time in Detroit and you'll find out that real secrets among the Big Three are rare. There's no elaborate spy network, but friends talk to friends and word travels fast among the automakers. This time, DeLorean got everyone's promise that they would keep this innovation a secret.

Pontiac quietly unleashed the GTO as an option package, RPO 382, for the 1964 Tempest Le Mans. DeLorean knew he couldn't get management to approve the GTO as a separate model, but the $295 option didn't need approval. Dealers did have to place five thousand orders before the option would be released, but that took only a matter of days. The GTO was not included in the Pontiac full line catalog that year, but Wangers did create a separate catalog with the tag line: "GTO, a device for shrinking time and distance." By the end of the model year, 32,450 GTOs had been sold.

Fueling those sales was the cover story of the March 1964 issue of *Car and Driver*, pitting the Pontiac GTO against the ultra-rare (thirty-eight built), ultra-exotic $18,000 Ferrari GTO racer. The magazine assured Wangers that they had already tested the Ferrari and were going to combine their test results of the Pontiac into the story. During the acceleration tests on December 29 at the Daytona Speedway, *Car and Driver* editor David E. Davis clicked off 0–60 in 4.6 seconds, 0–100 in 11.8 seconds. Quarter-mile numbers were 13.1 seconds at 115 miles per hour.

In the story, *Car and Driver* proclaimed, "The Pontiac will beat the Ferrari in a drag race, and the Ferrari will go around any American road circuit faster than the stock GTO." But, they added, "our test car, with stock suspension, metallic brakes and as-tested 348-bhp engine will lap any U.S. road course faster than any Ferrari street machine, including the 400 Superamerica." They also had one final jab at the Italian company: "Ferrari never built enough GTOs to earn the name anyway—just to be on the safe side though, Pontiac built a faster one."

Little did *Car and Driver* know that the red GTO used for the tests was running a stock-looking Royal-built 421 engine. Though they were told the GTO had been given the Royal Bobcat treatment, it only came out decades later that the 389 under the hood was something else. In fact, *Car and Driver* never tested a Ferrari GTO, and the entire story was something of a "what-if" fabrication. Ultimately, it didn't matter—the story was a huge success for both the magazine and the Pontiac GTO. The muscle car era was underway, and Royal Pontiac would play a part in it.

As GTO sales exploded, so did Royal Pontiac's. By 1966 they were selling more than one thousand Royal Bobcat kits annually, most through their mail-order catalog. The kit consisted of thinner head gaskets, blocked heat riser intake gaskets, larger carburetor jets, rocker arm locknuts, colder-running Champion J10Y spark plugs, and the necessary valve cover and valley pan gaskets to perform the modification. Since the 389 was particular about the ignition timing it could handle, the package also included a distributor recurve kit, which included Mallory points and condenser, and a new advance stop with lighter weights and springs. The kit also included Royal Racing Team Club decals, Royal Bobcat body stickers, a "GR-RRR" license plate, and Royal Pontiac license plate frames. While the ultimate and only true Bobcats were built at the dealership, the Bobcat kits turned any 389 Pontiac into a fearsome street machine.

Royal Pontiac Bobcat GTO 428 1968

General Motors created a new A-body platform for 1968, which meant the arrival of a new GTO. When it appeared, this car made everything else in the muscle class look positively boring. The shorter, more compact shape was sleek and free from excess trim, plus hidden headlights and the unique "Endura" rubber front

TOP: By 1969, the pioneering Pontiac GTO needed to get its mojo back, and the GTO Judge did just that. It was Jim Wangers's idea, though John DeLorean provided the name. But it took Royal Pontiac to deliver the real mojo for the Judge—when *Hot Rod* tested the Judge prototype, they posted a 14.41 at 99.55 miles per hour, while *Popular Hot Rodding* got their Royal Bobcat Judge to turn in a 13.42 at 108.42 miles per hour time. *Archives/TEN: The Enthusiast Network Magazines, LLC*

ABOVE: The actual 1964 Pontiac GTO used by *Car and Driver* in their famous Ferrari GTO vs. Pontiac GTO test has been restored. The magazine knew the GTO had been given the Royal Bobcat treatment, but they never knew a 421 replaced the factory 389 under the hood. *Tom & Kelly Glatch*

bumper made the GTO stand out in a crowd. The shorter wheelbase made the GTO more nimble, and under the hood the famed 389 was now punched right up to the corporate limit of 400 cubic inches. Sadly, the tri-carb induction system that had been a part of GTO lore right from the start was gone, due to another corporate dictate, but the new Carter Thermoquad four-barrel carburetor made up for the loss of two barrels. Add the top option of Ram Air induction and you had a very capable 360-horsepower performer.

The median age for muscle car owners in 1968 was twenty-seven years. Target a car for that demographic, get it right, and you have a sure-fire winner. As history attests, Pontiac got it right.

Royal Pontiac knew what was coming and was ready to turn its vehicles into Bobcats. Like all Pontiac engines, the big 428 was exactly the same size as the 400 in the GTO. In their February 1968 issue, *Car and Driver* reported on the transformation:

continued on page 20

The Blackbird Sings

This black-and-gold 1968 Pontiac Firebird 400 was not a Royal Bobcat, but the legendary "Blackbird" became an important piece of Royal Pontiac history—and Woodward Avenue lore.

Beginning in the 1950s, Woodward Avenue had a reputation for cruising and, sometimes, a little "competition." But by the late 1960s things had changed. The kids still played with their cars on Woodward, but the serious street scene had moved.

In a 1993 interview with your author, the late Tom Hoover, the Chrysler engineer known as "Godfather of the Hemi," talked about that era.

> By then the street races in Detroit had graduated from North Woodward. The cars had become so fast, it simply wasn't safe anymore. We would congregate at 10 Mile Road and Northwestern, then go out on I-696.

Tom Hoover's green 1966 Hemi Coronet was the king of I-696. With a set of A990 aluminum heads "borrowed" from Chrysler engineering, the modified Hemi was producing 560 horsepower, but the Coronet was also Hoover's daily driver, so it couldn't be too extreme. "It would run 116, even 117 in the quarter mile—just the way I drove it to work. I never made a pass in that car with the headers uncapped."

That Coronet also served as a development car for Chrysler's performance program. "It was good generally for our image as an engineering organization, how successful our organization was, to have the car to beat on I-696." But as employees of any of the manufacturers, it was imperative never to get caught.

> I kind of regret it now, but I never took any pictures of the car in an environment where it would be incriminating. I didn't want to have any evidence. Any time we did any serious racing I always had Ted Spehar drive. I'd be elsewhere . . . it could jeopardize the whole [racing] program if we were caught. Ted was under contract with Chrysler, but he wasn't an employee. It gave us some breathing room.

Tom Hoover's Coronet, with his trademark '57 Plymouth wheel covers—"I won the 1957 Nationals in a Plymouth; those became my good luck symbol"—ruled the roads until another legendary street machine was built, "The Silver Bullet."

"We managed to get the '67 GTX 440 four-barrel engineering test car into Jimmy Addison's hands," Hoover recalled. "We managed to funnel the right parts to Jimmy."

Addison worked at Spehar's Sunoco station on Woodward.

> My green car would run 117 miles per hour, but the Bullet would go 130. No nitrous, no funny stuff. It would run about 10.30 at 132 miles per hour. He ran it on slicks all the time; if it rained, Jimmy stayed home.

That became the silver target to aim for, and Wangers had a plan.

Milt Schornack and Brian Ballish from Schornack's Royal Automotive built the mighty 455 engine, with help from Pontiac engineers.

The times reported in *Popular Hot Rodding* and *Super Stock and Drag Illustrated*—11 seconds at 127 miles per hour—were purposely sandbagged to fool any competition. It held the unofficial title of "Fastest Car on I-696."

The black '68 Firebird 400 was purchased new by Tony Knieper, the parts manager for Stan Long Pontiac in Detroit. The Ram Air I 'Bird with column-shift automatic was ordered for Tony's brother, Ed, to replace the well-known '67 Firebird they were racing. Tragically, both brothers were killed in a June 1968 accident as they were towing the '67 back from the Great Lakes Dragaway in Wisconsin. Their family sold the barely used '68 Firebird to Wangers.

The car sat at Milt Schornack's Royal Automotive until 1970, when Wangers finally got Schornack and Brian Ballish to build "The Silver Bullet's" nemesis. Russ Gee and Bill Collins from Pontiac supplied an extra-strong 455 block. Tom Nell, Herb Adams, and other Pontiac engineers lent a hand. The Firebird was lightened extensively, and Wangers added "Light Peach Pearl" stripes as worn by the Royal Bobcats.

Ever the marketing man, Wangers got *Popular Hot Rodding* and *Super Stock and Drag Illustrated* to run stories on the development of the Blackbird, but the times reported in the magazines—11 seconds at 127 miles per hour—were purposely sandbagged to fool any competition. Driven by street racing legend John "Cheater" Politzer, Wangers's "Blackbird" now became the target. "It was very successful in and around the Detroit area and made a name for itself," Milt Schornack recalled. "Even the hot cars from down river would come all the way up, hunting for that car."

The Blackbird changed owners and engines over the years, but in 1994 Wangers was able to buy the car back. Wangers was relocating to California and needed to downsize; in 1997 he *gave* the Blackbird to Dr. Eric Schiffer. Dr. Schiffer, a chiropractor in the Detroit suburb of West Bloomfield, runs the Royal Pontiac Club of America. The club is dedicated to preserving Royal Pontiac's history, and holds social events throughout the year to celebrate Detroit's Woodward Avenue heritage. Who better to restore and occasionally fly the scourge of I-696?

Jim Wangers added the "Light Peach Pearl" stripes to give the "Blackbird" the Royal Bobcat look.

Royal Pontiac Bobcat GTO 428 1968

 # PRODUCED: unknown

ENGINE: 428-cubic-inch V-8

HORSEPOWER: n/a

TORQUE: n/a

¼-MILE TIME: 13.8 at 104 mph

continued from page 17

And now, speed-crazed sports fans, Royal Pontiac has outdone all previous piffling efforts with a car that should send Ralph Nader right into shock . . . . Yes, friends, for a mere $650 exchange, Royal will snake out that overworked little engine in your GTO and slide in the 428, all prepared for action.

This wasn't just a stock 428—it was a fully prepped and blueprinted Big Indian, built by Royal's engine master, Milt Schornack, producing far more than the rated 390 horses.

"Sleek and bulging with muscles, the 428 GTO is ready, even eager, to take matters into its own hands and send passersby scurrying up the nearest tree." The results: 0–60 miles per hour in 5.2 seconds, 0–100 miles per hour in 12.9 seconds, and the quarter in 13.8 seconds at 104 miles per hour. That's with cruising 3.55:1 gears.

Royal Pontiac RA V GTO 1969

For 1969, the option list grew with two more performance engines: the 366-horsepower Ram Air III, and the top-shelf 370-horsepower Ram Air IV. Those Ram Air cylinder heads were designed to move some serious air, but rumor had it something better was brewing in Pontiac Engineering's lair.

"Every winter, I made some arrangements to send a few of our press cars to Florida to do some timely magazine stories," Wangers wrote in *Glory Days*.

> Winter in Detroit put us out of business, and that meant no good performance press in the spring, when it was most important. In January of 1960, we brought out new '69 Ram Air IV Royal Bobcat to Florida. It was painted Crystal Turquoise with a special white accent, indicating a Royal Bobcat treatment. We wanted to remind people of the original 1962 Catalina Bobcat. This car would later appear in more magazine stories than any other car in Royal's history, fourteen in all. And it was fast. With a blueprinted Ram Air IV, a close-ratio four-speed, and a 3.90:1 rear end, it ran the quarter mile in the low 12.7s at 113 mph.

But Pontiac had developed a special "tunnel-port" cylinder head, based on the design used by Ford. Originally developed for the Trans Am racing series, its huge ports didn't work with the destroked 303-cubic-inch engine needed for that series. But as an over-the-counter Super Duty–like component mounted on a 400-ci engine . . . .

"We were asked by Pontiac Engineering to include the Ram Air V engine in our Florida testing. If it worked well, they agreed to let us get some very timely press, and satisfy the magazine writers," recalled Wangers.

Installed on the engine in the Turquoise Bobcat GTO, they underwent some side-by-side testing under the Florida sun. With the Ram Air IV, the GTO ran about 12.7 at 113 miles per hour. With the Ram Air V heads, they got to 12.82 at 114 miles per hour before spinning a rod bearing. "I think if we had been able to make more runs, we would have improved on those times," Wangers said.

> It was obviously more powerful that the blueprinted Ram Air IV, but remember, it was a committed racing engine. Unfortunately, Pontiac decided not to pursue a return to NASCAR racing, thus the Ram Air V engine project was allowed to die. No reports of our Ram Air V experience in Florida were ever released to the press.

That Turquoise Bobcat GTO has been restored to its as-tested state. A second Ram Air V GTO, painted Espresso Brown with Hurst Gold trim, was also built by Royal Pontiac, and that car has been restored. Unlike unicorns and the Loch Ness monster, at least two of the mythical Ram Air V Pontiacs exist today.

But as the 1960s wound down, changes were looming. Ace Wilson Jr. was rarely at the dealership, and his father was tired of babysitting his son's business. Royal Pontiac was sold, though Schornack created Royal Performance to continue some of the legend. DeLorean was promoted to general manager of Chevrolet, the most prized general manager position in the company. Without DeLorean as his champion at Pontiac, Wangers left MacManus, John & Adam to work with his friend, George Hurst, at Hurst Performance. America's performance pioneer was gone, but Royal Pontiac laid the foundation for the next half century of supercars.

Royal Bobcat GTO RA V 1969

 # PRODUCED: 2

ENGINE: 428-cubic-inch V-8

HORSEPOWER: n/a

TORQUE: n/a

¼-MILE TIME: 12.82 at 114 mph

TOP: If you were the advertising account manager for Pontiac in 1969, what would you drive? This is the Royal Bobcat GTO Judge owned by Jim Wangers. Wangers had suggested the concept to spark GTO sales, but John DeLorean gave it the "Judge" name.

ABOVE RIGHT: No question who owned this '69 Royal Bobcat GTO Judge.

ABOVE LEFT: This Judge didn't give much warning as to what it was packing—Royal Pontiac, not Pontiac Engineering, built the first Judge prototype.

The famous 1969 Royal Bobcat RA V GTO that was supposed to have been featured in *Hi-Performance CARS* magazine has been restored to its Florida test form. A bearing spun before significant speeds could be posted and no reports were ever released to the press. *Tom & Kelly Glatch*

ROYAL PONTIAC: SUPERSTAR PIONEER

Chapter 2

Yenko Chevrolet

Pure Genius

Some people are jacks-of-all-trades, which implies that they are masters of none. Much rarer is the "Renaissance man," an ideal evolved from Renaissance Italy from the concept taught by Leon Battista Alberti (1404–1472) that "a man can do all things if he will." Leonardo da Vinci was the quintessential classic Renaissance man. Example of a modern one? Don Yenko.

Yenko was not your typical gearhead. Born on May 27, 1927, he was class president in high school all four years, graduating as class valedictorian. He learned to fly at age fourteen, and he was an accomplished sculptor. Perhaps the most demanding of his interests was jazz piano, requiring superb technique plus the rare ability, as sax legend Charlie Parker said, to "forget all that and just wail." Don Yenko possessed a genius-level IQ of 140.

Yenko served as a meteorologist in the air force. After his discharge, he earned a degree in business administration from Penn State University, where he was president of the school's debate club. But Yenko had Chevrolet in his DNA; in 1957, he started managing his father's business, Yenko Chevrolet, in Canonsburg, Pennsylvania.

Yenko built ninety-nine 427 Chevelles, which put the Chevelle finally in the same supercar class as the Hemi Roadrunners and Coronets. *Super Stock and Drag Illustrated* was able turn the quarter mile in 13.70 seconds at 104.01 miles per hour.

22

TOP: Don Yenko's first race was in 1957 at New Smyrna Beach Airport near Daytona, Florida, in a stock three-speed Corvette with modified exhaust. He had been on vacation and got involved when he saw a sign that read "Enter for Sports Car Racing Here." He finished third. Later, of course, his cars would become legend at the racetrack, as seen here. *Yenko Family*

TOP, LEFT: Don Yenko's father, Frank, opened a Durant dealership, Yenko's Central Service, in Bentleyville, Pennsylvania, in 1929. *Yenko Family*

ABOVE: Few could have anticipated how legendary the Yenko name would become. From a modest lot like this one, the Yenko myth grew. *Yenko Family*

Frank, Don's father, had opened a Durant dealership, Yenko's Central Service in Bentleyville, Pennsylvania, in 1929. When Durant folded during the height of the Great Depression, Frank Yenko opened a Chevrolet dealership in the same location. In 1947, the Chevy dealership moved to 575 West Pike St. in Canonsburg, about 22 miles from downtown Pittsburgh.

According to a story from Chevy's house publication in the 1960s, *Corvette News*, Don Yenko's first race was in 1957, at New Smyrna Beach Airport near Daytona, Florida, in a stock three-speed Corvette with modified exhaust. He was on vacation and saw a sign that read "Enter for Sports Car Racing Here." Bluffing his way onto the track by giving the person at the gate an imaginary competition driver's number, Yenko found himself racing between veterans Paul Goldsmith in a newly released four-speed Corvette and Marvin Panch in the highly modified '57 Thunderbird "Battlebird." Both of these racers had factory support with the latest equipment. Though Yenko ran the entire race stuck in second gear, he finished in third place, with flames shooting from the rear of his car—the modified exhaust on Yenko's Corvette had set the differential housing on fire. He was twenty-nine years old.

With his new-found success in road racing, Yenko set up an area in the dealership devoted to Corvette performance, Yenko Sports Cars. The Sports Car Club of America (SCCA) B-Production National Champion in 1962 and 1963, and runner-up in 1964, he switched to A-Production and was Midwest Divisional Champion in 1965 and 1966. Sponsored by DX Oil, Yenko was able to buy the first 1967 L88 Corvette built, and, with Dave Morgan and Jerry Grant driving, was first-in-class and tenth overall at the Sebring 12 Hours of Endurance that year. The next year, Morgan and Hap Sharp was first-in-class and tenth overall at the 24 Hours of Daytona in the same Yenko Corvette. Then, in 1971, Yenko finished first-in-class and an amazing fourth overall at Daytona, sharing his C3 Corvette with Tony DeLorenzo and John Mahler.

Yenko Stinger 1965 Corvair

Thanks to the dominance of Carroll Shelby's Cobras and GT350 Mustangs, Yenko "got tired of looking at the rear bumper of Mark Donohue's Mustang" in B-Production competition. Yenko told author Greg Rager in *Muscle Car Review*, "I was racing when Carroll Shelby came out with his cars. I was pretty much a GM devotee as well as a Chevrolet dealer, so I got to thinking I'd like to be Shelby's counterpart in Chevrolet." The first result was the Yenko Stinger.

"I had already been talking to GM about building a sports car smaller than the Corvette," Yenko recalled.

> I suggested doing something with the Corvair. I coordinated with Dave Coe and Vince Piggins at GM, and with Dick Rutherford, Don Stickles, and Jerry Thompson at Chevrolet, who had already formed RST Engineering. We all decided to go for an SCCA letter-class car.

RST did the development work and testing to build 140 horsepower Corvair Monza engines into competitive race engines. By the end of 1965, RST was producing 210 horsepower from the air-cooled flat six.

With Chevrolet's support and RST Engineering's engines for the racing Corvairs, Yenko placed a special Central Office Purchase Order (COPO) for one hundred Corvair Corsa Sport Coupes, which included special dual master cylinder braking systems and 3.89:1 rear-axle-ratio differentials. One hundred cars was the magic number needed for SCCA homologation and, since the SCCA only allowed two-seat sports cars, the Stingers had carpeting where the rear seat was supposed to be installed. This might have been the first time a COPO, a tool for ordering fleets of taxis or trucks with special equipment, was used for a special build of performance cars from Chevrolet. One more sign of Yenko's standing with Chevrolet: Chevy owned the "Stinger" name, but he was allowed to use it.

The Yenko Stingers were available in a number of variations. Stage I was the basic 140-horsepower Stinger "recommended for street use," which included fiberglass rear-pillar landau panels and Stinger emblems, special fiberglass engine lid with spoiler, and dark blue stripes over white paint. Also included were tuned exhaust and carbs, good for 160 horsepower. Stage II was the "high-speed touring, rallying, or dual-purpose race machine," with higher compression, high-performance cam, and 175 horsepower. Stage III was the SCCA racers, getting as much as 240 horsepower from the RST Engineering powerplants. Stage IV was for "high-speed touring" and Stage V included fuel injection for "ultimate horsepower for off-street driving," but neither were SCCA legal. Perhaps only eight Stage IV cars were built, and possibly no Stage V cars.

Prices ranged from $2,200 for Stage I cars to over $3,100 for the Stage IV Stingers. The smallest Chevrolets dominated D-Production racing for years, including the 1967 National Championship for Jerry Thompson in his Stinger YS-005. Yenko's personal secretary, Donna Mae Mims, also raced her pink Stinger to many victories. After the original one hundred Stingers were built, Yenko created another eighty-five of the modified Corvairs over the next fifteen years. While not a supercar in the strictest sense, these little bombs paved the way for bigger and better things at Yenko Chevrolet.

Yenko Stinger Corvair 1965–1967

PRODUCED: 185

ENGINE: 164-cubic-inch flat-six

HORSEPOWER: 160 (Stage I); 190 (Stage III)

TORQUE: n/a

¼-MILE TIME: 13.6 at 97 mph (Stage III)

TOP: Other than a few small emblems, the only clue indicating that this is a 1967 Yenko Super Camaro 450 is the fiberglass Stinger hood.

ABOVE: All '67 Yenko Super Camaros were converted at Dick Harrell Speed Shop in East St. Louis, Illinois, and later sent to Yenko's dealer network across the country.

Yenko 450 Super Camaro 1967

- **# PRODUCED:** 54*
- **ENGINE:** L72 427-cubic-inch V-8
- **HORSEPOWER:** 425
- **TORQUE:** 460 lb-ft
- **¼-MILE TIME:** 13.50 at 100 mph

*Some experts claim there were 60 built

Yenko 450 Super Camaro 1967

Yenko could see the handwriting on the wall: the Corvair was doomed. The rear-engine Corvair was really no less safe than a Gullwing Mercedes-Benz 300 SL—both featured "swing-axle" rear suspension—but Ralph Nader's exploitative, anti–General Motors book, *Unsafe at Any Speed*, pretty much killed it. "Actually my timing couldn't have been worse," said Yenko. "The last one hundred or so cars sold very slowly." Chevrolet had already changed the Corvair to fully independent rear suspension by 1965, a year before the publication of Nader's screed, but the media frenzy sealed the Corvair's fate. As a Chevrolet dealer and friend of Chevrolet's racing director, Vince Piggins, he also knew of the imminent release of the Camaro. For 1967, all attention turned to Chevy's new pony car.

When it was introduced, the Camaro's top powerplant was the 295 horsepower 350 V-8, while the 325 horsepower 396 big-block was available after November '66. Working with famed drag racer Dick Harrell, Yenko developed a 427 conversion package for the Camaro. Yenko knew road racing, but the emphasis on the Yenko

TOP: Dick Harrell added a Stewart-Warner tach, three SW gauges, and the Yenko emblem to the glove box door. *David Newhardt*

ABOVE: The L72 427 engine was stock but "Yenko Tuned"—that was enough for most people!

26   CHAPTER 2

TOP: The Dick Harrell Speed Shop built this Butternut Super Camaro 450 based on an RS/SS model with disappearing headlights.

ABOVE: You can barely see the fiberglass Stinger hood from this angle, especially without a contrasting stripe.

RIGHT: This 1967 Camaro doesn't even say "427" on the spoiler, featuring only the small plastic "Yenko" emblem.

YENKO CHEVROLET: PURE GENIUS

TOP: Though Don Yenko made his mark racing Corvettes, he never produced a special Corvette model. His shop could, however, "Yenko Tune" any Corvette, like this '68 L71 coupe.

ABOVE: A "Yenko Tuned" Corvette would have been tuned by Warren Dernoshek, master mechanic for Yenko's race team.

Camaro would be *drag racing*, and even the seemingly limitless Yenko knew his limitations. Teaming with Harrell, a legendary drag racer known as "Mr. Chevrolet," was perfectly logical.

Whether a 350 or 396 car, Harrell replaced the original engine with a 427-ci L72 crate engine, the same fabled powerplant that was optional on the 1966 Corvette. The L72 was originally rated at a staggering 450 horsepower, still considered by some the most powerful Corvette engine from the 1960s; by October 1965, though, the engine was downgraded to 425 horsepower, probably to placate the insurance companies. Dyno tests reveal the 450 horsepower number was probably correct: stick-shift Yenkos received the 450 designation, while automatics were called the Super Camaro 410, as Yenko's horsepower designations matched the NHRA's factor for these cars.

With this much power on tap, Yenko also upgraded the suspension and brakes to match, and added his own styling touches. These included Yenko graphics and the unique fiberglass Stinger hood from Applied Plastics. All '67 Yenko Camaros were converted at Dick Harrell Speed Shop in East St. Louis, Illinois, where the L72 427 engine, Stewart Warner gauges, M/T headers, R/C bell housing, Autolite spark-plug wires, and Traction Master traction bars were added. To manage the weight and power of the L72, the front suspension was upgraded with Tuftrided spindles and shot-peened tie rods, steering relay, steering knuckles, steering arms, and ball studs. The Super Camaros were sent to Yenko Chevrolet, and some were then sold by dealers who were part of Yenko's network. Just one 350 Camaro was converted; the rest were 396 cars.

How fast was Yenko's missile? We have a pretty good idea. A Chevrolet engineer, Doug Roe, invited *Car Life* magazine to take his 427 Camaro development car for a blast. "That's my pet," Row stated. Why would a Chevy engineer build such a beast when corporate edicts banned their manufacture? "We want to keep abreast of what some of our customers are doing," he told the magazine. Those customers with reputations for performance included Yenko Chevrolet. With 4.88:1 gears, headers, open exhaust, and Goodyear slicks, Roe was able to crack a 13.5 second quarter at around 100 miles per hour, and felt he could get in the 12s with a little work.

Over 220,000 Camaros were produced that first year, but just 54 received the Yenko treatment (though some believe the number was 60). The typical cost for a Yenko Camaro in 1967 was about $4,100, over a grand more than a basic SS396. But speed costs money, right?

Yenko Super Camaro 1968

Building even fifty-four Yenko Camaros was a lot of work. It was also inefficient, with perfectly good engines and other components pulled from brand-new cars, only to be replaced with more new items. Then there was the logistics of shipping the cars from the St. Louis area to western Pennsylvania. Ever the analytical businessman, Yenko had to find a better way.

First, he severed ties with Harrell; it may have been due to a clash of egos, or just because of labor and transportation costs. Then, with 396 Camaros now mainstream, Yenko only bought 375-horsepower L78 396 cars for conversion. Instead of replacing the entire engine, Yenko purchased just 427 L72 short-blocks. Now his mechanics could reuse the original cylinder heads, intake and exhaust manifolds, and engine accessories.

Upgrading suspensions on the '67 Camaros was equally challenging. This time, Yenko used the COPO route again. COPO 9737, better known as the Sports Car Conversion option (named for Yenko Sports Cars), made life easier for Yenko's crew. The COPO

Yenko Super Camaro 1968

- **# PRODUCED:** 64
- **ENGINE:** L72 427-cubic-inch V-8
- **HORSEPOWER:** 425
- **TORQUE:** 460 lb-ft
- **¼-MILE TIME:** n/a

TOP: Don Yenko took conversion of the 1968 Camaros in-house. Styling touches included Pontiac 14x6 Rally II wheels, "Yenko" and "427" emblems, and a unique fiberglass hood.

ABOVE: The 1968 Yenko Camaros came with Pontiac 14x6 Rally II wheels with a special "Y" in the center caps and Firestone Wide Oval red-stripe tires.

9737 package included upgraded cooling and brakes, along with a 140-miles-per-hour speedometer, heavy-duty springs, larger anti-roll bar, M-21 close-ratio four-speed transmission, and a 4.10 posi rear differential. COPO 9737 was exclusive to Yenko that year.

For 1968, all Yenko Camaros started life as COPO 9737 cars with 396 engines. Since much of the work was now done right at Chevrolet, Yenko's mechanics could concentrate on engine upgrades and a few styling touches. These included Pontiac 14x6 Rally II wheels with a special "Y" in the center caps, Firestone Wide Oval red-stripe tires, "Yenko" and "427" emblems, and a unique fiberglass hood. Also added were Stewart Warner gauges and a Yenko emblem on the glove box. His mechanics were paid $140 per Camaro.

By year's end, a total of 64 '68 Yenko Camaros had been built, some of the most desirable supercars of the 1960s. But for Yenko, these cars came at a cost: "In 1967 and 1968, I had to cover the cars with my own warranty, with no backing from the factory at all," Yenko remembered. Considering the kind of abuse these Camaros could undergo, it was an increasing burden on Yenko Chevrolet.

Yenko Camaro sYc 1969

In 1968, Yenko was able to use the COPO to build a nearly perfect Camaro; the only thing missing was the 427 engine. Except for the Corvette, General Motors' management would not allow an engine over 400 cubic inches in anything smaller than a full-sized automobile. Chevrolet finally relented in the following year, thanks to pressure from Piggins, and allowed the 427 to be ordered on

Yenko Camaro sYc 1969

 # PRODUCED: 201

ENGINE: L72 427-cubic-inch V-8

HORSEPOWER: 425

TORQUE: 460 lb-ft

¼-MILE TIME: 12.59 at 108.07 mph

BELOW: Just 10 of the 201 Yenko Camaros built in 1969 were painted Olympic Gold, but only this Yenko, a pre-production car, had white stripes while the other nine had black stripes. This Yenko was pressed into duty in the spring of 1969 for a story in *Super Stock & Drag Illustrated* magazine, with famed drag racer Ed Hedrick at the wheel. Hedrick was racing Yenko's Super Stock Camaro at the time, and his times at the York US30 track revealed the street Yenko's true potential. By the third run, on street tires and headers with mufflers, he was down to 12.59 seconds at 108 miles per hour. Later, on slicks and open headers, Hedrick turned a 11.94-second pass, faster than the $7,400 ZL-1 Camaro the magazine featured in a previous issue. *Archives/TEN: The Enthusiast Network Magazines, LLC*

Like the COPO Camaros, COPO 9562 was available to all dealers, arriving from the factory with the Super Sport blackout grille with "bowtie" emblem, the Super Sport hood, black rear cove panel, twelve-bolt differential with 4.10:1 gears, and the standard Malibu interior.

a COPO. Perhaps it was because GM knew 454-ci engines were coming in 1970, or maybe it was the high visibility and positive press that Yenko's Camaros were receiving. No matter: for 1969 Yenko could get just about everything he wanted right from Chevrolet, all his crew needed was to add the "Yenko" trim.

Under COPO 9561, the Yenko Super Camaros were delivered right to Yenko Chevrolet, complete with L72 427 engine, Air Breathing hood with built-in sealed plenum chamber and throttle-operated solenoid valve, and positraction rear end with 4.10:1 rear axle ratio, or optional 4.56:1 rear gears. Transmissions were the close-ratio four-speed transmission or Turbo Hydromatic three-speed automatic transmission with column shifter (or optional floor shift and console). Power front disc brakes with steel wheels, optional Rallye wheels, or Yenko's own Atlas alloy wheels completed the package.

Once at the dealership, the distinctive "sYc" stripes, emblems, and embroidered headrests were added. Yenko's daughter Lynn and her friends were paid $5 per car to apply the stripes. Most importantly, these were true factory Chevrolets that came with the usual GM warranty. "A lot of local GM officials in other parts of the country didn't want to recognize the COPO as a GM car," said Yenko. "I have to give a lot of credit to the late Vince Piggins, who was a good friend of mine at GM. He went around the country putting out fires for me, telling all the zone managers these cars were in fact under full GM warranty."

The result was a spectacular performer. Ed Hedrick, a well-respected drag racer who had taken the "Dragonsnake" Shelby Cobra to a national championship, peeled off some demonstration runs at the York US 30 strip for *Super Stock and Drag Illustrated*. Yenko's Olympic Gold '69 Camaro prototype was running headers, a "massaged" L72 with M21 four-speed, and 4.10:1 gears. Hedrick turned a best 12.59 at 108.07 miles per hour on Firestone Wide Oval street tires, 11.94 at 114.60 on slicks. While the average sYc Camaro probably couldn't match this performance, it was indicative of what the car could do in the right hands.

Hedrick also raced an sYc Camaro, winning the 1969 NHRA Division One Super Stock Eliminator Championship. He scored the most points of any Chevy, and Chevrolet won the NHRA Manufacturer's Championship that year. Since GM had an anti-racing ban, drag racing was dominated by Ford and Mopar racers, so Yenko's victory was especially sweet. Hedrick's Yenko Camaro was featured on the cover of *National Dragster*, and Chevrolet sent copies to every dealer.

With their tasteful graphics, stellar performance, factory warranty, and availability through the thirty-six dealers in Yenko's network, the Yenko sYc Camaros were an instant hit. "We did extremely well the first eight months of the year, then the insurance companies caught up with us and started flatly refusing to insure the cars at any amount of money," Yenko recalled.

> This turned the last 100 or so cars into really distressed merchandise. We had a heck of a time selling them. I'll tell you, we'd take anything for them, even to the point of losing money. We even seriously considered transplanting our leftover 396s into the COPO cars just to try to get rid of them. Luckily they finally did sell.

COPO 9561 was not exclusive to Yenko Chevrolet, so other performance-minded dealers like Dana Chevrolet in Los Angeles and Berger Chevrolet in Grand Rapids, Michigan, could order the cars, but Yenko sold 201 of the instant legends—171 with four-speeds, 30 with automatics—all with the Yenko touch.

Yenko Chevelle sYc 1969

The Yenko Super Camaro hit the sweet spot for performance, but there was a whole legion of supercar buyers out there who wanted something a little bigger. For 1969, Yenko took the same formula and applied it to the midsize Chevelle.

Central Office Purchase Order 9562 added all the factory goodies, including the L72 427, onto the Chevelle instead of the Camaro. Like the COPO Camaros, COPO 9562 was available to all dealers, coming from the factory with the Super Sport blackout grille with bow-tie emblem, the Super Sport hood, black rear cove panel, twelve-bolt differential with 4.10:1 gears, and the standard Malibu interior. There were actually eight different variations of the COPO, though only Yenko's got their special stripes, emblems, and embroidered headrests to match the sYc Camaros.

In a reprise of *Super Stock and Drag Illustrated*'s Yenko Camaro test, the magazine tested a Yenko Chevelle a few months later. Running on stock tires at normal pressure, author Ro McGonegal was able to deliver a 13.83 at 102.97 quarter mile. Pretty good, but

> the rear tires were chopped to 20 psi and the front F70s were stuffed with 45. The trick worked—13.70—104.01 . . . . So look at it this way, if you want the roominess of a larger car, the scat of a smaller one, and the distinction of the grand touring class, the Yenko 427 Chevelle may just be your thing.

Yenko built ninety-nine 427 Chevelles, which put the Chevelle finally in the same supercar class as the Hemi Roadrunners and Coronets. What about Chevy's own super Chevelle, the 454-powered 1970 LS6? Empirical data and seat-of-the-pants evidence shows the LS6 was close, but no cigar—the COPO 9562 Chevelles were faster.

Yenko called his operation the "Leading U.S. Producer of Hi-Performance Chevrolet-Based Vehicles." Yenko Sports Cars had developed into a true automotive specialist. Like his friend and inspiration, Carroll Shelby, had done with Ford, Yenko had complete cooperation and support from Chevrolet, yet he was building the cars Chevy could not.

Yenko 427 Nova 1969

"That was the wildest thing we ever did," Yenko admitted to *Muscle Car Review*. Chevy's Nova and Camaro may have been spawned from the same platform, but the Nova was lighter. Being a compact sedan, it was also less conspicuous than a performance pony car. The perfect basis for another 427-powered Yenko supercar?

Since Chevrolet would not install the L72 427 in a Nova under a COPO, Yenko had to go back to his engine transplanting ways with these cars. Plain 396 Novas were ordered from Chevrolet without the Super Sport trim. Yenko then performed the L72 swap, added "Yenko" and "427" emblems, and nothing else. The cars were the ultimate "sleeper," with little to call attention to them. There was just one issue.

"The car was a beast, it was almost lethal," Yenko recalled.

> In retrospect, this probably wasn't the safest car in the world. It was way overpowered, and it really didn't have the right kind of suspension. To get the car to hook up at all, you had to have tires that were at the leading edge of the technology at the time. With the proper tires and the right driver, we had it clocked at 0–60 in under four seconds.

It was probably a good thing that Yenko only sold thirty-five of the 427 Novas. "I was really worried about that car, it was not for amateurs," he said.

Yenko Deuce 1970

Don Yenko called the Yenko Deuce his "insurance beater." A play on the Chevy II name, the Deuce featured a 350-ci LT1 small-block engine introduced in 1970. The solid-lifter LT1 was Zora Duntov's answer to the late, lamented fuel-injected Corvette engines. As Corvette's chief engineer, Duntov championed the superior weight distribution and improved handling of high-performance small-block Corvettes over the brute force propulsion on the big-block engines. He finally got his way with the LT1, which was also fitted to the Z28 Camaro that year. Producing 360 horsepower at 6,000 rpm in the Z28, 370 horsepower in the LT1 Corvette, the fabled LT1 engine came with forged TRW aluminum pistons, giving 11:1 compression. Also included were a heavy-duty starter, four-bolt main cap block, Tuftrided crank, special hi-lift cam, baffled oil pan, and transistor ignition. A high-rise aluminum intake, Holley 780

Yenko Chevelle sYc 1969

- **# PRODUCED:** 99
- **ENGINE:** L72 427-cubic-inch V-8
- **HORSEPOWER:** 425
- **TORQUE:** 460 lb-ft
- **¼-MILE TIME:** 13.70 sec at 104.01 mph

Yenko 427 Nova 1969

- **# PRODUCED:** 35
- **ENGINE:** L72 427-cubic-inch V-8
- **HORSEPOWER:** 425
- **TORQUE:** 460 lb-ft
- **¼-MILE TIME:** n/a

Hello and Good-Bye
My brief time with Don Yenko

BY GREG RAGER

As a fledgling freelance journalist, I was extremely apprehensive about my assignment. *Musclecar Review* editor Paul Zazarrine left no doubt for what was expected: "Go to Cannonsburg [Pennsylvania] and interview Don Yenko. Let *no* stone go unturned—you have as many pages as you need."

Don was an easy interview, answering my questions without hesitation, adding details where he saw holes needing filling. His memory was impeccable, and he opened his personal files to me for whatever I might need.

Fast-forward roughly two months: I received advance copies of the magazine with the interview, and made arrangements with Don's secretary to again visit the dealership on March 3, 1987, to give Don his copy. "I'll clear his calendar—you have him for the entire day," was Norma's response.

After reading (and loving) the feature, Don asked my plans for the rest of the day. I told him I had none. "Come on," he said, "we're going flying." And fly we did, in two of his three planes (mostly in a Cessna 210), visiting four different airports. Don had one and *only* one thing on his mind: he wanted to do his autobiography, and he wanted me to write it with him. No rational or logical begging off could dissuade him. Don was obviously a man used to getting what he wanted, and he wasn't buying my "I'm just a beginner at this" excuse.

"Hey, you wrote this—you can write my book," he said.
"But Don, we live 80-plus miles apart."
"Johnstown [my hometown] has an airport, doesn't it?"

Game, set, match—we agreed to think about what each of us wanted the book to be, and meet at the Johnstown airport for breakfast in two weeks. That was the last time I saw Don Yenko alive. He and three passengers died in the Cessna 210 two days later.

At his funeral we were treated to a recording of Don playing jazz piano (his greatest passion in life) along with the graveside services where Don had prearranged a mini air show to be performed over the gravesite during interment. I was unable to attend the going away party later that night at Don's favorite watering hole, where drinks were on Don, thanks to a fund set up for just that purpose.

Don had expressed one hard and fast stipulation where the book was concerned. "It has to be funny, because life's been a gas."

Greg Rager photographed this truckload of 1969 Yenko Camaros and Chevelles being delivered to Colonial Chevrolet in Norfolk, Virginia. Yenko would only sell complete truckloads of cars to his dealers. In December 1986 Greg interviewed Don Yenko. That story was published in *Musclecar Review*, just days before Don Yenko perished in a plane crash. *Greg Rager*

RIGHT: Always prophetic, Don Yenko saw the market changing in 1970. He debuted the Stinger II in 1971, a sporty Vega with the usual Yenko touches—front and rear spoilers plus Yenko stripes and emblems—plus a turbocharged four-cylinder engine. *Road & Track*, *Hot Rod*, *Car Craft*, and *Popular Hot Rodding* all loved the new Stinger, but Big Brother (the EPA) killed the project. *Archives/TEN: The Enthusiast Network Magazines, LLC*

BELOW: Don Yenko called the Deuce his "insurance beater." "We built 200 of the cars," he said, "and never heard a peep from the insurance companies." There were no "350" or "LT1" emblems, just the "Deuce" name. The Yenko Deuce could be ordered in 8 different colors.

Yenko Deuce 1970

 # PRODUCED: 175
ENGINE: LT1 350-cubic-inch V-8
HORSEPOWER: 360
TORQUE: 380 lb-ft
¼-MILE TIME: n/a

cfm carb, and 2½-inch exhaust helped the LT1 breathe. In other words, this was a mild race engine.

Yenko had Chevrolet create COPO 9010 to build an LT1-powered Nova right on the assembly line. Combined with Yenko's COPO 9737 Sports Car Conversion package, the Deuce had the powerful 350 engine with the suspension upgrades his 427 Novas never got. Those COPO 9737 upgrades included F40 heavy-duty suspension with a $^{13}/_{16}$-inch-diameter front anti-roll bar and a slightly smaller rear anti-roll bar, larger valving shock absorbers, and heavier springs.

"The insurance companies wouldn't insure a 427 Camaro, but a 350 Nova/Chevy II was a normal family car in 1970," said Yenko about his motivation for making the Deuce.

> It was not of the agent's concern that the 350 was the solid lifter LT1 Corvette motor. That car turned out to be a very nicely balanced package. We built 200 of the cars and never heard a peep from the insurance companies.

When *Car Life* tested the SS350 Nova in their January 1970 issue, they called it "a family car that goes well and handles better, a good car for a driver with passengers, or a fancier of trim and options in small packages." They got 0–60 in 9.3 seconds, and toured the quarter mile in 16.5 at 85.0 miles per hour. Now imagine that same basic sedan with real performance suspension and brakes, and a screaming 360-horsepower 350. That's the beauty of the Deuce.

Offering them for around $4,300—almost a grand more than the SS350 Nova—Yenko sold a total of 175 Deuces: 122 four-speed, 53 automatic. "All we were concerned with was the fun we were having building the cars," Yenko told *Musclecar Review*. "Sure we were making money, but we had a really good time with everything we were doing at the time."

The Post-Performance Years

Yenko planned to bring back the Deuce for 1971, and developed a COPO Nova powered by the new 400ci Chevy small-block. He also built a prototype '71 Camaro called the Super-Z, which would have used the same 400 engine. Sale of the Deuce was disappointing in 1970, and Yenko realized the market in 1971 was hardly receptive to potent Novas or Camaros.

He also debuted the Stinger II in 1971, a sporty Vega with the usual Yenko touches—front and rear spoilers plus Yenko stripes and emblems—with a turbocharged four-cylinder engine. *Road & Track*, *Hot Rod*, *Car Craft*, and *Popular Hot Rodding* all loved the new Stinger. The SCCA also promised to allow it to compete in D-production once five hundred were built. But the Environmental Protection Agency put a stop to the project.

Yenko then created a catalog and sold the Turbo Vega components aftermarket. His shop did the occasional one-off custom conversion, too. Then, in 1981, Yenko tried to reignite the magic with the Turbo Z Camaro. Performance was a thing of the past, but Yenko's turbo package promised to deliver decent performance without messing with the internals of the Camaro's engine. The '81 Z28 could barely muster a 17-second quarter mile, while the Turbo Z whistled down the strip in 14.52 at 97.81 miles per hour. Yenko offered a basic Stage I upgrade for $10,500, while the completely tricked-out Stage II cost $17,300, substantially above the base Z28's $8,000 price. Just nineteen Turbo Z Camaros were sold, only two of which were the Stage II versions. Car building wasn't fun anymore.

But Yenko was hardly sitting still. He competed in air races with actor Jack Lord (of *Hawaii 5-O* fame), played jazz piano and guitar, flew his Cessna 210M for business and pleasure, and did all the other things that met his criteria for fun. The dealership moved to McMurray, Pennsylvania, and became a Honda dealer. In early 1987, he talked to author Greg Rager about writing an autobiography. Then, on March 5, 1987, while flying into Charleston, West Virginia, Yenko's Cessna 210M, call letters N1230M, landed hard on the runway. The weather was light winds with broken clouds, yet the highly experienced Yenko lost control of the Cessna, and he and his three passengers perished.

Yenko Turbo Z Camaro 1981

 # PRODUCED: 19

ENGINE: LM1 350-cubic-inch V-8

HORSEPOWER: n/a

TORQUE: n/a

¼-MILE TIME: 14.52 at 97.81 mph

Don Yenko in his Subaru showroom. (Yenko Chevrolet had become Yenko Subaru in the late 1970s.) *Yenko Family*

Chapter 3

Mr. Norm's Grand Spaulding Dodge

The High-Performance King

Out of the thousands of new car dealers in the United States in the 1960s and early 1970s, just a handful understood the youth market. But only one took selling to the performance market and made it an art form: Norm Kraus's Mr. Norm's Grand Spaulding Dodge.

During the era when performance reigned supreme, Mr. Norm's was king. The Dodge dealer on the corner of 3300 W. Grand Avenue and Spaulding Avenue in Chicago's Humboldt Park neighborhood simply dominated the Mopar performance market. How dominant was it? Fully *one half* of the Dodge performance cars sold in America came though Grand Spaulding Dodge. Not bad for two brothers who wanted nothing to do with selling Dodges.

The 1970 Dodge Demon was an attractive car built on the same A-body platform as the Dart; Mr. Norm's made the Demon even better.

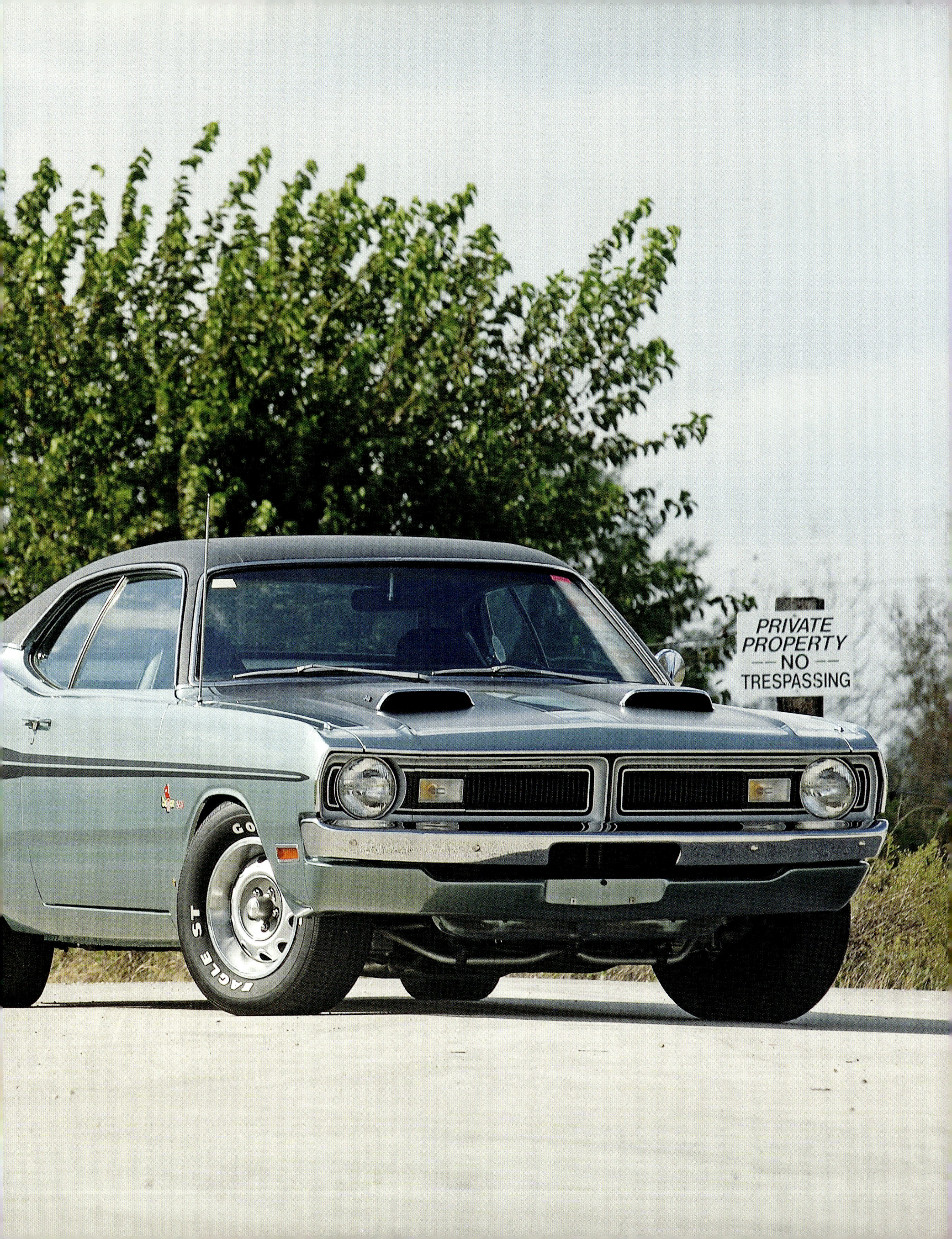
PRIVATE
PROPERTY
NO
TRESPASSING

TOP: In 1964, you could "Get with the GO Group" in a Hemi-powered Mr. Norm's Dodge, two years before Chrysler introduced the Street Hemi. *Norm Kraus*

ABOVE: Norm Kraus selling used cars in the 1950s. *Norm Kraus*

ABOVE, RIGHT: Grand Spaulding Dodge at its prime. *Norm Kraus*

RIGHT: Today, Mr. Norm's is just an old building where they used to sell some of the most competitive vehicles around. You could buy it and sell, well, whatever you'd like.

38 CHAPTER 3

Kraus's father Harvey opened a gas station on the corner of Grand and Spaulding in 1936, two years after Norm's birth. As teenagers in the 1940s, Norm and his brother Len began working there, making three cents a gallon pumping gas, checking fluids, and cleaning windshields—all the things service stations used to do. In 1956, the brothers decided to try selling used cars on the corner of their father's station. They made a tidy $60 profit on the first car they flipped. At age twenty-two, Norm Kraus was in the used car business.

Then something unexpected happened: a 1956 Chevy Bel Air convertible came into the shop equipped with 265 V-8 and three-speed manual gearbox. They placed a classified ad in the paper. With space at a premium, they wrote "Call Mr. Norm" on the ad. The next morning, I must have had twenty-five calls," Kraus told *Hemmings*.

> By 10 a.m. I had already delivered it. By 11, my brother, who was out buying cars, called me and I said, "Do not buy a regular car again. Buy all four-speeds." We got an education in performance from our customers.

The legend of Mr. Norm was born.

In the early 1960s, representatives for Dodge approached the brothers about establishing a new car dealership. Based on the Kraus brothers' reputation in the Chicago area, it made sense, but they initially turned down the offers. Chrysler rocked the automotive world in the late 1950s with their "Forward Look" cars, then the company made some market missteps and lost huge market share. Even the once-popular De Soto brand was dead by 1960. No wonder Norm and Len were skeptical. But once they saw what was in the pipeline for Dodge, including the 413 Max Wedge cars, they accepted. In 1962, at age twenty-eight, Norm Kraus was the youngest Dodge dealer in America. "I think the first month we sold about thirty-five cars. From that day on, it was totally performance."

By 1963, a brand-new dealership building was on the corner of Grand and Spaulding. A Clayton chassis dynamometer was available for installation the next year. "The first 383 we put on our dyno registered 180 horsepower," Norm recalled. "I said, 'What the hell is going on here? Let's set it up and see what she'll do.'"

Due to the inconsistencies of mass production, few performance cars of the era were generating the kinds of horsepower the manufacturers advertised. With a little work, Norm's mechanics got the Dodge up to 235 horsepower. "That's gonna be done on every car that goes out. Every high-performance customer is going to get a free dyno tune. When we sold a high-performance car, we had the car dyno'd right in front of the customer."

With salesmen typically aged twenty-one to twenty-seven, Mr. Norm's welcomed potential youth market buyers. When a new Dodge performance car was sold and tuned on the dyno, the sales process continued, as described by Norm:

> When completed, the dyno man would put a dyno sticker on the left rear quarter glass.

The car was then taken to the prep area where everything was checked out, including the installation of special ordered performance equipment (wheels, tires, headers, hi-rise manifold, headers, gears, etc.). When completed, a [Mr. Norm's Sport Club] members sticker was installed on the right rear lower glass or, upon request, the front lower right side glass.

Finally, the car was brought in front to be delivered to the customer with a key tag, T-shirt, and a license plate frame.

Then the customer was showed all the equipment that was installed and how to operate the vehicle. I came out when available and personally thanked the customer and let him know the sale did not stop there—it was just completed and I assured him we were there for any service necessary.

All new car buyers became members of the Mr. Norm's Sport Club. Others could join the club for $3. It was a social club with benefits, like discounts on all parts, invitations to Mr. Norm's Sports Car Clinics, 1,000-mile and 4,000-mile tune-ups, and occasional concerts by a local Chicago-area band, the Buckinghams. Norm knew talent—the Buckinghams later went national with songs like "Kind of a Drag" and "Hey Baby (They're Playing Our Song)," and were called "The Most Listened-to Band in America" by *Billboard*. Norm also had the Buckinghams record a jingle for Mr. Norm's radio ads, which were played frequently on WLS radio. The 50,000-watt station could be heard all over the country at night, thanks to the AM radio phenomenon called "signal skip" or "bounce." Since enthusiasts all over the nation were hearing the Buckinghams sing—"Get with the Go Group," "Be in the Go Group," and "Meet Mr. Norm"—Mr. Norm's offered any potential buyer a one-way ticket to Chicago to pick up the Dodge of their dreams and drive it home.

Customers of Mr. Norm's also got unprecedented access to the latest in Mopar performance technology. When Chrysler dropped the 426 Hemi on an unsuspecting world at the 1964 Daytona 500, only the top factory-sponsored stock car and drag race teams had access to the new, secret engine. The competition tried buying them at dealers, but they knew nothing about the Hemi . . . well, except Mr. Norm's. Just two years after opening the Dodge dealership, a 1964 ad for Grand Spaulding Dodge proclaimed "Get With The GO-Group With A Great New Hemi-Ram!" They claimed the Hemi-Ram, a Dodge Polara with a race Hemi transplant, was "the only production car in America guaranteed to run in the 11's—right off the showroom floor!" Remember, this was two years before Chrysler released the Street Hemi, and a year before the race Hemi's general availability.

A speed merchant like Grand Spaulding Dodge could have a bad reputation. Instead, "We have parents come in here with their kids and say 'I don't want him to have this or that,'" Norm Kraus told *Esquire*. "Later they come back and thank us for selling their son a car. They say, 'I know where he is now. He's working on the car.' The kids stop here before they go home after coming back from Vietnam."

Dodge Dart GSS 440 1968

Mr. Norm's influence with Chrysler was again evident in 1967. "Dodge was supposed to give us a high-performance Dart, to be competitive against the Malibu or the Camaro," said Kraus.

> And they said they had a high-performance engine for us. When we got the car in, the car came with a 273. Which right away I called up Dodge and said, "I thought we were getting a 383." "Our engineers said it couldn't be done." That was the challenge.
>
> I wanted the same thing that Ford and General Motors had. Give me something why the customers want to buy a Dart, why they want to buy a 383. Put a 330 horsepower engine in a car that's under 3,200 pounds, you got a little performance, if I could get it to the ground. And we knew how to get it to the ground.
>
> I called Denny (Hirschbeck) back in Parts, and I said, "Let's get a Dart in, and let's get a 383 engine, let's put it in a Dart, let's see what it takes to get it there." The next morning he comes in says "It's done."

Norm's mechanics cut off a quarter inch of the K-member to clear the oil pan and a hole near the oil pump was drilled and tapped so a modified engine mount could be attached. A heat shield was fabricated to keep the brake proportioning valve functioning in the tight confines, and a pinion snubber was added. Norm was proud of their accomplishment: "What an idea! What a performance car that we have here right now. This is the beginning of performance for Mopar."

Now what to call their creation? Dennis Hirschbeck in Parts was again summoned to find a letter to add to the Dart GTS emblem. "The only 'S' was this red 'S,'" recalled Norm. "I said 'Fine, it'll stand out. Now it'll be the GSS, which stands for Grand Spaulding Special.'"

First, Norm Kraus called *Car Craft*, and they flew to Chicago to test the 383 Dart prototype. The *Car Craft* testers were impressed:

> With the hood open, all you can see is cubic engine, as this "baby" occupies all the space from firewall to radiator and shock tower to shock tower. The fit really isn't that bad, though, as the stock engine compartment sheet metal retains its standard form . . . . The stock E-70x14 tires are worthless on this car, as there is no way they can handle the torque this engine puts out . . . . Even so, the initial times through the quarter mile were impressive. How does a 13.71 with a top speed of 105 miles per hour sound?

Then Kraus drove the Dart to Detroit. Dodge General Manager Bob McCurry was impressed, pointing out the heat shield by the brake proportioning valve. "Look at what the kids from Chicago built," he said to Dodge's top engineers. They were also impressed, and the 383-powered Dart GTS became a factory option for 1968.

Unfortunately, the competition didn't rest. The SS 396 Camaro became available to the public in 1968, and Ford dumped the unloved 390 in favor of the 428 Cobra Jet in the Mustang; The 383 in the Dart GTS didn't seem quite as impressive as it had the year before. Kraus knew that, if the 383 fit in the Dart, Chrysler's 440 Super Commando would, too. But building such a car at the cramped, ultra-busy dealership was out of the question.

Chrysler had turned to Hurst Performance to build the Hemi Dart and 'Cuda Super Stock drag racers for them. With Hurst's experience shoehorning a huge engine into the Mopar A-body—combined with their facility in the Detroit area to implement mass conversions—it made sense that Kraus turned to them. Chrysler's minimum order was 50 units, but for a dealer with at least 350 performance Dodges on hand at any time, that was well within the realm of possibility. All Dart GSS cars came with Chrysler's outstanding three-speed 727 TorqueFlite automatic, since it was feared a four-speed would destroy the Dart's 8¾-inch Sure-Grip differential, which was packed with 3.55:1 gears (no Dana 60 axle was available for the A-body). Power steering, power brakes, and air conditioning wouldn't fit in the tight engine compartment. The GSS rode on E70x14-inch Firestone Red Streak Tires.

Each 1968 Dart GSS was a special order vehicle, built as a 383 car, but it was delivered to Hurst Performance without the drivetrain, the same way the Hemi cars came down the line. The broadcast sheet for these models read "BUILD LESS ENG TRANS CARB AIR CLNR." Hurst then dropped in the 440 engine. Each modified Dart was inspected by Dodge service personnel at Hurst, then shipped directly to Grand Spaulding Dodge. The Hurst Performance conversion L68-1703 cost $363.65, and Grand Spaulding sold them for $3,788.00. With GTOs and many other performance cars selling for over $4,000, the GSS was a real deal. Or, as the Mr. Norm's ad said, "The mighty midget that's got what it takes to take what they've got!"

A year later Chrysler, continued the process, now referring to the car as the Dart GTS 440. Hurst Performance in Madison Heights, Michigan, continued to do the conversion. Built in batches on December 1, 1968, and January 14 and 31, February 14 and 21, March 29, and April 27, 1969, a total of 640 of the "M Code" 440 Darts were produced. No longer exclusive to Grand Spaulding Dodge, many were still sold by Mr. Norm. Those "kids from Chicago" did good!

Dodge Dart GSS 440 1968

- **# PRODUCED:** 50
- **ENGINE:** 440-cubic-inch V-8
- **HORSEPOWER:** 355
- **TORQUE:** 480 lb-ft
- **¼-MILE TIME:** 13.71 at 105 mph

TOP: The 1969 Dodge Dart GSS was a good-looking yet deceptive performance machine, packing a 440 Magnum punch. Only Grand Spaulding Dodge had it.

MIDDLE: Other than the "Bumble Bee" stripe and "GSS" emblems, the competition became wise to 440 power.

ABOVE: Denny Hirschbeck only had a red "S" in the Parts Department when creating the 383 Dart prototype. The tradition stayed with the production GSS 440.

LEFT: The 440 Magnum fit, barely. Norm Kraus autographed this masterpiece in '05.

MR. NORM'S GRAND SPAULDING DODGE: THE HIGH-PERFORMANCE KING   41

Dodge Demon GSS Tri-Power 1970–1971

Change was in the air in 1970, and those close to the performance market knew it. Carroll Shelby knew that Ford couldn't sell all of the 1969 Shelby Mustangs they built, and the leftover cars were VIN'd as 1970 models. Yenko knew the market was changing, too, so he introduced his "insurance fighter," the Yenko Deuce Nova. And America's "Hi-Performance Car King," Mr. Norm, was keenly aware of what was happening.

Chrysler introduced the Dodge Demon and Plymouth Duster in 1970 to great reviews. Both cars wrapped a modern coupe body on the venerable A-body platform, and both offered performance 340 versions. The 340 under the hood was packed with the best of everything: 2.02-inch intake valves and 1.60-inch exhaust valves, a high-rise dual-plane intake with 850-cfm Carter Thermoquad carburetor, a forged steel crank, and an oil pan with windage tray. It was a potent package in the lightweight A-body, and the 340 would float the valves at about 7,000 rpm, which was the signal for four-speed drivers to shift. Chrysler rated it at a very conservative 275 horsepower.

This became the basis for Mr. Norm's next Grand Spaulding Special. There wasn't much more you could do to the 340 for street purposes, except give it more air. This time, Norm followed Chrysler's lead. The Trans Am–inspired AAR 'Cuda and Challenger T/A were powered by essentially the same 340, except it was equipped with a setup of three two-barrel carburetors, which, along with a different head, was rated at 290 horsepower. Three "deuces" was hardly new, as hot rodders pioneered them in the 1950s, and GTOs and Corvettes had them in the 1960s; so did the Coronet 440 "Six Pack" and Road Runner "6 Barrel" cars of 1969 and 1970. The system was simple: in around-town driving, only the center two-barrel carb was used; stomp the loud pedal and the Holley floodgates open on all three carburetors. This meant better economy in normal driving, better airflow for wide-open driving than a single four-barrel.

Using parts ordered from Chrysler, the Demon 340 GSS was equipped with a similar 2x3 setup. One special Mr. Norm touch was a beautiful cast-aluminum air-cleaner cover with the stamp "Tri-Power." Loyal Mopar owners probably never realized this cover was a Ford part dating back to the early 1960s!

How fast was the Demon 340 GSS Tri-Power? No vintage road test data exists, but the tri-carbed 1970 Challenger T/A was good for 0–60 in 5.8 seconds and the quarter mile in 14.3 seconds at 99 miles per hour. It's easy to imagine that a dyno-tuned Demon GSS Tri-Power could do even better. That's one wicked Demon!

Dodge Demon Supercharged GSS 1972

Mr. Norm's 1972 Dodge Demon 340 GSS became essentially the prototype for today's performance cars. It was a new automotive era, one where ever-larger engines, higher compression, and wilder cams could no longer be used to create speed. He knew that significant modifications of the factory engine would raise the government's ire, so he performed an old hot rod trick: he installed a Paxton supercharger. The Granatelli brothers' centrifugal supercharger allowed Studebaker to wring good horsepower out of its Avanti, and Shelby was able to give a few GT350 Mustangs big-block-like performance. Now, in this brave new post-muscle world, the decade-old Paxton blower offered Mr. Norm a new performance tool.

The supercharger fed 7 pounds of boost to a custom-cast aluminum airbox around the factory carburetor. Mopar's 340 had its compression lowered to 9:1 in 1972 to accommodate the government-mandated move to lead-free gas. The lower compression allowed Mr. Norm's to supercharge this engine without internal modifications. The GSS package also included oversize pulleys, modified fuel pump and pressure regulator, heavy-duty oil pump and valve spring retainers, and Sure-Grip 3.55:1 rear axle. It was a slick solution that boosted the factory 340 from a wheezing 240 horsepower all the way to a stout 360 horses. And, before delivery, every GSS was tuned on Mr. Norm's Clayton chassis dyno.

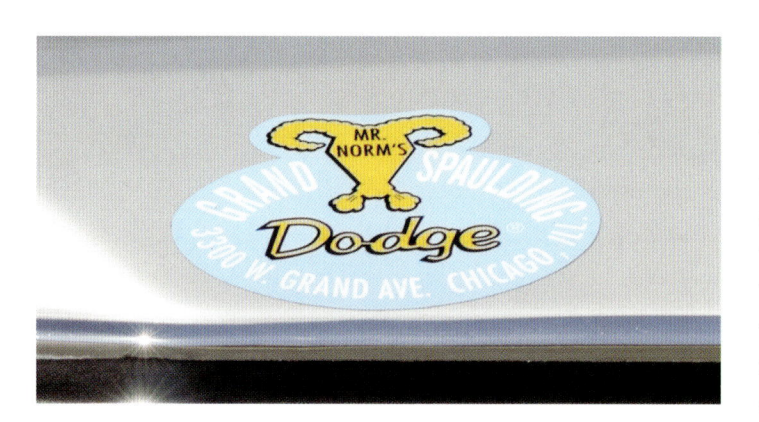

All performance cars sold through Mr. Norm's Grand Spaulding Dodge received this sticker. *David Newhardt*

Dodge Demon GSS Tri-Power 1970-71

 # PRODUCED: Unknown
ENGINE: 340-cubic-inch V-8
HORSEPOWER: 290
TORQUE: 340 lb-ft
¼-MILE TIME: n/a

TOP: The Dodge Demon 340 was a quick compact, especially up to 60 miles per hour or so. Mr. Norm's Demon GSS was even faster. The competition would not see the "GSS" decals until it was too late. This Dodge Demon GSS 340 is highly desirable with its "Plum Crazy" paint.

ABOVE: Sporty and quick, the Dodge Demon 340 could raise eyebrows and burn rubber.

LEFT: Mr. Norm's added the Edelbrock intake manifold and three Holley 2-bbl carbs that the special Challenger R/T models got. Mr's Norm's added their own touch, the cast aluminum "Tri-Power" air cleaner cover. Don't tell any Mopar fans, but that cover was a *Ford* part.

MR. NORM'S GRAND SPAULDING DODGE: THE HIGH-PERFORMANCE KING   43

TOP: By 1972, most dealers and manufacturers had given up on the performance market—not Mr. Norm's Grand Spaulding Dodge. The supercharged Demon GSS was only offered in 1972. Norm Kraus remembers that "about 100" were sold. This is the only one built in "Corporate Blue," better known as "Petty Blue."

ABOVE, LEFT: The 1972 Supercharged Demon GSS was the last of the breed. In 1973, Grand Spaulding Dodge began offering conversion vans instead of performance cars. Mr. Norm's Grand Spaulding Dodge became the world's largest Dodge dealer that year.

ABOVE, RIGHT The Granatelli brothers' Paxton centrifugal supercharger allowed Mr. Norm's to boost the low-compression '72 340 to 360 horsepower. The beautiful cast airbox is a nice touch, created by Norm Kraus.

RIGHT: Mr. Norm's added a Mopar hood tachometer to the supercharged Demon GSS.

The base price was a reasonable $3,695.00, but these were truly custom cars, and Mr. Norm's could make them as plain or as fancy as the customer wanted. That bought 0–60 in about 5.6 seconds, and the quarter mile in around 13.92 at 106 miles per hour. That's a true muscle machine. Some records from Mr. Norm's performance years were lost in a flood, but Kraus remembers that "about 100" GSS cars were converted out of the 8,750 1972 Demon 340s built by Dodge.

The 1972 Demon GSS was the last performance car Mr. Norm's would build. Sensing the potential explosion in the conversion van market, Kraus turned his efforts in that direction. In 1974, Grand Spaulding Dodge became the world's largest Dodge dealer by volume, thanks both to conversion van fever, and also to the request to supply "fleet" vehicles to the Chicago police, Illinois State Patrol, and other municipalities. Kraus sold his portion of Grand Spaulding Dodge to his brother in 1977 and went on to pursue other interests.

Today, Kraus is in his eighties, but he's still involved in building new Dodges even faster, including Mr. Norm's GSS King 'Cuda and Hurst GSS Supercat Hellcat, sold through Kosak Dodge in Merrillville, Indiana. He also makes appearances at Mopar events throughout the country. Grand Spaulding Dodge may be long gone, but Norm Kraus is still the Hi-Performance Car King!

Dodge Demon Supercharged GSS 1970

 # PRODUCED: about 100

ENGINE: 340-cubic-inch V-8 w/ Paxton supercharger

HORSEPOWER: 360

TORQUE: n/a

¼-MILE TIME: 13.92 at 106 mph

Even in his eighties, Norm Kraus was still involved with performance Dodges, like this Hurst GSS Supercat Hellcat, sold through Kosak Dodge in Merrillville, Indiana. *Norm Kraus*

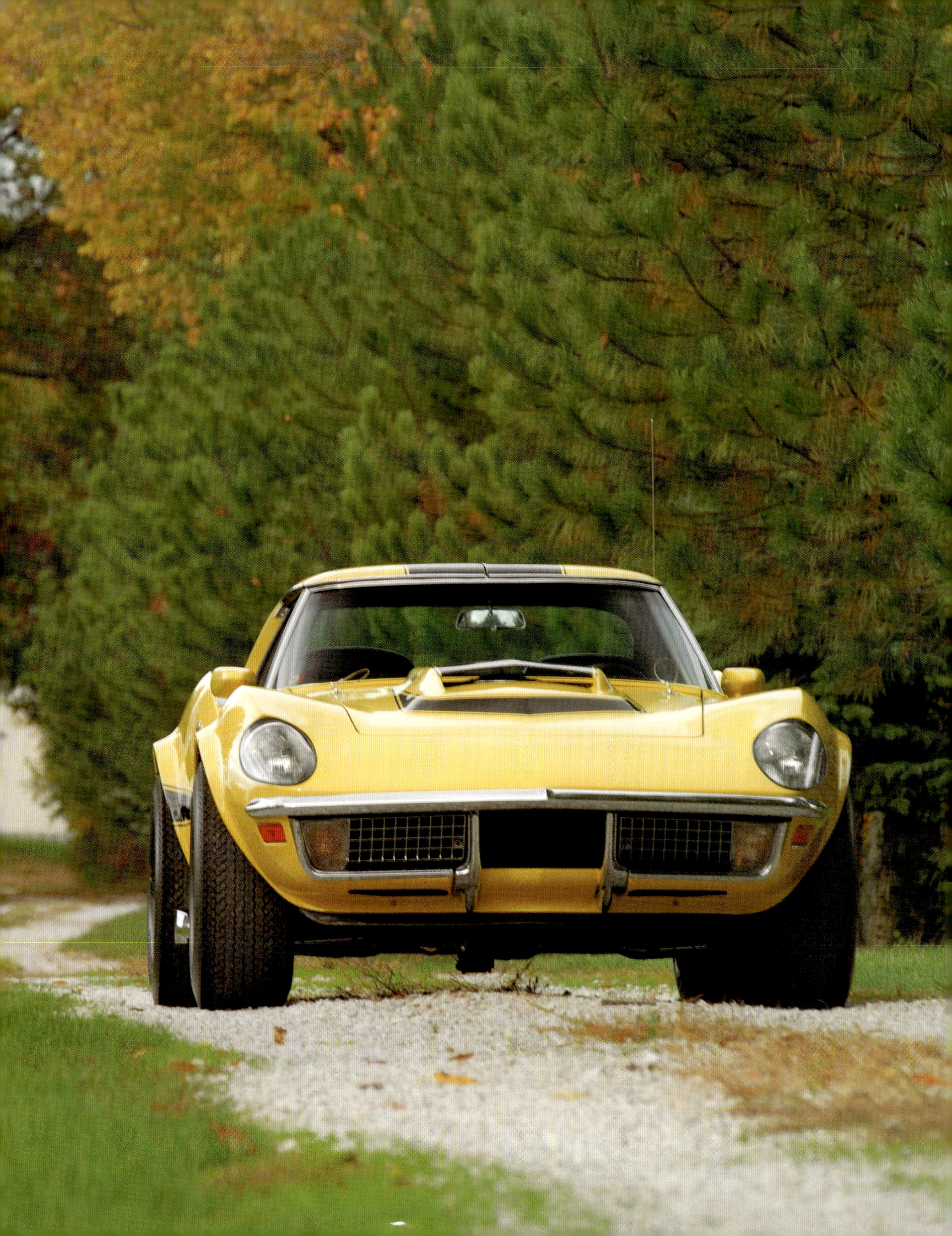

Chapter 4
Baldwin Motion
New York Minute Muscle

They do things differently in New York City: people walk fast, talk fast, drive fast, work fast, live fast. There's even Texas slang for the phenomenon: doing something "in a New York minute." They do things big and bold there, too, where big business gets done in the shadow of tall buildings, reflecting the glitz and spectacle of Times Square.

Maybe that explains the motivation behind Joel Rosen's cars. The Chevrolets his Motion Performance built and sold through Baldwin Chevrolet were supremely fast, with maximum impact. These weren't fast "sleepers" that hid in the shadows waiting for victims. No, Baldwin Motion cars were in your face, daring anyone and everyone to take them on. And they could defeat those takers—guaranteed.

Rosen was born in Brooklyn in 1939, and his family didn't own a car until he was sixteen, but Joel was a gearhead just the same. He graduated from James Madison High School at sixteen and his dad bought him a 1955 Oldsmobile. That manual trans three-on-the-tree Olds became the first "canvas" for Rosen's high-performance artistry—at various times it featured three deuces, lake pipes, a McCullough supercharger, and a floor-shifted Cadillac-LaSalle transmission. Then he

Joel Rosen replaced the Corvette's pop-up headlights with single fixed units. The Phase III GT started at $10,500, and, in the fine tradition of luxury Grand Touring vehicles, each one was custom-built.

Joel Rosen and John Silva called it the "Maco Shark" to avoid any legal issues with General Motors' trademarks, and six cars were custom-built for customers.

did a stint in the air force, becoming an aircraft engine specialist. "I had some mechanical background, but really learned the finer points of engines and tuning. We fixed a lot of those C-119s, the 'Flying Boxcars.'"

Upon his discharge, Rosen became co-owner of a Sunoco gas station, Neclan Service Station, on the corner of Albany and Atlantic Avenue in Brooklyn. When not turning wrenches on customer's cars, Rosen and his wife raced their '58 fuel-injected Corvette. Drag racing, road racing, hillclimbs—you name it, the Corvette competed in it. As the Corvette won, Rosen's business grew.

Fascinated with engines and the art of making them more powerful, Rosen bought a Clayton chassis dyno in 1963. It was then that the business changed direction.

> The name Motion came from a high-performance electronic ignition called "Motion EI" that I had installed on many Corvettes, including my own, a '58 Fuelie. I figured anything would sound better than Neclan Service Station! We were really the only one on Long Island that had a dyno and oscilloscope, and turned that into a major tuning business.

When business outgrew the Brooklyn location, Rosen incorporated as Motion Performance in 1966 and set up shop at 598 Sunrise Highway, Baldwin, Long Island, New York, about 10 miles from John F. Kennedy International Airport. A family Chevrolet franchise, Baldwin Auto Company, was less than a mile away, on the corner of Merrick Road and Central Avenue. Founded in the 1920s by August "Gus" Simonin, the dealership was managed by his son, Ed Simonin, and Ed's brother-in-law, Dave Bean. Like most dealers, Baldwin Chevrolet really didn't understand the youth market. Recognizing the advantages that dealerships like Nickey Chevrolet and Yenko Chevrolet had over the typical speed shop, Rosen approached the Baldwin Chevrolet owners.

The Fantastic Five

"Baldwin Chevrolet was a local mom-and-pop Chevy dealership, and Joel was friends with John Mahler, the parts manager," said Marty Schorr, a friend of Rosen's who edited *Hi-Performance CARS* magazine.

> It all started with a Baldwin Chevrolet- and CARS-sponsored 427 Camaro race car powered by an L88. Later, we put our heads together and pitched a program to Baldwin Chevrolet for a full line of supercars called "The Fantastic Five" that included the Camaro, Chevelle, Nova, Biscayne/Impala, and Corvette.

> We wanted to build and sell new cars to the public with anything everybody wanted on them, and they gave us the ability to do that.

With his partners at Baldwin Chevrolet, Motion Performance could now offer automobiles across the spectrum, from Corvettes to Biscayne. You want a mind-blowing two-seater? The Baldwin Motion SS-427 Corvette was the ticket. A family-sized sleeper? Try the "Street Racer's Special," the SS-427 Biscayne two-door sedan for just $2,998. In between were the SS-427 Nova, SS-427 Camaro, and SS-427 Chevelle.

ABOVE: The Baldwin Motion Maco Shark design was based on the 1965 Mako Shark II show car built by Chevrolet Studio III. *General Motors Heritage Collection*

RIGHT: Gary Kupfer airbrushed the lighter color to mimic the coloration of the actual shortfin mako shark. He also molded in Firebird taillights.

The most popular ticket was the SS-427 Camaro, starting at $3,795. Buyers got something they couldn't get from the factory: a 425-horsepower L72 427 engine. Baldwin Chevrolet ordered a four-speed SS396 Camaro, then turned it over to Motion Performance to replace the 396 with the L72, which alone added around 100 horsepower. A loaded SS396 could run $4,500, so the base SS-427 was a real bargain, or at least the basis for something more outrageous. As Schorr put it in *Vette* magazine:

> Unlike similar products from Rosen's popular and well-connected Chevrolet dealer competition, Baldwin-Motion 427 Camaros and Chevelles were never re-badged COPO cars. Truth be told, neither Rosen, myself, or the people at Baldwin Chevrolet knew about COPO cars in 1969, and didn't find out about their existence until years later!

Since Chevrolet couldn't build a 427 Camaro, Chevelle, or Nova, the Fantastic Five made sense. But why buy a 427 Impala or Corvette from Baldwin Motion? Air conditioning is one reason. Chevrolet engineering wouldn't allow air conditioning on their highest horsepower engines, since drive belts could be thrown at the kinds of rpm these engines could reach. But buy a 396 Impala, or a lower horsepower L36 or L68 Corvette, and Rosen could add the mighty 425 horsepower L72 and retain the existing accessories.

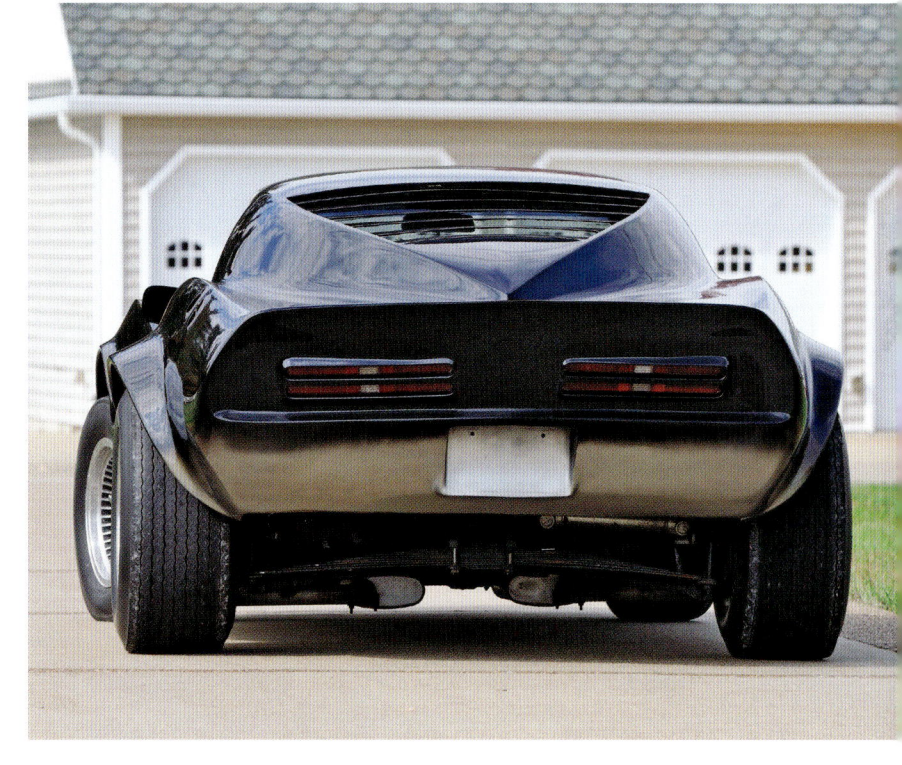

Baldwin Motion cars had warranties, too: 90 days or 4,000 miles on the powertrain and 24 months/24,000 miles on the rest of the car. Speed parts were excluded, and there was no warranty on any engine with internal engine modifications. In addition, because these were dealer-delivered Chevrolets, GMAC financing was available.

If one of the Fantastic Five wasn't quite fast enough, well, there was always Phase III.

BALDWIN MOTION: NEW YORK MINUTE MUSCLE 49

Baldwin Motion Phase III GT 1969-1971

- **# PRODUCED:** 12
- **ENGINE:** 427-cubic-inch V-8
- **HORSEPOWER:** 500
- **TORQUE:** n/a
- **¼-MILE TIME:** n/a

The Baldwin Motion Phase III

Like other performance dealers, Baldwin Motion offered upgraded levels of modified performance. Most high-performance dealers started with mild Phase I to wild Phase III. Not Rosen, who only offered Phase III. With that wild extreme of performance came a guarantee:

> We think so much of our Phase III Supercars that we guarantee they will turn at least 120 mph in 11.50 seconds or better with an M/P-approved driver on an AHRA or NHRA-sanctioned drag strip. Phase III Supercars are completely streetable, reliable machines that will run these times off the street.

ABOVE: The blueprinted 427 was equipped with a 1,050-cfm Holley four-barrel carb and low-restriction air filter on an aluminum high-rise manifold. *David Newhardt*

TOP: The Baldwin Motion Phase III GT was unveiled at the 1969 New York International Auto Show. The Baldwin Motion Phase III GT replaced the '68 Corvette's "sugar scoop" rear window with a flush unit. Triple taillights were molded into the fiberglass. *David Newhardt*

CHAPTER 4

"If the car wouldn't deliver, the customer could get his money back," Rosen told *Vette*. "That never happened though." After years of racing and dyno work, Rosen knew exactly what was needed to build the most extreme of street machines. Proof of that came from their racing program. Driven by Rosen, Bill Mitchell, and Dennis Ferrara, Baldwin-Motion drag racing Camaros were consistent AHRA and NHRA Modified Production national record holders from 1967 to 1972. Mitchell often fought another Chevy legend, Bill "Grumpy" Jenkins, for the NHRA A/MP record.

The key to Rosen's success was in dropping the most extreme engines in the Phase III cars. While most dealers were content with calling their modified L72-powered cars Phase III, Rosen usually started with the legendary full-race L88 aluminum heads and went from there. Suspensions were modified with the widest street tires, heavy-duty springs and shocks, and traction bars necessary to keep some of this power on the pavement. Motion Performance called it their "Super-Bite" suspension, and it did as much as the tire technology of the day allowed to prevent nothing but tire smoke.

Finally, to make sure the whole East Coast knew what you were driving, Motion Performance turned to local sign painter, Gary "The Local Brush" Kupfer, who painted the big, bold Phase III stripes for which Motion cars were known. "I did all of them," said Kupfer. "Every year Joel modified them a little bit, it was the same basic stripe but he'd say 'Let's make it a little wider along the trunk.' Those were his ideas but I physically did all the work."

Then Schorr went out and marketed the cars through his public relations talents, or as stories in *CARS* magazine. "I had first access to all the hot Chevrolets and was involved in their marketing," said Marty.

> Back then, Rosen couldn't get a West Coast magazine to even come out to his shop, let alone cover his cars. Yenko and Nickey Chevrolet were selling COPO cars in 1969 and were getting all the attention, but no one in the New York area had ever seen those cars. The West Coast car magazines didn't touch Joel's cars until the *Car Craft* story on a Phase III Vega titled 'King Kong is Alive and Well in Long Island, New York.' And that was after Baldwin Chevrolet had closed its doors.

Those West Coast magazines were missing out on something big: next to the Ford-built Shelby Mustangs, Motion Performance was the biggest specialty builder of performance cars in America.

Baldwin Motion Phase III GT 1969–1971

Rosen may have spent most of his time building Camaro supercars, but he started with Corvettes, which were always special to him. That was evident at the 1969 New York International Auto Show, where the Baldwin Motion Phase III GT was unveiled.

Built on a leftover '68 435-horsepower Corvette, the Phase III GT was Rosen's vision of a world-class grand touring machine. The blueprinted 427 was equipped with a 1,050-cfm Holley four-barrel carb and low-restriction air filter on an aluminum high-rise manifold. Ignition was Motion's Super/Spark CD system, and M/T finned valve covers gave the engine sparkle. Tube headers fed factory-chambered sidepipes. The dyno-tuned Phase III was rated at 500 horsepower. The suspension received special shocks, bushings, and springs, along with a single traction bar. The widest Goodyear Polyglas tires available were mounted on slotted alloy wheels.

But it was the exterior of the Phase III GT that turned heads. Rosen replaced the Corvette's pop-up headlights with single fixed units, while the recessed "sugar scoop" rear window was replaced with a flush unit. The fiberglass modifications, along with the paint, were the work of Gary Kupfer.

Finished in Monza Red, the Phase III GT made its mark amid the brand-new factory offerings at one of the most visible car shows in the world.

As Marty Schorr recalled,

> At the '69 New York International Auto Show, Zora [Duntov] escaped his handlers and came over to see the car—which he loved—and to talk to Joel and me. He would get very dramatic, with flowery prose, and loved to discuss Corvette handling dynamics and fuel-injected engines. Joel and Zora had a great rapport and would often meet for drinks when Zora was in town.

The Phase III GT was on the cover of the August 1969 issue of CARS, one of the most popular issues ever. Schorr also used the car for the cover of the Motion Performance 1969 catalog, in dramatic monochrome mezzotint artwork.

The Phase III GT started at $10,500, and in the fine tradition of luxury grand touring vehicles, each one was custom made. "We started building Phase III GTs to order in 1969, with production ending in 1971," Rosen told *Vette*.

> The GT was just too expensive for the audience that we had cultivated for big-block Camaros, Chevelles, Novas, and our $3,000 SS-427 Street Racer Special Biscaynes. The most expensive GT built, the air-conditioned '70 Daytona Yellow GT that Thomas Squire ordered on February 2, 1970, went out the door for over $13,000 including delivery to Los Angeles, California. It's one of only three GTs accounted for today. Although we only sold a few GTs, we ended up doing an incredible business marketing individual GT body parts and conversion kits to shops that specialized in customizing Corvettes.

At more than double the cost of the most expensive factory Corvette, just twelve Phase III GTs were built between 1969 and 1971. But in the same way Pininfarina and Bertone could custom-build a Ferrari, Rosen gave the all-American Corvette the same kind of grand touring exclusivity.

TOP: Driving the Baldwin Motion 1970 Phase III Camaro, *Hi-Performance CARS* commented: "You have to be either totally bent or a dedicated big-bucks street rat to go this route for daily city transportation."

ABOVE, LEFT: A story in *CARS* magazine about the 1970 Baldwin Motion Phase III Camaro told the whole story: 500 horsepower at 6,500 rpm; 500 lb-ft of torque at 4,800 rpm.

ABOVE, RIGHT: Under the fiberglass hood was the requisite giant Holley on an aluminum high-riser, Motion capacitor discharge ignition, Hooker equal-length headers, Schiefer clutch and scattershield, and a Flex-A-Lite fan.

LEFT: Motion's "Super Bite" suspension was improved and did an admirable job of planting 500 horses.

52 CHAPTER 4

Phase III Camaro 1970–1973

When Chevrolet introduced the new 1970 Camaro, they kept the 375-horsepower L78 396 the top engine. But Chevelles and Corvettes got a 454 version of the famous 427 engine. Talk about a monster motor—and a whole new "canvas"—on which Rosen could apply his performance art.

A story in CARS about the 1970 Baldwin Motion Phase III Camaro told the whole story: 500 horsepower at 6,500 rpm; 500 lb-ft of torque at 4,800 rpm. Under the fiberglass hood was the requisite giant Holley on an aluminum high-riser, Motion capacitor discharge ignition, Hooker equal-length headers, Schiefer clutch and scattershield, and a Flex-A-Lite fan. Motion's Super Bite suspension was improved and gave better grip, but Rosen stayed with the early-style sidepipes, since they fit better than the '70 Camaro's. Equipped with 4.88:1 gears, this was a serious street racer, as the CARS story noted: "You have to be either totally bent or a dedicated big-bucks street rat to go this route for daily city transportation."

The Camaro didn't get any track time for the story, but the standard Phase III guarantee applied, so the potential in the strip was obvious. What CARS wrote could be applied to any Baldwin Motion Phase III vehicle: "While the Phase III 454 Camaro is a groovy-looking car, it can't be appreciated unless it's driven and driven hard. It's not for stop and go driving and it's not for the city swinger. The suspension is too stiff, the engine is too potent and it just doesn't make sense."

Still, for such an extreme machine, the '70 Phase III Camaro was surprisingly habitable. Normally, a drag-oriented 4.88:1 would result in an engine that turned ridiculous rpm at highway speeds. For this reason, Rosen often installed a Hone-O-Matic 30 percent overdrive unit.

> I was able to drive a 4.88-geared 454 Camaro on the parkways at over 70 mph without any excessive rear end whine or engine noises. With OD engaged I was able to cruise with an effective ratio of 3.42-to-1. All this translates into a dual-purpose screamer with cruising potential and decent economy.... So the OD unit probably pays for itself in wear and tear and fuel economy alone, not to mention the beauty of owning a truly dual-purpose machine.

The Hone overdrive was expensive—a $750 option—but it made Motion's cars more than just stoplight racers, which the CARS article emphasized:

> With the OD engaged you can cruise—provided the "Man" doesn't play race driver—at 100 mph and get the feeling you're in an expensive GT car. It's responsive at any speed.... It starts to get a bit light up around 125 mph, which with the 3.42 gearing, isn't exactly the redline.

If it was fast on the street, imagine what a full-race Phase III 454 could do on the track. Dennis Ferrara took over the driving chores for Baldwin Motion, and their new '70 Camaro brought new terror to the strip. During the Camaro's first full season in 1971, Ferrara set the NHRA A/Modified Production record and won Modified Eliminator at the Division 1 WCS Grand Finale at ATCO Dragway, and took the NHRA National Open at New England Dragway. He also finished second in the Division 1 points race.

A new decade, a new Camaro, and the legend continued.

Motion Maco Shark Corvette 1970–1974

During 1965, Chevrolet Studio III was busy designing what would be the third-generation Corvette, the 1968 Sting Ray. That design by Larry Shinoda and Henry Haga was either loved or hated for its high, peaked fenders and overall voluptuous shape. Just as the Mako Shark I show car of 1962 teased the design of the '63 Corvette, the Mako Shark II concept of 1965 revealed the basic shape of the '68 Corvette.

For some, though, the third-generation Corvette was a disappointment compared to the Mako Shark II. John Silva was one of those people; he created the fiberglass pieces to turn an ordinary C3 Corvette into a shark. Rosen, always looking to push the Corvette's boundaries, saw Silva's kit and made a deal. They called it the "Maco Shark" to avoid any legal issues with General Motors' trademarks, and six cars were custom-built for customers. Motion Performance also sold the kits through their catalog.

Like the Phase III GT, the Maco Sharks could be built as plain or as fancy as the customer desired. One was painted metallic blue with airbrushed white along the bottom of the body, somewhat like the Mako Shark II show car, and mimicking the colors of the actual killer shortfin mako shark that is found in tropical waters around the world. Kupfer did the paint, as he did on practically all Motion cars, using his airbrush skills to lightly paint fish scales over the blue. "I know sharks don't have scales," he said, but the effect is subtle yet dramatic.

Since the shortfin mako shark is the fastest shark in the world, it was the perfect name for Rosen's ultra Corvettes.

Baldwin Motion Camaro SS-454 Phase III 1970

 # PRODUCED: unknown*

ENGINE: 454-cubic-inch V-8

HORSEPOWER: 500

TORQUE: 500 lb-ft

¼-MILE TIME: n/a

*Joel Rosen knows the exact number of vehicles Baldwin Motion and Motion Performance have built but will not reveal it. He will verify any possible Motion car for a fee. It is estimated they built between 350 and 500 cars total.

TOP: You couldn't buy a high-performance Camaro in 1973, but Joel Rosen could build one for you.

ABOVE, LEFT: Black stripes and a small "Motion" emblem were fair warning enough.

ABOVE RIGHT: The muscle era was over by the time Joel Rosen built the 1973 Phase III Camaro. That's no low-compression '73 350 under the hood—it's an all-out Phase III 454.

Just three Manta Ray Corvettes were built by Baldwin Motion. This one has a 350/automatic; the other two were 454/four-speeds. Though it looks mostly like a Phase III GT, the Manta Ray features the rubber '73 Corvette front bumper.

Motion Manta Ray Corvette 1973

Imagine buying a Corvette for $6,749 and then discovering that it is the one-of-a-kind Motion Manta Ray. The seller didn't know what he had, and the buyer wasn't sure either. The buyer took a chance anyway.

"I only built three of them, all three in 1973," said Rosen to the new owner.

> The name of it is Manta Ray. One of them was wrecked when it was new; the other one has never been heard from. One of them was pearl yellow; one was orange with no stripe. The other two were 454/four-speeds; yours is a 350/automatic with air. The guy wanted a street cruiser.

And what a cruiser it is. Though it looks mostly like a Phase III GT, the Manta Ray features the rubber '73 Corvette front bumper. The 350 under the Motion hood is dyno tuned, with Hooker header dumping into the sidepipes. A 400 automatic with shift kit gets it to the pavement. Rosen was involved in prepping the engine during the car's refurbishment, though the paint is mostly original. What's a Motion Corvette worth today? In late 2015, the only remaining Manta Ray was for sale, with an asking price of $150,000.

Motion Super Vega 1971–1973

By the 1970s, the automotive world was changing, yet Rosen knew there was still a need for speed. Chevy's Vega compact looked like the perfect platform for another supercar. Bill "Grumpy" Jenkens had turned the Vega into an NHRA Pro Stock champion. If the Vega was good enough for Rosen's old competitor, it should be a good street machine. And if Yenko's turbo Vega sounded exciting, imagine dropping a Chevy 454 in place of the Vega's four-banger.

"When we got into the V-8 Vegas, Baldwin Chevrolet really didn't want to be involved, as they would be difficult to warranty and finance," said Schorr. "All of the Vega cars we built were called

'Motion Super Vegas.'" The Super Vegas took small car/big engine to the ultimate extreme. Such extremes attracted the West Coast press, and *Car Craft* featured the Super Vega in their January 1974 issue.

Packing a 454 into a Vega gave Motion Performance national exposure—too much exposure. "Thinking that Baldwin-Motion was bigger than it really was because of all the editorial coverage we received," said Rosen, "the EPA and DOT targeted us to make an example. They wanted to shut down the biggest specialty car builder, thus putting the fear of 'Big Brother' into everyone else."

He received a summons from the Justice Department, "U.S. Government Against Motion Performance." Citing the Clean Air Act of 1970, the Environmental Protection Agency threatened fines as high as $10,000 per anti-smog device removed. Some engines had three or four anti-smog devices.

Rosen and his lawyer negotiated a settlement with the Justice Department, agreeing to pay a $500 fine and to "cease and desist" building brand-new Baldwin Motion high-performance cars. That didn't put Rosen out of business, but he could no longer modify new cars and sell them through Baldwin Chevrolet. It's just as well, since Baldwin was going through turmoil of its own: sold in 1972, it was out of business by 1974.

Rosen and Motion Performance could still modify customer cars, and continued to do so, but only with the disclaimer: "This vehicle does not comply with DOT and EPA regulations and is for off-road use only," signed by both Rosen and its owner.

Motion Can-Am Spyder 1978–1979

If you ever got to see John Greenwood's "Batmobile" Corvette race cars running in the IMSA series in the mid- to late-1970s, it was a sight you'd never forget. His wide-bodied Corvettes were incredibly fast, boldly patriotic, and often victorious. This was the inspiration for the Motion Can-Am Spyder.

Long after most dealers left the performance business, Motion Performance was still building customer cars. The first Can-Am

ABOVE: This black diamond-pleat upholstery would have looked as good in a "lead sled" custom as in a late-1970s Corvette.

LEFT: The first Can-Am Spyder, built in 1978 during the height of John Greenwood's popularity, was displayed at the New York Rod and Custom Show as a show car. Under the bulging hood lurked a 530 horsepower, 466-cubic-inch Motion big-block.

Spyder, built in 1978 during the height of Greenwood's popularity, was displayed at the New York Rod and Custom Show as a show car. The red custom Corvette featured Kupfer's stripes to accent the bulging fenders; under the equally bulging hood lurked a 530-horsepower, 466-cubic-inch Motion big-block. That power was delivered through a M22 "rock crusher" four-speed and 4.11:1 gears, but also included a Hone-O-Matic overdrive to deliver maximum top speed.

Inside, the car's black diamond-pleat upholstery would have looked as good in a "lead sled" custom as in a late-1970s Corvette—but this was a show car, remember. Motion Performance built three more Can-Am Spyder Corvettes, all of them painted yellow, all powered by 350 small-blocks. Late in the decade, gasoline had skyrocketed to over $1 a gallon, and interest rates on new cars were over 13 percent and over 18 percent for used vehicles. Motion built between 350 and 500 over the years (Rosen won't tell the exact number), and his small crew built cars for customers all over the world.

Rosen did some other projects, like Motion-modified IROC Camaros and Monte Carlos, and dabbled in Buick Grand Nationals. Relocating to Florida, he and his wife run Motion Models, building one-of-a-kind ship models and aircraft for museums, the military, and collectors. Then, in 2005, Rosen and Schorr joined forces with Larry Jaworske and Joel Ehrenpreis. Their Launch Edition two-seat SuperCoupe, a recreated '69 Camaro powered by a fuel-injected 540-inch aluminum big-block, earned the GM Design Award at SEMA 2005 and set a record at Barrett-Jackson in 2006. Six years later, Rosen teamed with Howard Tanner of Redline Motorsports of Schenectady, New York, to revive the Motion name on modern Camaros.

Still, Corvettes hold a special place in his heart. "When I saw a Corvette for the first time more than four decades ago," Rosen told *Vette*, "it was love at first sight. That love affair is still very much alive. I still miss the freewheeling Baldwin-Motion days and, if the right opportunity came along, I'd jump back into building Corvette Supercars in a New York minute."

Chapter 5

Nickey Chevrolet

Quick (With a Backward "K")

The poet Carl Sandburg called Chicago the "City of the Big Shoulders." America's "Second City" is that kind of place. Big shoulders, big dealers. A gas station on the corner of Grand and Spaulding grew to be the largest Dodge dealer in the world. A few miles away, on Irving Park Road, another dealer that could also claim to be the largest: Nickey Chevrolet.

Brothers Edward and Jack Stephani bought Nickey Chevrolet in the midst of the Great Depression. Rather than change it, they kept the memorable name, with Jack running the showroom and Ed running the business. Sales grew with the economy, but a backward "K" changed things in 1957. Jack was vacationing in Florida when he noticed that a local business had reversed one letter in their name. He liked the way it grabbed attention, so in the fall of 1957 he hired the White Way Sign Company to create a sign with a backward "K." People would come in off the street to report the "mistake." The dealership gave those people a certificate for a free upside-down cake at a local bakery. Later, WGN radio would blare the jingle: Nickey, Nickey, Nickey, Nickey, Nickey Chevrolet . . . with the backward K!

In the late 1950s, Jack Stephani got involved in auto racing. Most notably, Nickey Chevrolet was the sponsor of Jim Jeffords's "Purple

The 1967 Nickey 427 Camaros had hoods that matched the Stinger of the 427 Corvettes that year; otherwise the body was bone stock.

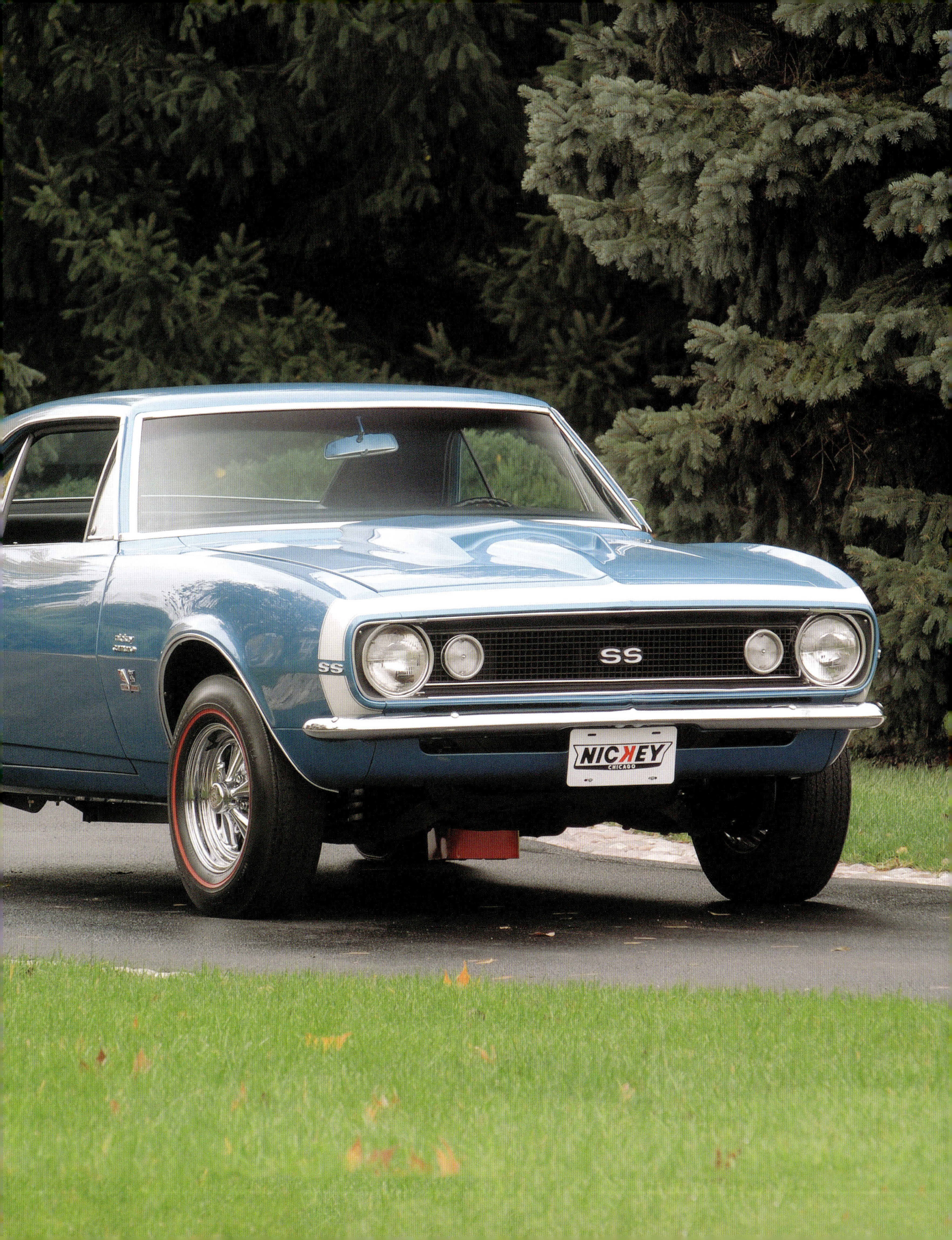
SS
NICKEY
CHICAGO

ABOVE: Nickey Chevrolet was the sponsor of Jim Jeffords's "Purple People Eater" Corvettes in SCCA B-production racing. Jeffords earned the National Championship in 1958 and 1959, winning twenty-nine of forty-two events. During the 1959 season, the Nickey Corvette never finished lower than second. *Tom & Kelly Glatch*

LEFT: Dan Blocker, John Cannon, and the "Vinegroon" made for a handsome cover of the June 1966 issue of *Sports Car Graphic*. *Author's Collection*

People Eater" Corvettes in SCCA B-Production racing. Jeffords earned the National Championship in 1958 and 1959, winning twenty-nine of forty-two events. During the '59 season, the Nickey Corvette never finished lower than second. They also bought one of Lance Reventlow's Scarab sports racers, and convinced GM to sell one of the three SR-2 Corvette race cars developed by Chevrolet Engineering, a move that was rare for GM.

Nickey Chevrolet's stature with General Motors was also evident when they received one of the first fifteen Z06 Corvettes in 1963. With the preparation of Nickey's racing manager, Ronnie Kaplan, the "Nickey Nouse" Corvette finished the Daytona American Challenge first in class, second overall, with one A. J. Foyt at the wheel.

In 1965, when Chevrolet introduced their first muscle car, the Z16 Chevelle, they sold the limited edition to a select list of buyers. Dan Blocker, who played Hoss Cartwright on the hugely popular TV show *Bonanza*, picked up his Butternut Yellow Z16 at Nickey Chevrolet. Blocker, the burley college football player turned actor, was a true gearhead, even building a hot rod around a V-12 engine from a Seagrave fire truck. Chevrolet was the sponsor of *Bonanza* on NBC, and the show's cast recorded a sales film introducing the 1965 Chevrolet lineup to dealers. Blocker had met Jack Stephani at the Twelfth Annual Bahamas Speed Weeks in 1965. John Cannon, driving Blocker's "Vinegroon" Genie Mk.10B sports racer, had finished second in the Nassau Trophy Race. Stephani offered Nickey's sponsorship in exchange for Blocker's promotional appearances.

Author Doug Marion was employed at Nickey Chevrolet the day Blocker's Z16 was delivered. "Chevrolet sent a fleet of prototype cars, pickups and semi-trucks to Nickey in order to hold a special weekend *Bonanza* festival. Select staff worked this weekend, playing host to the public and Midwest media," he wrote in *Super Chevy*.

Blocker, Cannon, and the "Vinegroon" (named after a venomous desert scorpion) also appeared on the cover of the June 1966 issue of *Sports Car Graphic*, with Nickey's logo on the door. They also won the United States Road Racing Championship race in Las Vegas that year, with Cannon again at the wheel.

While sports car fans were seeing the Nickey name in the winner's circle, the powerhouse dealership was preparing their assault on drag racing. In 1965, Nickey opened their High-Performance Center. Nickey's Vice President Al Seelig tasked Don Swiatek with developing this operation, housed in a 20,000-square-foot building. Eventually the parts business was generating $60,000 a month in sales from walk-ins and mail orders.

Nickey hired Dick Harrell to manage the High-Performance Center. The racer from Carlsbad, New Mexico, had developed a reputation racing Z11 Biscaynes with great success. Relocating to

Chicago, "Mr. Chevrolet" began another chapter in his legendary career, racing Nickey's Nova Funny Car.

Finally, Nickey Chevrolet formed an alliance with another Chevrolet legend, Bill Thomas. Based in Anaheim, California, Bill Thomas started roadracing Corvettes in 1956. Soon his C. S. Mead Motors Co. Corvettes won ninetten first overall out of twenty-four races entered in the highly competitive SoCal area. That caught Chevrolet's attention, and they hired him to develop more performance out of the new Corvair. They started work on Z11 Biscaynes that would be dominant in drag racing. When Shelby's Cobras started humiliating the new Z06 Corvettes, Chevrolet worked with Thomas to secretly develop the Cheetah sports cars. GM's racing ban in 1963 killed that project after only a few cars were built, but in 1965 he released the "Bill Thomas 396 Performance Handbook." For just $5, Thomas offered "the facts on what works and what doesn't work."

Nickey, Harrell, Thomas—this triumvirate of performance was ready.

Nickey 427 Camaro 1967–1968

The cover of the January 1967 issue of *TACH*, the official publication of the American Hot Rod Association, said it all: "The First Test Anywhere of Nickey 427 Camaro." Given the lead times in the publishing business work, the story by Bruce Young must have been written in September or October of 1966, right around Camaro's September 29 release date. "This was an answer to my prayers," Harrell said in the story. "A small, lightweight car that would be adaptable to the 427 engine. Right away I felt we could really have a winner."

TOP: Even at close range, it was hard to spot a Nickey 427 Camaro.
ABOVE: Two small Nickey emblems on the side and a Nickey sticker on the trunk were just about the only warning for potential takers.

The story detailed the swap of the stock 350 engine with the 425-horsepower L72 427, after which Dick Harrell got behind the wheel: "The stock Nickey 427 Camaro with 3.31 gears, street tires turned 13.20 and 108 mph. Not bad as the car smoked hides all the way through the first two gears." With $1,000 in upgrades, Harrell was able to get down to 10.80 and 128 miles per hour, and the reporter saw one of Harrell's modified 427s hit 600 horsepower on Nickey's dyno. They were equally impressed with the price, $3,711.65 for the base model, including a test drive by Harrell. They also named the Nickey 427 "TACH Performance Car of the Year."

The February 1967 issue of *Car Craft* also featured the Nickey 427 Camaro. "Almost no foot pressure was necessary to literally

Nickey 427 Camaro 1967

 # PRODUCED: unknown
ENGINE: 427-cubic-inch V-8
HORSEPOWER: 425
TORQUE: 460 lb-ft
¼-MILE TIME: 14.90 at 114 mph (slicks)

paste you to the back of the seat and the engine worked effortlessly in moving the Camaro through the gears." They added:

> In view of Nickey's planned production, it was determined that Nickey-built 427 Camaros would be eligible for AHRA Super Stock competition. As of this writing, these are the only 427 Camaros that will be allowed to run as a stocker . . . . To give you, the customer, even better and faster service, Nickey has recently established Bill Thomas Race Cars of Anaheim, California, as their associate on the West Coast. Thomas will carry the complete Nickey high performance parts line, as well as build 427 Camaros for Western enthusiasts.

Around sixty-nine 427 Camaros were built before Harrell left Nickey to open his own shop in East St. Louis. (Harrell would eventually be associated with Yenko's 427 conversions, then with Fred Gibb's COPO projects.) But they were the first, and they were touched by legends. That's the 1967 Nickey 427 Camaro.

Nickey 427 Camaro and Chevelle 1968

Nickey Chevrolet and Thomas continued their brisk 427 Camaro business into 1968, even if Harrell was no longer with them. One difference between Yenko's systematic approach to 427 conversions and dealers like Nickey was the upgrades performed after the 427 was installed. The stock Nickey 427 was a nasty piece, but *Popular Hot Rodding* found out what Phase II could get you.

Working with Thomas, PHR ran a '68 427 Camaro in Phase I form: "With the suspension worked over and the engine getting a boost with a Thomas 550 hydraulic cam kit, headers, and a Schiefer clutch and flywheel assembly we were [ready] for the drag test." Like the Camaro, it was good for elapsed times (ETs) in the 13.90–14.10 range, with traction the biggest factor. With the headers open and air cleaner removed, slicks brought it up to 12.30 seconds at 117 miles per hour.

Then came Phase II: Thomas RR 550 solid lifter cam, Offenhauser manifold with twin Holley 3,490 carbs, Schiefer 40-pound flywheel and clutch, and 4.56:1 gears.

We pushed 7,000 rpm shift points and crossed the line at 7,200 to net us top speeds of 124 mph. The ET was considerably better now at 11.43. Although our tests were limited by deadlines . . . we have every bit of confidence that the Nickey/Bill Thomas Camaro will top the '67 11.35 times."

Phase II was the maximum-performance package Nickey recommended for street use. Just imagine what Phase III was like.

When GM introduced their new A-body midsize cars in 1968, it seemed the Pontiac GTO got all the attention. Chevy fans got a new Chevelle, too, but for those who felt 396 cubic inches didn't cut it, Nickey had a solution. A 427 conversion was easy, or they could take the stock 396 and punch up the horsepower. Nickey's High Performance Center was willing to take just about any project. While you were at it, you could always get Nickey to add their "Traction-Action" traction bars or maybe a Stinger hood. Their advertisements and catalogs listed all the goodies you could buy and do yourself, or you could just let their experts do the work.

But Nickey didn't just stuff 427s into Camaros and Chevelles. There are reports they dropped the powerful 302 from the Z28 Camaro into some Chevelles and Novas as well. Corvettes were expensive and available with every engine imaginable in the late 1960s, but that wasn't good enough for some buyers, and Nickey could accommodate those owners. Live in another state? Like Mr. Norm's, Nickey Chevrolet would provide you with a one-way ticket from any location in the United States to go buy the Chevy of your dreams.

By 1969, the COPO Camaros and Chevelles were coming out, which eliminated much of the conversion business. Nickey sold those too, as well as Yenko's Chevrolets. The association with Nickey and Bill Thomas also ended, possibly since there was less of a need for their collaboration.

A year later, Nickey performed just two 454 Camaro conversions, though the performance parts business was still a huge success. Things were winding down.

Nickey 454 Nova 1973

"Buying a new muscle car right off the dealer's showroom floor has become a thing of the past," began the story in the May 1973 issue of *Hot Rod*. True, all the guys who were 27 in 1968 had become responsible 32-year-olds, and all new cars ran with low-compression, unleaded gas engines.

> But there are still a few performance enthusiasts who are willing to pay the price for the privilege of driving a genuine muscle car, and this is where Nickey Chevrolet of Chicago, Illinois, enters the picture . . . To satisfy the that market, Nickey is offering '73 Camaros, Nova's and Chevelles with a choice of powerplants. You can order the 370 horsepower 350 cubic-inch LT-1, 430 horsepower 427 ci L-88, or 450 horsepower 454 ci LS-6 engines coupled with either a four-speed Muncie or a Turbo-hydramatic transmission and virtually any positraction rear-end ratio you might want.

continued on page 66

62 CHAPTER 5

ABOVE: Nickey's High Performance Center was willing to do just about any project, including a 500-horsepower 396 Chevelle.

LEFT: Nickey's 1968 Chevelle also sported the '67 Corvette-style Stinger hood.

BELOW, LEFT: No 427 engine conversion here, but headers and internal mods brought this 396 up to 500 horsepower.

BELOW: Offenhauser manifold with twin Holley 3490 carbs from Thomas's hot setup. *Popular Hot Rodding* saw 11.43 seconds at 127 miles per hour with this and other mods.

NICKEY CHEVROLET: QUICK (WITH A BACKWARD "K") 63

The Other Speed Dealers

Fred Gibb Chevrolet

LaHarpe, Illinois, is not the end of the earth, but you can see it from there. Yet this small-town (pop. 1,385) Chevy dealer was a big player in the performance market.

Fred Gibb Chevrolet opened in LaHarpe in 1948. It was your typical rural Chevy dealer until 1967. That's when Herb Fox, the dealership's ace salesman, purchased a '67 Z28 Camaro and went drag racing. Fred Gibb accompanied Fox to the local strip in Cahokia, Illinois, and was hooked. Gibb sponsored Fox's "Little Hoss," and running in D/Gas they were 35–0 in 1967. A chance meeting with Harrell resulted in the dealership partnering with "Mr. Chevrolet." With Harrell's help, Fox took the AHRA Top Stock class in 1968 with a best time of 11.75 seconds.

Gibb was completely hooked. He noticed that Chevrolet only sold L78 396 Novas with four-speeds and, thinking there would be a market for these cars in Automatic-class racing, he leveraged the COPO and ordered the required minimum fifty L78 Novas with 400 Turbo Hydra-Matic transmission. Fox remembers selling all fifty COPO 9738s at sticker with no trade-ins—Harrell picked up about twenty of them.

Gibb earned legendary status the following year by ordering fifty Camaros powered by the all-aluminum ZL1 427 engine developed for Can-Am racing. Chevrolet thought the COPO 9560 cars would sell for around $4,900, so Gibb was shocked when the first trailer load arrived in LaHarpe on December 31, 1968—the ZL1 option cost $4,160 alone, sending the total well over $7,000. Gibb was able to sell thirteen of the monsters and convinced Chevrolet to take the other cars back to sell through other dealers. Eventually, sixty-nine of the famous COPO ZL1 Camaros were built.

Gibb died in 1993, but his wife, Helen, carried on her husband's legacy, attending many shows and meeting many fans. Even in her eighties, she drove her purple GMMG 2002 ZL1 Camaro prototype. Helen died in 2014 at age ninety-one.

"It was a great time in my life to have worked with Fred," Fox told *Hemmings*. "Not just any dealer could have done the COPO Novas and the ZL1s like he did."

Dana Chevrolet

Southern California was the birthplace of the car culture, yet no dealer specialized in performance cars there—at least until Dana Chevrolet opened in 1967. Payton Cramer had been working in Ford's controller's office when he was sent to California in the 1960s to help Shelby with his operation's finances. Cramer became Shelby's general manager until 1966, when Shelby's Mustang operations began moving to Detroit.

Cramer learned the performance business from Shelby, so, rather then move back to Detroit, he partnered with an L.A. Mercedes dealer, Paul Dombroski, to purchase a bankrupt Chevy dealership in Southgate, California. They named the revived dealership after the side street on which it was located. Not wanting to mix performance cars with the typical vehicles a dealership sells, Cramer and Dombroski found a building nearby and opened the Dana Hi-Performance Center.

A story in *Hot Rod* noted:

> The Dana plan of attack on the customer could well be called a "You Drive" approach, with all a customer having to do is supply the necessary capital for car preparation. One of the most interesting outgrowths of this idea is the interest in the 427-powered "Dana Camaro." In fact, a buyer can order his Camaro with "all the good stuff," and not even have to worry about having any work done until delivery day.

The Performance Center was run by Dick Guldstrand, one of the best Corvette and Camaro tuners ever. Dana sponsored a McLaren Mk. III in Can-Am racing, and Guldstrand's Z28 Camaro in Trans Am. Guldstrand also made history when his Dana-sponsored L88 Corvette led the GT class at Le Mans in 1967 for 11½ hours before breaking a wrist pin. Guldstrand's '67 L88 was clocked at 176 miles per hour on Le Mans' long Mulsanne Straight before failing.

After a disagreement between the partners, Payton Cramer sold his half of the dealership to Dombroski, who then sold it to Cormier Chevrolet. It only lasted eighteen months, but Dana Chevrolet left a major performance legacy.

Bob Tasca Ford

Ford Motor Company spent millions on Henry Ford II's "Total Performance" program in the 1960s, yet their international success didn't always translate into dealership sales. Bob Tasca knew drag racing was the grassroots sport that drove sales like no other, but he had to convince Ford management. Tasca had started at a Ford dealership in 1948, worked his way up to general manager, then struck out on his own, buying a struggling Ford dealership in Bristol, Rhode Island, in 1953. Sales went from 30 cars per year to 126 in just two months. A hurricane destroyed the

Fred Gibb's wife, Helen, was a regular at many Midwest Chevy shows until her death in 2014 at age 91. Here she's sitting in front of one of the 50 COPO 9738 Novas created by Gibb and Harrell. Even in her 80s she drove her purple GMMG 2002 ZL1 Camaro prototype. *Tom & Kelly Glatch*

dealership in 1954, but Ford offered Tasca another shop in East Providence, Rhode Island.

Tasca began drag racing Fords in the early 1960s, with Bill Lawton as his driver. Contrary to the old saying, Tasca discovered that racing on Sunday didn't necessarily turn into sales on Monday—at least if the dealer didn't have a compelling street machine to sell.

Tasca sold $100,000 in performance parts every month, so he knew what he was doing. Ford's decision to add the big 390 FE engine to the 1967 Mustang was a step in the right direction, but the 390 was a slug compared to Chevy's 396 or Pontiac's 400. Tasca had a 428 Police Interceptor engine installed in a 390 Mustang they had at the shop. They also added 427 heads and a 735-cfm Holley. The result was Tasca KR8 Mustang. *Hot Rod* featured the KR8 along with a ballot for readers to send to Ford. The result was overwhelming; in 1968, Ford began offering the 428 Super Cobra Jet Mustang.

In the same way that Mr. Norm's Grand Spaulding Dodge had influenced Chrysler's products, Tasca Ford showed the manufacturer what the customer wanted. Tasca grew to be the second largest Ford dealer in the nation—and made musclecar history along the way.

Berger Chevrolet

"If Chevy Makes It, Berger Has It," said the 1974 ad in *Hot Rod*. Grand Rapids is a nice city in western Michigan, but not one you'd expect to be a performance car destination. Long before companies like Summit and Jeg's dominated the mail order (or Internet) performance parts business, though, Berger Chevrolet was there.

William Berger opened his Grand Rapids Chevrolet dealership in 1926 after working for another dealer. Over the years, the dealership grew into the largest in western Michigan, with the facilities at 28th St. SE expanding several times. In November 1968, Berger opened its high-performance parts business. Berger had done a few "Berger Preferred Power" 427 Camaro conversions, and, in 1969, they'd sold a number of COPO cars; still, their focus was on parts. Berger hired a local NHRA Sportsman racer, Jim Luikens, to work in the new High-Performance Parts Department. Eighteen months later Luikens was manager.

"This was the time of Vietnam and a lot of soldiers would write us and tell us that they would be getting out of the service soon and wanted to build a hot car," Luikens told author John Gunnell in 2010.

> Early on, R. Dale Berger Jr. realized that, for every person who could afford a 427 Camaro conversion, there were millions of racers who built their own cars for circle track or straight-line competition. So he decided to specialize in selling the parts they would need to do that. Many times I would get up at 10 p.m. to open up for racers who needed parts for a race.

Mike Wawee was Berger's high-performance car salesman. "He fielded the letters from Vietnam and worked up quotes for them," Luikens remembered. "I thought the world of him for that. We just had a magical group that was in the right place at the right time."

Berger sponsorship could be seen on the NHRA Funny Car of "Jungle Jim" Liberman, Jim Bucher in *Top Fuel*, and J. D. McDuffie's NASCAR racer. "I felt like I was the everyman racer's friend back then," Luikens said. "But the catalytic converter came along, performance dried up and I left at a really good time." Before he left in 1975, Berger's performance business reached one million dollars in annual sales.

Matt Berger revived the dealership's performance business in 2003, building upgraded fourth- and fifth-generation Camaros. But it was Berger's performance parts business from 1968 to 1975 that kept the good times rolling.

Berger Preferred Power returned in 2010 with 550 supercharged horsepower in a new Camaro SS. Matt Berger revived the dealership's performance business in 2003, building upgraded fourth- and fifth-generation Camaros. *Tom & Kelly Glatch*

Nickey L88 Nova 1973

 # PRODUCED: 2

ENGINE: 427-cubic-inch V-8

HORSEPOWER: 430

TORQUE: 460 lb-ft

¼-MILE TIME: 12.03 at 116.57 mph (slicks)

continued from page 62

Hot Rod ordered up a '73 Nova Hatchback with the L88 engine and automatic. They decked it out with air shocks, traction bars, headers, electric fuel pump, and a Vitar 9-inch stall converter. Nickey built the car in seventy-two hours, then flew it to California in a Boeing 747. Of course, this was smog-laden California, so the magazine took it in for the required emissions testing. With a little carb tweaking, they were able to pass, and this nasty Nova was truly street legal.

Now, for the real test. *Hot Rod* got the Nickey Nova down to 12.03 at 116.57 miles per hour with slicks. "The Nova fulfilled the claims made by Nickey. It could be made to meet the most stringent emissions requirements and still deliver lightning performance. . . . Who says you can't buy performance in '73?" Nickey Chevrolet built two of these Novas that year.

Nickey 454 Camaro 1974

The Nova story in *Hot Rod* inspired a customer to order a special 1974 Camaro. The gentleman from Northbrook, Illinois, wanted the same Stage III Super Car Conversion as the Nova, but on a brand-new Camaro LT purchased in late November 1973. The car was supposed to get the 454 "450 horsepower Special High Performance Mark IV" engine, but the second owner speculates the dealership substituted an L88 using parts they had on hand, knowing what was about to happen. Chevrolet no longer sold the L88 as a complete engine, so Nickey built one from an L88 short-block by adding iron open-chamber heads, 12.5:1 pistons, and a Holley 780 on a low-profile LS6 intake manifold. The owner also wanted 3.08:1 gears for cruising, and 14x7 front and 15x8 rear Cragar SS wheels with Nickey centers. Days after the Camaro was delivered, the dealership closed for good, shuttered because of mounting business issues.

Down the road from the dealership, Seelig and Swiatek opened Nickey Chicago, a continuation of the performance side of the business that lasted until 1977. In 2003, a Chicagoland Chevy enthusiast, Stefano Bimbi, bought the rights to the Nickey name. Along with Swiatek, he opened Nickey Performance in St. Charles, Illinois, offering both modern and vintage performance Camaros. It's a nice reminder of the Original Super Car Headquarters.

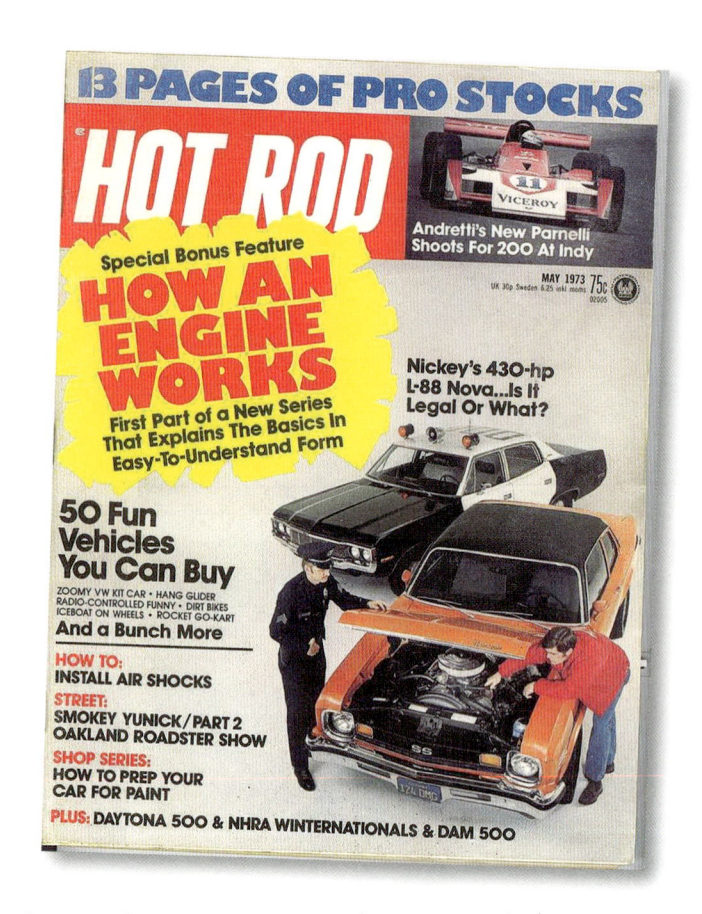

Nickey's 430 horsepower Nova was the cover story in the May 1973 issue of *Hot Rod*. The L88-powered Nova hatchback was not only fast, it was also fully California emissions compliant. *Author's Collection*

RIGHT: The January 1967 issue of *TACH* magazine featured "First Test Anywhere of Nickey 427 Camaro." *Nickey Chicago*

BELOW: "427 Makes Camaro 'Boss'" was another cover story on the Nickey/Bill Thomas 427 Camaro in 1967. *Nickey Chicago*

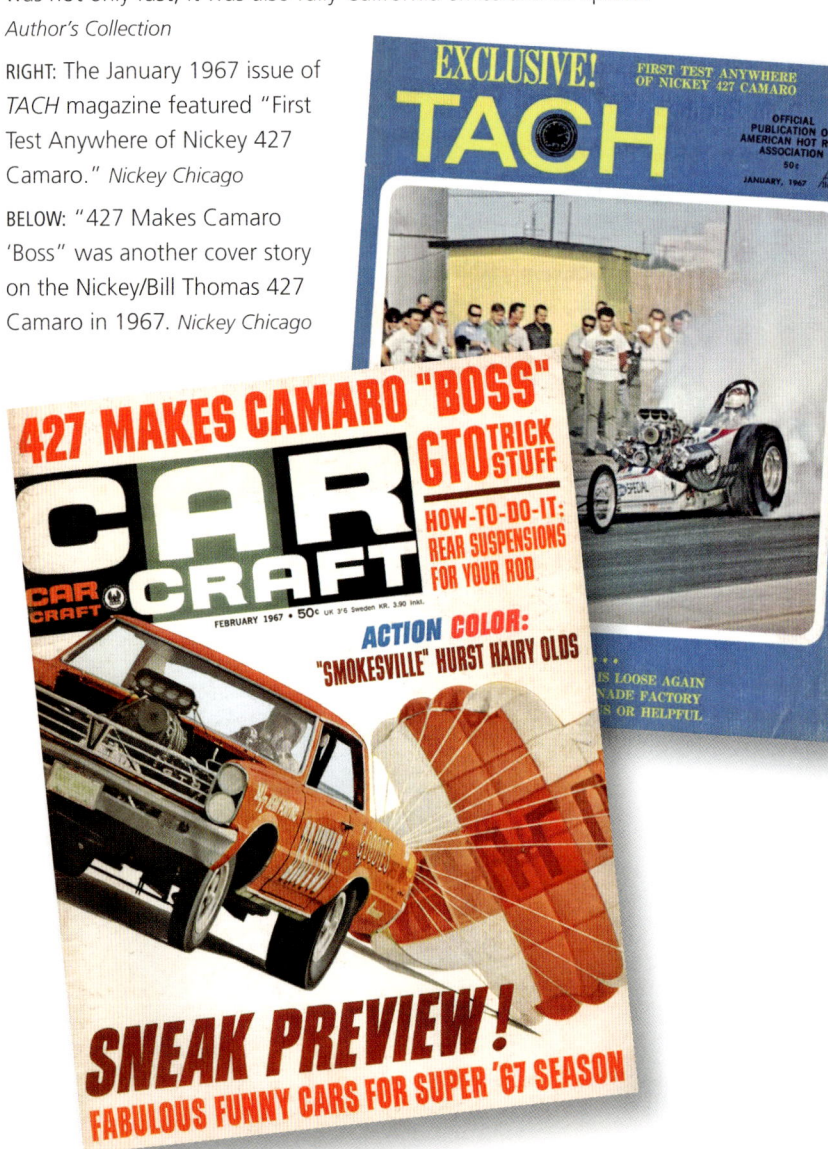

66 CHAPTER 5

TOP: The only modification to the Nickey-delivered 1968 L72 Corvette are the Hooker headers and side pipes, and T-70 Torque-Thrust wheels. Nickey could build anything.

ABOVE: Sun tachometer, oil pressure, and water temperature gauges were installed in the otherwise stock interior.

ABOVE: Corvettes were expensive and available with every engine imaginable in the late 1960s, but that wasn't good enough for some buyers. Nickey could accommodate his choosiest customers.

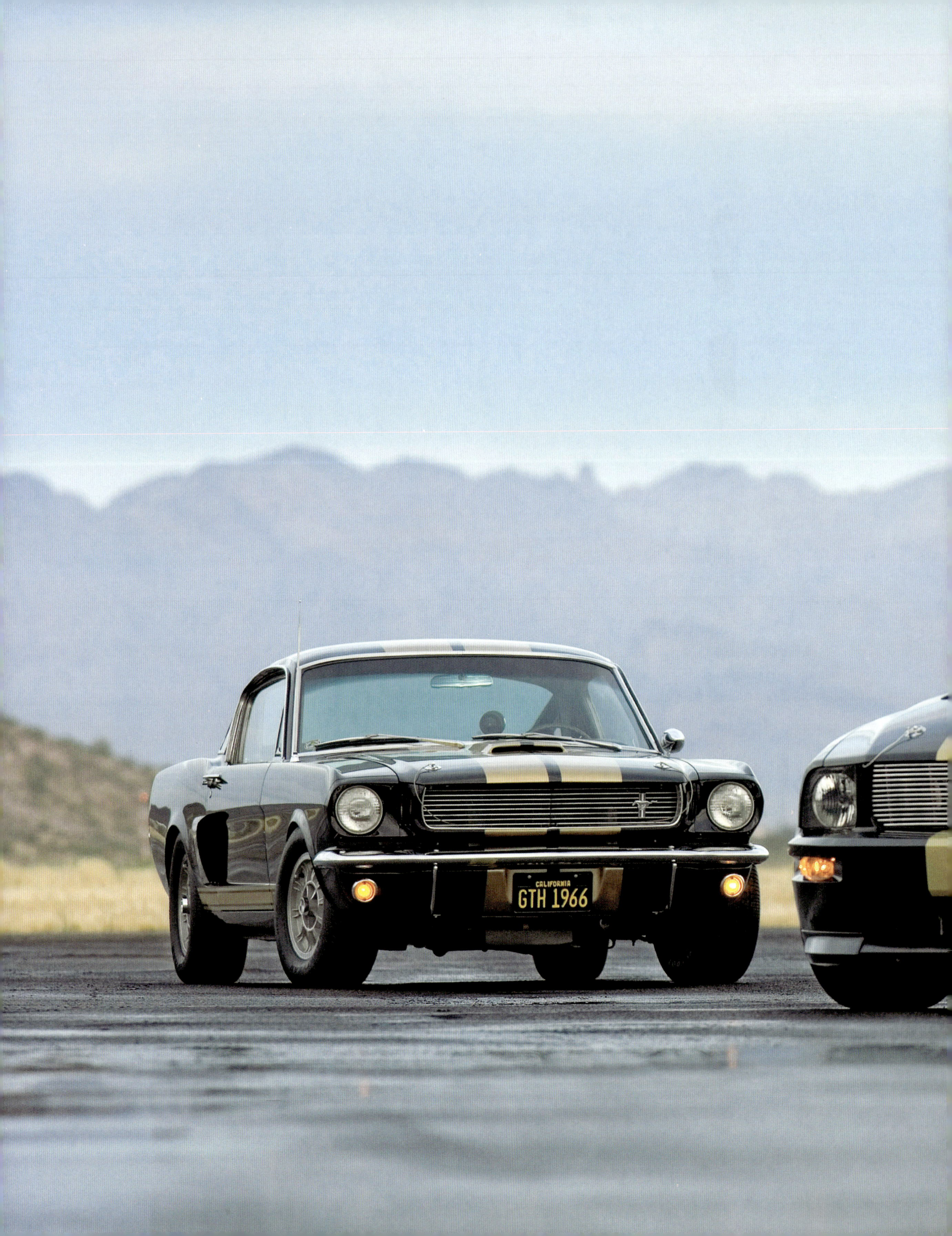
CALIFORNIA
GTH 1966

SECTION TWO

The Specialists

Chapter 6

Shelby American
The Legend, The Legacy

"Goddamn it, keep Shelby American alive," Carroll Shelby faintly ordered John Luft, the president of Shelby's company, just hours before he died. Shelby couldn't live forever—but his legend could.

Carroll Hall Shelby was born January 11, 1923, in Leesburg, Texas. He died eighty-nine years later in Houston on May 12, 2012. In between, he created a Texas-sized legacy unlike anyone's in the automobile business.

Heart issues kept Shelby bedridden for much of his childhood, but by his mid-teens he seemed to have outgrown them. He joined the Army Air Corps during World War II, training pilots in Texas. After the war he tried his hand at various occupations, including oil rig roughneck and chicken farmer.

In May 1952, a childhood friend, Ed Wilkins, asked Shelby if he would like to drive the MG TC in a sports car race. It was straight out of a Hollywood script: at age twenty-nine, with no racing experience, Shelby won. His next

RIGHT: On July 4, 1965, American Bob Bondurant and Frenchman Jo Schlesser took the checkered flag at the conclusion of the 12 Hours of Reims. Their victory sealed the 1965 World Manufacturer's Championship in the GT class. Bondurant and Schlesser drove this car, Cobra Daytona Coupe CSX2601, the sixth of the six legendary Daytona Coupes built by Shelby American.

PREVIOUS PAGES: After 36 years, Ford again teamed with Carroll Shelby, this time to create the 2006 Mustang GT-H, celebrating the fortieth anniversary of the Shelby GT350-H. At age eighty-three, Carroll Shelby was back in the Mustang business.

70

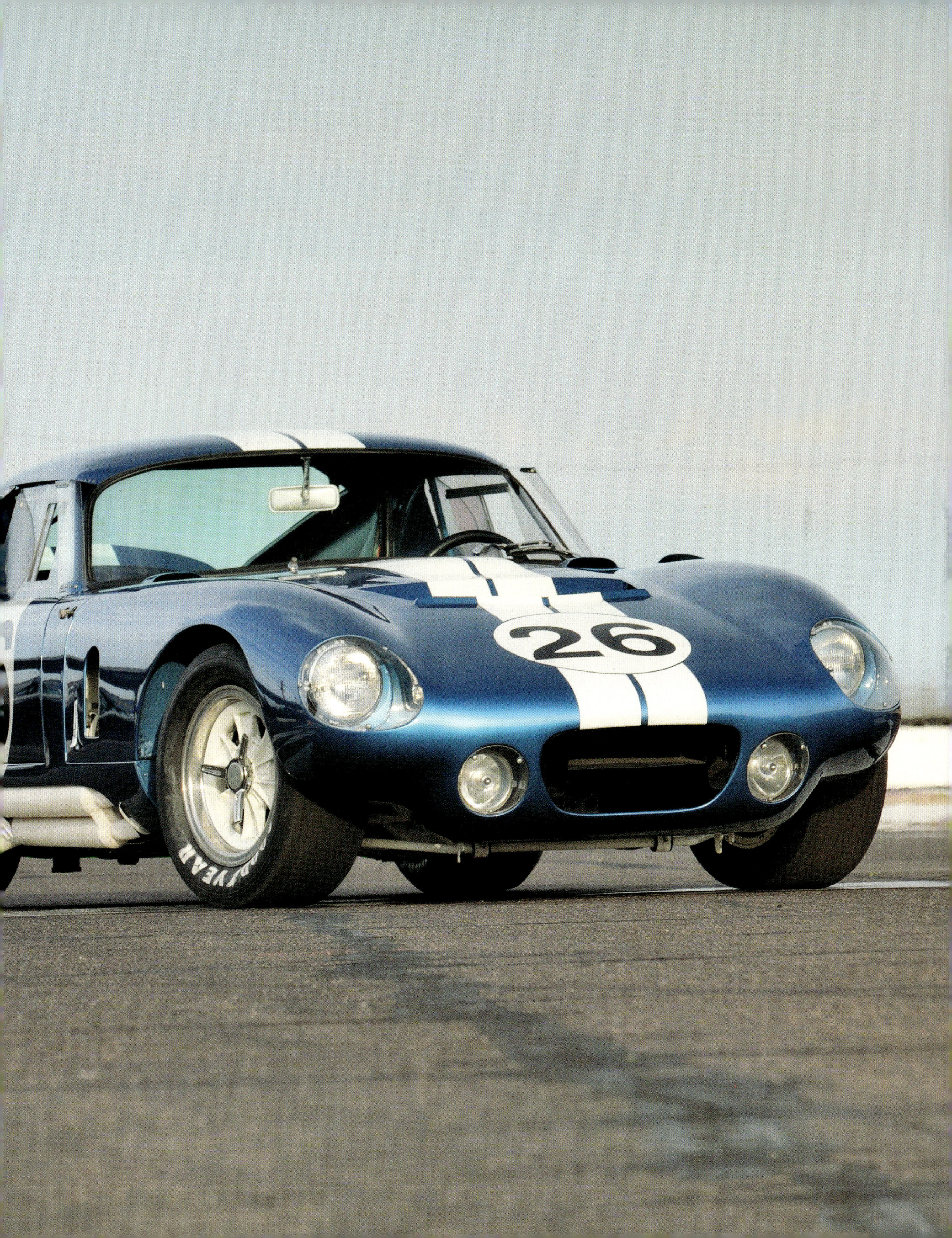
26
GOODYEAR

TOP: The most copied automobile ever, Shelby's 427 Cobra produced numbers that seemed impossible for the time. *Car and Driver* reported 0–100–0 in 14.5 seconds. Shelby's test driver, Ken Miles, actually did it in 13.8 seconds. Remember, that was more than a half-century ago! *Archives/TEN: The Enthusiast Network Magazines, LLC*

ABOVE: Carroll Shelby strikes a classic pose behind the wheel of one of his Cobras. *Ford Archives*

TOP, LEFT: When *Motor Trend* finally got to test the Cobra, Shelby had already upped the horsepower with the change from the 260 to 289 Ford V-8. They reported, "With a base price of $5995, the Cobra doesn't come cheap, but if you fancy yourself an enthusiast and you want the most out of your dollar, we'd recommend a serious look and a personal test drive in this car." *Archives/TEN: The Enthusiast Network Magazines, LLC*

LEFT: The first true Cobra, CSX2000, was completed in February 1962. *Sports Car Graphic* magazine got the scoop, being the first publication to test the car, which was featured in their May '62 issue. They called the Cobra "one of the most impressive production sports cars we've ever driven. Its acceleration . . . can only be described as explosive . . ." Afterward, *Road & Track* got it up to 153 miles per hour, while *Car Life* did 0–60 in 4.2 seconds. Those are impressive numbers today, and simply shocking in 1962. *Archives/TEN: The Enthusiast Network Magazines, LLC*

CHAPTER 6

One of those rides in 1953 was in a Cadillac-powered Allard J2. Sidney Allard built the sports cars in England, but he equipped them with powerful Lincoln and Cadillac V-8. Extremely fast but cursed with diabolical handling, few mortals could master the Allard. It was no problem for Shelby.

Arriving late to one event, Shelby drove the Allard wearing the striped bib overalls that he had on. The bibs became his trademark, along with a black cowboy hat—just another way the "Ol' Shel" deceived unsuspecting competitors.

Shelby's talents attracted the attention of Englishman John Wyer, head of Aston Martin's racing program. Shelby's first drive for Wyer was at the 12 Hours of Sebring. Though the Aston broke, Shelby's abilities were evident. Much of 1954 was spent in Europe racing for Aston Martin. By 1956, Shelby opened a sports car dealership in Dallas, and had his pick of first-line Ferrari and Maserati racers; two years later, he relocated to Modena, Italy, the home of those companies. Shelby drove Aston Martin's Formula 1 car and competed in Aston's DBR3 sports racer in the 24 Hours of Le Mans in 1958 and 1959. It was at the second Le Mans that Shelby and teammate Roy Salvadori triumphed on the biggest international stage of them all.

Shelby also received a gift in 1959: wealthy Texas oil man Gary Laughlin bought three Corvette chassis from Chevrolet and sent them to Carrozzeria Scaglietti in Modena, Italy, to be covered in an aluminum coupe body. Scaglietti had supplied bodies to Ferrari during the 1950s, and what resulted looked very Ferrari-like, but with the Corvette chassis and fuel-injected engines. Laughlin kept one for himself and gave the other two Italian/American hybrids to Shelby and a fellow Texan, Jim Hall.

Shelby's heart condition worsened in 1960, and he was forced to retire. Relocating to southern California, Shelby used his racing triumphs to score an exclusive Goodyear distributorship on the West Coast. He also opened the Carroll Shelby School of High Performance Driving at Riverside Raceway in 1961.

Then came the news: British sports car maker A. C. Cars Ltd. had a problem. The six-cylinder Bristol engine that A. C. used to power their Ace sports car was no longer being manufactured. Remembering the hybrid Cad-Allard and Scaglietti Corvettes, Shelby attempted to find an American V-8 that could fit the compact Ace. Chevrolet had the Corvette and wasn't interested, but Ford was just embarking on their "Total Performance" program. Ford was also just readying a small, light, 221-cubic-inch V-8, and they were happy to give one to Shelby for evaluation. The V-8's dimensions fit the Ace with minimal modifications, and the owners of A. C. Cars were receptive to fitting the V-8 into their Ace. They shipped an engineless car to California where, in a space rented from friend and hot rodder Dean Moon, the CSX2001 was born; it was the first Shelby sports car. Dean Moon recalled that "we got drunk, and drove it around an impromptu road course we had setup between the oil derricks. When it didn't break, even after all that rough treatment, well, then we knew we had a good car."

CSX2001 was the first production Cobra, and also one of the very first batch of cars shipped by air to early dealer Ed Hugus's European Cars in Pittsburgh, Pennsylvania. The first delivery arrived in July 1962.

SHELBY AMERICAN: THE LEGEND, THE LEGACY 73

Shelby Cobra 1962–65

According to Shelby, he had a dream one night in which the name "Cobra" came to him. Whether fact or another Shelby tall tale, the story only adds to the Cobra mystique. Ford Division's general manager, Donald Frey, loved the prototype and gave Shelby Ford's support. He also told Shelby about a larger version of the small V-8 to be released, now at 260 cubic inches. Shelby made some suggestions to A. C. Cars, after which a second car was on its way to California.

That first true Cobra, CSX2001, was completed in February 1962. The handcrafted aluminum body was polished metal when *Sports Car Graphic* tested it, calling the Cobra "one of the most impressive production sports cars we've ever driven." Afterward, each time a magazine tested the car, it was painted a different color; this was to give the impression that Shelby had completed a number of Cobras. *Road & Track* got it up to 153 miles per hour, while *Car Life* did 0–60 in 4.2 seconds. So the legend was born.

Peter Brock, a young former GM designer and Shelby's first employee, designed the famous Cobra emblem. To make sure it looked right in metal, Shelby had a local jeweler make the first prototype. After the first few Cobras were built, Shelby moved to larger quarters in Venice, California, in early 1963. After the first 75 Cobras, Ford's famous 289 engine became available. The 289 Cobra lost its first road race, at Riverside Raceway, to the new Z06 Corvettes. Speed wasn't the issue—the Cobra ran away from the Corvettes—but a rear hub broke. The Cobras rarely lost again, capturing the SCCA class championships from 1963 to 1968. Cobras were equally successful drag racing, setting numerous records. Shelby also built a number of 289 Cobra Federation Internationale de l'Automobile (FIA) Competition cars for European racing. Shelby's personal Cobra, CSX2589, was the last of the 289 cars.

ABOVE AND LEFT: CSX2001 was the first production Cobra.

ABOVE, RIGHT: Before racing the car in France, Vincent embarked on a program of modifying the car to essentially 1964 Cobra race specs. This included swapping the 260 engine for a full-race, Weber-equipped 289 and adding Halibrand 6.5- and 8.5-inch mag wheels (requiring modification of the fenders), sway bars, an oil cooler, a 36-gallon fuel tank, and a cutout at the leading edge of the hood to allow air to escape from the engine compartment. Parts were made available from A. C. Cars and the work was performed by the official Shelby garage in Europe, the Garage de Lorraine of Andre Chardonnet.

Shelby Cobra 260 1962

- **# PRODUCED:** 75
- **ENGINE:** 260-cubic-inch V-8
- **HORSEPOWER:** 260
- **TORQUE:** 269 lb-ft
- **¼-MILE TIME:** 13.8 at 112 mph

Shelby Cobra 289 1963-1965

- **# Produced:** 580
- **ENGINE:** 289-cubic-inch V-8
- **HORSEPOWER:** 271
- **TORQUE:** 314 lb-ft
- **¼-MILE TIME:** 13.8 at 104 mph

ABOVE: CSX2093 was the ninety-third Cobra built and is one of only eight cars modified with the Shelby-developed Dragonsnake package.

LEFT: The Dragonsnake raced with a Weber-carbureted 289 Ford V-8 that included Ballanger side-mount headers. The Dragonsnake package could cost as much as $8,990.

RIGHT: Early Shelby American magazine ad for the Cobra. Even police officers had to check out the fastest American car available in the 1960s and later. *Author's Collection*

LEFT: CSX2487 was invoiced to Shelby American on July 9, 1964, and shipped aboard the SS *Loch Gowan* to Hayward Ford Motors in Los Angeles.

LEFT: CSX3301 was the first car in the third production group of 427 Cobras. Completed at A. C. Cars for delivery directly to Ford Advanced Vehicles in Slough, England, the CSX3301 was purchased new by a Mr. Franck of Paris, France, who sold it to GT40 owner Jean-Pierre Van Den Doorn, also of Paris.

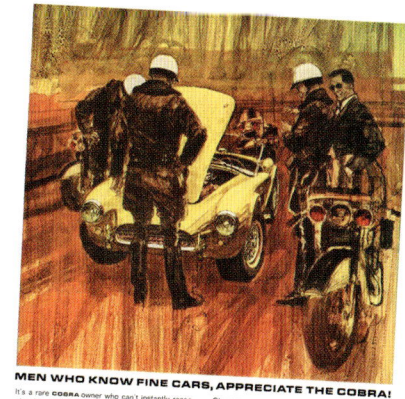

SHELBY AMERICAN: THE LEGEND, THE LEGACY 75

The Cobra Daytona Coupe: American Royalty

The stark, purposeful interior of Cobra Daytona Coupe CSX2601.

Before the French Revolution, the kings of France were crowned in the great cathedral in the city of Reims. On July 4, 1965, another coronation took place when American Bob Bondurant and Frenchman Jo Schlesser took the checkered flag at the conclusion of the 12 Hours of Reims. Their victory sealed the 1965 World Manufacturer's Championship in the GT class. Ford had finally defeated Ferrari.

Bondurant and Schlesser were driving Cobra Daytona Coupe CSX2601, the sixth of the six legendary Daytona Coupes built by Shelby American. While the FIA Cobra roadsters were practically unbeatable in US road racing, the European tracks were another story. The 5.138-mile Circuit de Reims-Gueux was a perfect example: two long straightaways of 1.53 miles and mostly fast, sweeping turns. Then there was Le Mans, with its infamous 3.7-mile long Mulsanne Straight, where prototype racers in the late 1980s touched 250 miles per hour before slamming into a tight 90-degree turn (two chicanes were added in 1990 to slow thing to around 200 miles per hour). If Shelby and Ford were to compete on Ferrari's home turf, their cars would need better aerodynamics.

Shelby turned to Brock for the solution. The young designer came up with a body similar to the all-conquering Ferrari GTOs, but it was lower and offered a few aero tricks of his own, including a tail and spoiler inspired by the work of German scientist Dr. Wunibald Kamm. Ford sent engineers from their Aeroneutronics Division to suggest ideas and run tests on the completed prototype. Shelby also had Benny Howard, a famous aero engineer, review the design. Howard said Brock's design simply wouldn't work. "I said to Carroll, 'Benny knows about airplanes. He doesn't know about cars,'" Brock told *Car and Driver*. "Carroll looked me in the eyes and said, 'You better be right.'"

The first coupe body, built on chassis CSX2286, was crafted of aluminum, and Shelby's master fabricator, Phil Remington, and his crew completed the Cobra in time for the 1964 Daytona Continental race in February. The name "Daytona Coupe" stuck. Driver Ken Miles was able to hit 186 miles per hour on Riverside Raceway's straightaway in testing, where the Cobra roadsters topped out at 160 miles per hour. With proof that Brock was right, the remaining five Daytona Coupes received aluminum bodies fabricated by Carrozzeria Gransport in Modena, Italy.

"The FIA considered the Daytona coupe just a variation of the roadster body, since it used the existing roadster chassis," Remington said. But as the Daytona Coupes began showing their superiority during the 1964 season, the FIA inspectors "hassled us endlessly, always making sure we weren't running anything that wasn't listed on the original homologation papers," Remington told author Wallace Wyss.

While the Daytona Coupes finished 1964 second in the championship behind Ferrari, Shelby's continuous improvements to the cars resulted in the historic championship in 1965, the only Manufacturer's Championship ever won by an American company.

What was considered ugly in 1965 is now one of the most copied cars ever. And the importance of the Daytona Coupes have not been forgotten a half century later. When the triumphant Bondurant/Schlesser Daytona Coupe CSX2601 went to auction in 2009, it sold for $7,250,000—by far the record for an American car to date. "Many vintage race cars have a strong American racing history to share . . . but no car can claim a finer race hour than the Shelby Daytona Cobra Coupe CSX2601," said Dana Mecum, president of Mecum Auction. "The legacy of its World Manufacturer's Championship win stays with us more than four decades later, reminding us of one the proudest moments in US race history and a competitive spirit of victory against all odds."

To celebrate the fiftieth anniversary of Shelby's Championship, the world's greatest vintage race car event, the Goodwood Revival in England brought all six Daytona Coupes together for the first time. "We're delighted to honor the fiftieth anniversary of Shelby American's World Sports Car Championship success by recreating the 1965 Sebring pits for what will be a wonderfully nostalgic display," said Lord March, Goodwood Revival founder.

When the triumphant Bondurant/Schlesser Daytona Coupe CSX2601 was auctioned in 2009, it sold for $7,250,000—by far the record for an American car to date.

Gathering all six Shelby Cobra Daytona Coupes for the first time in history was a difficult feat, but the support of their current owners demonstrates the importance of this racing achievement. Since Carroll Shelby's team was truly an international effort comprised of people and machinery from across the globe, the Goodwood Revival, the world's largest historic motor racing event, is the perfect place to tell the story of an underdog team who made motor racing history with their achievements.

PARTIAL COBRA DAYTONA COUPE RACE HISTORY

- 1964: 12 Hours of Sebring (GT class win, Dave MacDonald/Bob Holbert)
- 1964: 24 Hours of Le Mans (GT class win, fourth overall, Dan Gurney/Bob Bondurant)
- 1964: RAC Tourist Trophy (GT class win)
- 1964: Tour de France Automobile (GT class win)
- 1965: 24 Hours of Daytona (GT class win)
- 1965: 12 Hours of Sebring (GT class win)
- 1965: Italian Grand Prix at Monza (GT class win)
- 1965: Nürburgring 1000 (GT class win)
- 1965: 12 Hours of Reims (GT class win, clinched 1965 World Sportscar Championship)
- 1965: Enna-Pergusa (GT class win)
- 1965: 25 land speed records at Bonneville

Sunbeam Tiger 1964–67

If there was a problem with Shelby's Cobra, it was that most people couldn't afford one. At over $6,000, the Cobra cost almost $1,000 more than a fuel-injected Corvette—and how many people had the money on hand for one of those loaded Sting Rays? At least with the Cobra you got a hand-formed aluminum body, a large measure of exclusivity, and the kind of performance than ran circles around a "Fuelie" Corvette. All the same, speed costs money. With a little help from Shelby, though, there was an alternative.

The Sunbeam Alpine was one of those traditional British sports cars that proliferated during the 1950s and 1960s. When introduced in 1959, the Alpine had a pleasant, modern shape, with a nod to the huge fins made famous by the 1958 Chryslers. It handled well, had front disc brakes, and enjoyed some competition success. Like most British motorcars, though, the Alpine was saddled with a low-tech engine under the "bonnet"—a 97.2-cubic-inch four producing 90 horsepower.

Sunbeam was named after Sir Malcolm Campbell's 1926 land speed record car; it was owned by the Rootes Group. Like most

TOP: Second-generation Mark II Sunbeam Tigers got a 200-horsepower 289 V-8 upgrade. Just 633 of the total 7,083 Tigers built were Mark II models.

ABOVE: The $3,400 Sunbeam Tiger was an inexpensive alternate to the $6,000 Cobra. Shelby developed the Tiger, but Rootes Motors built it in England.

LEFT: Though the two-barrel Ford 260-cubic-inch engine only produced 164 horsepower, in the lightweight Sunbeam Tiger that was more than enough to humiliate much larger, more expensive machines. Vintage road tests showed 0–60 in 7.8 seconds with a top speed of 121 miles per hour. With a price around $3,400, the Tiger was a hit. *Archives/TEN: The Enthusiast Network Magazines, LLC*

British manufacturers during the 1960s, Rootes was rocked by labor turmoil and the poor English economy, so engine development was not financially possible. But Formula 1 legend Jack Brabham, who raced a factory-backed Alpine in Europe, had a suggestion: American V-8 power.

Ian Garrard, Rootes's West Coast manager, went to local dealerships with a yardstick, searching for a V-8 that would fit the Alpine's engine compartment. He found it in Ford's 221/260 powerplant. Knowing that Shelby's Cobras used the same engine, a meeting was arranged. Rootes agreed to pay Shelby $10,000 to develop a V-8-powered Alpine prototype.

Fitting the Ford engine and transmission in the Alpine was relatively easy—L.A. sports car maven Ken Miles built a similar prototype for Rootes for just $800—but the Shelby difference was in how their Alpine was engineered. To preserve the car's balance, Shelby master fabricator Phil Remington located the 260 V-8 further back in the engine compartment, a modification that required notches in the firewall. He also added rack-and-pinion steering and a larger cooling system. Dual exhausts were fabricated and routed through the frame rails. Garrard was thrilled with the little car's performance, especially compared with Miles's crude conversion. The Shelby prototype was shipped to England for inspection by management.

Lord Rootes, chairman of the company, drove the Shelby prototype and was delighted with the V-8 Alpine, approving it for production immediately. Instead of turning construction over to Shelby American, though, the car was built by Jensen Motors in England. Lord Rootes's friend, Henry Ford II, agreed to ship 3,000 260-cubic-inch 2-barrel engines to Rootes Group. With this, the Sunbeam Tiger was born.

Selling for $3,400, the Tiger was a hit! Though the two-barrel Ford engine only produced 164 horsepower, in the lightweight Tiger that was more than enough to humiliate much larger, more expensive machines. A Tiger, modified by Shelby, won the 1964 SCCA B-production Pacific Coast Divisional Championship Race at Willow Springs, California, beating Jaguars, Corvettes, and even Cobras. Tigers also set records in drag racing and won the famous the 1965 Monte Carlo Rally.

Shelby American designed performance kits for the Tiger, sold through Sunbeam dealers. Sunbeam produced 6,450 of the 260 Tigers, known as Mark I cars, in 1964 and 1965. When Ford's supply of 260 engines ran out, Tigers received the newer 289 V-8, making 200 horsepower. These Mark II Tigers also received a pretty egg-crate-pattern grille, a Shelby-like stripe on the side, and other minor changes.

Compared to traditional British sports cars, *Road & Track* commented:

> Like the Tiger I, the Tiger II is difficult to fault within the framework of what it is and what it is intended to be. It is a great pleasure to drive a small car that simply has gobs and gobs of power for its size. It makes a nice noise when you twist the key, it burbles confidentially along at very moderate revs in fourth gear, and it does everything with almost disdainful ease.

Just 633 of the total 7,083 Tigers built were Mark II models. Rootes was bought by Chrysler in 1964 and had the embarrassing distinction of building a Ford-powered sports car (the Mopar 273 V-8 wouldn't fit). Side badges were changed from "Powered by Ford" to "Sunbeam V8," but the new owners stayed true to the Tiger's heritage. Chrysler has been criticized by some as killing the Tiger after the 1967 model year, but the new US government regulations enacted in 1968 actually doomed the Tiger, the Austin Healey 3000, the original Mini, and many other imports from the US market. Without the US market, great cars like the Tiger and the Healey died on the vine.

Though not produced by Shelby, the Tiger was given the Shelby touch, and the amazing little sports car is an important part of the Shelby legend. How important? In 1995, when Shelby auctioned off many of the vehicles and items he'd accumulated over the years, one car remained in his possession: his personal Sunbeam Tiger. Enough said.

Shelby Mustang GT350 1965–66

Ford Motor Company had a problem. Despite the international success of the Cobra, it just wasn't a Ford. Marketing made sure the car was called the "Cobra powered by Ford," but it had about as much relevance to the cars in Ford showrooms as the "Lotus powered by Ford" that won the Indianapolis 500 in 1965. Ford's "Total Performance" message needed a halo, and Ford's "halo" car was the Mustang.

Ford didn't need to sell more Mustangs—it represents the single greatest new car launch in automotive history. By 1965, Ford had three plants working overtime to meet the demand for Lee Iacocca's "secretary's car." But no one would consider the Mustang a bona fide supercar.

The Shelby GT350 fulfilled the potential of the Mustang that Iacocca never saw. They were built to meet the Sports Car Club of America's rules to allow them into the production class. SCCA rules mandated that a minimum of one hundred cars be built for entry into the production classes. Feeling that one hundred race cars would not sell, Shelby built a slightly toned-down street version. He proudly displayed the new GT350 to the automotive press at Riverside Raceway on January 27, 1965.

Wimbledon White K-Code Mustang GT 2+2 Fastbacks from Ford's San Jose, California, plant were trucked to Shelby's new buildings at Los Angeles International Airport. They were built without rear seats, both to reduce weight and to meet the SCCA's rule allowing only two-seat sports cars. Shelby was allowed to modify either the engines or the suspension—but not both—to be considered "production."

TOP: On January 27, 1965, the Shelby GT350 made its debut at the Los Angeles International Auto Show. *Ford Archives*

ABOVE, LEFT: Shelby once said, "The only time a 'Vette would see Victory Circle was if a Shelby GT350 didn't show up." *Ford Archives*

ABOVE, RIGHT: Eleven 1966 GT350s were equipped with the Paxton supercharger, Autolite 4100 four-barrel carburetor and Carter high-volume fuel pump. The $670 blower boosted horsepower from 306 to 395.

LEFT: Full-page magazine ads for the GT350 emphasized that the vehicles were: "Hand assembled in Southern California in limited quantities by the craftsmen who are responsible for the championship Ford-powered Cobra sports car."

80 CHAPTER 6

They chose to upgrade the suspension, adding Traction Master over-axle traction bars to the rear axle, mounted to brackets inside the car in the space formerly occupied by the rear seat. The battery was moved to the trunk for better balance. The front upper A-arms were relocated by an inch, and a beefy anti-roll bar was added, while special Koni shocks were mounted all around to support the stock K-code springs. A quicker gear ratio was added to the manual steering box. The front brakes were 11-inch Kelsey-Hayes discs with heavy-duty pads; the rear brakes 10x3-inch drums (¾-inch wider than stock) with sintered metallic linings. A racing Detroit Locker differential delivered the power to the rear wheels. Those wheels were wide steel or optional cast-aluminum Cragers, with 130-mile-per-hour 7.75x15 Goodyear Blue Streaks mounted. "The words here are: control, limit, locate, stiffen, and snub," wrote *Motor Trend*.

Under the fiberglass hood designed by Brock was a stock 271-horsepower "HiPo" 289, to which Shelby added an aluminum high-rise intake manifold and huge Holley four-barrel. Headers fed a pair of straight-through mufflers and pipes that exited in front of the rear tires. The engine also got a pair of Shelby's trademark Cobra valve covers. Brock also designed the GT350 side stripes and wide blue "Le Mans" stripes running over the hood, top, and trunk. You probably won't see a '65 GT350 without the Le Mans stripes today, but most cars were not shipped with them—they were a dealer-installed option.

Every major magazine featured the GT350. *Motor Trend* commented:

> Not everyone will appreciate the cockpit noise and firm ride, but we're sure no enthusiast will ever complain . . . . The GT350's best handling qualities won't show with halfhearted cornering, though. You have to corner hard enough to take all the slack out of the suspension in one direction. Then you get (on smooth surface) a sensation of superb stability, and you can feel the tires really bite . . . .

> The GT-350 is one car that'll never put you asleep at the wheel. We recommend it as a sure cure for all strains of boredom. It positively exudes character—something rare in this day of follow-the-crowd compromises and design by large committees.

By the end of the 1965 model year, Shelby American produced 504 street GT350 Mustangs and 34 GT350R racers. The GT350R dominated SCCA B-production racing, sending the small-block Corvettes and Jaguar XKEs to the showers in 1965, 1966, and 1967. Mission accomplished! Or, as Shelby once said, "The only time a 'Vette would see Victory Circle was if a Shelby GT350 didn't show up."

The GT350 returned for 1966, just a bit kinder and gentler. The rear seat returned, deafening side exhaust was removed, and simpler under-axle traction bars were installed. Brock removed the rear roof vents and replaced them with Plexiglas. New exterior colors were offered—Raven Black, Sapphire Blue, Ivy Green, and Candy Apple Red—along with Wimbledon White. *Car and Driver* opined:

> For '66 the car has been considerably refined . . . though it's still a tough, for-men-only machine, requiring strong arms to twist the steering wheel, strong legs to push the pedals, and strong kidneys to survive the ride. The exhaust pipes, which used to end just ahead of the rear wheels (stock-car style, and right under your ear) have been lengthened and rerouted to terminate aft of the rear axle. This change has made the noise level more bearable, and almost solved the problem we mentioned last year of exhaust fumes seeping

Light, simple, and engineered for speed, the first Shelby GT350 was made to be driven–HARD. This magazine press car shows the effects of those highly publicized road tests, which further spread the Shelby legend to enthusiasts. *Archives/TEN: The Enthusiast Network Magazines, LLC*

There are only 1000 of these for rent in the entire world. Hertz has them all.

It's the Shelby G.T.350-H.
Only Hertz rents it.
Cobra engine. Disc brakes. High speed wheels and tires. Stick shift or automatic. Rally stripes. High performance shocks. Torque controlled rear axle. The whole load.
Why a rent-a-car with all this performance? We could have gotten a fleet of high-powered pseudo-sports-cars. But we figured you'd want to try a champion. Not just another imitation.
So we got the one car that holds the Sports Car Club of America National Championship.

And you can rent this 4-seater G.T.350-H from Hertz in most cities for a day. Or longer. But *only* from Hertz.
Two stipulations. You have to be at least 25 years old. And you have to hurry. (It's all on a first-come-first-serve basis.)
So make your reservation today. One local phone call reserves your car here. Or just about anywhere in the country.
Call the only rent-a-car company that offers you a championship G.T.350-H.
Hertz.

Let Hertz put *you* in the driver's seat. (Isn't that where you belong?)

Don't have the $3704.62 to buy a GT350? Then rent one! In September 1965, Shelby American General Manager Peyton Cramer made a deal with Hertz Rent-a-Car to produce the GT350H. The rates varied, but in the New York City area you could rent a GT350H for $17 a day (or $70 a week) and 17 cents per mile. You had to be at least twenty-five years old and a member of the Hertz Sports Car Club. *Author's Collection*

into the cockpit. The ride seems more supple, though still what the British call "gratifyingly stiff," and the noisy, ratcheting-type, limited-slip racing differential is gone (thank heavens; it used to scuff the inside rear wheel around a turn and then unlock with a crack like a breaking suspension member).

If you didn't have the $3704.62 to buy a GT350, you could rent one! In September 1965, Shelby American General Manager Peyton Cramer made a deal with Hertz Rent-A-Car to produce the GT350H. The rates varied, but in the New York City area you could rent a GT350H for $17 per day (or $70 per week) and 17 cents per mile. You had to be at least twenty-five years old and a member of the Hertz Sports Car Club. The first eighty-five cars built by Shelby had the standard four-speed, but after the first cars returned to Hertz with fried clutches, reason prevailed and subsequent GT350H cars had three-speed automatics.

Most of the Hertz Shelbys were Raven Black with Bronze Powder side and Le Mans stripes, though fifty each were painted Candy Apple Red, Wimbledon White, Sapphire Blue, and Ivy Green. Ford

said, "The idea was to put high-performance, special-edition Shelby Mustang coupes into the hands of racing enthusiast–minded rental customers." Great idea!

If the standard GT350 wasn't fast enough—*Car and Driver* recorded 0–60 miles per hour in 6.6 seconds and the quarter in 15.2 seconds at 93 miles per hour—Shelby offered a supercharged version. Andy Granatelli's Paxton Products approached Shelby about getting a supercharged GT350. Paxton received a car on loan and, when Granatelli's brother Joe returned, legend has it Andy raced Carroll Shelby in a Cobra—and the Mustang won. A special model was considered, but the supercharger simply became a factory option. The $670 blower boosted horsepower from 306 to 395, but just eleven buyers added the option in '66.

Shelby built 2,377 GT350s in 1966, including 1,001 for Hertz. Shelby also built four convertible prototypes, three for Ford, and one for singer Bob Shane of the Kingston Trio. There was no need to make any more GT350R racers; the thirty-four built in 1965 were enough to dominate SCCA B-production.

Shelby Cobra 427 1965–1966

While the 289 Cobras "owned" the Z06 Corvettes on the racetrack, a credible threat was on the horizon. As early as 1963, Mickey Thompson had built and raced a Sting Ray coupe equipped with the 396-cubic-inch NASCAR Mark II "Mystery Motor," and it was known at the time that a similar Corvette was being readied for production. Shelby also knew the 289 Cobra was at the end of its development cycle, since the engine could only reliably produce 400 horsepower, and the archaic leaf spring independent suspension was at the point of being a liability.

This time, Shelby specified a design to A. C. Cars that corrected all those faults. The frame was made much stiffer and designed to carry the weight and power of Ford's 427/428 FE engines (the original Cobra frame was more flexible than a Model T Ford). All new coil-over suspension was designed by Klaus Arning, and the brakes, wheels, and tires were made bigger. The aluminum body was stretched and bulged to accommodate the bulk: 6 inches longer and 7 inches wider, though the wheelbase remained the same 90 inches. Quite simply, it was a Cobra on steroids.

The first 427 Cobra, CSX3001, arrived from England in November 1964. Street Cobras used a version of the 428 Police Interceptor engine, while competition Cobras got the famed 427 "Side Oiler." Then there was the Cobra S/C, as in Semi Competition, a hybrid of the street and race Cobras, which could be easily converted into a full race machine. Special equipment included sidepipes, quick-jack lifting points instead of bumpers, a paperclip-style roll bar, wide Halibrand magnesium wheels, and a quick-filler gas cap atop the right rear fender. The first one hundred cars were designated to be S/C models so that the car could compete in FIA races, but only fifty-three were completed before Henry Ford II made his special request of Shelby to take on

Ferrari in the prototype class with the famous Ford GT racers. The 427 engine and billowing sidepipes of the S/C Cobras made them the stuff of legends.

Starting at $7,495, the new 427 Cobra was beyond comprehension. *Car and Driver* exclaimed: "Not long ago, the Cobra 427 would have been the hot setup on any racetrack. Now it's a civilized street machine!" Their November 1965 road test revealed a shocking statistic: 0–100–0 in 14.5 seconds. A driver could go from dead stop to 100 miles per hour and back to a dead stop in less than 15 seconds! Shelby's test driver, Ken Miles, actually did it in 13.8 seconds.

Car and Driver continued:

> The 427 Cobra does accelerate and decelerate at unbelievable rates, as the above figures should imply. What's more, it is a more civilized machine than the original 289 Cobra that brought the fabulous Shelby organization into being four years ago. It handles properly, thanks to a completely new all-independent suspension system that is traceable to the deft hand of Klaus Arning, the Ford Motor Company genius responsible for the impeccable handling of the Ford GT . . . .
>
> One might expect a Cobra with an engine displacing 427 cubic inches to be an absolute beast on the street. It is utterly to the contrary, with a positively placid disposition at low speeds.

The magazine warned, though, that:

> The car will break traction to speeds beyond 100 mph and imprudent applications of power will send the tail-end slewing sideways . . . the fact remains that the Cobra 427 is not an automobile for novices.

The last 427 Cobra, CSX3358, was built by A. C. Cars the last week of December 1965. Ford no longer needed the Cobra; they had conquered the world's racetracks and the mission was accomplished. Shelby had all they could do to keep up with Mustang GT350 demand while also running Ford's road racing operations. Shelby built just 998 Cobras—75 260 Cobras, 580 289 Cobras, and 343 427 Cobras—in just four years. Yet it remains the true definition of "iconic"—the ultimate American supercar.

Shelby Mustang GT350 & GT500 1967

The Mustang evolved from an inexpensive, fun car into something more mature. It was no longer the only player in the pony car market, with the new Chevy Camaro, Pontiac Firebird, and Mercury Cougar (Mustang's sister) poised to take away market share. The revamped Plymouth Barracuda hoped to do the same.

With that in mind, Ford grew the Mustang 2 inches in length and 2.5 inches in width. That made it a little roomier all around, and wide enough to fit Ford's FE series engines. Ford chose the 320 horsepower, 390-cubic-inches version for the top-of-the line Mustang GT, and that kept the Mustang in the game against the 396 Camaro and 383 'Cuda with 0–60 miles per hour in 7.4 seconds and a top speed of 115 miles per hour. Good, but not great.

True greatness came from Los Angeles in the form of the 1967 Shelby GT500. Two young designers on loan from Ford, Chuck McHose and Pete Stacey, used a few fiberglass pieces creatively to give the GT500 a distinctive look. The fiberglass hood was 3 inches longer over the grille, and the headlight surrounds were replaced to match. A fiberglass trunk lid integrated a "ducktail" spoiler, and the cast rear fender endcaps were replaced with fiberglass items that blended into the spoiler. The pair also added scoops in front of the rear tires, scoops on the "C" pillars of the fastback roof for interior ventilation, and wide taillights sourced from the Cougar, without the chrome surrounds. Driving lights were added to the Shelby grille, centered in the states that allowed it, farther out near the headlights in the states that didn't. The GT500 looked fast just standing still.

Shelby Cobra 427 1965-1966

 # PRODUCED: 316

ENGINE: 427-cubic-inch V-8

HORSEPOWER: 485

TORQUE: 480 lb-ft

¼-MILE TIME: 12.2 at 118 mph

Ford was becoming more involved in Shelby's business, and 1967 GT500 ads were combined with regular Mustang promotions. 1967 Shelby GT500. *Author's Collection*

ABOVE: The bigger, more powerful 1967 Shelby GT500 hit the sweet spot between performance, comfort, style, and price. At $4,195, the GT500 cost $152 less than the 1965 GT350, yet packed a 355-horsepower 428-cubic-inch engine. *Road & Track* concluded, "All in all, the GT500 is a more civilized vehicle than the original GT350 from which it descended. It rides better, is has more amenities and it is far more attractive. It isn't so closely related to a racing car, perhaps, but we have a feeling that it will appeal to a larger number of buyers than any previous Shelby American automobile." The numbers bear that out: 1,175 GT350 and 2,048 GT500 Shelbys were sold that year. *Archives/TEN: The Enthusiast Network Magazines, LLC*

MIDDLE, LEFT: Imagine blasting through the canyons above Los Angeles in a '66 Shelby GT350. Now imagine doing that for $17 a day. That's what the Shelby GT350H brought to Hertz Rent-a-Car customers. Stories of these cars being raced, then returned to Hertz much worse for the wear, abound. Most were equipped with automatics, since the clutches of the first cars had to be frequently replaced. Go figure. *Archives/TEN: The Enthusiast Network Magazines, LLC*

BOTTOM, LEFT: *Sports Car Graphic* editor Jerry Titus flogged the 1965 Shelby GT350 to the limit. He had known Carroll Shelby since 1957, managing the shop that maintained Shelby's Type 61 "Birdcage" Maserati. When Titus did the same with the first competition Shelby GT350R, he came within a second of Shelby's test driver, Ken Miles, at Willow Springs raceway. Due to that performance, Titus was made a member of Shelby's team, and won nine SCCA B-production races and the national championship driving a GT350R that year. *Archives/TEN: The Enthusiast Network Magazines, LLC*

And it was fast, thanks to the 355-horsepower 428-cubic-inch FE engine Shelby sourced from Ford's Thunderbird. Producing 44 more horsepower than the high-winding 289 in the '65 GT350, the GT500 cost $152 less than Shelby's first Mustang. But it was a still a Shelby, which included the roll bar and shoulder straps like the original GT350, and a dished wood-rimmed steering wheel. Stiffer springs and Gabriel shocks kept things under control.

No longer was the GT500—and the returning GT350—"a tough, for-men-only machine." It was "a styled-up fastback that should appeal to a wider audience than the previous Shelby Mustangs," as *Road & Track* called the $4,195 GT500. "The suspension of the GT500 is stiff and the ride could be described as extra-firm.... The car is extremely easy to drive. The engine lights off with a whump, there's a clunk-jump when the shift lever is moved into gear, and if you mash the gas pedal, you'll GO."

If the 428 engine had a fault, it was its weight. The GT500 came in at 3,520 pounds, the GT350 at 2,800. Perhaps the best performance option was the GT350 with the optional Paxton supercharger, adding $549 to the GT350's $3,995 base, but generating 395 horses.

R&T concluded that:

> All in all, the GT500 is a more civilized vehicle than the original GT350 from which it descended. It rides better, has more amenities, and it is far more attractive. It isn't so closely related to a racing car, perhaps, but we have a feeling that it will appeal to a larger number of buyers than any previous Shelby American automobile.

The numbers bear that out: 1,175 GT350s and 2,048 GT500s were sold. But keeping up with the demand was challenging Shelby American. They had quality issues with the fiberglass parts, and the cars demanded a lot of hand rework. In late 1966, Shelby American lost the lease of their two large buildings at Los Angeles International Airport due to runway expansion. "Even if our lease hadn't expired, we did not have the capacity at the airport to build the number of Shelbys that Ford wanted to sell," said Payton Cramer, Shelby American's general manager at the time.

For the remainder of the 1967 model year, the Shelby Mustangs would be built at A. O. Smith Inland, a large automotive supplier in Ionia, Michigan (ironically, they had once supplied Corvette bodies). From here on the Shelby Mustangs would be built by Ford.

Shelby Mustang GT350 & GT500 1968–1970

When *Car Life* tested the new 1968 Shelby GT500KR ("King of the Road"), they noted that "every year the Shelby Mustang is a little less Shelby and a little more Mustang." The GT500KR didn't look it, with new fiberglass front fenders, hood, and grille surround bumping up the Shelby's appearance a notch. The convertible versions of the GT350 and GT500, with a stylish integral roll bar, were also new. Then there was the GT500KR, which replaced the GT500 when the 428 Cobra Jet engine became available on the

In 1967, Carroll Shelby built one GT500 Super Snake as a tire–testing vehicle for Goodyear. It featured the same powerplant used in the GT40 Mk II that won Le Mans in 1966, producing 600 horsepower. Built by Shelby "post-title," the Super Snakes were GT500s given the Shelby touch—like 660 supercharged horsepower (or an optional 800 horsepower engine).

Mustang. But *Car Life* could feel a difference. Shelby still designed the upgrades and specified the equipment, and the cars were still exciting—just different.

The GT500 was straight-line fast, that's for sure. The original 428 engine was nothing great, but the Cobra Jet benefited from heads and intake derived from the Le Mans champion 427 Side Oiler. Ford still rated it at 335 horsepower (wink, wink), but 400 or higher was more likely. With a street-friendly 3.50:1 rear gear, *Car Life* was able to see 0–60 in 6.9 seconds and blasted the quarter mile in 14.57 at 99.55 miles per hour. What was missing was the suspension and brakes that matched the power.

The GT350 returned, but gone was the 271-horsepower "HiPo" 289, replaced with a garden-variety 302 with "Cobra" trim producing 250 horsepower. You got the show of the Shelby without much go. The Paxton supercharger was still an option.

The June 1968 issue of *The Hertz System* newsletter announced the reintroduction of the new Shelby GT350H to the Hertz Sports Car Club. Hertz touted the sports car look and feel of the cars but emphasized that anyone could drive them. They were fully optioned, including tinted glass, Tilt-Top steering wheel, and air conditioning. The Shelby American World Registry identified 227 Shelby built for Hertz. Though not the supercar GT350H of 1966, the new Hertz cars were a great way to spend a vacation.

TOP: When *Car Life* tested the new 1968 Shelby GT500KR ("King of the Road") they noted that "every year the Shelby Mustang is a little less Shelby and a little more Mustang." With a street-friendly 3.50:1 rear gear, *Car Life* was able to see 0–60 in 6.9 seconds and blasted the quarter-mile in 14.57 at 99.55 miles per hour.

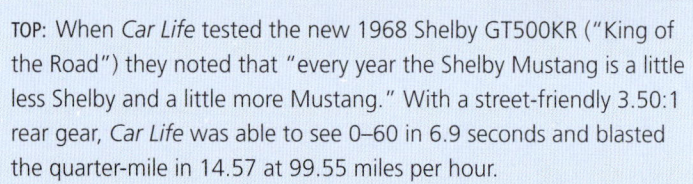

ABOVE: *Road & Track* concluded, "All in all, the GT500 is a more civilized vehicle than the original GT350 from which it descended. It rides better, it has more amenities, and it is far more attractive."

ABOVE, RIGHT: The convertible versions of the GT350 and GT500, with a stylish integral roll bar, were also new.

86 CHAPTER 6

TOP: The June 1968 issue of *The Hertz System* newsletter announced the reintroduction of the new Shelby GT350H to the Hertz Sports Car Club. Hertz touted the sports car look and feel of the cars, but that anyone could drive them.

ABOVE, LEFT: A Paxton supercharger was still a rare option on the '69 GT350.

ABOVE, RIGHT: Both the GT350 and the GT500 returned in 1969, in both new "SportsRoof" and convertible form. The 1969 Shelby Mustangs looked even less like a Mustang, with a large, full-width grille surrounding the headlights. Lucas fog lamps were mounted below, and the fiberglass hood sported no less than five NACA ducts.

Both the GT350 and the GT500 returned in 1969, in both new "SportsRoof" and convertible form. But as the Mustang again became larger, so of course did the Shelby. The Shelby Mustangs looked even less like a Mustang, with a large, full-width grille surrounding the headlights. Lucas foglamps were mounted below, and the fiberglass hood sported no less than five National Advisory Committee for Aeronautics (NACA) ducts. But the GT500KR's performance was no better than the stock Mustang GT Cobra Jet, and the GT350 received a mild 290-horsepower 351 Windsor.

When *Car and Driver* took a GT350 preproduction car for a spin, they called it "a garter snake in Cobra skin, affixed with dozens of name plates reading 'Shelby,' 'Shelby-American,' 'Cobra,' and 'GT 350,' as if to consistently re-assure the owner that he is driving the real thing and not a neatly decorated Mustang (which it is)." They concluded,

So what do we have in the Shelby Cobra GT 350, 1969 style? Certainly not what Carroll Shelby and his gang of merry men dreamed up five models previously. It is really a dolled-up version of the new Mustang Grande—a baby 'Bird, as we said before.

Buyers knew the "real thing"—by the end of 1969 around 789 Shelbys went unsold, and new VIN numbers made them 1970 models. It was the end of an era, but an era that changed the game. Author Joe Scalzo in *Car Life* commented, "After the Shelby came the Z28 Camaro, the Boss Mustang, the 'Cuda 340, the AMX. This

TOP: When *Car and Driver* took a 1969 GT350 for a spin, they called it "a garter snake in Cobra skin."

ABOVE: To celebrate the 40th anniversary of the GT350H Mustangs built for Hertz Rent-a-Car, Hertz worked with Shelby American to create 500 GT-H Mustangs built on the new S197 platform. Carroll Shelby was back in the Mustang business. The new Shelby Mustangs had the familiar black with gold stripes of the original GT350H cars, and were equipped with the optional FR1 Power Pack for an additional 25 horsepower, and the FR3 Ford Racing Handling Pack. *Ford Archives*

LEFT: Carroll Shelby sold the "Cobra" brand to Ford for $1. Ford would use it on Torinos and Mustang IIs.

88 CHAPTER 6

ABOVE: Carroll Shelby also created limited-edition versions of Chrysler's hot compacts. For the 1980s, they were quick enough; with fewer than 1,000 built of each, they offered that Shelby exclusivity and mystique. *FCNA*

RIGHT: When Lee Iacocca became head of Chrysler, he turned to Carroll Shelby to give his products what Iacocca called "pizzazz." Carroll Shelby created the Chrysler Shelby Performance Center (CSPC) in Whittier, California, and took the good-looking Charger compact to create the quick Shelby Charger. *FCNA*

is why the Shelby Mustang was important. It speeded up and influenced the development of the Ponycars and supercars."

With the Shelby Mustangs out of his control, and Ford's participation in racing coming to an end on November 19, 1970, Shelby was out of the automobile business. Burned out from nearly a decade of intense automotive work, Shelby moved on to big game hunting in South Africa.

The Chrysler Years 1982–1991

A call from his old friend from Ford, Lee Iacocca, got Shelby back in the automotive game. Iacocca was hired as Chrysler's chairman and CEO in 1979, with the objective of saving the company from bankruptcy. Iacocca famously did that, cutting costs by basing nearly every Chrysler product on variations of the front-drive "K-Car" platform. Once the company was growing again, he turned to Shelby to give his products what Iacocca called "pizazz."

Shelby created the Chrysler Shelby Performance Center (CSPC) in Whittier, California, and took the good-looking Charger compact to create the quick Shelby Charger. Then came the Shelby Daytona and the Omni GLH ("Goes Like Hell"), many with powerful turbocharged four-cylinder engines. It was the GLH Turbo that caused BMW to pull an ad that claimed their 535i as the "fastest four-door sedan sold in the US."

ABOVE: Carroll Shelby created the Chrysler Shelby Performance Center (CSPC) in Whittier, California, to develop performance versions of Chrysler's compacts. Shelby also created limited-edition versions of those cars with increased performance. For the eighties they were quite quick, and with less than 1,000 built of each, had that Shelby exclusivity and mystique. *Archives/TEN: The Enthusiast Network Magazines, LLC*

SHELBY AMERICAN: THE LEGEND, THE LEGACY   89

On March 11, 1986, Shelby Automobiles, Inc. was incorporated at 12444 E. Putnam St., Whittier, California. Shelby was back in the specialty car game. His hot, limited-edition Mopars included the Charger GLHS, Shelby Lancer, and the Shadow-based Shelby CSX. Though they were all front-wheel-drive, for the 1980s they were quick, and, with less than 1,000 built of each model, they offered that Shelby exclusivity and mystique.

While he was working for Chrysler, Shelby also consulted on the development of the spiritual successor to the Cobra, the Dodge Viper. The Viper wasn't his idea, but he knew where to make improvements to the design. In 1991, when the Dodge Viper paced the Indianapolis 500, Shelby was at the wheel.

Shelby Series 1 1999

Throughout his automotive career, Shelby took other companies' vehicles and made them better. The Shelby Series 1 was his attempt to build a sports car from the ground up.

The goal of the Series 1 was to be small, light, and powerful. Sound familiar? But Shelby wanted to do it with the latest technology. His cars featured an aluminum honeycomb chassis, carbon-fiber body, rear-mounted six-speed transaxle, and a 4.0 DOHC Aurora V-8 sourced from the Indy Racing League. Shelby Automobiles moved from California to two new buildings on the site of the Las Vegas Motor Speedway.

News of the project surfaced around 1994, but the 249 cars built were 1999 models. Building a car in 1999 was a totally different proposition than putting together the Cobra in 1962. There were numerous delays and, eventually, lawsuits. GM underwent another reorganization, and Shelby lost Oldsmobile's support. Huge costs were incurred in testing, and certification required conformance with 1999 Federal Motor Vehicle Safety Standards.

When *Car and Driver* finally got to test a Series 1, they recorded an impressive 0–to–60 time of 4.1 seconds and a quarter-mile pass of 13.0 seconds at 112 miles per hour. Then it broke. Frank Markus in *Car and Driver* lamented,

> The thing is Frankensteined out of lots of production GM parts, as I'd have done it after a zillion trips to the local junkyard. One sits on this car rather than in it, as in most home-built rods with tuck-

'n'-roll bench seats. And finally, it blows up every time you try to drive it . . . .

Venture Corporation, a supplier of carbon fiber components to the auto industry, purchased much of Shelby American in 1999. Then, in 2004, Venture Corporation went bankrupt (not due to the Series 1), and Shelby's new company, Shelby Automobiles, Inc., was able to purchase enough components to build a few Series II cars. What was supposed to be a $99,975 sports car became a $181,824 disappointment.

Shelby Cobra Continuation 1996–Today

Think of it: just 998 Shelby Cobras were built in the 1960s. Today, they are simply too valuable to drive—and they're out of the reach of most of the people who would love to own one. You could buy one of the knockoff Cobras, or you could own the genuine article: a brand-new Shelby Cobra.

This was the one piece of Shelby American that Venture Corporation did not acquire. It began when Shelby hired Tom D'Antonio. D'Antonio built Cobra knockoffs in Phoenix, Arizona, but instead of taking him to court—as Shelby did with many Cobra copycats—he recognized D'Antonio's machines as the best reproductions around and made him part of the company. They are billed as "continuation" models, the only authentic Shelby Cobras you can buy new today.

"Our authentic Cobra factory chassis are built by Shelby American, Inc., in Las Vegas, Nevada, and delivered with the Shelby American Manufacturer's Statement of Origin (MSO). The CSX6000 427, CSX7000 FIA, CSX8000 Slabside, and CSX9000 Daytona Coupe are all authentic Shelbys," reads their literature. Continuation Cobras start at $89,995 with fiberglass bodies, or $154,995 with handcrafted aluminum shells, just like A. C. Cars delivered in the 1960s.

Shelby can't sell a complete car, thanks to Uncle Sam's regulations, but dealers mate the completed Cobra with the customer's engine. The Carroll Shelby Engine Company in Windsor, California—a company separate from Shelby American but licensed to use the Shelby name—can provide an authentic powerplant, with 289 engines starting at around $25,000.

It's not a Cobra from the 1960s, but it's the next best thing. It's also the real thing.

Shelby GT-H 2006–2007

Ford introduced the first completely redesigned Mustang in 2005, and a special model was shown at the 2006 New York Auto Show. To celebrate the fortieth anniversary of the GT350H Mustangs built for Hertz Rent-a-Car, Hertz worked with Shelby American to create 500 GT-H Mustangs built on the new S197 platform. The new Shelby Mustangs had the familiar black with gold stripes of the

---

Shelby Series 1 1999

- **# PRODUCED:** 249
- **ENGINE:** 244-cubic-inch V-8
- **HORSEPOWER:** 320
- **TORQUE:** 290 lb-ft
- **¼-MILE TIME:** 13.0 at 112 mph

Carroll Shelby with the 2010 Shelby GT350. Already in his eighties, Carroll Shelby was back in the Mustang business.

original GT350H cars and were equipped with the optional FR1 Power Pack for an additional 25 horsepower, as well as the FR3 Ford Racing Handling Pack. Though the engine was stock, Shelby replaced the standard 3.31:1 rear with 3.55:1 gears. The 500 cars produced were only available for rental from Hertz.

At age eighty-three, Shelby was back building Cobras and Mustangs. The Mustang deal was the culmination of Ford and Shelby reconciling their differences from decades before, working together for the betterment of both companies. In 2001, Shelby was invited to consult on the Ford GT supercar to be unveiled in 2003 in honor of Ford's one-hundredth birthday. Ford and Shelby later created the CS-1 concept car, a modern interpretation of the famous Shelby Daytona Coupes.

Finally, in 2006 came the deal to build the GT-H Mustangs for Hertz, a company wholly owned by Ford at the time. "It all happened over the course of about three months," Paula Rivera, Hertz's public affairs manager, told *Road & Track*.

> We have an original Shelby GT350H in the lobby of our corporate headquarters. We see it every day. As we were developing the Fun Collection program, our vice president of fleet, Walt Seaman, said "Why not this—again?" Once we started talking about this idea with Shelby and Ford, everyone got on board.

Shelby also built GT-H convertibles for Hertz in 2007. Ford and Shelby were a team again. As *Road & Track* concluded, "What's even more heartwarming to Shelbyphiles is that this is real. It's not a licensee agreement, an arrangement with a subcontractor, or a backyard Shelby clone operation . . . . And the man who owns the place is a Texan named Carroll. Just as it should be."

Shelby Mustang GT-H 2006-2007

 # PRODUCED: 1000 (500 coupes, 500 convertibles)
ENGINE: 281-cubic-inch V-8
HORSEPOWER: 325
TORQUE: 330 lb-ft
¼-MILE TIME: 13.6 at 102 mph

SHELBY AMERICAN: THE LEGEND, THE LEGACY

TOP: In 2012, Shelby celebrated the 50th anniversary of Shelby American with a special GT350 model. "Few thought that Shelby American would make it in the car business for fifty years," Shelby said. "We built the first Cobra in a rented garage and then GT350s in an old hangar. But our company is still here, manufacturing the best cars that I've ever made. The next fifty years will be even better for Shelby American."

ABOVE: Shelby announced the Shelby GT based on the new 2015 Mustang, including an optional 627-horsepower Ford Performance supercharger. *Shelby American*

Shelby GT500 Super Snake 2007–2014, 2015–Today

The original Shelby Mustangs were built by Ford, then shipped across town to Shelby American, where perfectly good parts were removed and replaced with high-performance parts and paint and trim updated, then the vehicles were shipped back to Ford. If this sounds inefficient and expensive, it was. With this in mind, Ford moved production of the new 2007 Shelby GT500 Mustangs to the same Flat Rock, Michigan, assembly line as lessor 'Stangs. Unlike the late 1960s, when Shelby's involvement decreased, the newest Shelby Mustangs represented a true collaboration between Shelby, his team, and Ford.

Shelby Mustang Super Snake 2013–2014

 # PRODUCED: n/a
ENGINE: 355-cubic-inch V-8
HORSEPOWER: 850
TORQUE: n/a
¼-MILE TIME: 12.0 at 129 mph

CHAPTER 6

Don't own a GT500, but want some of that Shelby magic for your 2007–2014 Mustang (even if it's a V-6)? The GTS should do the trick.

Some things just can't be done on an assembly line, though. Corporate prudence is also a factor when it comes to hand-finishing. For that, there's the Super Snake. Built by Shelby "post title," the Super Snakes are GT500s given the Shelby touch—like 660 supercharged horsepower (or an optional 800 horsepower), unique carbon-fiber body panels, Borla cat-back exhaust, 3.73:1 gears, and 20-inch Shelby/Alcoa wheels stuffed with massive six-piston brakes. There are other options, too, like Eibach adjustable coil-over suspension and custom leather interior upgrades. The Super Snake starts at around $30,000 on top of the cost of the GT500. "You provide the 2007 or later Shelby GT500 (regardless of mileage)," says Shelby, "and we'll take it from there!"

Shelby GTS 2007–2014

The Super Snake starts with the best, the GT500, and makes it better. What if you don't own a GT500, but want some Shelby magic for your 2007–2014 Mustang, like a V-6? That's what the GTS did.

The GTS package started at $9,995, which added the bodywork, upgraded Baer brakes, Borla exhaust, new springs, shocks and anti-roll bars, plus the requisite Shelby badges and plaques. From there the sky was the limit.

As *Motor Trend* found out:

> If there's one place where the GTS shines, it's in grip. The car pulled an impressive 1.01 average g on our skidpad and ran the figure-eight course in 24.9 seconds at 0.75 g average—impressive numbers. That's a substantial improvement over the stock V-6 Mustang, which pulled 0.96 g average and needed 25.8 seconds at 0.71 average g to get around the figure eight. It's also a big improvement over the Mustang GT, which pulled 0.94 g and needed 25.3 seconds at 0.75 average g to complete the figure eight.

Of course, starting from a GT500 made more sense, and the Super Snake was a much better Shelby all around, but the GTS was an attractive alternative—though it's no longer available. In 2012, Shelby also made a limited edition 50th Anniversary GTS—fifty in white with gold stripes, fifty in black with gold stripes—to celebrate the 1962 founding of Shelby American. Like all Shelbys, you could pick it up at the museum in Las Vegas.

Shelby 1000 2011–2014

The Super Snake is more Mustang than most people can handle. For those who can't get enough, Shelby created the Shelby 1000. That's right, one thousand (or more) horses under the carbon-fiber hood. "The Shelby team spent hundreds of R&D hours addressing each component to ensure they work together and provide unparalleled performance," says Shelby. This is a complete rebuild of a 2011-to-2014 GT500 into an understated stealth machine. The Shelby 1000 starts at $149,995 on top of the cost of the GT500, or $154,995 for the non-street-legal 1100 horsepower Shelby 1000 S/C. That's a small price to pay for the ultimate Mustang.

"When we had Carroll in Vegas to drive the 800-horse version of the Super Snake," explains Shelby's Gary Patterson, "we all expected to get a bunch of accolades and 'attaboys' after he finished driving the car. But even before the car had stopped rolling, Carroll was asking us when we'd have a 1000-horse Mustang."

According to *Road & Track* in 2012:

> If you think the new Shelby 1000 is simply a boosted 1000-horse Super Snake, think again . . . this post-title Shelby has been totally reengineered to handle the supercharged 5.4-liter V-8's claimed 1,000 horsepower at 6,450 rpm and 750 lb-ft of torque at 4,500 rpm . . . . We can't think of a more fitting way to celebrate the 50th Anniversary of Shelby American.

SHELBY AMERICAN: THE LEGEND, THE LEGACY

Shelby Raptor/Baja 700
2010–Today

A Shelby pickup truck? Ford's Raptor is a game-changing truck, and Shelby recognized that. "The Shelby Raptor became a star the moment we launched it at the New York Auto Show in 2012," said Joe Conway, co-CEO of Carroll Shelby International and CEO of Shelby American. "Carroll had a love for trucks and brought his high-performance, 'Texas style' to the drawing board when he envisioned the Shelby Raptor."

A 2.9-liter Whipple supercharger, with bigger throttle bodies and injectors, plus a more robust heat exchanger, pushes the Shelby Raptor from 411 horsepower to 575. The $17,995 package also adds suspension and interior upgrades, and great Shelby graphics. Other options can give the Shelby Raptor the owner's personal touch.

In April 2015, Shelby announced the Baja 700. "In the best Shelby tradition, we took our already high-performance 575 horsepower Shelby Raptor and made it even more capable," said Shelby American Vice President of Operations Akos J. Feher.

Fifty lucky owners will have the baddest, best-handling, and best-looking Shelby truck we offer. Not to mention, all of the interior fit-and-finish people expect from Shelby. It's a truck that can thrive under the most extreme conditions.

"The Shelby Baja 700 is striking in looks and, most of all, its capabilities," said Vince LaViolette, Shelby American senior designer and test driver. "The off-road performance suspension system allows the Shelby Baja 700 to go most anywhere and stand out as it does so. We believe that we've built a truck with ultimate performance and off-road capabilities."

Shelby has gotten into upgrading Ford's other high-performance machine, the Raptor. This is the 2015 Shelby F-150, delivering 700 horsepower. *Shelby American*

Shelby Continuation Daytona Coupe 2015 celebrates the 50th anniversary of the Shelby Cobra Daytona Coupe's historic 1965 World Manufacturer's Championship. Shelby American COO Keith Belair says the aluminum models are "faithful to the six built during the 1960s," while the fiberglass examples are "true to the spirit of the Coupe, but reimagined as if it had remained in production over the years." The total combined production run for both body styles is capped at fifty examples, each wearing a commemorative badge celebrating the 50th anniversary of the original. Fiberglass models start at $179,995, aluminum versions at $349,995. And they're true Shelby Cobras. *Shelby American*

Shelby Continuation Daytona Coupe 2015

One more celebration took place with the fiftieth anniversary of the Shelby Cobra Daytona Coupe's historic 1965 World Manufacturer's Championship. That was an event that deserves a special commemoration, as only Shelby can do it, with the Shelby Continuation Daytona Coupe, available in a hand-formed aluminum body like the originals, or in fiberglass.

Shelby American COO Keith Belair says the aluminum models are "faithful to the six built during the 1960s," while the fiberglass examples are "true to the spirit of the Coupe, but reimagined as if it had remained in production over the years." The total combined production run for both body styles is capped at fifty examples, each wearing a commemorative badge celebrating the fiftieth anniversary of the original. Like the other continuation Cobras, the Daytona Coupes must be sold without engine or transmission, though Shelby American will provide an aluminum-block 289 V-8 with a serial number identical to the rolling chassis for those looking for a historically accurate powerplant. Like Shelby American's continuation-series Cobras, each Daytona Coupe will carry a CSX serial number.

Other new products include the Shelby GT and GT EcoBoost Mustangs, built on the all-new Mustang released in 2015. These continued innovations should quell any fears that Shelby American would not continue after the death of Carroll Shelby. "There has been no one like Carroll Shelby," Belair said, "and never will be. However, we promised Carroll we would carry on, and he put the team, the products and the vision in place to do just that."

Few people can create a legacy that continues long after they leave this world. That is the true measure of greatness.

SHELBY AMERICAN: THE LEGEND, THE LEGACY   95

Chapter 7

Hurst Performance
Detroit's Image Maker

P. T. Barnum, creator of the Greatest Show on Earth, understood marketing. He wrote, "Without promotion something terrible happens . . . nothing!" George Hurst understood that concept, too.

Born in 1927 in upstate New York, Hurst grew up in New Jersey. At age sixteen—and in the midst of World War II—he joined the Navy. Discharged in Warminster, Pennsylvania, after a decade of service, Hurst relocated to nearby Abington. His ability to install modern overhead-valve V-8s in older automobiles became widely known; people came to him with problems, such as replacing a Lincoln's flathead V-12 with a Cadillac V-8. He fabricated all the motor mounts he used, but then teamed with an engineer, Bill Campbell, who refined Hurst's ideas into products that could be manufactured on a large scale.

Together, the new Hurst-Campbell company began offering motor mounts for a variety of engine conversions. Other companies offered similar products at lower cost, but Hurst's products gained a reputation for the finest quality and engineering. In 1961, Hurst began offering his trademark shifters. As the American automobile market began a rapid transition from three-on-the-tree to three- or four-on-the-floor, Hurst was there with the floor shifter to make the conversion. Even

The Hurst Pontiac Grand Prix SSJ was based on a customized Grand Prix built by Jim Wangers. Unlike the factory-built Hurst/Olds, this was a post-title conversion that involved ordering a new Grand Prix with specific options, then having Pontiac drop ship the car to Hurst Performance. The Hurst upgrades were strictly cosmetic and only about five hundred were built between 1970 and 1972, starting at $1,147.25 for the conversion. *Archives/TEN: The Enthusiast Network Magazines, LLC*

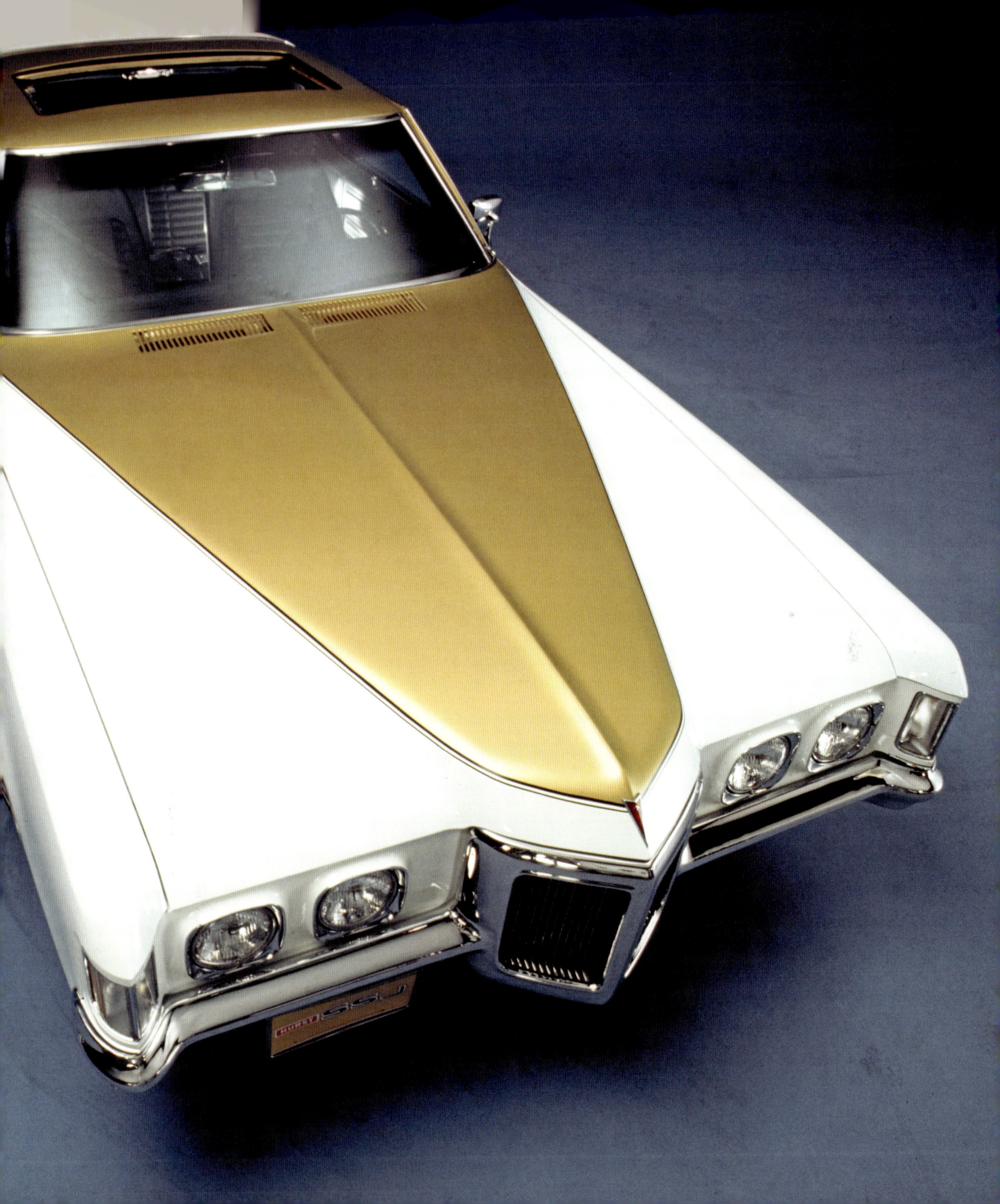
SSJ

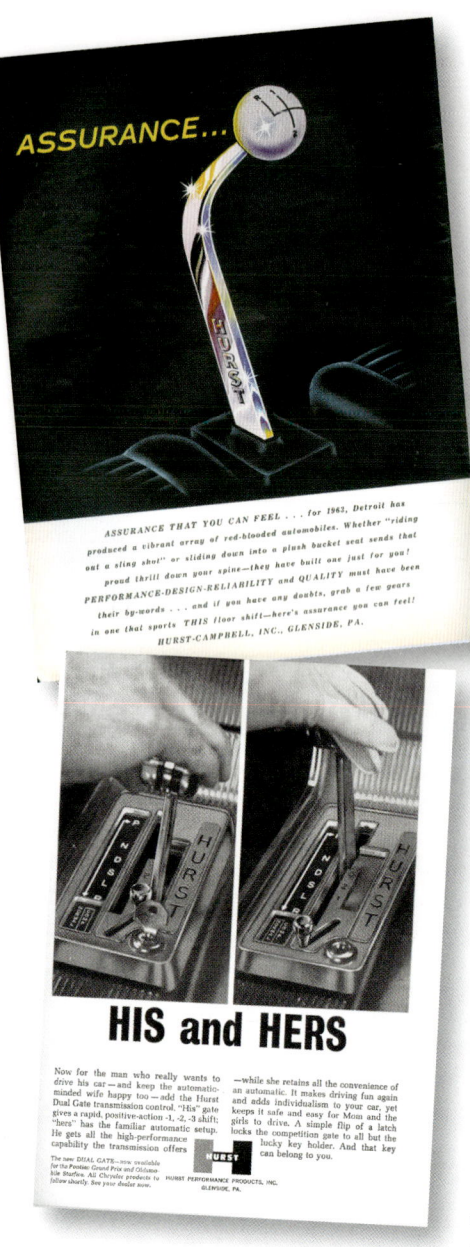

Hurst-Campbell placed this expensive, full-page color ad in the November 1962 issue of *Motor Trend*, their 1963 Auto Show Issue. It made the small company look much larger than it really was, part of George Hurst's marketing to grow the company. Hurst shifters were installed on the 1962 Pontiac Super Duty Catalinas, the first time Hurst served as an OEM supplier to a manufacturer.
Author's Collection

The full-page ad in *Motor Trend* introducing the Hurst Dual Gate shifter for automatic transmissions; November 1962.
Author's Collection

as the manufacturers began offering cars with floor-mounted shifters, Hurst's brilliant "Golden Shifter" was far superior; in the shifter's first year of manufacture, Chrysler began offering the Hurst product as an aftermarket item.

Hurst's shifter stormed the market: it was built like a rock, with solid linkage and a positive movement between the all-important 2–3 gear change. His confidence in his products led him to offer an unconditional lifetime guarantee. Detroit took notice, and in 1964, when the revolutionary Pontiac GTO hit the streets, it was equipped with a Hurst Golden Shifter at the factory. Hurst also tackled the automatic transmission market, introducing the famous Hurst "Dual-Gate" that allowed a driver to shift sequentially through the gears, or just run the motor in drive.

For all his creative genius, Hurst was just as skilled at promoting his products. Racing was a natural market for his shifters, and Hurst participated in all the major American racing organizations. He also conceived two outrageous exhibition drag racers: the twin-engine all-wheel-drive "Hurst Hairy Olds" Cutlass and the mid-engine "Hurst Hemi Under Glass" Barracuda. Traveling to these events was Hurst's "shifty doctor," Jack "Doc" Watson, who consulted with racers, adjusted and repaired their Hurst shifters, and acted as ambassador for Hurst-Campbell products. A succession of contests and Hurst-equipped giveaway cars helped promote their products, and a number of "Miss Golden Shifter" girls kept the Hurst name in the forefront.

Having witnessed the serious, sometimes fatal crashes that plagued auto racing in the 1960s, Hurst began developing the "Hurst Rescue Tool," patented in 1965. This idea, which developed into the "Jaws of Life," has saved tens of thousands of crash victims over the years.

Along with a new manufacturing plant in Warminster, Pennsylvania, Hurst-Campbell created the Hurst Performance Research Center in Madison Heights, Michigan, right in the neighborhood of the Big Three. The facility would be used for developing prototypes for the automakers and building Hurst's exhibition drag racers, as well as functioning as headquarters for Hurst's specialty manufacturing services.

Hurst/Olds 1968

A well-known Detroit maxim, attributed to Bunkie Knudsen, goes: "You can sell an old man a young man's car, but you can never sell a young man an old man's car." And Oldsmobile had an image. Even their name said it: *old*.

In their June 1968 issue, *Car Life* commented on this fact:

> This unfortunate lack of recognition is primarily due to a couple of attitudes: General Motors still maintains the tentative advertising approach to racing it adopted several years ago in the name of safety; and despite the demonstrated potency of several Olds products, the Oldsmobile name still retains most of its old-time aura of expensive, luxurious, gentility.

They honestly tried. In their 1968 advertising campaigns, they called their performance cars "The Youngmobiles for Oldsmobile" and told potential buyers to "Cut loose in a Cutlass S." Nothing worked.

Back in the days before social media, it could take years to create a positive image in the marketplace; it took even longer to reverse a negative impression. At one time, Oldsmobile owned the prominent performance persona. For example, in 1949 Olds set the automotive world on fire with the introduction of the first mass-produced overhead-valve V-8 engines for their mid-market cars. Oldsmobile's Rocket 88 became America's choice for performance cars, and they were what NASCAR champions like Lee Petty and Buck Baker picked out of the herd in that era.

Soon, though, Oldsmobile found itself behind value-priced Chevrolet and Ford, placing third by sales among America's automakers. By the mid-1950s, Oldsmobile was no longer the hot carmaker: Pontiac, Chevrolet, Ford, Chrysler, Plymouth, and Dodge were all working hard to build a performance image for themselves.

The last sporty Oldsmobile, the J2, was built in 1957. A big and beautiful car, it was hardly a high-performance automobile. At the dawn of the 1960s, Oldsmobile was down to sixth in annual sales. Coincidence?

In 1967, John DeLorean, Jim Wangers, and George Hurst sought the go-ahead from Pontiac management to build a 428 Firebird. Hurst's first original equipment manufacturer (OEM) customer was Pontiac, and Hurst reciprocated when it came to

Some thought it radical. Some thought it ridiculous. Either way, the Hurst SC/Rambler 390-cubic-inch hood scoop helped make the car really, really fast.

loyalty. Nevertheless, the proposal was a clear violation of the 400-cubic-inch limit imposed by General Motors on their divisions for anything smaller than a full-sized automobile (or the flagship Corvette). Threatened by a possible Bell Telephone–style breakup of the world's largest corporation, GM management felt that taking up an image of social responsibility was more important than a new hot rod—they shot DeLorean's proposal down. Of course, thanks to the success of the pioneering Pontiac GTO, that division didn't have an image to rebuild.

A discussion with Oldsmobile Chief Design Engineer John Beltz resulted in Doc Watson building a concept that might fly with Olds management. It would be an "executive hot rod," a "gentleman's hot rod," that is, an exclusive automobile with as much emphasis on handling and creature comforts as on straight-line performance. Watson delivered on the concept, taking a black '68 Olds 4-4-2, installing a 455 engine from a Toronado, and adding Gold stripes to create Hurst's favorite combination. Watson also installed foldaway headlights in the factory grille using Pontiac GTO components, and an innovative "air brake" rear spoiler that would rise when the brakes were applied. Hurst absolutely loved to drive the car—it became his personal transportation.

Late in 1967, Doc Watson delivered his proposal to Oldsmobile, offering to build this same car in limited quantities:

Hurst Olds 1968

 # PRODUCED: 515
ENGINE: 455-cubic-inch V-8
HORSEPOWER: 390
TORQUE: 500 lb-ft

How do you get prospects in the front door of the dealership? That's the number one problem that plagues all new car merchandising and keeps new car designers up at night.

Following is a proposal for a vehicle that can help solve that problem, plus open new venues for Oldsmobile image building.

That vehicle is the HURST OLDS!!

A vehicle keyed to the performance oriented enthusiast automotive market.

A vehicle that can help Oldsmobile reestablish themselves as the leader in the "super-car" market.

A vehicle that will give the "ACTION" styling of the 4-4-2 even more meaning to the automotive enthusiasts of this country.

The basic Hurst Olds consists of:

1. A 1968 Oldsmobile 4-4-2
2. 455 cubic inch special W-30 engine
3. Turbo-Hydramatic (3-speed automatic) transmission equipped with a Hurst dual/gate transmission control.
4. 3.91 to 1 anti-spin rear axle.
5. Special H.O. exterior emblems.
6. The normal complement of standard General Motors safety devices plus the full line of Oldsmobile options.

A Hurst Olds would also be available with the following options . . .

1. Hurst custom paint job—A unique performance enthusiast oriented paint scheme of "Hurst Gold" Firefrost and Black. [This would be available only with the order of Black interior trim.]
2. A custom front-end treatment consisting of a restyled grille with hide-away head lamps. The reason for the styling technique is to establish a strong "competition look" identity . . .
3. A new concept in sports vehicle accessories, a "Braking Spoiler." This electrically operated "wing" is activated by stepping on the brake pedal . . . .

The main purpose for doing any vehicles in this manner at all is to gain notoriety for the project through the enthusiast press . . . .

HURST PERFORMANCE: DETROIT'S IMAGE MAKER

The 1968 Hurst/Olds prototype is on display at the Ransom E. Oldsmobile Museum in Lansing, Michigan. This '68 Hurst/Olds was equipped with a four-speed.

The Hurst/Olds returned in 1973, this time on the restyled Cutlass "Colonnade" coupe, powered by a 455 engine with either 275 or 300 horsepower, and for the first time available in either white or black with the customary Hurst Gold stripes. The '74 Hurst/Olds was similar, but this time the Olds 350 V-8 was standard, while the 455 was still optional. Hurst built 1,097 Oldsmobiles in 1973, another 1,903 in 1974, despite their rapidly diminishing horsepower.
Archives/TEN: The Enthusiast Network Magazines, LLC

The pitch caught the attention of General Motors Vice President E. M. "Pete" Estes—he must have understood how critically Oldsmobile needed a makeover, and so he gave his approval to Hurst's proposal. It helped that Hurst would be installing the 455 monsters in his shop, which distanced GM from the project. Oldsmobile Chief Engineer Beltz assigned Ted Lucas, Dale Smith, and Bob Stempel to assist Watson and Hurst. Hurst Performance, in turn, contracted with Demmer Tool and Die in Lansing to provide space and assistance for the conversions.

The end of the model year was fast approaching and Hurst had to hurry. Gone was the gold-with-black paint scheme, since gold wasn't an Olds option that year. Instead, the cars were painted "Peruvian Silver," a 1967 Toronado color that was still on hand. The hideaway headlights and popup rear spoiler were also canned, since development time was tight. Otherwise, production moved forward on a largely unchanged version of Watson's proposal. Even the projected price of $4,115.96 was close to the actual cost of the finished product: $4,288.

100 **CHAPTER 7**

A highly customized 1974 Hurst/Olds again paced the Indianapolis 500 that year. The Hurst/Olds returned to showrooms, but like in 1973, Cutlass convertibles were no longer offered by Oldsmobile, so the Hurst/Olds ragtop was history. But Hurst did build ninety-two full-size Oldsmobile Eighty-Eight convertibles with H/O badges and stripes for VIP use during the Indy 500's parades and festivities. *Archives/TEN: The Enthusiast Network Magazines, LLC*

At first, the plan was to build 500 Hurst/Olds vehicles. The dealers could sense how much this car would boost the Olds image in their showrooms: 2,600 orders were taken just two days after the announcement. Spreading out 500 cars among over 3,000 dealers was a challenge, with some major dealers getting more than one car and others receiving none. Thank Story Oldsmobile on Michigan Avenue in Lansing—the world's largest Olds dealer—for demanding an extra 15 cars be built. This brought the total up to 515: 451 "Holiday Coupe" hardtops, and 64 of the stronger, lighter "Sport Coupes," which were geared more for competition.

The Lansing assembly line produced the special-order Cutlasses, then the cars were shipped about 3 miles to Demmer's building on 728 Porter Street. There, the black paint, H/O emblems and trim, Hurst "Dual-Gate" shifter (all production Hurst/Olds were automatics), and walnut dash appliqué were added. A local pinstriper, Paul Hutton, was paid $20 per car to freehand-paint the white stripe between the silver and black. Doc Watson's contribution was recognized, as every car had a plaque on the glove box that read "Hurst/Olds by Doc Watson." The first Hurst/Olds was shipped on May 24; the last car was delivered on July 12.

Look at any photo of the temporary operation Hurst set up at Demmer's building and you'll see plenty of paint-and-trim activity, but nowhere is there a sign of engines being pulled and replaced. In fact, the 455 engines were installed right on the Lansing assembly line. No pictures were taken of this step, of course: heads would have rolled had top GM management found out about this flagrant infraction of the 400-cubic-inch rule. Instead, it stayed everyone's little secret—at least until all of the perpetrators had retired from General Motors. The clandestine operation was so well hidden that Bob Stempel, an engineer on the project, eventually advanced to chairman of the board of GM. While the cars were being assembled, though, there were likely some awfully tense people in Lansing.

Compared to Oldsmobile's 4-4-2 musclecar, the 455-powered H/O ran at least one half-second faster through the traps, thanks to the difference between 360 horsepower for the 400-cubic-inch 4-4-2 W30 versus 390 horsepower for the Hurst. Handling and braking were slightly better on the H/O, since the 455 weighed 12 pounds less than the 400. The lighter weight was right where it was needed for better cornering, and the extra power and torque could be felt easily. And compared to the competition, the Hurst/Olds was fast. For example, Lynn Welfringer of Tacoma, Washington, held the NHRA record for D/SA for years. As Oldsmobile's Chief Engineer Beltz told *Esquire*, "If an Olds wins, it's like ten Chevrolets winning."

Bud Lindemann, host of the 1960s Car and Track TV show, called it "the silkiest bomb ever nestled between four wheels." His tests saw a quarter-mile time of 13.24 at 107 miles per hour, which is about what other publications recorded. That was a good second faster than a '68 SS396 Chevelle, and right up there with the factory-built monsters like the Chevelle LS-6 that the GM divisions were finally allowed to produce in 1970. Just as impressive was the car's comfort and demeanor in regular traffic, about which Lindemann proclaimed: "It's a supercar that can honestly be termed a family car."

"The Hurst/Olds has all the muscle characteristics of the finest supercar, but without the objectionable interior noise and choppy ride," according to Hurst's promotions of the car. Clearly, they delivered. Decades later, the Hurst/Olds was still the benchmark for other specialists to meet, and one of the most desirable Oldsmobiles ever.

AMC Hurst SC/Rambler 1969

Hurst Performance Research tackled two other OEM programs in 1968. They began building 25,000 Dodge and Plymouth taxis for New York City, with lowered rear floors to meet the Taxi Authority's passenger room regulations. Hurst earned a tidy $43.50 for each taxi built. They also converted 50 Dodge 383 Darts into Dart 440 GSSs for Mr. Norm's Grand Spaulding Dodge in Chicago. Hurst's expanding specialty manufacturing operation continued into 1969.

"Factory assembly lines are set up to handle only high-volume components with standardized assembly procedures," said Wangers in a *Hi-Performance CARS* interview.

> You can't stick little extra gimmicks into this pattern. Like, say, you wanted to add a little fender decal and bolt-on rear spoiler to a certain model. You couldn't arrange to do this on the regular assembly lines. The stuff would have to be added "by hand" in a special shop after the car [was] built. And, of course, the factories don't have the space or manpower to do very much specialty stuff. This is where we come in.

Wangers had left Pontiac's ad agency and was now working for Hurst.

American Motors didn't have an image problem; they were essentially off the radar. The smallest of the Detroit automakers by far—GM built more Cadillacs in 1969 than AMC built cars that year—American Motors had a reputation for fine economy vehicles and not much else. They expanded into the larger cars in the 1960s, and bought Jeep from Kaiser. In 1968 they introduced two fine performance cars, the Mustang-fighter Javelin and the two-seater AMX, but AMC was so small it was difficult to get the message out.

The fact was, AMC made some very good cars. After Chrysler bought AMC in 1987, Bob Lutz, Chrysler's president and vice chairman at the time, stood in awe of what AMC had accomplished, writing that, "with almost no resources, and fighting a vastly superior enemy, they were able to roll out an impressive succession of new products." The challenge was to get potential buyers in the showrooms so they could see for themselves.

Dave Landreth, vice president of Hurst Performance Research Center, and Wangers hatched an idea to build a simple, fast car like the 1964 GTO. The Hurst SC/Rambler they proposed was designed around the NHRA F-stock rules, though they were completely street legal, and many never saw a drag strip. Based on AMC's thrifty compact, the American Rogue, Hurst specified that the 315 horsepower 390-cubic-inch engine, BorgWarner four-speed, and 3:54:1 "Twin Grip" differential used on the AMX be installed into the spunky American.

Unlike the Hurst/Olds, the SC/Rambler was built entirely in Kenosha, Wisconsin, on AMC's east assembly line. Hurst designed the hood scoop (made by Demmer Tool and Die), the SC/Rambler's bold graphics, and the patriotic paint scheme, with red on the sides and twin blue stripes on a Frost White base. The design hinted at the "A-Mark" logo that American Motors would adapt in 1970.

The SC/Rambler also featured popular aftermarket components, including a chrome Sun 8,000 rpm tach mounted on the steering column, adjustable Gabriel Air Shocks on the rear axle, Thrush Hush glass-pack mufflers, and, of course, a Hurst shifter. Hurst himself recognized that these were the components the youth market often added to their cars after they left the dealer; acting on his philosophy of delivering maximum value to customers, he

AMC Hurst SC/Rambler 1969

 # PRODUCED: 1,512
ENGINE: 390-cubic-inch V-8
HORSEPOWER: 315
TORQUE: 425 lb-ft
¼-MILE TIME: 14.4 at 100.44 mph

The performance magazines had a field day with the Hurst SC/Rambler. *Road Test* magazine wrung 14.14 seconds at 100.44 miles per hour quarter mile out of their SC/Rambler, while *Car and Driver* saw 0–60 in 6.3 seconds and 14.7 at 96.3 miles per hour on the strip. That's why *Car Life* magazine could claim, "We could turn quarter-miles in the mid-14s all day, with a full gas tank and two people." It was not known at the time that the ten SC/Ramblers in the press fleet were equipped with 3.91 gears, not the stock 3.55:1 rear end. *Archives/TEN: The Enthusiast Network Magazines, LLC*

TOP: Based on AMC's thrifty compact, the American Rogue, the Hurst SC/Rambler came with the 315-horsepower 390-cubic-inch engine, Borg Warner four-speed, and 3:54:1 "Twin Grip" differential used on the AMX. The Hurst SC/Rambler's patriotic paint scheme, with red on the sides and twin blue stripes on a Frost White base, hinted at the "A-Mark" logo American Motors would adapt in 1970.

LEFT, LOWER: The 315-horsepower, 390-cubic-inch engine of the Hurst SC/Rambler made these lightweight sedans the terror of street and strip, easily making low 14-second times.

RIGHT, MIDDLE: Hurst designed the functional hood scoop (made by Demmer Tool and Die). *Car Life* magazine called the functional hood "the world's most outrageous production cold-air scoop."

RIGHT, LOWER: The SC/Rambler also featured popular aftermarket components, including a chrome Sun 8,000-rpm tach mounted on the steering column. The only option available was an AM radio.

"Snarls softly and carries a big stick" is how Hurst's full-page ad for the 1969 H/O read.

had these items installed right on the AMC assembly line instead. Racing—on or off the track—was the intention, so the only option available on the SC/Rambler was an AM radio.

A batch of 500 cars was built starting in February 1969, but demand caught everyone by surprise, and more cars were ordered. That run began in March, and some of these cars were built with a second "B" series featuring a toned-down paint scheme. Apparently, the "A" series cars attracted too much attention—at least from the Law and insurance companies—and around 300 "B" cars just had small red and blue stripes on the Frost White body. Both "A" and "B" paint scheme cars were intermingled, so the VINs are not consecutive. By the time production ended, Hurst had built 1,512 SC/Ramblers.

Still, the bold, brash little scramblers caught a lot of other attention. An "A" series SC/Rambler was the cover story in the May 1969 issue of Super Stock & Drag Illustrated. AMC's marketing also cranked up the spin machine, with ads shouting, "It Only Hurts Them for 14 Seconds." Another ad bragged, "A Rambler that does the quarter mile in 14.3."

The shocking fact was this was an amazingly quick little compact, with one magazine getting a SC/Rambler to 12.6 seconds in the quarter mile with a little tune-up work. Performance is all about power-to-weight ratio, and, at 3,160 pounds, the bantam-weight SC/Rambler could humble heavier cars with much more power under their hoods. The compact rocket impressed *Car Life*. "We could turn quarter miles in the mid-14s all day, with a full gas tank and two people. At the press showing, with driver only and half a gallon in the tank, the car turned best ET of 14.14. Even the ads only claim a 14.3 ET" They called the functional hood "the world's most outrageous production cold-air scoop" and boasted that the brakes "sent the decelerometer gauge up into area of 1 g." They concluded, "For three big ones, the Scrambler does the budget-super car thing well."

The partnership of Hurst Performance Research and American Motors succeeded in so many ways—stunning performance, in-your-face style, and ready-to-race goodies—all for a truly bargain price of $2,998. The Hurst SC/Ramblers may not have amounted to much of a sales spike, even for American Motors, but they got the attention of many who would never have given an AMC as much as a second look.

Hurst/Olds 1969

Oldsmobile's management and its dealers must have been pleased by the '68 Hurst/Olds success, and Hurst joined forces with them for another H/O in 1969. It took Hurst three attempts before Oldsmobile approved the program, but, by late January 1969, they were given the green light.

Hurst used the same formula for the 1969 car. The Cutlass coupes would be built in Lansing, then shipped to Demmer's facility for the Hurst treatment. This time, Hurst got the colors he wanted, Cameo White with Firefrost Gold stripes added by Hurst. Like the '68, Lansing built the cars with the 455 engine, but again the official word was that Hurst made the switch.

Hurst Olds 1969

 # PRODUCED: 916
ENGINE: 455-cubic-inch V-8
HORSEPOWER: 380
TORQUE: 500 lb-ft
¼-MILE TIME: 14.6 at 100.55 mph

There were 916 Hurst/Olds built in 1969, including five convertibles for Hurst employees. *Car Life* magazine called the 1969 Hurst/Olds, "a first-Cabin Supercar. It goes, stops, and turns in a manner befitting its stripes and scoops. A tiger surely has a right to go around looking like a tiger."

ABOVE: As in 1968, Lansing built the cars with the 370-horsepower 455 engine, but again the official word was Hurst made the switch.

ABOVE, RIGHT: Interior was mostly stock, with Hurst/Olds emblem on the glove box and Hurst Dual Gate shifter added.

RIGHT: Demmer Tool & Die made the twin-snorkel scoop on the hood that bragged "H/O 455."

BELOW, RIGHT: A three-speed Turbo Hydramatic featuring a Hurst Dual Gate shifter.

BELOW, FAR RIGHT: Hurst/Olds emblem returned, but the huge pedestal wing was new for '69.

HURST PERFORMANCE: DETROIT'S IMAGE MAKER

But the 1969 Hurst/Olds was hardly a clone of the original. Along with the bold paint job, the cars had a large pedestal wing on the trunk, and a Demmer-made twin-snorkel scoop on the hood that bragged "H/O 455." Kelsey-Hayes Rallye wheels, a Cutlass option, were included. The 455 engine delivered 380 horsepower at 5,000 rpm and a thundering 500 lb-ft of torque through a three-speed Turbo Hydramatic featuring a Hurst Dual-Gate shifter.

"Snarls softly and carries a big stick" is how Hurst's full-page ad for the 1969 H/O read. Compared to the quietly seductive '68 "Gentleman's Hot Rod," the new car was much more brazen. *Car Life* recorded times of 0–60 in 6.2 seconds, and averaged 14.1 for the quarter with a best of 14.06. It seemed the Hurst/Olds slipped some in the super car ranks, yet *CL* concluded: "The Hurst/Olds is a first-Cabin Supercar. It goes, stops, and turns in a manner befitting its stripes and scoops. A tiger surely has a right to go around looking like a tiger." Buyers loved this beast, and 916 were built, including five convertibles for Hurst employees.

AMC Rebel Machine 1970

Flush with the success of the SC/Rambler, Hurst and AMC joined forces again to produce the Rebel Machine for 1970. AMC replaced the compact American with the new Hornet sedan in 1970, so the SC/Rambler couldn't be continued. But AMC's midsize Rebel looked like a promising performance platform. Plymouth had incredible success with their midsize, low-cost, high-performance Road Runner in 1968 and 1969, and, of course, the iconic Pontiac GTO was the intermediate-class bogey everyone else aimed for.

Central to the Rebel Machine was the prominent, vacuum-operated hood scoop that integrated an 8,000-rpm tachometer in the rear edge. Pontiac pioneered an optional hood-mounted tach on the 1967 Firebird and GTO in an effort to make it more visible to the driver's line of sight, and Hurst's design, again made by Demmer, took that concept one step further. Hurst also designed another bold red/white/blue paint scheme, this time designed to accent the good-looking Rebel's lines, though on the Machine any of the Rebel's sixteen paint colors were available, and the patriotic scheme was a $75 option.

Under that scoop was a special version of AMC's 390 V-8, producing 15 horsepower more than the SC/Rambler's. A Hurst-shifted BorgWarner four-speed was standard, a three-speed automatic optional. Standard also were power front disc brakes, heavy-duty cooling package, free-flowing exhaust, and 3.54:1 gears. AMC engineers added heavy-duty springs all around, and their use of station wagon rear springs gave the cars a nicely "jacked-up" look. The Machine's interior was also above average, with comfortable vinyl high-backed bucket seats and a special steering wheel. And, unlike the SC/Rambler, the Machine had a long list of available options. A good-looking set of 15x7 styled steel wheels and Goodyear Polyglas GT tires rounded out the package. It was a lot of machine for $3,475.

AMC Rebel Machine 1970

 # PRODUCED: 2,326
ENGINE: 390-cubic-inch V-8
HORSEPOWER: 330
TORQUE: 430 lb-ft
¼-MILE TIME: 14.57 at 94.77 mph

The Machine was introduced at the NHRA World Championships in Dallas on October 25, 1969. AMC claimed the Machine was capable of quarter-mile times around 14.4 seconds at 98 miles per hour, surprisingly close to the SC/Rambler's performance. *Road Test* concurred, reporting 14.57 seconds at 92.77 miles per hour. They praised the Machine's handling, claiming, "You can also get around corners with sports car aplomb or the kind of handling that brings home the bacon in Trans Am racing." They also reported, "The brakes on the Machine are among the best yet tested on a muscle car," which "do an excellent job of bringing 4,000 lbs. of The Machine to a halt from 60 mph in about 142 feet." While not the ultra-high performance projectile of the 454-cubic-inch 1970 LS6 Chevelle and some of its peers, the scrappy Machine AMC and Hurst Performance put together was a compelling youth market car.

AMC's vice president of sales, William Pickett, was justifiably optimistic. "The Machine should provide strong sales competition in the rapidly emerging performance car market," he stated. But no one predicted that muscle car sales in 1970 would be nearly half the 1969 number, and the lack of demand for all performance cars hurt the Machine's sale. There is some dispute over the number of Rebel Machines sold, but 2,326 seems to be a credible figure, with around 1,300 buyers choosing the code 768 red-white-and-blue paint. The Machine would be another one-year wonder, but it got people in the showroom, and that alone made it a success.

Other sectors experienced difficulty in 1970. With the skyrocketing success of Hurst-Campbell, Hurst and Campbell took the company public in 1968. Along with the company's biggest investor, Larry Greenwald, each man owned 25.9 percent of the company, now valued at $18 million. Company accountant Louis Palitz owned another 11.3 percent. The remaining 10.4 percent, or 250,000 shares, was sold to Hurst employees and became available on the stock market. That raised much-needed capital to expand the company, but, when Campbell left Hurst in 1969 and then sold his shares to Sunbeam Electric Corporation of Chicago, the balance of power shifted. Greenwald later sold his shares to Sunbeam. Why the maker of toasters and blenders was interested in taking over the world's preeminent performance company is unclear, but that meant

"Faster on the getaway than a Volkswagen, a slow freight train, and your old man's Cadillac" is how AMC introduced the Hurst-upgraded 1970 Rebel Machine. *Author's Collection*

Hurst was now a minority shareholder, and Sunbeam management gave him the powerless title of chairman of the board. He resigned in December 1970 from the company that he'd founded. Hurst was in good company—Walt Disney and Steve Jobs are but two of the many business giants who suffered the same fate.

One factor leading to Hurst's ouster from his company was the failure of the 1970 Hurst/Olds program. As in previous years, Hurst built prototypes and made proposals to Oldsmobile management. The new Hurst/Olds was bright yellow and powered by Oldsmobile's 350-cubic-inch engine as an alternative to the 4-4-2, which was now powered by the Olds 455. Instead, Oldsmobile chose to copy Hurst's proposal and build it in-house. Called the Rallye 350, it was hardly a sales success, but it did outsell both Hurst/Olds cars from the previous years combined. The 1970 Hurst/Olds debacle was a serious blow to Hurst Performance's income and image, and Sunbeam management was not pleased.

With the performance car market dying—and without the visionary leadership of George Hurst—the company continued to build limited-edition automobiles, including a mammoth 1970 Chrysler 300H with Hurst trim, a batch of Yenko "Deuce" Novas for Don Yenko, and a series of Hurst Pontiac Grand Prix SSJ conversions in 1972 to 1974. The Hurst/Olds returned in 1972, 1973, and 1974, but they were nothing more than trim-and-badge specials, and even the Hurst-developed cold-air scoops were missing. Yet, by 1972, Oldsmobile had moved back up to third in sales, behind Chevrolet and Ford. Coincidence, or Hurst image magic?

Sunbeam was purchased by Allegheny International in 1981, who then sold Hurst to former employee Dick Chrysler. Even Hurst's Rescue Tool was sold, this time to a North Carolina manufacturer, Hale Products, who trademarked the "Jaws of Life" name.

Hurst, ever the innovator and promoter, attempted a number of other business ventures. Then came the headline in the *Los Angeles Times*:

GEORGE HURST, 59, INVENTOR OF THE "JAWS OF LIFE," FOUND DEAD

May 19, 1986

George Hurst, an inventor who developed a tool to pluck drivers from their wrecked race cars, which was later adapted as the "jaws of life" rescue device widely used by police and firefighters, has been found dead in the garage of his Redlands town house.

Redlands Police Capt. Lewis Nelson said Hurst's body was found Tuesday.

David Hammock, deputy coroner inspector for San Bernardino County, said no cause of death could be determined pending completion of toxicological tests. He said his office was investigating the possibility of carbon monoxide poisoning, adding that there was no evidence indicating suicide.

Hurst was 59 and had no known health problems, a family spokesman said.

He was the founder of the Hurst Performance Product Co. and was associated with high-performance vehicles and automotive advances, particularly in the area of car transmissions. His Hurst Shifter, a floor-mounted gear shift for performance cars, made him a wealthy man.

The company has since been sold several times, said Chuck Lamerel of American Bristol Co., seller of the jaws of life. The jaws of life tool was originally developed by Hurst in the 1960s to rescue drivers in crashes at the Indianapolis Motor Speedway and then adopted by rescue agencies throughout the country, Lamerel said.

Billy Closson, a friend and owner of Custom Engineering Inc. of Redlands, said Hurst had been working most recently on a cable winding device for use in towing. "There is no reason at all to think he was despondent," Closson said. "He had everything in the world going for him."

Whatever the cause of his death, the fact is that George Hurst accomplished more in a decade than most people do in a lifetime. Hurst shifters, now made by B&M Automotive, are still the gold standard, and countless lives have been saved by his Jaws of Life innovation. And, of all the muscle cars to come out of Detroit, Hurst's machines are some of the most unique and desirable of the era. Successful indeed.

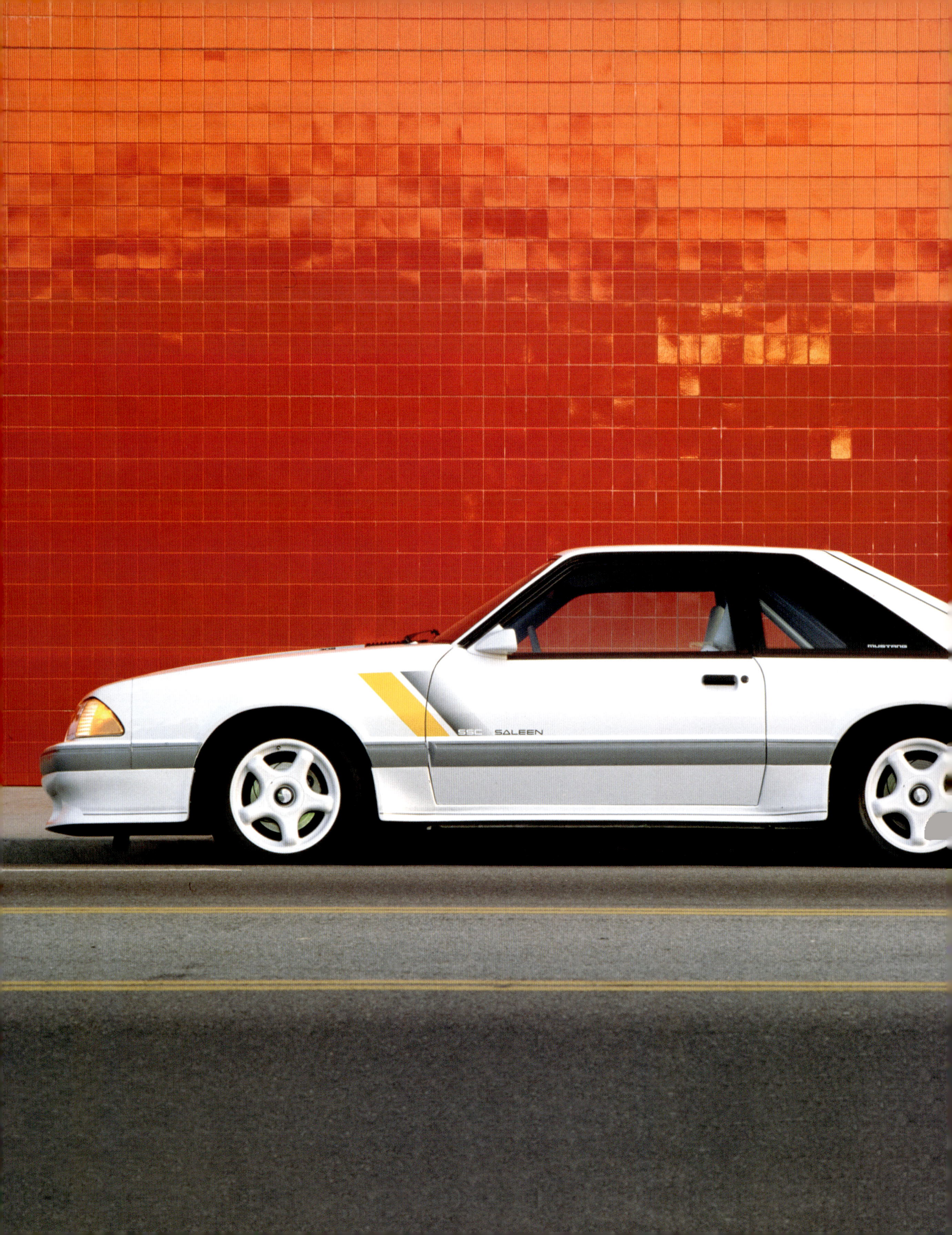
SSC
SALEEN
MUSTANG

Chapter 8
Saleen Automotive
The Mustang Reborn

"These are the best Mustangs I have ever built," said Steve Saleen at the introduction of the Saleen White Label Mustang on February 2, 2015. "We are in for a thrill ride as this car will take us to levels we have never seen before." The event was more than the release of yet another Saleen supercar: it was the culmination of a thirty-year thrill ride filled with triumphs, accolades, challenges—and rebirth.

Like many other automotive success stories, Saleen seems to have that gearhead gene. Born in 1949, Saleen's father, a manufacturing executive, bought a Porsche 356 while Steve was at the University of Southern California earning a business degree. That Porsche sparked Steve's interest in road racing, and in 1973 he raced a 1965 Shelby GT350R, winning his first event. Saleen went on to race in the Formula Atlantic open wheel series, setting thirteen records and finishing third in the 1980 finals behind champion (and future Indy 500 winner) Jacques Villeneuve.

But Mustangs had a special place in his heart. "I was, at an early age, bitten by the racing and Mustang heritage bug," he explained.

In 1989, Saleen Automotive began a tradition of celebrating every five years of business with a special edition. The SSC was the first Saleen to feature a modified engine, including Saleen-designed high-flow SSC heads, Saleen-modified upper and lower intake manifold, SVO 1.7 rocker arms, 65mm throttle body, Saleen SSC-designed headers, and Walker Dynomax low-restriction exhaust system. The result was 292-horsepower (stock was 225) and 325 lb-ft of torque. Like previous Saleens, the SSC was completely fifty-state EPA compliant. Total production for Saleen in '89 was 895, including 161 SSC Mustangs. *Archives/TEN: The Enthusiast Network*

TOP: Quick, sure, refined—Steve Saleen's version of the uniquely American breed of machine known as a pony car. This first Saleen Mustang was finished on June 1, 1984, built from a white GT he'd bought from his sister, Robyn Lee. That first Saleen Mustang, serial number 84-0032, made its debut at Sears Point Raceway the same month. Even the first Saleen Mustang was the complete performance package. Saleen built three Mustangs in 1984. *Saleen Automotive*

ABOVE: "Since I started building cars in 1984, my goal has always been to go above and beyond where anybody has been before," said Steve Saleen of the 2015 Black Label Mustang. "This will by far be the most refined and advanced Mustang we have built to date." The reviews were excellent, with *Hot Rod* calling the Black Label "More Powerful than a Hellcat, More Affordable than a Z28." *Saleen Automotive*

LEFT: Steven M. Saleen. *Saleen Automotive*

110 **CHAPTER 8**

Entered in the SCCA Escort Showroom Stock Endurance Series, the Mustangs won the demanding 24 Hours of Mosport in 1986, repeated the feat in 1987, and completed the "threepeat" with this 1-2-3 finish in 1988. "We use the race team as both a test bed for our street cars and a showplace to our buyers to point to," Saleen said. "Racing victories play an important role in the image of a car. We wanted our drivers to be able to say to Porsche, Firebird, 300 Turbo ZX, Supra Turbo, and Camaro owners, my car whips yours in one of the toughest racing formats in the world. People who are buying our cars know they're driving winners." *Saleen Automotive*

I was very Ford oriented in the late '60s and early '70s. I had a '65 Shelby, a '66 Shelby, and my dad had a '66 289 coupe. I also had a '67 GT fastback that looked like Steve McQueen's car from Bullitt, except that mine had a 390 in it, and I put dual quads on it. I then went on to a '69 Boss 302.

America was coming out of the "malaise" of the 1970s, and, in 1982, Ford was bringing back the Mustang GT. The time seemed right for Steve Saleen.

Saleen Mustang 1984–1989

A quick flick of the wrist puts a set on the throttle-induced oversteer. The chassis settles immediately, reeling in the next corner like a tournament fishing rod. A firm stab of the brakes squats the car on all fours as the shift lever pulls cleanly to the next lower gear. With the power back on, the car slings itself around the corner. Quick, sure, refined. The car—Steve Saleen's version of the uniquely American breed of machine called the pony car.

Motor Trend had just driven something we hadn't seen since the mid-1960s: a limited-edition, handcrafted Mustang built for a total driving experience. "We don't build this car for the average driver. In our view, that would be a horrendous waste of effort," Saleen told *Motor Trend*.

Saleen had worked out an arrangement with Ford to build this supercar. "Without factory support and a commitment to excellence by everyone involved, you might as well not start," Saleen emphasized. The cars were sold with a complete Ford three-year, 36,000-mile warranty, but to do that Saleen couldn't touch the engine. With the 5.0-liter only producing 175 horsepower in 1984, that meant chassis mods and aerodynamics had to produce.

The first Saleen Mustang was finished on June 1, 1984, built from a white GT purchased from his sister, Robyn Lee. Saleen was sharing space in Petaluma, California, with race fabricator Joe Carr. That first Saleen Mustang, serial number 84-0032, made its debut at Sears Point Raceway the same month, where it was displayed with Saleen's Trans Am racer. Saleen took orders for two more Mustangs that weekend, and cars 84-0051 and 84-0052 were built over the summer. The Saleen Mustangs exuded a feeling of being a complete package. These were more than just tuner cars—Saleen was determined to be a manufacturer.

continued on page 115

Saleen Mustang 1984-1989

PRODUCED: 344
ENGINE: 302-cubic-inch V-8
HORSEPOWER: 200
TORQUE: 285 lb-ft
¼-MILE TIME: 14.7 at 92 mph

SALEEN AUTOMOTIVE: THE MUSTANG REBORN

Phil Frank: Driven Design

Creating the 2007 Saleen S302H Parnelli Jones editions should have been easy.

The Mustang was a modern interpretation of the 1970 Boss 302 Parnelli Jones raced in the SCCA Trans Am championship that year. Some Grabber Orange paint and "Boss" stripes should be all that was needed, right?

Not if you're Phil Frank. Since 1994, the Seattle-based designer had been giving Saleen's vehicles the carefully crafted look that makes them so special.

Well, if you start at the front fascia, the obvious elements are the lamp splitters, then the chrome grille trim front and rear, a very subtle detail is in the shape of the bottom front intake. I mimicked the 1969 stamped sheet metal valance panel, which gives the inner edge opening a bit more authenticity; compare the two and you will see. There is also a highlight line at the bottom of the front fascia that carries into the side skirts and rear fascia to add a bit of sparkle above the grounding blackout parts—this makes the car seem long and low.

That's the difference between an accomplished designer and the rest of us. The details continued:

The rear was kept really simple by moving the plate up into the blackout area between the lamps and, of course, adding the authentic Boss wing, but I made sure that it could not be installed incorrectly to produce lift like so many 1969 cars you see driving around. The interior was a nice departure from black as I brought in the Grabber Orange, some pattern and small details such as the

RIGHT: Phil Frank's Senior project at San Jose State University in 1991 was a full-size foam car model called the "Illicit," "the design of which actually points the way for the design DNA of all Saleen's that I've worked on." *Phil Frank*

BELOW: Frank's sketches show the design evolution of the Saleen S7's exterior. Early sketches featured more of the Illicit's form. *Phil Frank*

The Saleen S7's structure is primarily steel tube and aluminum sheet, with the carbon fiber body bonded to this structure. The result was stronger than the contemporary Ferrari Enzo. *Phil Frank*

Frank, at left, and Saleen with the Saleen S7. "I was the only aesthetic designer and CAD modeler for the exterior and interior, which is extremely rare in automotive design, so all the beauty and mistakes I take equal credit for," Frank said. *Phil Frank*

chrome PJ badges in the upper bolster; this pattern was inspired by another early Mustang interior.

The result, as with all Saleen Mustangs, was spectacular.

Design comes as naturally to Frank as speed to Saleen. "I was born of two creative parents, so creativity is in my DNA." His father, Phil Sr., drew a popular cartoon in the San Francisco Bay area, and also restored seven Model A Fords, two MG TCs, an MG SA Tickford Drophead, and a Jaguar MKII. His mother and sister are accomplished artists.

As a kid I was always working with my hands, figuring stuff out, making hybrid 1:18 scale car models with working suspension or Dremel Tool-powered Lego dragsters.

I kept it up when I went to San Jose State University in California and studied Industrial Design with an emphasis on transportation design to learn the skills of the profession. What I learned is you have to work harder than the next guy if you want to get anywhere. So that is what I've always done.

The long relationship between Frank and Saleen was due to a chance meeting.

For my senior project at San Jose State University in 1991, I built a full-size foam car model called the "Illicit," the design of which actually points the way for the design DNA of all Saleens that I've worked on. After I graduated I

The Saleen S7 was tested in the University of Glasgow's wind tunnel. The S7 generates enough downforce that it can be driven upside down and remain in contact with the pavement. *Phil Frank*

SALEEN AUTOMOTIVE: THE MUSTANG REBORN 113

For over 30 years, Saleen Automotive has been a preeminent specialty manufacturer. *David Newhardt*

"If you start at the front fascia, the obvious elements are the lamp splitters, then the chrome grille trim front and rear, a very subtle detail is in the shape of the bottom front intake, I mimicked the 1969 stamped sheet metal valance panel which gives the inner edge opening a bit more authenticity; compare the two and you will see," Frank says of the 2007 Saleen S302H Parnelli Jones edition. *David Newhardt*

was invited to the 1993 SEMA Show to display it alongside a number of other designers, companies, schools, and such that provide design services. In typical Steve style, he wandered by on the last hour of the last day and commented that the car was neat and he needed help designing the 1994 Mustang. He gave me his card and wandered away, so that is where it all began.

Frank's first project was designing the one-off Saleen RRR Mustang for comedian Tim Allen. "Steve basically just told me what he was after and I just rendered up three or four variations, and as they were for Tim, I drew a crazy RRR caveman driving!" Then came the 1994 Saleen S-351 built on the new SN-95 Mustang. But Frank's masterpiece is the Saleen S7 supercar.

I was the only aesthetic designer and CAD modeler for the exterior and interior, which is extremely rare in automotive design, so all the beauty and mistakes I take equal credit for, with the exception of a number of early cars that had an engineering "designed" front lip spoiler that was all wonky. Luckily I was able to correct that after the first year of production.

Due to the racing focus of the S7, and the rapid development time, Frank couldn't completely refine the design.

The interior needed more design refinement and better execution, but there is only so much that can be done when someone doesn't want to spend the required time and money. The same can be said of the engine bay. But the body had no compromises from my perspective.

Viewing Frank's sketches of the S7 is an exercise in beginning to see like a designer.

He joined Saleen full time in 2006, just before the Great Recession hit, then moved to Saleen's SMS Supercars to develop the automotive design and branding of those cars. Today, Frank is principal product and industrial designer at Microsoft, and continues his design business, *pfd. He's also done work for Galpin, Lingenfelter, Edelbrock, and others.

Saleen was a unique situation for the time. All the manufacturers have developed their own internal performance groups and it is next to impossible to compete with their cost and performance structure. You can buy a 202 mph Shelby GT 500 for under $60K!

Saleen/Parnelli Jones Limited Edition 2007

 # PRODUCED: 500

ENGINE: 302-cubic-inch V-8

HORSEPOWER: 430

TORQUE: 390 lb-ft

¼-MILE TIME: 13.3 at 106.9 mph

continued from page 111

The "Racecraft" suspension upgrades included Bilstein shocks and struts, heavier spring rates, lower crossmember supports, and Eagle GT P215/60HR15 tires on 15x7 Hayashi gold mesh wheels. The lowered stance, combined with the aero package Saleen created—a front air dam, rear spoiler and valance, side skirts, and clear headlight covers—reduced drag and increased downforce. The interior upgrades included a Saleen instrument cluster, custom floor mats, upgraded seats, and a custom stereo. Note the serial numbers? In the same way Carroll Shelby had repainted his first two Cobras numerous times to give the impression there were more than just a couple of cars, Saleen numbered his first year's production to imply that many more cars had been built. It worked: the *Los Angeles Times* reported his production that year at fifty.

In 1985, Saleen moved to the Los Angeles area, and actual production took off—140 that year, followed by 201 in 1986. By 1986, the Mustang GT now had 200 horsepower, but Saleen's improvements—still without touching the engine—were dramatic:

Test	1986 Saleen Mustang	1986 Mustang GT
0–60 mph	6.0	7.6
¼ mile	14.70 at 92.0 mph	15.60 at 89.8 mph
Skid pad	0.79 g	0.88 g

Just as dramatic was Saleen's performance on the racetrack. Entered in the SCCA Escort Showroom Stock Endurance Series, the Mustangs won the demanding 24 Hours of Mosport in 1986, repeated the feat in 1987, and completed the "threepeat" with a 1-2-3 finish in 1988. The team also won the series championship in 1987, and all '88 Saleens had dash plaques that read "Saleen Autosport Mustang—1987 SCCA Escort Endurance Champion."

"We use the race team as both a test bed for our street cars and a showplace to our buyers to point to," Saleen said.

> Racing victories play an important role in the image of a car. We wanted our drivers to be able to say to Porsche, Firebird, 300 Turbo ZX, Supra Turbo, and Camaro owners, "My car whips yours in one of the toughest racing formats in the world." People who are buying our cars know they're driving winners.

Saleen's philosophy was working: 279 cars were sold in 1987 and 709 in 1988.

Saleen Mustang 1989–1993

In 1989, Saleen Automotive began a tradition of celebrating every five years of business with a special edition. The SSC was the first Saleen to feature a modified engine, and their literature details the mods: Saleen-designed high-flow SSC heads, Saleen-modified upper and lower intake manifold, SVO 1.7 rocker arms, 65mm throttle body, Saleen SSC-designed headers, and Walker Dynomax low-restriction exhaust system. The result was 292 horsepower (stock was 225 horsepower) and 325 lb-ft of torque. Saleen also removed the rear seat in a throwback to the original Shelby GT350. Along with the usual Racecraft suspension, the SSC featured a hand-tailored, glove-leather interior. Like before, the SSC was completely fifty-state EPA compliant. Ford forgot to celebrate the Mustang's twenty-fifth anniversary; Saleen did it for them. Total production for Saleen in 1989 was 895, including 161 SSC Mustangs.

Saleen also celebrated the company's fifth anniversary by entering the Indianapolis 500. He purchased three cars and attacked the Brickyard. A news item in the *Los Angeles Times* reveals how the month of May went:

> Steve Saleen spun in turn four and slammed into the wall virtually head-on. He was awake and alert, but had to be helped from the car and was expected to stay overnight Saturday at Methodist Hospital for further examination with back pain.

All three cars crashed and he didn't qualify. "Looking back it was the right thing to do at the wrong time," he told *Los Angeles Magazine*. "From a marketing perspective, the concept was to expand our sphere of influence to new Saleen buyers. But we didn't have the resources to race at that level, and a bad month of Indy killed us."

The SSC returned in 1990 as a regular production item, now known as the SC. Just 13 SC Mustangs were sold in 1990, out of 256 total. The next year was worse, with only 102 cars sold. Saleen's motto, "Power in the Hands of a Few," was taken a little too far in 1992, and only 17 Saleen Mustangs were delivered. America was falling into a serious recession and, combined with the expense of the failed Indy 500 attempt, Saleen Performance was broke and ready to close its doors. "The recession hit, and we had dealers going broke and not paying us for their cars," said Saleen. "It was a lethal combination."

Enter Tony Johnson. He owned a number of successful original equipment automotive businesses and was looking to buy a Saleen Mustang. Instead, upon hearing of Saleen's plight, he made a significant investment (he never said how much) and became the financial manager of the company. Saleen Performance was back.

In 1993, Saleen returned to SCCA competition with a supercharged SC in the World Challenge series. They also celebrated their tenth anniversary by offering ten SA-10 Mustangs. Production was

Saleen Mustang SC 1989–1993

- **# PRODUCED:** 27
- **ENGINE:** 302-cubic-inch V-8
- **HORSEPOWER:** 304
- **TORQUE:** 326 lb-ft
- **¼-MILE TIME:** 13.7 at 102.27 mph

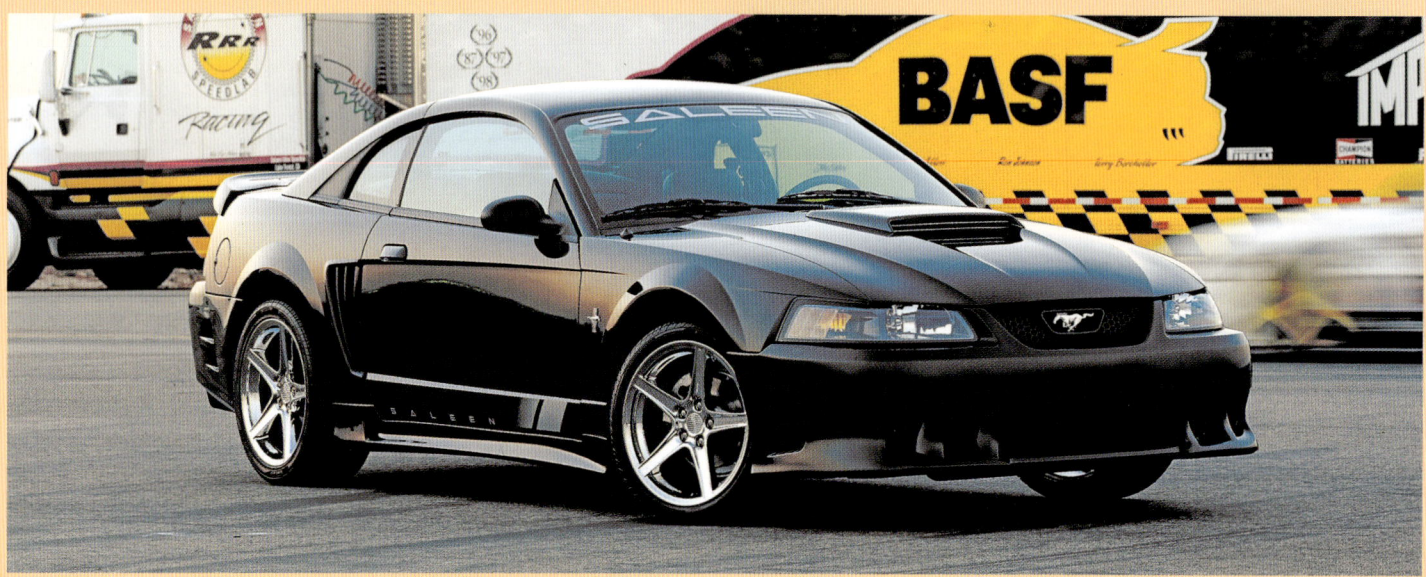

TOP: In the same way young Ford designers Chuck McHose and Pete Stacey created the Shelby Mustang look, Phil Frank redesigned all of the typical Saleen body mods to work with the new Mustang's body. Saleen introduced the S281 in 1996, a more affordable supercar based on the 4.6-liter SOHC engine. It was a huge success: 193 coupes and 234 convertibles sold. 467 more were delivered in 1997 and 1998. This is a 1998 Saleen S281. *Saleen Automotive*

ABOVE, MIDDLE: Paint manufacturer BASF has been a partner with Saleen since 1995. Together the two companies have created a number of unique paints for Saleen vehicles, the first being the chameleon-like "Mystic" hue, the latest the Sunset Yellow of the 2015 Saleen Black Label Mustang. *Saleen Automotive*

ABOVE, LEFT: As a major subcontractor of the Ford GT program, Saleen opened a facility in Troy, Michigan, to sub-assemble Ford's supercar. *Saleen Automotive*

ABOVE, RIGHT: Any Mustang lover's dream. The Irvine facility produced 989 Saleen Mustangs in 2000, 916 in 2001, and 835 in 2002. *Saleen Automotive*

ABOVE, LEFT: The serial number of Saleen vehicles is always located below the driver's side headlight. Saleen vehicles never have the serial number "6," due to a mistake from early in Saleen history: a secretary had missed issuing the serial number "6," and the tradition stayed.

ABOVE, RIGHT: Ford introduced a significant upgrade to the Mustang in 1994, and Steve Saleen took advantage of it. Saleen offered the S351 and SR models, built on Mustangs that were stripped to a bare shell, then reassembled and upgraded to perfection. "Saleen wanted the '94 bearing his name to be a quantum leap above anything else based on the Mustang; he was looking for a real Neil Armstrong moment," said *Mustang Monthly* magazine. *Archives/ TEN: The Enthusiast Network Magazines, LLC*

LEFT: The Phil Frank–designed "Boss" stripes couldn't say "Boss," only "302," since Ford owns the trademark to that name.

back to 101 that year, and one of those was a special Mustang, the RRR, built for comedian Tim Allen. For this one-off, high-visibility Mustang, Saleen turned to a young designer named Phil Frank.

Saleen Mustang 1994–2004

Ford took the venerable Fox platform, updated 80 percent of it, and created the first new Mustang in fifteen years—and a new pony car for Saleen to improve. In the same way, young Ford designers Chuck McHose and Pete Stacey created the Shelby Mustang look, Frank redesigned all of the typical Saleen body mods to work with the new Mustang's body, and two new engines were created: the 371-horsepower S351 and the supercharged 480-horsepower SR, both based on the 351-cubic-inch mill from the SVO Lightning truck.

"Saleen wanted the '94 bearing his name to be a quantum leap above anything else based on the Mustang; he was looking for a real Neil Armstrong moment," said *Mustang Monthly*. Both cars were based on Mustangs that had been stripped to a bare shell, then reassembled and upgraded to perfection. The new Saleens were introduced later in the 1994 model year, so only forty-four S351s and two of the wild SRs were sold.

There was a reason for the huge rear spoiler and extreme horsepower of the SR: Saleen used that model to reenter the SCCA World Challenge with Allen and the Saleen/Allen RRR Speedlab Mustangs in 1995. The same year, Saleen introduced the

Saleen Mustang S351 1994-1998

PRODUCED: 257

ENGINE: 351-cubic-inch V-8

HORSEPOWER: 371

TORQUE: 422 lb-ft

¼-MILE TIME: n/a

Saleen Mustang S281 S/C 1999-2004

PRODUCED: 1,899

ENGINE: 281-cubic-inch V-8

HORSEPOWER: 365

TORQUE: 400 lb-ft

¼-MILE TIME: n/a

SALEEN AUTOMOTIVE: THE MUSTANG REBORN   117

The 2006 Saleen S7, originally designed by Phil Frank. *Kimballstock*

Saleen S7 2001

 # PRODUCED: 30
ENGINE: 427-cubic-inch V-8
HORSEPOWER: 550
TORQUE: 560 lb-ft
¼-MILE TIME: 11.60 at 126 mph

Saleen S7 Twin Turbo 2005

 # PRODUCED: 30
ENGINE: 427-cubic-inch V-8
HORSEPOWER: 750
TORQUE: 700
¼-MILE TIME: 10.90 at 140 mph

Speedster package for an S351 convertible. *Motor Trend* wrote of the supercharged '96 S351 R:

> At 119.3 mph, the S351 R is the fastest production street car (not a tuner special) *Motor Trend* has ever tested in the quarter mile, outrunning even the Saleen SR prototype we drove last year. At the quarter-mile mark, the Saleen pulls away smartly from the 113.4-mph Viper, and accelerates away from the Mustang Cobra at a rate of 17.6 mph—like Carl Lewis at a full run. That's teleportation. That's the Saleen S351 R.

This was also the year that Saleen formed a strategic partnership with paint manufacturer BASF. Together, the companies have created a number of unique paints for Saleen vehicles, the first being the chameleon-like "Mystic" hue. Saleen introduced the S281 in 1995 as well, which was a more affordable supercar based on the 4.6-liter SOHC engine. It was a huge success: 193 coupes and 234 convertibles sold. In 1997 and 1998, 467 more were delivered. Saleen/Allen RRR Speedlab Mustangs also captured the SCCA Manufacturers' and Drivers' Championship titles in 1998. Following tradition, ten special SA-15 Mustangs celebrated Saleen's 15th anniversary.

Saleen unveiled the 1999 S281 and S351 Mustang at Planet Hollywood, featuring a dynamic new design combined with lower cost and a higher level of performance. In 2000, the S351 was dropped, the last of the old "Windsor" engines. To replace it, Saleen created the S281 Extreme model, powered by the new Twin Screw Supercharger.

Saleen S7 2001, 2005

It's a dream many car enthusiasts have, but very few can attempt. For Saleen, eighteen months of rapid development were on display at the Monterey Historic Races on August 19, 2000—the Saleen S7.

"With the design of the S7, I was aiming to create a visually exciting and iconic car," designer Frank explains.

> Its muscular fenders convey the power beneath; its sinuous edges and M. C. Escher-like surface transitions create a sense of movement and drama. The stance is taut and predatorial. Vents, intakes, and splitters were all designed to conjure up images of a shark while serving aerodynamic and cooling purposes. The nose and tail reflect traditional Saleen styling cues with a new level of refinement.

Building a supercar from the ground up is a daunting and incredibly expensive endeavor. It bankrupted John DeLorean, with sad results. But Tony Johnson, Saleen's financier, thought he knew the challenges. John Coletti, the Ford product design engineer who led the 1994 Mustang development, recalled his conversation with Johnson to *Automotive News*: "I remember taking Tony aside and telling him, 'Have you gone off your rocker? Do you have any idea how big of a money pit a sports car can be?' And Tony simply smiled and said he was trying to have a little fun."

The S7 was built around a steel-and-aluminum structure with carbon-fiber body panels bonded to it. The result was stronger than the contemporary Ferrari Enzo. An aluminum 427-cubic-inch engine derived from Ford's NASCAR powerplants propelled the machine, with horsepower quoted at 550 for 6,400 rpm. Just as impressive was the torque: 500 lb-ft at almost any place in the powerband. Thanks to ground effects tuned in the University of Glasgow's wind tunnel, the S7 generated enough downforce that it could be driven upside down and remain in contact with the pavement! Yet the shape is slippery enough that the car could reach a theoretical 223 miles per hour.

"The car, when seen in person, has an amazing presence," said Saleen. "It is quite long and wide, and only 41 inches high, which adds to its exotic appearance. We wanted a 'form-follows-function' look, but also one that was beautiful. I'd say we succeeded!"

The first cars built were S7R racers, which, in typical Saleen fashion, triumphed on the track: class win in the 12 Hours of Sebring in 2001, the GTS-class pole at Le Mans the same year. The subsequent street S7 cars were mildly civilized versions of the S7R. When *Car and Driver* was finally able to test the $400,000 S7 in 2003, they were impressed:

> The S7 did not disappoint us: 0 to 60 arrived in 3.3 seconds and 0 to 100 in 7.6 seconds, and the quarter mile went by in 11.6 seconds at 126 mph. The S7 is simply ridiculously fast, and it's the quickest production car built in the US. It comes within a hair of keeping pace with the $1 million McLaren F1, which didn't meet US emissions regulations, and the Ferrari Enzo, which does . . . . You do feel everything on the road—cracks, reflectors, possibly cigarette butts. The larger dips and road undulations are soaked up quite well, but the little stuff comes through loud and clear. If the road is smooth and curvy, however—and you're not afraid of the cops—you can carry an incredible amount of speed in the S7. We measured 1.02 g on the skid pad—second only to the Ferrari Enzo for a street car on street tires . . . . If driving a slightly civilized version of a Le Mans racer sounds cool to you, there's only one choice.

Saleen built thirty S7s, then in 2006 the S7 Twin Turbo debuted, still using the giant 427 Ford in back but with double boost. Asked *Car and Driver*, "Do 750 horsepower and 140 mph in the quarter make for street cred in the supercar class?" They discovered the answer:

> Do it right, and you'll scorch the quarter mile in 10.9 seconds at 140 mph. We hit 60 mph in 3.4 seconds, 100 mph in 6.2, and 160 mph, which was as fast as we could go at the short track placed at our disposal, in 15.6 seconds. The S7 Twin Turbo has enough power to easily get below three seconds to 60, but despite trying about a dozen full-power launches, which bothered the car not one whit, such a time needs a higher-traction surface than we had available.

Another twenty-nine S7 Twin Turbos were built, along with fifteen S7R racer cars.

If you've see the movie *Bruce Almighty*, you've seen the Saleen S7—it's the car that God drives.

The first Saleen S7 cars built were S7-R racers, which, in typical Saleen fashion, triumph on the track: class win in the 12 Hours of Sebring in 2001, the GTS-class pole at Le Mans the same year. *Phil Frank*

SALEEN AUTOMOTIVE: THE MUSTANG REBORN

Ford brought back the legendary Boss 302 in 2012. Like the Trans Am–inspired 1969–1970 Boss 302, the modern version balanced raw speed with superb cornering and braking. The normally aspirated 302 produced 444 horsepower with a wide powerband. Fully adjustable shocks and three modes of speed-sensitive steering controlled those horses. *Motor Trend* declared it "the best, most well-rounded Mustang ever." *Archives/TEN: The Enthusiast Network Magazines, LLC*

Saleen Mustangs 2005–2009

In 2005, when Ford introduced their own supercar, the Ford GT, they turned to Saleen for help with the paint and subassembly. Setting up the plant in the Detroit area, though, and the cost of building this facility—and the falloff of sales as buyers waited for the next-generation Mustang—were hurting Saleen. Factor in the expense of creating the S7, and the company faced an additional financial bind. The *Los Angeles Times* reported in 2004:

> After nearly running out of money last year, the company was recently revitalized by a cash infusion, believed to be in the neighborhood of $20 million, from Los Angeles-based private equity investor Hancock Park Associates. The investment firm is now Saleen's majority owner.

When the 2005 Mustang was introduced, the new Saleens it was based on were attractive. The S281 models continued on the new Mustang, and the S302 was added in 2007. The retro look of the '05 Mustang became the basis of the H302 series, celebrating Mustang's success in the Trans Am series in 1969 and 1970, including the Parnelli Jones and Dan Gurney models.

On May 14, 2007, Saleen resigned from the company he had founded. The decision may have been prompted by this May 2, 2007, press release:

> ASC Incorporated announced that Hancock Park Associates, a private-equity firm based in Los Angeles, has signed a definitive purchase agreement for the automotive "open air" roof-systems unit and the automotive design-services unit of ASC from its owner, American Specialty Cars Holdings LLC. Terms of the transaction were not disclosed.

Just a few weeks later, the *Los Angeles Times* reported:

> Steve Saleen made his name selling hyperfast, hyperexpensive cars that were hand-built at his company's Irvine factory. The auto industry will be watching to see how that high-end expertise translates to Saleen's new career: running a company that aims to import the first Chinese cars to the American market. The former race driver is the new chief executive of Irvine-based ZX Automobile Co. of North America Inc., which was formed to import low-priced cars and trucks from China.

It wasn't Saleen's only business venture. A few months later, he announced the founding of SMS Supercars. The Chinese deal fell through in a few years, but SMS Supercars kept going.

SMS Supercars 2010–2012

In 2010, Saleen's new company, SMS Supercars, released their first products, the 460 and 460X Mustangs. They were beautifully designed, beautifully crafted Mustangs, just as you would expect from Steve Saleen. But they were not "Saleen" Mustangs.

The company that he had formed in 1984 was now run by Hancock Park Associates. They sold all assets in California, merged with ASC, and relocated to Pontiac, Michigan. And they continued to build and sell Saleen Mustangs—or at least they made the effort. Like Apple without Steve Jobs, or Hurst Performance without George Hurst, the old Saleen was putting up a brave fight. Then, on February 2, 2009, Saleen was sold to MJ Acquisitions. The company had only built thirteen Mustangs by that time. On November 2, 2009, new CEO Mike Shields published an open letter:

> Since acquiring Saleen Performance Vehicles earlier this year, we have been working tirelessly to usher this iconic brand into a pulse-quickening new chapter . . . . We are also committed to the brand's future, and are actively developing the next generation of Saleen products. In July, we presented the 2010 Saleen 435s in Myrtle Beach. Deliveries of this potent V-8 coupe began in September.

The end came a little over a year later, with a March 2011 press release stating: "Saleen Performance Vehicles announced that it will end production of their Saleen Mustang vehicles in order to focus on aftermarket parts. The final vehicle, a 2011 Saleen S302, will end a lineage that stretches back to 1983."

During this time, SMS Supercars built a new campus in Corona, California. Following the SMS 460 and 460X came the normally aspirated 302 and supercharged 302 SC in 2011. Then, in 2012, SMS introduced their "Label" series, White, Yellow, and Black. SMS also broke tradition, introducing upgraded Camaro and Challenger automobiles. It's not the first time Steve Saleen had deviated from Mustangs: they've built performance vehicles based on the Ford Ranger, Explorer, F-150, and Focus, but they were always Fords. Through 2014, just fourteen Camaros and fifty-six Challengers

Saleen's spectacular campus in Corona, California, is now home to their production line, paint facility, R&D skunk works, and all other operations. *Saleen Automotive*

The entry-level 2015 Saleen White Label is powered by a naturally aspirated 450 horsepower 302-cubic-inch V8 and has an MSRP of $42,754. *Saleen Automotive*

have been produced. Saleen has also produced a performance upgrade for the Tesla S sedan, the Saleen GTX.

For a while, the two companies coexisted, but when Saleen Performance Vehicles was sold to MJ Acquisitions, it was no longer legally the company Steve Saleen had founded. He lawyered up, and in 2012 won the battle to retain the "Saleen" name. He also bought what was left of the old company and integrated it with SMS Supercars to become Saleen Automotive. There wasn't much left—devoted Saleen enthusiasts soundly rejected the brand after the MJ Acquisitions sale. Saleen was again Saleen.

Saleen S302 2015

"Since I started building cars in 1984, my goal has always been to go above and beyond where anybody has been before," Saleen said. "This will by far be the most refined and advanced Mustang we have built to date." The gala event at the Kim Sing Theatre in Los Angeles on March 20, 2015, unveiled the third part of Saleen's Mustang offerings, the 750 horsepower Black Label, to go with the Yellow Label and White Label models. The reviews were excellent, with *Hot Rod* declaring the cars "More Powerful than a Hellcat, More Affordable than a Z28."

But there were dark clouds brooding over the event. Saleen's financial statement in July 2015 included this language: "The Company's independent auditors, in their audit report for the year ended March 31, 2015, expressed substantial doubt about the Company's ability to continue as a going concern." Yet the company's founder remains optimistic. "With the 2016 model year approaching, I am seeing real forecasts not only for our current vehicles but also for the performance aftermarket segment that are exceeding my expectations."

Don't bet against Steve Saleen—he's been on this thrill ride before.

Saleen S302 Black Label 2015–

 # PRODUCED: n/a
ENGINE: 302-cubic-inch V-8
HORSEPOWER: 750
TORQUE: 600 lb-ft
¼-MILE TIME: n/a

The 2015 Saleen Yellow Label is powered by a 715-horsepower 302-cubic-inch supercharged V-8 and has an MSRP starting at $54,495. *Saleen Automotive*

Chapter 9

Callaway Cars
Automotive Artistry

Flip open the hood on one of the Callaway Twin Turbo Corvettes built between 1987 and 1991 and your eye will be immediately drawn to the twin intercoolers atop the engine. Handcrafted of stainless steel by Vinnie DiScipio, with flawless welded seams and a gleaming polished finish, the workmanship of the intercoolers and accompanying ductwork is breathtaking.

What can't be seen are the nearly 1,000 other parts that made up the Twin Turbo package, most manufactured in-house by Callaway, all finished and assembled to the same standard. The motto of Callaway Cars is "Powerfully Engineered Automobiles," but at the same time his automobiles are the essence of craftsmanship.

Reeves Callaway never planned on creating supercars:

I was one of those young men that was really in pursuit of trying to win the World Championship in Formula 1. And if you had no money, you pretty much had to start at Formula Vee or Formula Ford. My contemporaries were Emerson Fittipaldi, Rick Mears, and folks like that, and they all started in Vee. I got a job virtually right out of college for America's largest racecar manufacturer, which was Autodynamics. I took my place sweeping the floor, and managed to be the welder/fabricator during the day that built the parts to allow people to build their own Formula Vee, they were all sold as kits. I did manage to win the North

Introduced in late 1986, the Callaway Twin Turbo Corvette was an official Regular Production Order option, B2K. The early Twin Turbo Corvettes looked stock, with the exception of the Dymag alloy wheels.

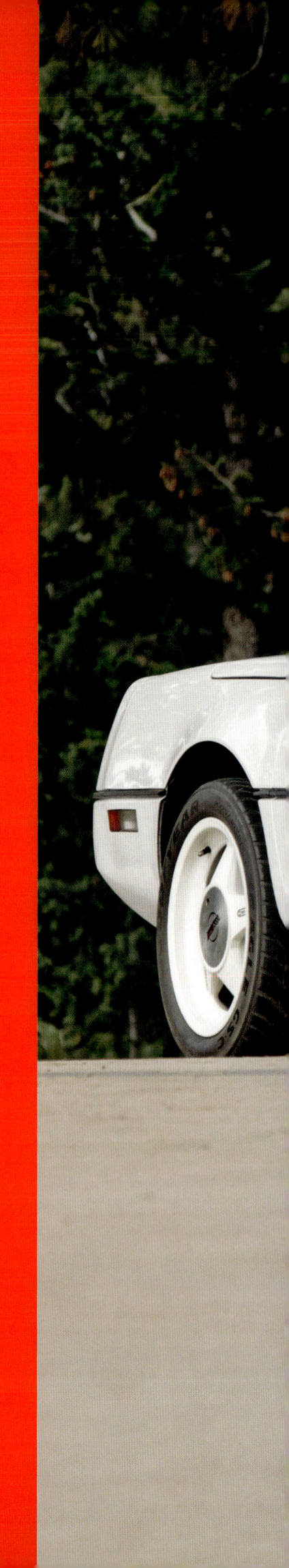

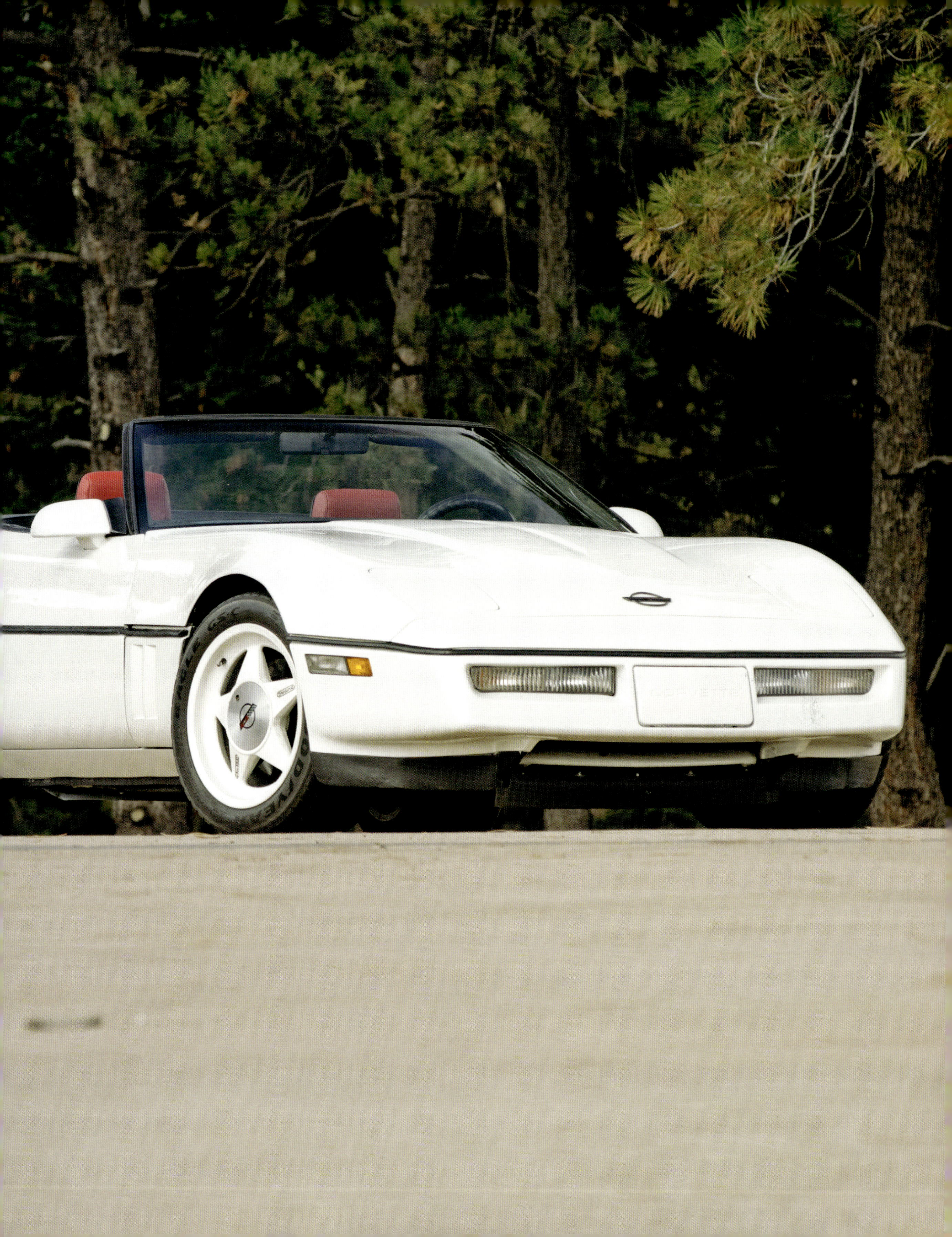
EAGLE GS-C

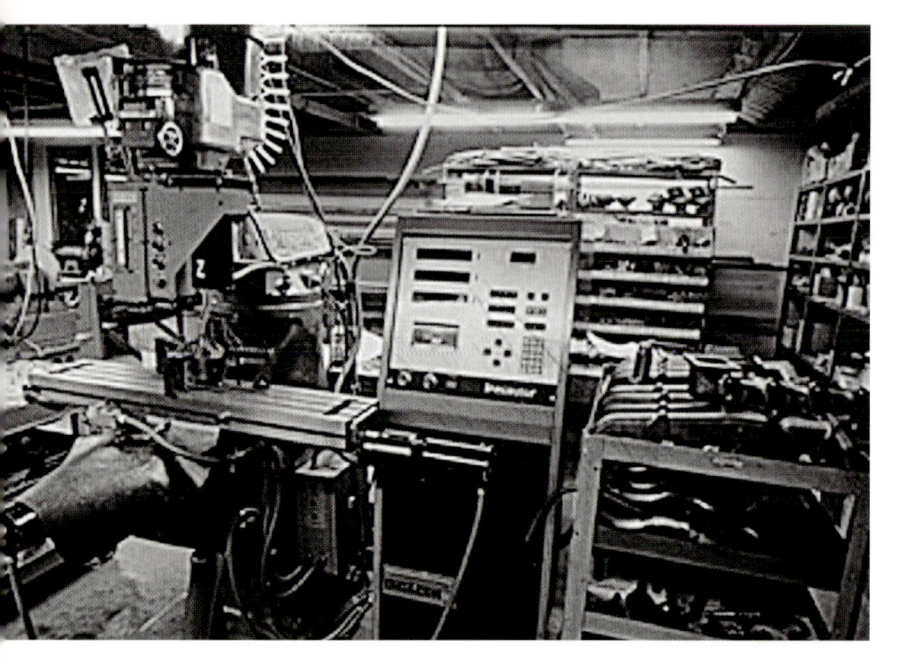

ABOVE: Callaway created his first turbocharger kit for the BMW 320i while he was an instructor for the Bob Bondurant School of High Performance Driving. *Reeves Callaway*

RIGHT: Callaway's turbocharger kits were built in his home garage shop in 1977. *Reeves Callaway*

Atlantic Road Racing Championship in my first year out. I made it to the National Championship the next year (1973) and manage to win that. It should be noted that Roger Penske did not call me, he called Rick Mears.

That was the end of his racing aspirations.

Callaway was selected to be an instructor at Bob Bondurant's School of High Performance Driving at Lime Rock Park, Connecticut.

I was penniless, and when Bondurant called looking for instructors—and this is going to date me—he was looking for drivers that were slightly over the hill. The others were David Hobbs, Sam Posey, who was sort of my hero, Nick Craw, and Jim Busby.

The school used BMW 320i sedans, which handled well but lacked serious horsepower. This led Callaway to create a turbocharger setup for the 320i in his garage. A small story by Don Sherman in *Car and Driver*, which implied that Callaway was actually selling these turbo kits, created enough demand for Callaway to start producing turbo upgrade kits for VW, Audi, Porsche, BMW, and Mercedes-Benz cars. Founded in 1977, his company started with five men and one woman working in his home's garage—until business outgrew the space.

Callaway's first OEM turbo conversion was for the lovely Alfa Romeo GTV6.

Here we are running a turbocharger kit-making operation out of the back of my house in Old Lyme, Connecticut, and Alfa North America was having a terrible time with their competition, which was the Maserati BiTurbo. Alfa North America asked us to make a series of cars that were both powerful and emissions compliant—and live up to their reliability standards.

The ever-methodical Callaway assigned "C" project numbers to his company's major projects, and the Alfa project was numbered C3.

We geared up for our big shot at fame and fortune, we were about 30 cars into the production run, and Alfa North America closed its doors and went back to Italy. Our first OE program was now homeless. But one of those cars wound up at General Motors' "war room" under (Corvette Chief Engineer) Dave McClellan's tutelage.

C4—Callaway B2K Twin Turbo Corvette 1987–1991

When Chevrolet introduced the all-new fourth-generation Corvette in 1984, it was truly world class in every way—except in horsepower. The Cross-Fire Injection engine that carried over from the 1982 model produced just 205 horsepower; the new Tuned-Port Injected L98 engine introduced in 1986 delivered 230 horsepower.

Since the late 1970s, Chevrolet engineers had been experimenting with turbocharging as a way to increase horsepower while still meeting stringent EPA regulations. It made sense, since General Motors had pioneered turbos on production cars on their 1962 Olds F85 and Chevy Corvair Monza models. Turbocharging the relatively low-production Corvette would be a huge challenge for Chevrolet, since there was little room in the Corvette's engine compartment, and no current production engine could safely withstand the stress of turbocharging. But the Callaway Alfa GTV6 Twin Turbo floating around the Tech Center made an impression.

Over 1,000 parts went into the Callaway Twin Turbo conversion; most were machined by Callaway.

124 CHAPTER 9

Reeves Callaway drove the Sledgehammer from Connecticut to the TRC test track in Ohio, where John Lingenfelter ran it at a record-setting 254.76 miles per hour. Callaway then drove it back home. The 254 miles per hour Sledgehammer was the first Callaway Corvette to feature the Aerobody nose and tail designed by Paul Deutschman.

"Dave McClellan called and said, 'We have this little GTV6 Twin Turbo, and it's the dead ringer for the performance of the '84 Corvette,'" said Callaway.

"How did you do that?" That was the call you always wait for in the aftermarket business, we were always in search of a relationship with an OE, and here was America's producers of sports cars asking, "Would you be interested in turbocharging some Corvettes?"

With that, the regular production order (RPO) B2K, "Callaway Twin Turbo," was born. "That was how it all unfolded, it was the call from Dave McClellan, very simple, no contract, only a handshake kind of agreement," said Callaway.

When introduced in 1987, it produced a stunning 345 horsepower and an earthshaking 465 lb-ft of torque, though the option cost $19,995 over the Corvette's $27,999 base price for the coupe or $33,172 for the convertible, plus any other options. But what price perfection? Over 1,000 parts went into the Twin Turbo conversion, taking seventy to seventy-five hours for the Callaway crew to make the magic. To endure the double dose of boost, the stock L98 engine received complete balance and blueprinting, with four-bolt main bearing caps and a forged crankshaft. Strong 7.5:1 compression Mahle pistons were added to withstand the 10-psi kick provided by a pair of water-cooled Rotomaster T04 turbos mounted low, next to the engine. A total of thirty-six heat shields were added to keep the cockpit comfortable, and a larger radiator was installed. Surprisingly, the factory fuel-injection system was adequate, but Callaway's Micro Fueler II enrichment system was added to supply the increased need for fuel at high speed.

Those first Twin Turbos were the ultimate in stealth, looking nearly factory stock with only the addition of twin NACA ducts on the hood to feed those beautiful intercoolers and special Callaway badges. Strong alloy wheels made by Dymag in England were also available. The B2K option was fully warrantied by Chevrolet, plus the cars came with a fifty-page addendum to the owner's manual, so any competent Corvette mechanic could work on them.

For the first time in many years, the Corvette was again a true supercar, capable of actually hitting 178 miles per hour. But would there be any demand? Callaway recalled: "Do you know many cars Chevrolet thought they would sell? Marketing said, 'Really, a $50,000 Corvette? We think we can sell twenty-five cars.'" But just before the 1987 Corvette model year began, a one-page story appeared in *Road & Track*, previewing what the Twin Turbo would be like. "Remember when telephone systems had lights on them? The lights on our telephone system all lit up simultaneously, and didn't unlight for a year."

One Twin Turbo was built at the end of 1986, and by the end of the '87 model Chevrolet had sold another 188 B2K Twin Turbos, 123 coupes, and 65 convertibles. But more than owning simply the fastest car in the country, those first Callaway owners got a piece of automotive perfection. "After the car is tested and tuned, it's handed to Reeves Callaway to take home," David Kaplan, Callaway's marketing man at the time, told *Corvette Fever*.

This man signs his name, essentially, to all these cars and there isn't a fussier or more knowledgeable Corvette person than Reeves Callaway. He's very good at this. He notices absolutely any flaw,

CALLAWAY CARS: AUTOMOTIVE ARTISTRY

whether it's ours or Chevrolet's, and makes sure it's fixed. So we give him a pad, a paper, a pencil, and a car every night for him to take home. When Reeves can't generate a list, the car's finished.

What Ferrari, Porsche, or Lamborghini owner could say the same of their automobiles?

Callaway upped the ante for 1988 to 382 horsepower and 562 lb-ft of torque, while factory Corvettes still generated 245 horsepower. The B2K option now cost $25,895. As with the 1987 model, a Callaway-modified TH400 automatic transmission was available for an additional $6,500. Chevrolet sold another 125 Twin Turbos that year, fueled by such glowing road tests as this one in *Car and Driver*:

> Here's how you get The Big Rush in a Callaway Twin-Turbo Corvette: at 75 mph, slide the gear lever from sixth to fifth and plant your right foot hard. The twin turbochargers whoosh, the seat scoops you up from behind, and the Callaway lunges ahead like a roller coaster taking the big plunge. Before you know it, you're catapulting past the 125-mile mark—and the beast is showing no signs of slowing down. It's ripping the air to shreds, surging ahead so fast that you've got to squint to make out the world in front of you. You try to tell yourself that this car can't be eating up the triple digits this fast. But it is.

As rumors of a "king-of-the-hill" Corvette being prepared by Chevrolet began to surface, though, there was plenty of activity back at Old Lyme. "It was important to remember that Chevrolet's Corvette group really wanted to be taken seriously and admired by the rest of the automotive engineering community worldwide," said Callaway. "They wanted to show that they were as good or better than Porsche, Mercedes, Ferrari, whoever. And one of the showcases was those magazine events that were based on top speed."

GM rules dictated any development vehicle be crushed after use, so Callaway asked: "Couldn't we build just one car, with an adjustable amount of horsepower that would allow us to run just fast enough to win the event, and then essentially put the car away until the next year, and save all that money?'" And the Callaway Sledgehammer project was born.

"Everyone was testing at 200 miles per hour, the low 200s," said Callaway.

> We better make sure that our car can go 250, but never run it that fast in the hands of a magazine, we'll run it just fast enough so we could just win by a few miles per hour. So we designed the car to be stable enough at 250, and to have enough power to reach 250, but we had to go test it before we turned it over to a magazine.

The letter received by Callaway's chief engineer, Tim Good, told the story:

> Dear Mr. Good,
> The Transportation Research Center of Ohio (TRC) was pleased to support the testing performed on the Callaway Twin Turbo Corvette. On October 26, 1988, using Alge timing equipment Model Numbers S3 and P3 for the timer and printer, respectively, we recorded a top speed of 254.76 mph for your vehicle driven by Mr. John Lingenfelter of Decatur, Indiana. The strip chart is enclosed. To the best of my recollection, this is the fastest speed ever recorded at TRC. We compliment Callaway on the achievement.
> Sincerely,
> Kay Latimer
> Project Manager
> Transportation Research Center of Ohio

Of course, this was no ordinary Corvette. A production 1988 Twin Turbo, #51, was selected to be the Sledgehammer. John Lingenfelter, master engine builder and NHRA champion, was brought in to construct the special engine and drive the beast on the track. Carroll Smith, who had helped Carroll Shelby win the 1965 Manufacturers Championship with the Daytona Cobras, came on to modify the chassis and suspension. Tony Cicale, aerodynamicist for a number of CART open wheel teams, helped find the balance between low drag and adequate downforce for these ultra-high-speed runs. Finally, to wrap this car with a distinctive yet functional body, Callaway contacted a designer whom he greatly admired, Paul Deutschman of Montréal, Canada.

C4 Callaway B2K Twin Turbo Corvette 1987–1991

 # PRODUCED: 510

ENGINE: 350-cubic-inch V-8

HORSEPOWER: 345 (1987) 403 (1991)

TORQUE: 465 lb-ft (1987) 575 (1991)

¼-MILE TIME: 13.2 at 108.00 mph (1987)

"What Paul Deutschman has done here is complete the design of the whole car. He got an opportunity to do everything from the beltline down first and now this is his first addressing of the top side of the vehicle," Reeves Callaway said. *Tom Glatch*

The team used the most conservative engine Lingenfelter prepared, producing 898 horsepower (some generated over 1,000 horsepower). Goodyear supplied a set of stock-looking Gatorback tires that were specially made for 250-plus miles per hour. Lingenfelter put the Sledgehammer through its paces on the huge 7-mile-long TRC oval, but "the weather went to hell in a hand basket, and we had to drive home, so we never really knew how fast it could go," said Callaway.

That's right, Reeves Callaway drove the Sledgehammer from Connecticut to Ohio and, after this record-smashing run, drove it back home. Callaway had built a 254-mile-per-hour car that was docile at lower speeds, also completely equipped with functioning factory Bose sound system and air conditioning. "And you know what happened? No one ever showed up for one of those high-speed tests again," laughed Callaway. "That was the end of high-speed testing!"

The Callaway Sledgehammer was officially the fastest street vehicle in America, a record that took over a decade to break. The publicity it generated was immeasurable. Twin Turbos for 1990 also were now available with Deutschman's distinctive body mods from the Sledgehammer, the "Aerobody," for an additional $6,500, and existing Twin Turbos could also be upgraded. But 1990 was also the year Chevrolet introduced its own homegrown supercar, the "King of the Hill" four-cam 32-valve ZR1.

No doubt the ZR1 stole some the Callaway's thunder, as just fifty-eight Twin Turbo cars were sold, but it was hardly a replacement for the turbocharged beast. "How do you want your power?" *Road & Track* asked in a cover story titled "King vs. Kong." "With a whoosh and a whir of vanes, or a rousing crescendo of multitudinous valves and bellowing pipes?" They discovered that the two super Corvettes were almost identical in acceleration and top speed, but the driving experience was very different.

> One the one hand, the ZR1 is blessed with an engine that loves to rev; it's at its sonic best between 5,000 and 7,000 rpm. In fact, few drivers can resist the impulse to delay gear changes just a little longer than necessary, just to listen to the four-cam V-8's unique sound. On the other hand, there's the Callaway, which winds no higher than any other two-valve 'Vette, but picks up speed with an uncanny rush when boost builds up. It's almost too refined, lacking the snarl of its opponent. The only aural giveaway to the Callaway's extra performance is a muted whoosh from the turbos when they're putting out maximum pressure.

With the Aerobody option, no one would confuse a Callaway with a ZR1 or any other Corvette.

The end of the B2K Twin Turbo Corvette came in 1991. The 1992 Corvette would be powered by an all-new engine, the first radical redesign of the venerable small-block since its debut in 1955. A total of 510 B2K Corvettes had been built since its introduction, a truly remarkable number. But 10 of the last Twin Turbos that Callaway built would leave a most lasting impression.

On display at the 1991 Greater Los Angeles Auto Show was possibly the most gorgeous Corvette ever: the Callaway Speedster.

TOP: Beginning in 1990, Chevrolet actually offered two supercars, the ZR1 Corvette (red) and the Callaway Twin Turbo (white). Both produced about the same horsepower, but the driving experience was very different. *Tom Glatch*

ABOVE: Both supercar Corvettes had very different appearances, especially if the Callaway was an Aerobody. *Tom Glatch*

Painted "Old Lyme Green" with a "My Favorite Blue" leather interior, the Speedster made an incredible visual statement. "What Paul Deutschman has done here," Callaway told *Corvette Fever*, "is complete the design of the whole car. He got an opportunity to do everything from the beltline down first and now this is his first addressing of the top side of the vehicle."

Libby-Owens-Ford provided the "EZ Cool" glass that surrounded the cockpit, and that stunning interior was completely redone by Callaway's German leather craftsmen. No top or tonneau to ruin the sleek lines was offered. But the Speedster was more than heart-stopping flash, as these cars packed a 450 horsepower Twin Turbo punch. The price was heart stopping, too: $150,000.

Though not part of the RPO B2K program, Callaway built two Twin Turbo Super Speedsters based on ZR1 Corvettes. This one was built in 1993 and made its debut at the 1993 Cypress Gardens Corvette Show.

The Speedsters were featured on many magazine covers and were prominent in advertising. Today, as the cars near the quarter-century mark, the design is still timeless. It was a fitting sendoff for the first true American supercar in a very long time.

C6—Callaway SuperNatural Corvette 1992–1996

Callaway worked with many other manufacturers over the years (for example, project C5 was for Aston Martin), but Callaway is best known for his Chevrolets. Like AMG to Mercedes-Benz, or Abarth to Fiat, "as a specialist, it's that symbiotic relationship you are always looking for," he said.

The new LT1 engine effectively killed the Twin Turbo. "You couldn't have turbocharged it," said Callaway. The LT1 utilized a reverse-flow cooling design, "and that made it ineligible to turbocharge. It could barely stay together in stock form." Callaway then introduced the SuperNatural® package, employing tuned, "natural" aspiration principles in the engine design. "The Twin Turbo cars had gotten too expensive to build, and no one wanted an $80,000 Corvette. Doing those cars normally aspirated was an effort to bring the cost down to a reasonable level."

There were 400-, 435-, 440-, and 450-horsepower versions for the LT1, and 475 and 490 horsepower upgrades for the ZR1's LT5 engine. No longer a factory option, cars could either be ordered and shipped directly to Callaway's facility in Connecticut, or they could be sent to a select authorized installer. An existing '92–'96 Corvette could also be sent to Callaway for conversion. Owners could also purchase the SuperNatural components from Callaway, but only Corvettes sent to Old Lyme for conversion could be given the complete Callaway treatment, including the Aerobody upgrade.

To prove the abilities of the SuperNatural design, Callaway built two special Corvettes to compete in the most popular race in the world, the 24 Hours of Le Mans. Callaway Competition was established in Leingarten, Germany, to prepare the cars and handle the logistics, and Deutschman designed a special body to maximize the GT2 class rules. The C6 LM worked as designed—in 1994 Callaway qualified first in GT2, 18th overall. For the next year, the LM cars continued to have success, capped by their return to Le Mans, where they qualified 1st, 4th, and 5th in GT2 and finished 2nd and 3rd in class, 11th and 13th overall.

Though no longer part of the RPO B2K program, Callaway also built two more Speedsters—this time Twin Turbo ZR1 Speedsters! Pumping out over 775 horsepower, they remain the ultimate Twin Turbo Corvette.

C7–Callaway C7 1993–1996

The Callaway C7 was an attempt to build a supercar from the ground up. Before a road car was built, Callaway built two C7.R racers to compete in GT1 competition. Deutschman designed the sleek body to fit the maximum dimension of the class, and the entire body/chassis unit was formed out of carbon-fiber composite. Power was by a fuel-injected SuperNatural 383-cubic-inch LT1 V-8 driving a rear-mounted transaxle. Weighing just 1,780 pounds, the power-to-weight ratio of the C7.R was just 3.6 pounds-per-horsepower, far lower than the competition.

At its debut in the 1997 Rolex 24 Hours of Daytona, the C7.R led its class, until an electrical fire took it out. A rule change ended the racing career of the C7.R, and, sadly, Callaway dropped the project before any $300,000 street machines were built.

C8—Callaway SuperNatural Camaro 1993–2002

When Chevrolet introduced the fifth-generation Chevrolet Camaro, powered by the LT1 engine, it made sense for Callaway to offer the SuperNatural package newest four-seater. The same engines offered for the Corvettes could be ordered, along with suspension and brake upgrades. Deutschman also designed a special body package called the "CamAeroBody." Callaway offered all components individually, or a Camaro could be sent to Old Lyme for conversion.

Motor Trend took a C8 for a spin in their March 1994 issue:

> The C-8 costs little more than a Corvette LT1, but is quicker than a ZR-1 from 0-60 mph and through the quarter mile. At about $40,000, the C-8 is capable of blasting from rest to 60 mph in 4.6 seconds, covering the quarter mile in 13.2 seconds at 106.4 mph, and diverting attention from a Madonna flag-raising ceremony.

While a number of Camaros were given the SuperNatural treatment, only 18 Callaway C8 Camaros were built.

C8 Callaway SuperNatural Camaro 1993–2002

 # PRODUCED: 18
ENGINE: 383-cubic-inch V-8
HORSEPOWER: 400
TORQUE: n/a
¼-MILE TIME: 13.2 at 106.4 mph

C9—Callaway Impala SS 1994–1996

A SuperNatural version of the cult classic, Chevy's 1994–96 Impala SS? Sure, why not?! Along with a 404-horsepower 383-cubic-inch LT1, Callaway added Brembo 13.1-inch front, Koni adjustable shocks, Eibach coil springs, ForgeLine alloy wheels, and stout BFGoodrich Comp T/A ZR tires (275/40ZR17 front, 315/35ZR17 rear).

Motor Trend wrote:

> Broad shoulders, nasty black paint, and fat-boy tires are prima facie evidence of evil intent. The initial tap of the throttle jolts the driver into a zesty frame of mind. Classic V-8 reverberations rumble through the 2.5-inch stainless-steel exhaust system, but that doesn't fully prepare the driver for the windfall of torque released when throttle plates are cracked to explore the SuperNatural dimension.

ABOVE: To prove the abilities of the SuperNatural design, Callaway built two special Corvettes to compete in the most popular race in the world, the 24 Hours of Le Mans. In 1995 the Callaway LM qualified 1st, 4th, and 5th in GT2 and finished 2nd and 3rd in class, 11th and 13th overall. *Reeves Callaway*

CALLAWAY CARS: AUTOMOTIVE ARTISTRY 129

Callaway learned from the C7 project "that building a car is the most capital-intensive pursuit there is." With the C12, Callaway took the excellent engineering of the C5 Corvette, and transformed it into his own supercar.

> Steering and braking responses are equally forthright. This Impala perfectly impersonates a Corvette in four-door clothing . . . .

The article recorded that "The dash to 60 mph took only 5.9 seconds, 1.4 seconds quicker than stock. The quarter-mile ticket reads 14.0 seconds at 100.3 mph, beating the standard model by 1.6 seconds and 10.2 mph."

Callaway also mentioned that the same SuperNatural power could be given to any 1994–1996 Caprice or Buick Roadmaster wagon—wouldn't that have been cool?—but, like the C8 Camaro, only the Callaway-built Impala SSs are considered a Callaway C9, and records show just eighteen were built.

C12—Callaway C12 1997–2001

"GM builds the Corvette to a cost, we built the Callaway C12 to a standard," said Callaway. Based on the fifth-generation Corvette platform, the C12 supercar was designed to compete at Le Mans in the GT2 class, and provide world-class performance and comfort on the street. Callaway learned from the C7 project "that building a car is the most capital-intensive pursuit there is."

With the C12, Callaway took the excellent engineering of the C5 Corvette and transformed it into his own supercar. It was built in conjunction with the IVM Engineering Group of Germany, and included a flawless carbon composite body designed by Deutschman, 440-horsepower SuperNatural LS1 power, huge four-piston brakes with 355mm slotted rotors, and redesigned coil-over suspension. Interior and paint finishes were available at the request of the customer.

Costing around $170,000, just nineteen C12 coupes and convertibles were built for very exclusive owners like Dale Earnhardt Jr. and Sony Music president Tommy Mattola (who was then Mariah Carey's husband). Two C12.Rs were also built, shocking the racing world when one qualified on the pole of the 24 Hours of Le Mans in 2001. Just imagine Mariah Carey cruising down the Pacific Coast Highway in her husband's silver C12 convertible.

C15—FIA GT3 Z06.R Corvette 2007–2014

Callaway Competition built a total of ten Z06.R racers for the European FIA GT3 series and the regional ADAC Masters and Belcar series. In the first two years of competition, they earned FIA GT3 championships, the Manufacturer's Championship in 2007, and the Driver's Championship in 2008. They earned another FIA GT3 Driver's Championship in 2010. Regionally, Callaway's Z06.R custom cars won the ADAC GT Masters Team Championship in 2009 and Driver's Championship in 2013. This was quite an accomplishment for Callaway Competition, headed by Director and Team Manager Ernst Woehr.

"I have to tell you we did all this without any help from GM," Callaway proudly states.

> We raised all the money, we bought the cars from GM Europe, and we designed, prepared, constructed, and built four race teams. These cars are not thinly disguised tube-frame cars, these are actual production cars with actual production bits. This speaks very well for the car.
>
> We built these cars at Callaway Competition in Leingarten, Germany, virtually the same town as Audi. Down the street is Mercedes in Stuttgart, less than 30 minutes away; across the road is Porsche, 25 minutes away. This is car-building heaven. Our guys all came up through the Audi system, and I'm very proud of that, it's a hard, tough apprenticeship. The cars are absolutely gorgeous; there is nobody that makes a better racecar than Callaway Competition. I've never seen a better-prepared racecar; this is beyond the Penske

level of preparation. And the cars really, really work. The sign of a good race car is when you put different levels of talent in the car and everybody comes back and says, "Wow, I can drive this car all day." And these are the guys that have gotten out of the other competing brands. That means it's built well, handles well, and is predictable for a wide range of drivers, and that's what we need because we're in the business of selling racecars to race teams.

And lessons learned with these race cars are applied to Callaway's street Corvettes.

C16—Callaway C16 2007–2013

Like the C12, the Callaway C16 was Callaway's ultra-fast, ultra-exclusive sports car, this time based on the sixth-generation Corvette platform. Callaway described the C16 as "our technology demonstrator, it's our calling card. It's our vision of what a great front-engine, two-seat, rear-drive sports car can be." Starting with a Corvette coupe or convertible, each C16 was built to order. The C16 featured a sensuous composite body, again sculpted by Deutschman, with three variations available—coupe, convertible, or a new take on the original Speedster theme. "We replaced every body panel on the automobile," says Callaway. "Look at the body panels; we made those from scratch. Additionally we took the 121 pieces of the interior, sent them to our leather craftsmen in Germany, and a month and a half later we got a leather interior that belongs in a Bentley."

C9 Callaway SuperNatural Impala SS 1996

 # PRODUCED: 18
ENGINE: 383-cubic-inch V-8
HORSEPOWER: 404
TORQUE: n/a
¼-MILE TIME: 14.1 at 100.30 mph

C12 Callaway 1997–2001

 # PRODUCED: 19
ENGINE: 378-cubic-inch V-8
HORSEPOWER: 650 Coupe/Convertible; 700 Speedster
TORQUE: 585
¼-MILE TIME: n/a

ABOVE: Costing around $170,000, just nineteen C12 coupes and convertibles were built for very exclusive owners like this one for Dale Earnhardt Jr.

LEFT: Callaway's German leather craftsmen created the interior of the C12.

Like the C12, the Callaway C16 was Callaway's ultra-fast, ultra-exclusive sports car, this time based on the sixth-generation Corvette platform. Reeves Callaway described the C16 as "our technology demonstrator, it's our calling card." *Callaway Cars*

"I think a very cool element is how the helmets are handled on the Speedster," Reeves Callaway said. "They are encapsulated by the rear deck, that's what gives the headrest their form. When the deck is opened, the helmets are there for the taking." *Callaway Cars*

Callaway is proud not only of the craftsmanship of the C16, but the design. "I think a very cool element is how the helmets are handled on the Speedster. They are encapsulated by the rear deck, that's what gives the headrest their form. When the deck is opened, the helmets are there for the taking." There are also no rearview mirrors on the Speedster to ruin the flow of the design; three hidden cameras take care of that. No door handles, either: hidden D-spots magically open doors when a hand touches them.

Reducing unsprung weight was a set of Callaway/Dymag wheels, featuring forged magnesium centers with carbon-fiber rims. Measuring 19x10 in front, 20x12 at rear, they were shod with "AdvantSport" tires developed by Yokohama specifically for the C16, 285/30ZR19 front and 325/25ZR20 rear.

Standard power was a supercharged LS3, delivering 560 horsepower at 6,200 rpm and 529 lb-ft of torque at 4,750 rpm. The Performance Package was optional, with 616 horsepower and 582 lb-ft of torque. All at an EPA-friendly 18 city/28 highway miles per gallon.

The C16 cost $173,000 for the coupe, about $8,000 more for the convertible. The unique Speedster cost just over $300,000. There were no options: all C16 cars were fully equipped, and the buyer only needed to choose the colors.

Callaway built just twenty-six of these ultra-exclusive supercars, but before one was delivered to its owner, *MotorWeek TV* got a rare taste of the C16 experience for its popular TV show. "This C16 was an owner's car and we, as well as Callaway, were reluctant to subject it to all of our normal tests. But Callaway says the C16 is capable of a 0–60 of 3.2 seconds and a top speed of 206 miles per hour, and there is little doubt in our minds that this supercar can do it."

C17—The Callaway Supercharged Corvette 2007–2013

When Chevrolet introduced the C5 Corvette in 1997 and C6 Corvette in 2005, Callaway continued to perform SuperNatural upgrades to those cars. But 2007 brought a number of changes to the company. Reeves Callaway moved to California to open a new headquarters in Santa Ana, with his son, Pete, as general manager of the West Coast operation. Callaway also introduced their new sixth-generation Corvette project; code C17, the Callaway Supercharged Corvette. For the first time since 1991, Callaway was again applying positive manifold pressure to Chevy engines, this time with supercharging.

"It looks like a standard Corvette, it has just a subtle hood change, and a great set of Callaway wheels, and we sold it through

132　CHAPTER 9

In 2007, Callaway introduced their new sixth-generation Corvette project; code C17, the Callaway Supercharged Corvette. "So for virtually half the price of a ZR1 you got a hand-built automobile that is very exclusive, but perhaps met your needs better since it could be an automatic or a convertible," Reeves Callaway said. The new LS3 in later Corvettes was bumped up to 580 horsepower and 510 lb-ft of torque using a Magnuson MP-122 supercharger on SC580 models, while the 606-horsepower SC606 cars used the Magnuson TVS2300 blower. Corvettes with LS7 engines were transformed into the SC652 with a monster 652 horsepower. *Callaway Cars*

twenty-nine prominent Chevrolet Dealers nationwide as an option for $18,900," said Reeves Callaway.

> The cars were shipped to us from Bowling Green, they were built at either our East Coast plant or our West Coast plant, and then sent off to the dealer destination. The program produced a car that was a fabulous performance bargain. We included all the right stuff but kept the cost down. If you wanted greater than Z06 performance, we gave it to you as an automatic, or as a convertible.

Remember, the Z06 was only available with a fixed roof and manual transmission, so Callaway was offering a very unique Corvette at an attractive price.

In 2007, the magic came from the 6.2-liter LS2 that included a Magnuson MP-112 supercharger, high-flow injectors, their own fuel-system controllers, and a liquid-to-air intercooler. The new LS3 in later Corvettes was bumped up to 580 horsepower and 510 lb-ft of torque using a Magnuson MP-122 supercharger on SC580 models, while the 606-horsepower SC606 cars used the Magnuson TVS2300 blower. Corvettes with LS7 engines were transformed into the SC652 with a monster 652 horsepower.

> So, for a price from the high-sixties to the mid-seventies you had a seriously fast car that could go nose-to-nose with a ZR1. From a 0–to–60 point of view they are nanoseconds apart, from a quarter-mile point of view they are milliseconds apart, and from a top-speed point of view they are nearly the same, as the Callaway version will do 202 mph. So for virtually half the price of a ZR1 you got a handbuilt automobile that is very exclusive, but perhaps met your needs better since it could be an automatic or a convertible.

And the Callaway Corvette warranty paralleled the factory five-year/100,000 mile warranty, with an additional three-year/36,000 mile for the Callaway components. The Callaway also got 31 mpg at a steady-state 70 miles per hour.

And, in 2009, a limited production of twenty-nine Reeves Callaway Signature Edition Supercharged Corvettes was produced, one for each dealer in the Callaway Dealer Network.

Motor Week got some track time in a C17 during the same test of the C16, and reported:

> The result is performance that betters a Z06 'Vette and keeps six grand in your pocket! The Callaway Corvette and the C16 represent very different levels of performance and price, but with the same pedigree. Both cars transcend their Corvette roots, and give credence to Callaway Car's claim of being a specialty manufacturer, not merely a tuner. Matching or besting Chevy's factory Hot Rods is no small feat and that's powerfully engineered, indeed!

C18 Callaway Camaro 2010–Today

The all-new model gave Callaway another platform for their supercharged Chevy engines, just as the fourth-generation Camaro had done for the SuperNatural powerplants. True to the Callaway philosophy, they offer a complete package, with chassis and styling upgrades to go with the 572-horsepower blast under the hood.

In 2010, Callaway also produced the Hendrick Motorsports 25th Anniversary Camaros, with just twenty-five cars built to celebrate Rick Hendrick's twenty-five years of NASCAR racing success. The first of the limited-edition Camaros—which featured special Hendrick Motorsports interior, exterior, and under-hood treatments—was shown at Chevrolet stand at the 2009 SEMA Show in Las Vegas.

How did Callaway's work transform the new Camaro? Calvin Kim of *Road & Track* wrote:

The Callaway C18 Camaro is a complete package, with chassis and styling upgrades to go with the 572-horsepower blast under the hood. *Callaway Cars*

Another platform for the supercharged LS engines is Chevrolet's Tahoe, Silverado, and Suburban trucks. "Callaway is leveraging its performance image into a whole new arena of vehicles, significantly enhancing a variety of Chevy pickups and SUVs. It's a Callaway you can drive every day," said Chris Chessnoe, Callaway's program manager. *Callaway Cars*

While we regret not being able to acquire any handling numbers, we did burn up a few tanks of gas getting acquainted with the Callaway on highways, byways and city roads, and can say its drivability nearly matches the stocker. The difference comes from the super-sized burst of g's upon acceleration with a mild whine from the blower under full-throttle loads. Part-throttle operation is smooth, tip-in predictable and we experienced no surging issues on quick, highly loaded on-off throttle applications, similar to what you'd experience driving uphill on a tight mountain road. Although our tester came out to nearly $60,000, the base package with the suspension option is all you need to significantly up the performance of your Camaro SS. What you get with that is a certified sleeper: a 572-horsepower daily driver with a warranty!

Then there is Chevy's own Super Camaro, the Z28, introduced in 2014. Not to be outdone, Callaway has created its own version, the Camaro Z28 SC652. Based on the SC652 Corvette's power unit, the Callaway version jacks the stock Z28's power 52 horses. That makes 0–60 0.3 seconds faster than the factory version, the quarter mile in 11.5 at 114 miles per hour. Chevrolet chose not to supercharge the Z28, preferring to shave 300 pounds from the front of the vehicle. Owners who prefer the power of a ZL1 with the aerodynamics and chassis mods of the Z28 now have an option, a Callaway option.

C19 Callaway SportTruck 2011–Today

Chevrolet's Tahoe, Silverado, and Suburban trucks offer another platform for the supercharged LS engines. "Callaway is leveraging its performance image into a whole new arena of vehicles, significantly enhancing a variety of Chevy pickups and SUVs. It's a Callaway you can drive every day," said Chris Chessnoe, Callaway's program manager.

A Callaway truck? Susan Carpenter in the *Orange County Register* got to experience one:

Transplanting the heart of a Corvette into the muscular body of a pickup is an intriguing proposition. Pressing the accelerator pedal, the power was instantaneous as I accelerated through its six gears to cruising speed on the highway, then maneuvered into the twisties. The SC540 handles like a very tall sport car, even though the front and back ends are both lowered to make it level and keep its fanny in line. Even lowered, the truck can haul 10,700 pounds, and the additional power actually helps its ability to pull—not that I used it to haul anything. Demographically, I'm unlike the SportTruck's core buyer, who's more likely to have a stable of elite vehicles than a herd of cattle. In terms of how I used the truck, though, I was similar. I carried nothing but my purse.

Imagine a SportTruck pulling a Corvette Limited Edition Ski Boat—now that's a gearhead's dream team!

C20 Callaway Corvette 2014–Today

Taking everything they learned from the fabulous C17 Supercharged Corvette, Callaway has done the same for Chevrolet's latest sports car. One interesting innovation is Callaway's third-generation supercharger, which no longer resides under a modern version of the classic Corvette "power bulge." Instead, it pokes through the hood, beautifully exposed to the elements—part of the blower's unique intercooling system designed to deliver consistent power all day long.

ABOVE: You know those stylized "Sting Ray" emblems on the Corvette's front fenders? On the Callaway C20, they're supercharged! *Callaway Cars*

LEFT: A supercharged Callaway C20 Stingray Corvette rests inside the Callaway offices. *Callaway Cars*

Chevrolet produces some amazing supercars of their own, like the Z06 and ZR1 Corvettes, so why even consider the Callaway? *Automobile* tested both and concluded:

> Compared with the base Chevrolet Corvette C7 (without performance exhaust), output in the SC627 climbs 172 horsepower (to 627 at 6,400 rpm) and 150 lb-ft (to 610 at 4,400 rpm). So equipped, the SC627 ripped to 60 mph in just 3.6 seconds and flashed through the quarter mile in 11.7 seconds at 123.7 mph. What the SC627 delivers is its own unique flavor. It outguns the standard C7 while being sleeker and less flashy than the Z06—a stealth rocket (that prominent blower up front notwithstanding). It sounds completely different than Chevy's own supercharged 'Vette, too, blaring to the redline with a decidedly higher-pitched exhaust note and a seemingly more linear flow of power. (The Z06 switches from mild to wild in an instant.) And just as Callaway says, I drove the hell out of the car all day and never saw the various temperatures budge a whit above normal.

As always, Callaway sweated the details on this car. You know those stylized "Sting Ray" emblems on the Corvette's front fenders? On the Callaway, they're supercharged!

C21 Callaway AeroWagon Concept 2013

What does the future of Callaway Cars hold? In 2013, they unveiled the C21 Callaway AeroWagon concept, their take on the classic grand touring "shooting brake." If the thought of a high-speed station wagon seems strange, look no further than the Ferrari FF. The Deutschman-designed body panels will be manufactured using Callaway's proprietary Resin Transfer Molding process. It will not have the four doors or all-wheel drive of the Ferrari FF, nor will the AeroWagon quite match the Ferrari's 651 horsepower. This Callaway will, however, will have a top speed of 202 miles per hour, and still be socially responsible by delivering the best fuel economy of the supercar segments, far surpassing the FF's 11 city/16 highway EPA mileage. It will also cost a fraction of the FF's $295,000 price tag.

Callaway has also committed to building a new version of the championship-winning Z06.R, based on the seventh-generation Corvette. Callaway's GT3 fighter will be constructed and sold in Europe only through Callaway Competition.

After nearly forty years, Callaway Cars is not slowing down. Builders have come and gone during that time. By carefully choosing projects and always staying true to their vision, Callaway Cars has survived and thrived.

Here's just one example why: Callaway C16 number 006, a pearl-white coupe, was ordered by Sheikh Khalid of the United Arab Emirates. The first time the Sheikh drove his new supercar, he called Reeves Callaway from inside the cockpit. "He was crying, the man was in tears," says Callaway proudly. "Here is a man who can afford anything he wants, and the C16 exceeded his expectations that much." Automotive artistry has a way of doing that.

In 2013, Callaway unveiled the C21 AeroWagon concept, their take on the classic Grand Touring "shooting brake." Callaway is planning on selling the AeroWagon, which is based on the SC627 Corvette. The Paul Deutschman—designed body panels will be manufactured using Callaway's proprietary Resin Transfer Molding process. The Callaway will have a top speed of 202 miles per hour and still be socially responsible by delivering the best fuel economy of the supercar category. *Callaway Cars*

CALLAWAY CARS: AUTOMOTIVE ARTISTRY

HALL OF FAME
OFFICIAL PACE CAR
73rd INDIANAPOLIS 500 MAY 28 1989
TURBO

# Chapter 10

PAS, Inc.
Performance DNA

Sometimes it all comes together perfectly. The right circumstances, the right products, and the right people. Then—bam!—something special happens. Production Automotive Services, Inc. (better known as PAS, Inc.) was the result of the combination of Prototype Automotive Services of Farmington Hills, Michigan—owned by Jeff Beitzel—and Triad Services of Troy, Michigan—owned by Chuck Mountain and Mike Pocobello. Together, these companies had the kind of performance DNA only possible in the Motor City.

Spend any time in the Detroit area, and you'll see hundreds of companies that support the Big Three in various ways. Some have famous names, like Roush and Saleen, but most are known only among the Motor City inner circle. Prototype Automotive Services developed prototype vehicles for the automotive manufacturers, specifically those related to drivetrain. Beitzel's team of about thirty-five people performed custom engine building and testing along with competition, show, and pace cars.

Callaway's third-generation supercharger on the C20 pokes through the hood, beautifully exposed to the elements, as part of the blower's unique intercooling system designed to deliver consistent power all day long. The SC627 rips the Callaway C20 to 60 mph in just 3.6 seconds and blasts through the quarter mile in 11.7 seconds at 123.7 mph. *Callaway Cars*

Triad Services also created prototypes and concept vehicles, such as the Buick Wildcat, Cadillac Solitare, and the Cadillac Voyage, the latter featured in the 1993 Sylvester Stallone and Wesley Snipes movie, *Demolition Man*. Pocobello started at Chevrolet Engineering and developed Corvettes with Zora Duntov, as well as working with Jim Hall and the Chaparral racing team. He left Chevrolet for a position with the racing team, and was the development engineer on some of the legendary Chaparral Can-Am cars, such as the "Sucker Car," which was equipped with separate engine-driven fans to induce downforce. Mountain came from Ford and the GT40 program and became one of the owners of Kar Kraft, which continued to develop the GT40 and manufacture the Boss 429 limited-production Mustangs.

Pontiac 20th Anniversary Trans Am 1989

GM had built two Trans Ams in 1986 with the Buick Turbo 3.8-liter engine, one automatic and one manual transmission. In order to fit the engine package, the passenger side frame rail was cut to make room for the exhaust downpipe. This was a problem, since the car would have to be recertified at great expense to put into production. These cars also adapted the engine to the standard Trans Am transmissions, another certification issue.

The original mission was for the Prototype team to create an updated Firebird and investigate the packaging to see if production would be feasible. Bill Owen of Buick, a hot rodder at heart who was the primary force behind the Buick Turbo V-6 engine, stepped in at this point and came up with the idea to use the cylinder heads from the front-wheel-drive 3300 V-6, which would narrow the width of the engine and make room for the downpipe. It worked, even though the downpipe had to be installed just right for the engine to fit well.

The second challenge was the transmission. Prototype developed the "horseshoe" transmission bracket so that the entire Grand National package, along with the different heads, would fit. The first production-buildable Turbo Trans Am was made.

Pontiac 20th Anniversary Turbo Trans Am 1989

- **# PRODUCED:** 1,555
- **ENGINE:** 236-cubic-inch V-6
- **HORSEPOWER:** 250
- **TORQUE:** 340 lb-ft
- **¼-MILE TIME:** 13.40 at 101 mph

Lloyd Reuss, executive vice president for GM's passenger car groups at the time, drove the gray-on-gray prototype and decided he wanted it to be the 20th Anniversary Trans Am. Beitzel announced at the Prototype Christmas party that "we are going to build 1,500 of these cars." Building that number was beyond what a small shop like Prototype Automotive Services could handle, so they merged with the Triad Group and created PAS Incorporated as their manufacturing arm.

Then, on October 20, 1988, it was announced that Turbo Trans Am would be the Indianapolis 500 pace car for the 1989 event. The *Orlando Sentinel* reported:

> In the past, most pace car builders, Pontiac included, have modified the specific cars that actually led the charge at the Brickyard. Not so this time, says Pontiac: It will pick three cars from the pool of 1,500, add the required safety lights, and hit the track at 40 mph for one lap, then 80 and, finally, 130.

The 20th Anniversary Trans Am was the first entirely stock car ever to pace the Indy 500, even on pump gas.

All the 20th Anniversary Turbo Trans Am pace cars were elegantly dressed in white with a saddle-colored cloth interior. The classiness extended to the cloisonné "20th Anniversary" emblems and winged Indianapolis 500 badges. "Pontiac realized this machine didn't need a billboard to make its case," said the special 20th Anniversary brochure. PAS was able to specify the rare 1LE brake package developed for the Canadian Players Cup race series, which included 12-inch discs front and 11.7-inch rear, with Corvette two-piston aluminum calipers up front, single-piston Corvette calipers in back, combined with a baffle in the fuel tank to keep from starving the fuel pump around corners.

Now the hard work began. For quality reasons, Pontiac chose their Van Nuys, California, plant over the Norwood, Ohio, plant to supply to GTA Firebirds to be transformed into 20th Anniversary Turbo Trans Ams. PAS rented a 40,000 square foot. building at 770 E. Epperson in City of Industry, located near Van Nuys, with good access to the Pomona Freeway.

Think automotive work is glamorous? Scott Kelly, engineering liaison to GM for Prototype/PAS, vividly remembers: "I had five days off in 1988. I lived out of a motel in Studio City for three months straight." But that work helped set up the PAS California operation, and he trained the Van Nuys assembly workers on how to build the 20th Anniversary Turbo Trans Am.

There were four levels to that assembly process:

AA—Engine manufacturing. Buick-Olds-Pontiac built the LC2 code engine with most components and shipped them to PAS.

BB—Engine/transmission module assembly. At PAS, they mated the engine to the 200-4R four-speed automatic transmission, installed the wiring, intercooler, downpipe, and catalytic converter. The engine was then crated and shipped to Van Nuys under one part number and called a "powertrain module."

TOP, LEFT The 1989 Pontiac 20th Anniversary Turbo Trans Am Pilot #5. This Firebird was used as a press demonstrator on the West Coast; it was driven by Validation Engineer Scott Kelly while in California. Later, it was converted into a convertible by American Sunroof Corp. (ASC) for Prototype Automotive Services owner Jeff Beitzel. *Scott Kelly*

TOP, RIGHT: Some of the 162 1989 20th Anniversary Turbo Trans Ams used during the month of May at the Indianapolis Motor Speedway, here shown ready for shipment. The cars used to support the Indianapolis 500 activities were equipped with T-tops and cloth interior. Around one hundred were sold to GM employees for $25,854.83 after the race. *Scott Kelly*

MIDDLE, LEFT: PAS Validation Engineer Scott Kelly with the 1989 Turbo Trans Ams used during the month of May at the Indianapolis Motor Speedway. *Scott Kelly*

MIDDLE, RIGHT: The front cover of the 20th Anniversary Turbo Trans Am brochure prominently displayed the unique cloisonné emblem. No wonder thieves stole them off the cars on the transport trains, until PAS started boxing them in the trunk. *Author's Collection*

ABOVE: Every Turbo Trans Am owner's dream—some of the 162 cars used during the 1989 Indianapolis 500 festivities. *Scott Kelly*

PAS, INC.: PERFORMANCE DNA 139

CC—Assembly. Van Nuys assembled a basic white GTA with the Turbo V-6 assembly, but without the back seats, inlet hose, and air cleaner, and without the special 20th Anniversary emblems. "Van Nuys could not finish the car, because we (PAS) were the manufacturer-of-record for certification reasons," Kelly recalled. "One of the reasons they wanted us to own the certification is we had the 'gas guzzler.'" This helped preserve Pontiac's compliance with the government's fuel economy regulations. Thanks to a lot of effort, "we didn't hit gas guzzler and we met fifty state emissions, so we didn't get the penalty." As engineering liaison between Pontiac and PAS, one of Kelly's tasks was to "go through the bill-of-materials for a GTA, and we had to add and delete until we had the bill-of-materials right for the package. So when the car went down the assembly line, it was built like any other car."

DD—Finishing and testing. The mostly complete Firebird was driven on a hauler and shipped back to PAS for completion. There PAS installed the special seats, the safety stickers, and finished up under-hood work, all with the kind of care and attention no mass-produced vehicle could receive. "We went through a checklist, went under-hood and under-body, we checked every bolt," Kelly said. "We put them on a chassis dyno, and made sure the engine ran good on all cylinders, checked emissions, and verified that the fans kicked on."

Every Anniversary Trans Am was inspected at the end of the Van Nuys line by a PAS inspector who was a retired Van Nuys employee. "We had an inspection pit, and if we identified an issue, the car was sent to 'final repair' and corrected before being delivered to the PAS plant," Kelly recalled.

After the DD level, the cars went on a hauler back to Van Nuys, into the car corral, and then into the distribution system. "The first cars were shipped with emblems," Scott Kelly recalled, "but people stole them off the trains, doing so much body damage that we stopped sending them with emblems and started sending them in a box to the dealerships."

More than just classy, the Turbo Trans Am was by far the fastest production American automobile during to the 1980s, both in acceleration and top speed. The Turbo V-6 was listed as producing 250 horsepower at 4,400 rpm, but, like the Buick GNX, actual horsepower was just above 300. "The quickest I ever saw one go was 0–60 in 4.6," said Kelly. "Csaba Csere did it at the Chrysler Proving Grounds in Chelsea, Michigan, the first time he did it I couldn't believe it, that can't be right, and he did it twice more with an optical sensor data acquisition system so I couldn't argue with it."

Unlike some of the "ringers" manufacturers supplied to the media in the 1960s, this was a completely stock Turbo Trans Am. "There was no speed-limiter on the chip even in production. We published 152 miles per hour top speed because that was the limit of the V-rated tires. We used to test the cars at TRC. Gregg Palm and I did the top speed runs; we got 157 out of it." To back that up, *Motor Trend* saw 162 miles per hour at the Arizona Test Center in their "Flat-Out Fastest American Cars II—the Sequel," in the June 1989 issue.

After that experience, Csere wrote in the June 1989 issue of *Car and Driver*:

> Our test car scorched the drag strip with a 0–60-mph blast of 4.6 seconds and a quarter-mile run of 13.4 seconds at 101 mph. That means, as we go to press, that the turbocharged Trans Am is the quickest 0–60 sprinter available in any US production-car showroom—at any price . . . . This is a car for muscle-car mavens, pure and simple.

Buick had absolutely no trouble selling all the GNXs it could build—mostly because they delivered old-time horsepower as few modern cars can. We're willing to bet that Pontiac won't be holding any muscle car clearance sales, either.

Csere sadly lost the bet. At $31,198, the 20th Anniversary cars were expensive, but most cars were ordered by dealers with both T-tops and leather, driving the price into Corvette territory. Even Kelly discovered the 20th Anniversary coupe with leather he ordered for himself was "upgraded" with T-tops by the zone manager. Thankfully, he learned this the day the car was scheduled for assembly, called a friend at GM, and put a stop to it.

PAS built the contracted total 1,550 production 20th Anniversary cars, plus five preproduction "pilot" cars. Four were T-top cars and one was a hardtop. One of the T-top cars was converted by ASC for PAS President Beitzel into a convertible. The 162 cars used to support the Indianapolis 500 activities were equipped with T-tops and cloth interior, and around 100 were sold to GM employees for $25,854.83 after the race. Thanks to the zone managers, the optional T-tops were ordered on 1,539 (99 percent) of the cars, and 1,348 (87 percent) had the leather interior option.

They didn't sell as planned, but they were hardly a failure. A quarter century later, the unique 1989 Turbo Trans Am still has performance that rivals many modern vehicles, and they stand as the high point of American supercars from the 1980s.

The Turbo Trans Am was supposed to be repeated for 1991, but the lack of sales for the '89 cars forced GM to cancel the program. "We actually built two '91 Turbo Trans Am prototypes and completed some of the development testing before the program was cancelled," Kelly recalled.

GMC Syclone 1991

 # PRODUCED: 2,995

ENGINE: 262-cubic-inch V-6

HORSEPOWER: 280

TORQUE: 350 lb-ft

¼-MILE TIME: 14.10 at 93 mph

A Syclone power module, built by PAS, ready for delivery to GM's Shreveport, Louisiana, plant for installation. *Scott Kelly*

GMC Syclone 1991

"GMC hired ASC/McLaren to build a prototype turbocharged GMC Sonoma pickup after meeting with us (PAS) to talk about what it would take to build a fast pickup truck based on the S-10," Kelly said, "and when we found out McLaren was paid to do their version, the PAS owners said, look, we're just going to do this." He continued:

> We went and bought a truck, we took one of our Trans Am 3.8 Turbos, we made an adapter plate for a 700R4. Knowing that the light S-10 would not have any traction, we decided to make it all-wheel-drive. One of Mike Pocobello's friends from General Motors was a transfer case engineer, we engineered a transfer case right off the end of the 700R4 that would hold up to this. So we built an all-wheel-drive Syclone with the Turbo Trans Am engine in it. They (McLaren) used a Turbo Grand Prix engine. I reworked a Sunbird Turbo instrument cluster and wired the first Syclone in an all-nighter at Triad.

It took a drag race to determine who would build the Syclone. The day of the competition it was pouring rain. The two-wheel-drive ASC/McLaren truck lined up against the all-wheel-drive PAS truck. Guess who won?

PAS had already shut down their temporary operation in California, and, using the same business model, established a similar facility just down the road from the Shreveport, Louisiana, plant that built the GMC Sonoma trucks. This time, John Koss was in charge of the PAS Louisiana operation. For the production Syclone, PAS used the full-time all-wheel-drive system that was optional on the Chevy Astro van, which shared the same chassis as the S-10/Sonoma, delivering the power 35 percent front/65 percent rear.

A significant change from the PAS prototype was the use of GM's Vortec 4.3-liter V-6 instead of the Buick 3.8-liter Turbo. "The Buick-Oldsmobile group said they would absolutely not build another of those 3.8 Turbos," said Scott Kelly.

This Norman Rockwell—like photograph by famed Detroit illustrator/photographer Charles Schridde emphasized the heritage of the GMC Syclone. *GM Media Archives*

If we could have gotten the Syclone project on top of the Turbo Trans Am project, then the numbers would have made enough sense to keep the line going. The line had been shut down at the end of the Buick Grand National, and it was a challenge to get that line up to make the Turbo Trans Am.

Following the model of the Turbo Trans Am, PAS, Inc. established a similar four-level build plan. First, PAS received the 4.3-liter Vortec V-6 engines from GM's famed Tonawanda, New York, engine plant. Unlike the 3.8-liter, which came from Buick built for turbocharging, PAS had to modify the 4.3-liter V-6 to withstand the pressure of forced induction. "We validated the whole engine [for emissions and durability]," Kelly explained.

> We changed the pistons, we actually created our own cast-iron exhaust manifolds that the turbo would bolt right on to, we custom cast our own intake manifolds as well. We did our own 20k and 50k dyno durability accelerated testing. We worked with GM, of course, because everyone has a stake in making sure it was a reliable vehicle.

The "powertrain module" was sent into the Shreveport truck plant for assembly into the black Sonoma pickups, which were then hauled back to PAS for finishing. They added a Mitsubishi TD06-17G turbo, a water-to-air intercooler, and a modified 48mm throttle body borrowed from the L98 Corvette. PAS also installed the unique fiberglass air dam and tonneau cover, embroidered seats, and the gauge cluster from the Sunbird Turbo, complete with boost gauge. Finally, the completed Syclone was sent back to the assembly plant for distribution to the dealers.

The result was 280 horsepower and 350 lb-ft of torque in the 3,500-pound pickup. The Syclone prototype was first shown at the Chicago Auto Show on January 23, 1989. "Introducing today's technological brainstorm, the new Syclone," GMC declared. "This truck moves in the spirit of the muscle cars of the 1960s, but with the technology of the '90s!" The 1978 Dodge "Lil' Red Wagon" may have been the first factory performance truck, but they were still just a semi-powerful, stylish short-box pickup. The Syclone was something quite different.

The Syclone began production on January 17, 1991. "Think of it as a Porsche 911 that really 'hauls,'" announced the full-page ad in USA Today. To prove its point, GMC listed the specs of the new Syclone next to that of the Porsche 911 Carrera 4. Yes, the specs were amazingly similar—except that the all-wheel-drive Porsche cost around $50,000 more than the GMC.

"The Syclone will beat a brand-new $122,000 Ferrari 348ts," wrote Car and Driver in one of its apples-to-oranges road tests.

> The Syclone's turbo, torque converter, and adhesive-tape traction are devastating from 0 to 60. Above 80 mph, it pays for its truck shape. It clears the quarter mile in 14.1 seconds, compared with 14.5 seconds for the Ferrari, but the Ferrari is moving 6 mph faster (99 mph versus 93). The Ferrari grabs the lead very soon after the quarter and never looks back. Its top speed is 166 mph. The Syclone's is 126.

This was the first time a truck ever graced the cover of Car and Driver.

Now, if it happened to be raining, that Ferrari (or most any other exotic) would be left in the Syclone's rooster tail, thanks to the AWD. Grabbing the pavement were P245/50-16 Firestone Firehawk tires on 16x8 alloy wheels, unique to the Syclone. Brakes were discs front, drums rear, but the Syclone was the first truck ever equipped with four-wheel anti-lock brakes. The hunkered-down suspension was stiffened with heavier springs and sway bars. The only transmission available was the Corvette's 700R4 automatic. Car and Driver continued: "It also happens to be pretty darn good at the other moves we Americans expect of sports cars. It beats the Ferrari at braking, too, drawing to a stop from 70 mph in 183 feet, four feet shorter. Cornering grip is less but, at 0.80 g, it is still respectable."

By the end of the '91 model year, PAS had built a total of 2,995 of the $26,000 Syclones, including 113 for export, known as "Saudi" trucks. The export trucks didn't need to meet the US government's regulations, so they were equipped with a metric dash cluster, leaded fuel chip, and a resonator in place of the catalytic converter and non-tinted glass.

Ten Syclones also were modified for Marlboro to be given away in a special promotion for the cigarette company that year. They were painted PPG "Hot Lick Red," then shipped to ASC (American Sunroof Corp.) for a Targa top conversion. ASC also installed a pair of Recaro seats with five-point racing harnesses, a CD changer, and a set of Boyd Coddington wheels.

Plans were underway for the Syclone's return in 1992, and PAS has already built two pilot trucks when the '92 model was cancelled. A third truck, VIN'd as a '92 model, was part of the Marlboro giveaway. The cancellation was simple: many of the '91 Syclones remained at the dealers, who had a difficult time selling the expensive supertrucks. Sound familiar? They were expensive, and, due to the performance suspension, could only haul 500 pounds, so they were none too practical. Still, if the Buick GNX was Darth Vader's car, the Syclone was the Sith Lord's high-speed cargo carrier.

GMC Sonoma GT 1992

"One of the reasons our cars were built was to get showroom traffic. GM wanted these trucks in the magazines, they wanted the 'wow' factor for the dealers," according to Kelly. That's why the GMC Sonoma GT was also created.

Unlike the Syclone, these GMC S15 trucks were built at the Pontiac West assembly plant, so the modifications took place at the PAS facility in Auburn Hills, Michigan. The cost was dramatically less than the Syclone's, at $16,770. The Sonoma GT got the Syclone's interior, with black or gray cloth seats and red piping, console with floor shift, and the Sunbird gauge cluster (without the boost gauge).

Outside, the Sonoma GT also received the same air dam and tonneau cover as the Syclone, along with the lowered suspension, four-wheel anti-lock brakes, and stylish alloy wheels. Other than the basic black of the Syclone, the Sonoma GT could be ordered in Frost White, Apple Red, Bright Teal, Forest Green, and Aspen Blue. But under the hood was a stock high-output L35 Vortec 4.3-liter V-6 producing 195 horsepower, and standard automatic transmission. Missing were the turbocharged engine and AWD.

"It may wear the Syclone's hand-me-downs, but it deserves better" wrote Don Schroeder in Car and Driver.

> The Sonoma GT certainly can't match the Syclone's 0-to-60 time of 5.3 seconds, but at 7.6 seconds, it's hardly a slug . . . . GMC backs up the Sonoma GT's power with decent grip, 0.79 g, and equally respectable braking, 211 feet from 70 mph, thanks to a rear-wheel anti-lock system. For a "sport" truck, it's the most athletic for its price, and its performance is nothing to snicker at.

You might think a great-looking compact truck priced reasonably would sell like hotcakes. You'd be wrong. "I was quite surprised we only sold 806," said Kelly.

GMC Sonoma GT 1992

 # PRODUCED: 806

ENGINE: 262-cubic-inch V-6

HORSEPOWER: 195

TORQUE: 260 lb-ft

¼-MILE TIME: 16.10 at 84 mph

GMC Typhoon 1992–1993

"Good news for those who thought the GMC Syclone was a great idea, but couldn't justify buying a two-seat pick-'em-up any more than they could a Corvette or a Miata: a Typhoon is blowing in your direction." So wrote *AutoWeek* in their October 21, 1991, issue. "What we're talking here is one stormin' sport/ute. The second chapter of GMC's effort to rewrite its image from good-for-you heartland virtue to bi-coastal bad boy, the Typhoon is a regular $30,000 hot rod."

All of the development that went into the Syclone could be applied to the GMC's S-15 two-door Jimmy. The same engine/transmission module with AWD, the same suspension and brakes, the same front air dam. Even the same interior mods went into the Typhoon. While still available in basic black, the Typhoon could also be ordered in a variety of colors, like the Sonoma GT.

AutoWeek continued:

> It'll blow from 0–60 mph in an estimated 6.5 seconds. That's a second and a half longer than it takes Syclone to reach the mile-a-minute mark, but in exchange for a little less rush you get a lot more plush. If your family and the gendarmes would sit still for it, Typhoon is capable of howling all the way to 120 mph with four up.

PAS, Inc. built a total of 4,697 Typhoons: 2,497 for 1992, another 2,200 for 1993. That seemed like a success compared to the sales performance of Syclone and Sonoma GT. But it could have been better, Kelly explained:

> When we did the Typhoons in '92, we got halfway through the model year and they still weren't selling. So we ended up making our own posters and doing our own marketing blitz. So for '93, which was the last year of that body style, we were going to build 3,000 for that year, and we actually had orders for 4,500. However, GM got sued for the Chevy 454 SS, they promised they were only going to make so many for the collectors, and they made so many more thousands of them, and they got sued by the people that bought them thinking they were getting a limited-production vehicle. GM lost. So GM said, absolutely not, you cannot build the other 1,500."

So why not carry the Typhoon over into the 1994 model year?

> We could not build them for '94, because GM went to a new body style, and they went to the CPI [center port injection] engine, and we would have had to revalidate the engine all over again for emissions. GM did not sign up for that in time and we could not have met the model year.

PAS did build two Typhoon-like four-door Oldsmobile Bravada SUVs to pitch the concept to Olds and Cadillac and one Chevrolet Syclone, but all were turned down.

The buzz was changing from performance to alternate fuels in the early 1990s, so PAS also built thousands of the first-production Natural-Gas Powered Chevrolet and GMS 1500 pickups with a patented, under-throttle body injection (TBI) injection unit. These trucks were completed at the same PAS facility in Auburn Hills,

Typhoon Dyno Test at the end of line. Scott Kelly

Michigan, as the Typhoon and Sonoma GT. Unfortunately, the technology was too early, and the injectors of the day—and the natural gas infrastructure—caused a major reliability and PR issue, and GM recalled the vehicles.

The time was right. The products were right. And the performance DNA of many talented automotive people came together for five great years to build some of the best engineered and most interesting supercars and trucks America has ever seen. Many of PAS, Prototype Automotive, and Triad Services people are still in the prototype, racing, and performance automotive industry.

Sadly, Jeff Beitzel and Mike Pocobello have both passed away. Chuck Mountain has retired to Florida. Scott Kelly, through Mike Pocobello, worked for Jim Hall's Indycar team in the mid-1990s after PAS closed, and has been doing business consulting . . . and in contact with most of the Prototype guys. Could history repeat itself?

GMC Typhoon 1992–1993

PRODUCED: 4,697
ENGINE: 262-cubic-inch V-6
HORSEPOWER: 280
TORQUE: 350 lb-ft
¼-MILE TIME: n/a

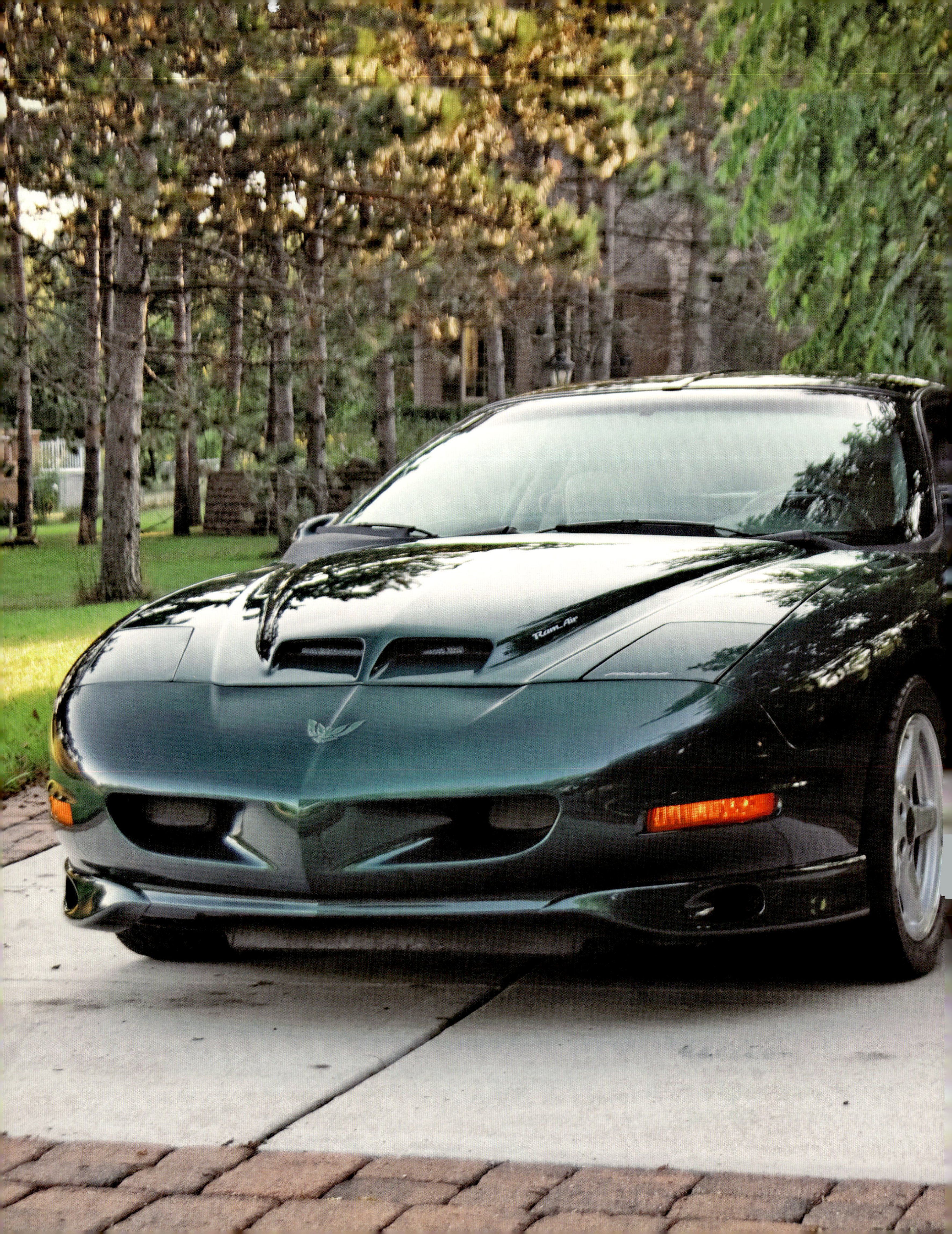
Ram Air

Chapter 11

Street-Legal Performance
Power Play

Ed Hamburger is one of those rare individuals who is part entrepreneur, all gearhead. From 1970 to 1978, his small-block-powered Plymouth Dusters and Dodge Challengers gave the competition fits in NHRA Super Stock racing. He became one of the best in the nation in tuning the Carter Thermoquad carburetors, and was named 1976 NHRA Top Sportsman Wrench. In 1986, he was inducted into the NHRA Northeast Division Hall of Fame, and is listed as one of NHRA's Top 50 racers.

As his New Jersey—based operation expanded, Hamburger turned his passion and skill in racing into his first business, Ed Hamburger's Hi-Performance Parts, which specialized in components for Chrysler's "A" block engines—"For 340s/360s Only" was the motto. He was also one of the first distributors for Mopar's *Direct Connection Catalog*. If you owned a Mopar in the 1970s, and you wanted to make it faster, you had his catalogs.

Clearly, Ed Hamburger had the Midas touch, both for cars, and for commerce. He founded his next business, Hamburger's Oil Pans, in 1978,

The 1996 WS6 was essentially the Firehawk power package, with the same twin-nostril cold-air hood and induction system, but this was added to Formula coupes only. Horsepower for the WS6 was 305 at 5,400 rpm versus the standard Formula's 285 horsepower. It was an extremely tempting option for just $23,339, versus $21,414 for the basic Formula. This '96 is owned by Jerry Boser of New Berlin, Wisconsin. *Tom & Kelly Glatch*

TOP: This is the first truck load of 1993 Firehawks leaving SLP Automotive Canada. It is believed the black Firehawk on top is the first built by SLP Canada (see sidebar on page 156). *Terry "Zeke" Maxwell*

ABOVE, LEFT: Ed Hamburger became one of the best in the nation at tuning the Carter Thermoquad carburetors (Super Stock required factory carburetors), and he was named 1976 NHRA Top Sportsman Wrench. *SLP*

ABOVE, RIGHT: In 1986, Hamburger was inducted into the NHRA Northeast Division Hall of Fame. He's listed as one of NHRA's Top 50 racers. *SLP*

BELOW: Hamburger's Hi-Performance Parts specialized in components for Chrysler's "A" block engines—"For 340s/360s Only" was the motto. He was also one of the first distributors for Mopar's *Direct Connection Catalog*. From 1970 to 1978, his small-block-powered Plymouth Dusters and Dodge Challengers gave the competition fits in NHRA Super Stock racing. *SLP*

146 CHAPTER 11

which was all the more proof of his talents. Creating an oil pan for racers is part engineering, part black art. Oil is an engine's lifeblood, so it must be circulated reliably under all g-force conditions, yet with minimal drag on the rotating crankshaft.

Hamburger's pans were the gold standard. John Force used them. So did Dale Earnhardt. In fact, at one time 85 percent of NASCAR competitors used them, along with road racing and drag racing competitors. But, by 1986, it was time for another challenge, and his company was sold to Mr. Gasket.

"Our mission was to provide late model Camaro and Firebird owners with a complete selection (One-Stop-Shopping) of 'Street Legal Performance' products that would enhance the performance, handling and fuel economy of their cars," SLP's website stated. And so SLP Engineering was born. In 1988, they introduced the industry's first emission-legal performance package for the third-generation Camaro and Firebird. You didn't find the usual "legal only for off-road activities" disclaimers on their products, and that was revolutionary. It led to a formal relationship with GM's Performance Parts division. Now enthusiasts could purchase SLP products directly from any GM dealer throughout the country.

The only thing left for Ed Hamburger was to create a complete, fifty-state legal, performance automobile.

Pontiac Firebird Firehawk 1991–1992

"Rocketing down the back straight at Road Atlanta, the speedometer buried deep in Never-Never Land, you recall the first of the High-Performance Ten Commandments: Thou can never have too much horsepower. In this car, 350 is just fine." Jim Campisano, writing in the October 1991 issue of *High Performance Pontiac*, was experiencing something completely unique in an American pony car.

> Of course, as you approach the final turn, you remember the eighth commandment: Thou can never have too much brakes. Tapping the whoa pedal, the gigantic Brembo disc brakes—the same as those that stop the Ferrari F-40—haul you down to a speed judicious enough to keep you from missing Turn 11. You downshift the six-speed gearbox and you're through the curve and headed toward the main straight.
>
> Six-speed? Brembo brakes? 350 horsepower? Sounds pretty exotic, right? Yep, except it's built in the good ol' U. S. of A.—and sold at your local Pontiac dealer.
>
> The Firehawk has landed.

Those numbers may not sound all that special here in the twenty-first century, but in 1991 they were shocking. From the factory, the top-of-the-line Pontiac Trans Am generated 240 horsepower through a four-speed manual transmission. They delivered decent performance and handling, but nothing close to the Firehawk's.

The price was shocking, too. In 1991, a Trans Am started at $18,105, the Firehawk cost $39,995, with the optional Ricaro driver's seat adding another $995. But the amount of work SLP did to these cars at their Toms River, New Jersey, shop justified the cost.

The Firehawk option required checking the regular production order code "B4U" on the order form. Beginning with a red Firebird Formula with automatic transmission and 1LE suspension, the cars were shipped from the either the Norwood, Ohio, or Van Nuys, California, assembly plant. Once at SLP, a new 383-cubic-inch small-block was fitted, built by SLP with nothing but the best: forged crankshaft, "pink" rods, cast pistons, and an SLP-designed cam. SLP also ported the aluminum heads and installed stainless steel valves. A Ryan Falconer manifold featuring 11.5 in runners and a 52 mm throttle body finished off the powerplant. SLP also added the ZF six-speed transmission used on Corvettes, and a bulletproof Dana 44 rear end. Revised spring rates and lowered suspension, upgraded shocks and struts, and larger anti-roll bars completed the package. It all rolled on 17x9.5 Ronal wheels and (what else) 275/4OZR-17 Firestone Firehawk tires. If this sounds more like a race car than a street machine, you're right.

But a second Firehawk, an actual race car, was also available, the $49,990 Competition Package. Intended for the Bridgestone Supercar series, the Competition Package replaced the standard 12-inch 1LE/Corvette brakes with 13-inch Brembo units, included the Ricaro seat, added a roll cage and weight-reducing aluminum hood, and deleted the rear seat.

Former Escort Challenge Series champion, Stu Hayner, campaigned one in the IMSA Bridgestone Potenza Supercar Championship series, and told *High Performance Pontiac*:

> I can't imagine a better-handling street car. We'll have to change the camber a little bit for the racetrack, but this is one helluva car. People have called the F-bodies primitive, and maybe they are, but this is fun to drive. I'm really looking forward to racing it. It should be very competitive.

Hayner finished third at the series opener at Lime Rock, behind an exotic Consulier GTP (hardly a "production" automobile) and a Corvette ZR1. At Road Atlanta, he finished sixth behind three Lotus Esprits and two Porsche 911 Turbos. By the end of the year, Hayner's Firehawk finished third in the championship behind Hurley Haywood (Porsche 911 Turbo) and Lance Stewart (Consulier GTP).

1991-1992 Pontiac Firebird Firehawk

- **# PRODUCED:** 25
- **ENGINE:** 383-cubic-inch V-8
- **HORSEPOWER:** 350
- **TORQUE:** 390 lb-ft
- **¼-MILE TIME:** 13.20 at 107 mph

SLP and Pontiac anticipated 250 Firehawks would be sold the first year. Instead, only 8 of the ultimate Firebirds were sold in 1991, 17 in 1992, with 2 orders cancelled. Cost was one factor, since the Firehawk package more than doubled the cost of the Firebird Formula on which it was based. Moreover, while the Firehawk was a superb track car, only a true believer or a masochist would love it on the street. Something needed to change.

Pontiac Firebird Firehawk 1993–1995

The new fourth-generation Firebird emerged for 1993, and so did a new Firehawk. The '93 Firebird was 90 percent all new, including the first complete makeover of the venerable small-block engine, the 350-cubic-inch LT1. With its sleek, modern shape and composite plastic body panels, the new Firebird was a stunning departure from the past. So was the assembly plant. GM moved the fourth generation F-body production from Ohio and California to their facility in Sainte-Thérèse, Québec, Canada. Opened in 1966, the Sainte-Thérèse plant was a modern assembly operation.

More good news: Pontiac again offered the Firehawk option. This time, Hamburger teamed with Canadian hot rodder Terry "Zeke" Maxwell to create SLP Automotive Canada. Maxwell founded Zeke's Automotive in the Montréal borough of Lachine to build high-performance street and race vehicles. By 1985, he had seven employees. Zeke's reputation, and his location about 20 miles from Sainte-Thérèse, made him the perfect partner to create the new Firehawk.

> I bought a lot of trick race parts from Ed starting in '76—special rings, quick-change cam timers—for all my race engines as he was the only guy smart enough to figure these things out. We hadn't talked in many years when he called in September '92 to talk about the Firehawk project. I told Ed that we had an 11,400 sq. ft. shop and a killer crew that could handle anything. Let's go!

Maxwell is also fluent in both English and French, which proved critical when operating in the French-speaking province of Québec.

But this Firehawk was very different from the first. Instead of creating a complete high-performance engine for the Firehawk, SLP replaced the hood and airbox system with a new twin-nostril "functional cold-air induction" hood to direct air into a low-restriction intake system, which used a Corvette airbox and filter. Otherwise, the engine was untouched, and no EPA recertification was needed. A slightly stiffer front anti-roll bar was added, creating a little more understeer to balance the increased power. Shorter lower rear control arms and a new Panhard rod were mounted in stiffer bushings to reduce wheel hop under hard acceleration. Five-spoke 17x9 Ronal aluminum wheels were wrapped with—what else?—275/40ZR17 Firestone Firehawk SZ tires. Finally, SLP installed Firehawk logos and attached a serial number plate to the ashtray lid. Unlike the original Firehawk, this one was also available in a convertible, though ragtops only got stock-size 245/50ZR16 tires, since the stiff sidewalls of the coupe's Firehawk SZ tires aggravated chassis flex.

1993-1995 Pontiac Firebird Firehawk

PRODUCED: 1,693
ENGINE: 350-cubic-inch V-8
HORSEPOWER: 300 (1993–95); 310 (1996–97)
TORQUE: 330 lb-ft (1993–95); 330 (1996–97)
¼-MILE TIME: 13.5 at 103 mph

The stock LT1-powered Firebird Formula generated 270 horsepower at 4,800 rpm, 325 lb-ft of torque at 2,400 rpm. SLP's free-breathing cold-air induction raised output to 300 horsepower at 5,000 rpm. Need more speed? The optional $1,199 Performance Exhaust Package generated 315 horsepower at 5,000 rpm, featuring a 3-inch intermediate pipe, freer flowing muffler, and two 2.5-inch tail pipes, all fabricated by SLP craftsmen out of stainless steel.

Once complete, the Firehawk went back to Sainte-Thérèse for distribution to the dealers. Because this was an RPO, code R6V, all Pontiac dealers could order a Firehawk. GM's three-year/36,000-mile warranty still applied, and GMAC financing was available.

"The whole arrangement is virtually transparent to the retail customer and the dealer," Ed Hamburger told *Automotive News* in May 1993. "The basic Firebird is a terrific performance value. We've just bumped that up a notch for the people who want something special with a little extra muscle." The Firebird Firehawk coupe sticker was $24,244, compared to $18,249 for the Firebird Formula on which they were based. SLP quoted figures from a *Motor Trend* test of 0–60 in 4.9 seconds, and 60–0 in 110 feet of braking power. "Know any other $24,244 sports car that can match that?" asked the Firehawk's brochure. "We don't."

F-body production got a late start at Sainte-Thérèse, with the first cars rolling off the line in November 1992, putting them in showrooms in early 1993. Unfortunately, the delay in the start of production meant SLP was delayed, too, with the first Firehawk was completed in May 1993. Due to this late start, only 201 Firehawks were built before the 1994 model changeover, although Pontiac had allocated up to 500 Firebirds to SLP.

Little changed in 1994, though an SLP-designed air cleaner replaced the Corvette unit of the '93 cars. Now, though, SLP had the entire model year to build their allocation of 500 Firehawks. Thanks to the success of that first full year, another 743 Firehawks were sold in 1995: 569 coupes, 102 convertibles, and 72 of the special Comp TA coupes. As production grew, so did SLP Automotive Canada, now with twenty-three employees and their own high-quality paint

SLP built 164 Comp T/A Formulas between 1995 and 1997. This is a batch of rare Comp T/A cars nearing completion. *Terry "Zeke" Maxwell*

equipment. SLP Automotive Canada created their own cold-air hoods in-house, using the same sheet-formed composite material as the factory hood, and the paint equipment was necessary to match the hoods with the Firebirds receiving Firehawk conversion.

Comp T/A Firebird 1995–1997

Back in the late 1960s, a new type of tire became available. The radial-ply tire originated in Europe, and was constructed differently than the bias-ply tires we knew and cursed back then. But, as with anything new, it was difficult to sell the benefits of radials. At the time, there were rumors of tread separation and unreliability, which made acceptance of radial tires a challenge.

No tire company did more to promote radial-ply tires than BFGoodrich. Their "Radial T/A" tires were the first American-made radials to be DOT rated, and they also received SCCA approval for track competition. To prove the superior handling and outstanding reliability of their tires, BFG pitted their Radial T/A street skins against the best racing tires of the day in the popular SCCA Trans-Am series throughout the 1970 and 1971 seasons. Sound impossible? So did most people, until Larry Dent put his "Tirebird" Firebird in the winner's circle in 1971 with a class win at Watkins Glen.

BFG contracted with Jerry Titus's T & G Enterprises to build the three Trans Am racers. The cars were blue with white stripes outlined in red, and raced in the Trans-Am series, the 24 Hours of Daytona, the 12 Hours of Sebring, and other SCCA events.

To commemorate the twenty-fifth anniversary of these amazing Tirebirds, Jim Mattison of Pontiac Historic Services proposed creating a limited-edition 1995 Tirebird, based on the upcoming WS6 option. Mattison had previously been a BFG distributor, and his ties with the company went back to the 1970s. He suggested painting them the same color combination as the original race cars, and he built a prototype to sell his case. He purchased an early '95 Formula, which was equipped with prototype WS6 components by Pontiac Engineering.

In 1970, T&G Racing began to campaign the BFGoodrich "Tirebird" in the SCCA Formula series, racing on Goodrich Comp T/A street tires. This ad from 1971 celebrated their first victory. The SLP-built Comp T/A Firebirds commemorated the feat twenty-five years later. SLP built 164 Comp T/As between 1995 and 1997; twenty years later, they are the rarest SLP cars. *Author's Collection*

STREET-LEGAL PERFORMANCE: POWER PLAY   149

"I was sworn to secrecy on the upcoming WS6 program," Mattison told *High Performance Pontiac*. "This car had all of the WS6 componentry added on. We even had to paint over the wheels to hide the WS6 badges on the center caps." GM Designer Jeff Denison took the original Tirebird color theme and updated it to match the Gen4 body. The prototype was shown at the Detroit Autorama that year, where it received a warm reception, but it became apparent that the hot rodders of the 1990s knew nothing about the road racer of a quarter century earlier.

Mattison had hoped his company, Automotive Services, would build the cars. Instead, it was decided to turn the project over to SLP, since they were going to build the WS6 anyway, and they had the Canadian/American infrastructure in place to do it. The "Tirebird" was changed into a silver anniversary "Comp T/A," and the cars were built on a Trans Am base instead of on a Formula's.

The 1995 Comp T/A became a premium package, with all the Firehawk goodies added to the Trans Am, wrapped in a silver skin with charcoal stripes based on Jeff Denison's original design. Of course, BFGoodrich 275/40ZR17 Comp T/A tires were included, though an extra set of BFG's Comp T/A RI Competition ultra-performance shoes could also be ordered. "It was a great way to test the WS6 without giving up any secrets," said Mattison, who stayed on to consult with SLP on the project.

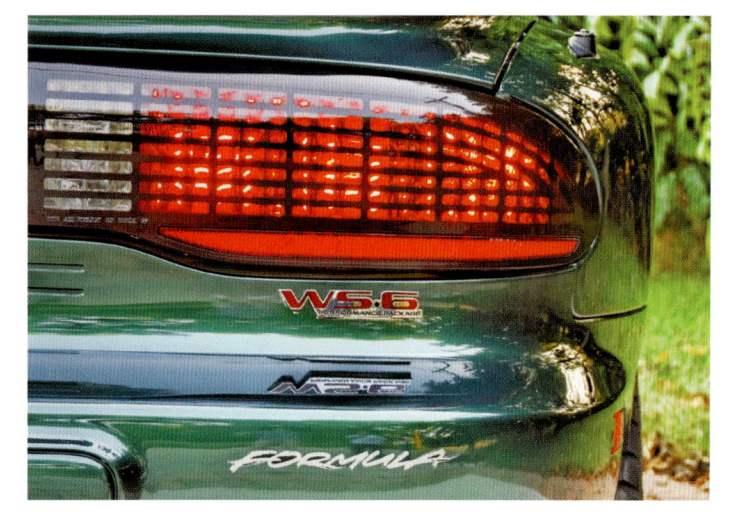

A build of 200 Comp T/A Trans Ams was planned, but only 72 packages were sold, which added $6,995 to the Trans Am price. Production was extended into the '96 and '97 model years, when another 45 and 47 were ordered.

While not quite the commemorative Tirebird that Jim Mattison had envisioned, the Comp T/A became the rarest and, many feel, the most desirable of the SLP Firebirds.

Pontiac Firebird WS-6 1996–1997

While the Firehawk was an unmitigated success for SLP, they added another performance vehicle to their lineup. The return of a legendary Firebird option code, WS6, came in 1996. Beginning in 1978, RPO WS6 had given the Firebird the best brakes and suspension the technology at the time could offer. You could spot an early WS6 by the 8-inch wide "snowflake" wheels and wider than standard tires.

The renewed 1996 WS6 was essentially the Firehawk power package—the twin-nostril cold-air hood and induction system—but it was only added to Trans Am coupes. Horsepower for the WS6 was 305 at 5,400 rpm versus the standard Trans Am's 285 horsepower. It was an extremely tempting option for just $23,339, versus $21,414 for the basic Trans Am.

SLP Automotive Canada geared up for the demand by moving to a 140,000-square-foot building in the Montréal borough of La Salle in July 1995. They now had forty-six employees and room for better workflow. They needed it, as 2,051 WS6 Trans Ams were built during the '96 model year.

"If all the Pontiac Trans Am had going for it was the 305 pavement-warping horses, it would still be one of America's most desirable cars," wrote Jack Keebler in the February 1997 issue of *Motor Trend*. "But the hottest Firebird also manages to set an aggressive exterior-design benchmark and rolls on an uncomplicated, well-executed, track-tuned platform. Mash the gas and it will romp 0–60 mph in 5.7 seconds and eat the quarter mile in 14.0 seconds at 101.9 mph." No wonder by December 1995 SLP Automotive Canada added a resin transfer molding (RTM) manufacturing facility in the Saint-Henri district of Montréal to produce cold-air hoods for the Firehawk and WS6, along with hoods for their latest project, the Camaro SS.

ABOVE: The rear of the 1996 Firebird Formula WS6 featured special badging. *Tom & Kelly Glatch*

LEFT: Like the Firehawks, SLP designed and manufactured the "cold-air induction" hood of the WS6. Together with the SLP air cleaner assembly below, 20 horsepower was added. *Tom & Kelly Glatch*

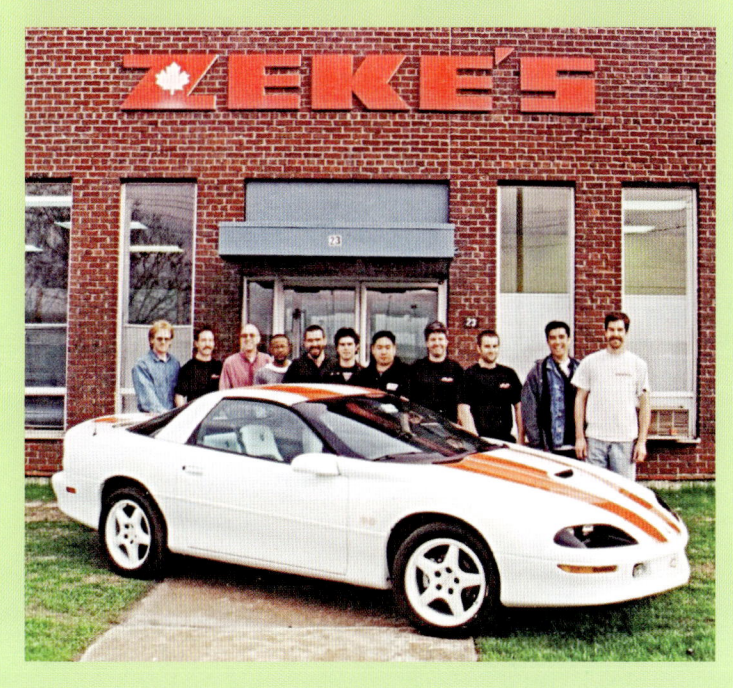

TOP, LEFT: A yard full of WS6 and Camaro SS, either completed or awaiting completion. *Terry "Zeke" Maxwell*

TOP, RIGHT: Four preproduction 1996 WS6 Firebird pilot cars. Shown are code 48U Dark Green Metallic, 41U Black, 81U Bright Red, and 13U Sebring Silver Metallic. The only other color available that year was 10U Arctic White. *Terry "Zeke" Maxwell*

ABOVE: The last 1997 Firebird WS6 built by SLP Automotive Canada. SLP lost the contract to build the WS6 after the 1997 models. *Terry "Zeke" Maxwell*

MIDDLE LEFT: SLP Automotive Canada management included John Sullivan, director, Operations; Terry Maxwell, general manager; Kevin Cuthbert, director, Composites and R&D; Dan LaSalle, manager, Paint. *Terry "Zeke" Maxwell*

LEFT: In 1997, SLP purchased the last 135 Corvette LT4 engines from GM. A total of 106 Camaro SS and 29 Firehawks were built. This small crew from the original "Zeke's Automotive" facility on 23 St. Joseph Street balanced, blueprinted, and dyno'd every one of the engines. *Terry "Zeke" Maxwell*

STREET-LEGAL PERFORMANCE: POWER PLAY

The WS6 option returned in 1997, but this time it was available on both Formula and Trans Am Firebirds. The package was also available on convertibles for the first time. Now that buyers could have their WS6 power a number of different ways, sales leaped to 3,804 units. By the summer of 1997, SLP Automotive Canada had a workforce of 237 employees.

Pontiac Firebird Firehawk 1996–1997

With the extraordinary value of the WS6, the Firehawk seemed like an afterthought. The Firehawk, which cost almost $3,000 less than a comparable '95 model, still possessed unique features that were unavailable on the WS6, which SLP's brochure pointed out:

- Engine oil cooler package
- Performance lubricants package with synthetic rear axle lube, semi-synthetic power steering fluid, and premium-quality, synthetic media engine oil filter
- Level II Bilstein sport suspension package
- SLP Hurst short throw-shifter with H-shift knob
- Torsen limited slip differential (includes performance lubricants package)
- American Racing Equipment chrome-plated aluminum wheels

The Firehawk was still the premiere Firebird, but not by the wide margin as before, and SLP Automotive Canada built just

1996-1997 Pontiac Firebird WS6

 # PRODUCED: 5,855

ENGINE: 350-cubic-inch V-8

HORSEPOWER: 305

TORQUE: 335 lb-ft

¼-MILE TIME: 14.00 at 101.9 mph

1997 Pontiac Firebird Firehawk LT4

 # PRODUCED: 30

ENGINE: 350-cubic-inch V-8

HORSEPOWER: 330

TORQUE: 340 lb-ft

¼-MILE TIME: n/a

TOP: TORSEN torque sensing differentials were assembled into the factory rear ends on this stand. *Terry "Zeke" Maxwell*

MIDDLE: SLP Automotive Canada moved into a 140,000-square-foot facility in the Montreal suburb of La Salle in 1996, giving them more room and the capacity for superior workflow. *Terry "Zeke" Maxwell*

ABOVE: A load of the rare LT4-powered 1997 Firehawk and Camaro SS cars ready for delivery back to GM. Just 29 Firehawk LT4 and 106 Camaro SS LT4 cars were built. *Terry "Zeke" Maxwell*

To differentiate the 1998 Firehawk from the WS6, SLP designed a new front fascia, featuring fixed composite headlights replacing the Firebird's pop-up units. Over 11 pounds were reduced from the nose, and there would be no mistaking a Firehawk coming up rapidly from behind. The US Department of Transportation wouldn't approve SLP's design; the six prototypes with these headlights had to be converted back to factory stock and the whole program was cancelled. Much time was lost, and SLP dropped the Firehawk for 1998. *General Motors*

41 cars in 1996, along with 45 Comp T/A coupes. The numbers improved somewhat in 1997, with 116 Firehawks and 47 Comp T/A cars sold. But a few of the '97 Firehawks sported special power. "This will be a very rare bird; just 25 to 30 SLP Pontiac Firehawks will emerge with the pumped 330-horsepower LT4 V-8 first seen in the '96 Corvette Grand Sport," reported *Motor Trend* in their August 1997 issue.

> The quick-revving LT4, with its increased-flow-rate injectors, reworked ports, bigger valves, high-lift cam, and higher-compression pistons, was created as a special optional variation on the standard LT1 small-block V-8. SLP Engineering got its hands on the last 150 or so of these hot engines and while some slid into about 100 30th anniversary Camaros, a few of the blueprinted strays will go into this special number of Firehawks.

The engines were balanced and blueprinted at SLP Automotive Canada's first home, Zeke's Performance shop in Lachine. And they were rare 'Birds indeed—just 29 production cars and one prototype were built. The price was a steep $40,378, but *Motor Trend*'s conclusion stated that "If low-altitude scouting is the mission with an occasional hunk of Mustang flesh as an in-flight snack, this bird is the hot ticket." Or, as they might say in French Québec, it was *la crème de la crème* of American performance cars.

Chevrolet Camaro SS 1996–2002

In hockey, a "power play" occurs, to quote the *Collins English Dictionary*, "when one team has more players taking part than their opponents, usually as a result of a penalty for foul play." Beginning in 1996, SLP staged a power play of their own. Along with the WS6 and Firehawk for Pontiac, they ganged up on the competition— Ford's SVT Cobra and the imports—by adding the Camaro SS to their lineup.

The hottest Gen4 Camaro was the Z28 model, which provided about the same performance as the Trans Am. Since the Camaro

Chevrolet Camaro SS 1996-1997

PRODUCED: 5,201

ENGINE: 350-cubic-inch V-8

HORSEPOWER: 305

TORQUE: 325 lb-ft

¼-MILE TIME: n/a

Chevrolet Camaro SS 1997 LT4

PRODUCED: 106

ENGINE: 350-cubic-inch V-8

HORSEPOWER: 330

TORQUE: 340 lb-ft

¼-MILE TIME: n/a

In 1996, SLP began producing the Camaro SS for Chevrolet. This is the first Camaro SS built (at left) along with a new-for-1996 Firebird WS6. *Terry "Zeke" Maxwell*

and Firebird shared all major components, it made sense to create an SLP version. Chevrolet also sold two to three times as many Camaros as Pontiac sold Firebirds, so it was also a good business move. Since both cars were built at Sainte-Thérèse, it was just a matter of convincing Chevrolet to let SLP do their magic—and the result would revive a storied name from the past: Camaro SS.

Chevrolet had built Super Sport versions of Impalas, Chevelles, Novas, and Camaros throughout the 1960s. Now, twenty-four years since the last Camaro SS was built, it was time to create another legend.

It's not surprising that SLP used similar cold-air induction techniques, as on the Firehawks, but the two cars were hardly identical. Where the Firehawk and WS6 brought in air through twin scoops at the front of the hood, the SS used a NACA duct mounted midhood. The technology goes back to the National Advisory Committee for Aeronautics in the 1950s, in the days before NASA, and is still a valid design: look at the hood of today's Dodge Hellcats. The SLP air box was mounted below this duct, where the charge then made a 180-degree turn into the throttle body. Like the SLP-blessed Firebirds, the SS made 305 horsepower at 5,500 rpm, or 310 horsepower at 5,500 rpm with the Performance Exhaust option. Either way, you got a ground-pounding 325 lb-ft of torque at just 2,400 rpm.

The 1996 Camaro SS also came with the 1LE suspension and 17-inch wheels. Because SLP had to match their cold-air hood to the Camaro they were converting, the only paint colors available were Arctic White, Bright Red, Black, Polo Green Metallic, and Bright Teal Metallic. Like the Firehawk, the Camaro SS, RPO R7T, could be ordered at any Chevy dealer. What was missing were some of the items that made a Firehawk a Firehawk, but those options—like the SLP Hurst short throw-shifter ($299), stainless-steel Performance Exhaust Package ($1,199), or Level II Bilstein Sport Suspension Package ($1,599)—could be added. Like the Firehawk, the Camaro SS was a great value, at $24,490. No wonder 2,269 were sold in the first year, while overall Camaro sales were half of the total for 1995.

The success of the Camaro SS came just in time to celebrate Camaro's thirtieth birthday in 1997. Chevrolet released a special 30th Anniversary Z28, dressed in Arctic White paint with Hugger Orange stripes, just like the famous 1969 Indy 500 pace car. The $550 Z4C option was popular, with 3,038 built in both coupe and convertible form. Of those, 957 passed through SLP Automotive Canada for the ultimate celebration: the 30th Anniversary Camaro SS. Better yet, 106 of those received the last of the LT4 engines produced by Chevrolet. Powered by the 330-horsepower mill developed for the 1996 Corvette Grand Sport, these would ultimately be the rarest of the Camaro SS cars.

Overall, 1997 was a good year for SLP, with 3,038 Camaro SSs sold. To keep up with the demand, they now had 245 employees at their three locations in the Montréal area.

Painted Firehawk and Camaro SS hoods, ready for installation. *Terry "Zeke" Maxwell*

The Camaro SS was new for 1996, the first Super Sport Camaro in twenty-four years. The SS used a traditional "NACA" duct mounted mid-hood for cold air induction. The car also came with the 1LE suspension and 17-inch wheels. Because SLP had to match their cold-air hood to the Camaro being converted, the only paint colors available were Arctic White, Bright Red, Black, Polo Green Metallic, and Bright Teal Metallic. The Camaro SS was a great value at $24,490. *Chevrolet*

TOP: A truckload of completed Camaro SSs ready to return to the GM plant in nearby Ste.-Thérèse. *Terry "Zeke" Maxwell*
ABOVE: The last load of 2002 Camaro SSs just before the closure of the Ste.-Thérèse plant and the end of the Gen4 F-bodies. *Terry "Zeke" Maxwell*

STREET-LEGAL PERFORMANCE: POWER PLAY 155

1993 Firebird Firehawk #001

This is the first 1993 Firebird Firehawk built by SLP, serial number 001. It was purchased new by the current owner, Tom Boser of Waukesha, Wisconsin.
Tom & Kelly Glatch

When Tom Boser graduated from the Milwaukee School of Engineering with a degree in Electrical Engineering, he decided to celebrate—he ordered a brand-new 1993 Trans Am from Wilde Pontiac in Waukesha, Wisconsin. Not wanting any garden-variety Trans Am, he ordered it with all the performance goodies available in the first year of the fifth-generation Firebird. A few weeks later, the salesman from Wilde Pontiac told Tom he could have all he wanted, and more, by ordering a new Firehawk. "We can add it to your existing order," the salesman said.

So Tom changed his order from a Trans Am to a Firehawk. Little did he realize he was getting the first Firehawk built by the partnership of Ed Hamburger and Terry "Zeke" Maxwell, SLP Automotive Canada. Boser spent the first year of ownership driving the Firehawk occasionally, showing it off at car shows and to friends. Since then, the Firehawk has become the centerpiece of Tom's collection of Pontiacs. Today, it shows just 644 miles on the odometer. It's never been washed (only polished) and is completely original.

Boser realizes there can only be one "number one," and this is it.

1993 Pontiac Firehawk Formula #001

RPO	Description
122	Graphite leather trim combination
12I	Interior trim graphite

17P	Wheel color silver
1SB	Package option 04
2FS87	Firebird Coupe
41U	Exterior color, Black
6EJ	Spring/Suspension—Front LH
7EJ	Spring/Suspension—Front RH
8TH	COMPONENT RR LH COMPUTER SEL SUSP
9TH	COMPONENT RR RH COMPUTER SEL SUSP
A31	Power windows
AAA	Standard Safety Features
AK5	Driver and passenger side inflatable restraint system (air bags).
AR9	Front bucket seats manual reclining (European style)
AU0	Remote keyless entry system
AU3	Power door locks
B35	Carpet rear floor mats
B84	Exterior body side molding
C49	Rear window electric defogger
C60	Air conditioning, manual controls
DG7	Right & left hand remote control electric outside mirrors
E7Z	SENSOR—VEH SPD—DELETE
FE2	Touring Suspension system ride and handling
G80	Limited slip positraction rear axle
G92	Performance rear axle 3.23
GU5	Rear axle gear ratio 3.23
IP2	Interior Design (P2)
J65	Power front & rear disc brake system
K34	Automatic electronic cruise control with resume & accelerate
KC4	Engine oil cooling system
KG7	Generator 125 Amp
LT1	Engine gas, 8 cyl, 5.7L(5.7P), MFI, HO
M29	Transmission Manual, 6-speed BorgWarner, 85mm, 2.97 1st, 1.44 3rd
MN6	6-speed manual transmission
NA5	Emission system, federal requirements
NP5	Leather wrap steering wheel
PW7	16x8 styled aluminum superlight wheel
QLC	P245/50ZR16 performance tires
R6V	Formula Firehawk option
STE	Ste.-Thérèse, Quebec assembly plant
U1A	Radio, AM&FM stereo, seek/scan, CD player, equilizer, includes clock
UB3	Instrument cluster (oil, coolant temp, voltmeter, tach, trip, ODO)
UK3	Steering wheel radio controls
UW2	10-speaker, quad front door mounted, dual rear sail panel, amplifier
V73	Vehicle Certification US
VK3	License plate front mounting package
W66	Merchandised Pkg Pontiac Firebird Formula
WS9	Model Conversion Pontiac Firebird Formula

ABOVE: All Firehawk and Camaro SS cars have a serial number plate installed. Tom Boser's 1993 Firehawk is serial number 001. *Tom & Kelly Glatch*

RIGHT: Firehawks came with stainless-steel exhaust tips and distinctive graphics. *Tom & Kelly Glatch*

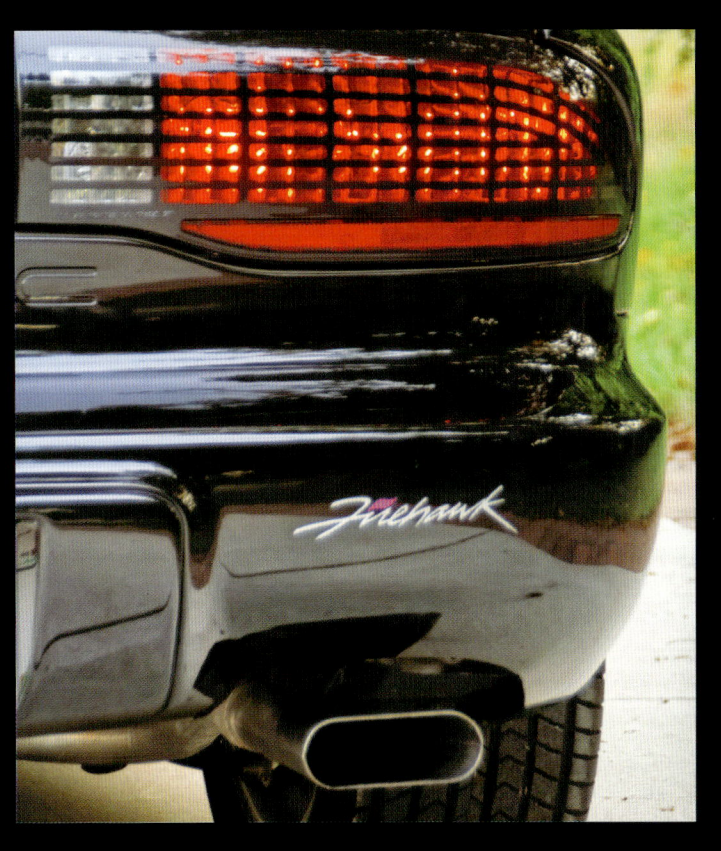

Finished 2001 10th Anniversary Firehawks ready to be delivered back to GM's Ste.-Thérèse plant for distribution to dealers. *Terry "Zeke" Maxwell*

Pontiac Firebird Firehawk 1998–2002

The next year should have been a great one for SLP. The '98 Firebird received a styling refresh and, under the hood, the top option was the spectacular LS1 engine right out of the fifth-generation Corvette.

Just at this moment, SLP lost the contract to build the WS6 for Pontiac. But SLP were still able to offer the top-of-the-line Firehawk, so all was not lost. To differentiate the Firehawk from the lesser WS6, SLP designed a new front fascia, featuring fixed composite headlights to replace the Firebirds' popup units. Over 11 pounds were reduced from the nose, and there would be no mistaking a Firehawk coming up rapidly from behind.

In another example of excessive government oversight, the US Department of Transportation would not approve SLP's design, though it was similar to the Camaro's. No DOT, no sale. The six prototypes with these headlights had to be converted back to factory stock, and the whole program was cancelled. A lot of time was lost, and ultimately SLP dropped the Firehawk for 1998, though they continued to build the popular Camaro SS.

The Firehawk returned for 1999, this time without the unique headlight design. You could still spot a Firehawk, since SLP used twin enlarged openings in the hood for air induction, rather than the strange quad "nostrils" of the '98 and later WS6. "1999 SLP Firehawk: Hottest Firebird Ever?" asked *Motor Trend* in their June 1998 issue. Testing one of the six fixed-headlight '98 prototypes against an immaculate '69 Trans Am and '71 455-horsepower, they concluded:

> The SLP Firehawk may be the most refined F-machine ever. Much of that feel and performance comes from the revisions made to

Pontiac Firebird Firehawk 1998–2002

 # PRODUCED: 3,699

ENGINE: 346-cubic-inch V-8

HORSEPOWER: 305 (1998–2000); 335 (2001–2002)

TORQUE: 335 lb-ft (1998–2000); 350 lb-ft (2001–2002)

¼-MILE TIME: 13.60 at 106 mph (2002)

the '98 models, and the rest comes from the SLP upgrades. The exhaust sound is still American V-8, but tempered with a richness and sophistication offered up by the new LS1 . . . . More polish or no, have no fear that the newest 'Bird has become soft: This car flat honks. The alloy V-8 is revvier than ever before, and the six-speed, especially with the Hurst stick, is a joy to row. Handling? How about 0.91 g on the skid pad, a number even racing versions of the older machines would have a tough time matching. It would also be no contest in the braking category, given the Firehawk's four-wheel discs with ABS and sticky 275 cross-section Firestones that help it anchor from 60 in just 115 feet.

Despite competition from the lower-cost WS6, Firehawk sales soared to 971 units in 1999. There was little change for 2000, and another 741 Firehawks were sold, 459 with the six-speed, 282 with automatic.

For 2001, SLP celebrated ten years of Firehawks, and rightly so—no specialist had produced factory-supported, dealer-delivered cars for as long as SLP. Based only on the Trans Am, the option code "QLC" 10th Anniversary Firehawk was dressed in black with gold stripes and wheels. It reminded some of the Smokey and the Bandit Tran Am Special Edition cars of the 1970s and early 1980s, but actually they had a connection with the first *X-Men* movie. "Although the car does not appear in the movie, it was showcased during recent 20th Century Fox media activities at The Essex House Hotel in New York City, where it served as the backdrop for interviews and photo sessions," read SLP's press release. "Going forward, SLP's Trans Am Firehawk will be highlighted at upcoming X-Men promotional venues, such as national comic book collectors' conventions."

A new, larger rear spoiler appeared on the 10th Anniversary coupes, along with a "super wide CHMSL" (center high mounted stop lamp), and all 2001 Firehawks received the Corvette's LS6 intake and could now produce 335 horsepower. The '01 Firehawk was priced at $3,999, while the 10th Anniversary cost $1,899 for a Trans Am coupe and $1,399 for the convertible. In all, 540 Firehawks were built, including 139 10th Anniversary cars.

But change was in the air. As early as 1997 the automotive press was reporting the death of the F-body. These were rather exaggerated—until GM made it known that 2002 would be the last year. In many ways, SLP saved the best for last, and Firehawks built after August 2001 gained a high-flow induction system, pushing horsepower 345 and torque to 350 lb-ft. Their brochure made sure potential buyers wouldn't confuse the non-SLP WS6 with the WU6 Firehawk:

Ordering Your Dream Car? Make sure your dealer adds General Motors' RPO Code WU6 to your Trans Am coupe, convertible, or Formula coupe car order. Why? Because it's not a Firehawk without the WU6 code. You cannot add SLP content on the WS6 Firebird.

Knowing there may never be another Firebird, enthusiasts stepped up and bought 1,501 Firehawks.

Chevrolet Camaro RS 2001–2002

If the Camaro SS had a fault, it was unattainability—the car was still out of reach for some buyers. Not that $32,000 for a basic 2001 Camaro SS was anything less than a bargain, it was just too expensive to buy, or too expensive to insure. SLP attempted to address that by reviving yet another name from the past: Camaro RS.

"Chevy's Camaro has always represented the best value in sports cars, and SLP's Camaro RS package (GM option code Y3B) is no exception," said the RS brochure. The $849 option included a unique look, with "Dual Heritage Racing Stripes" in black or red, gloss black grille with red "bowtie" emblem, and RS badges on the sides and rear. They included the Z28's exhaust for an extra 5 horsepower, and the 16x8-inch painted wheels from the same car could be added for $699. That brought the total to around $20,000, though the optional Z28 performance suspension would jack the price up still more. But the Camaro RS was powered by the base 231-cubic-inch L36 V-6 engine, with four-speed automatic or five-speed manual gearboxes.

Car and Driver's Aaron Robinson commented:

The exhaust change dubs real snarl into the 3.8-liter V-6's song and adds five horsepower, claims SLP, bringing the total to 205. Our test car with an automatic managed to cruise the quarter in 15.8 seconds at 86 mph—more than a second quicker than Burt's original Bandit Trans Am V-8. These days, that kind of power increase won't make you invulnerable on the avenue, but the looks and extra decibels might mean you never have to show it.

Zero to 60 was a snappy 7.5 seconds, too, and *Car and Driver* averaged 25 miles per gallon.

"Make no mistake, RS is true to its proud heritage, giving budget minded enthusiasts the look, sound, and overall performance they've come to expect from SLP and Chevrolet," the brochure concluded. With rising post-9/11 fuel costs and insurance premiums, the Camaro RS had great sales potential. Instead, just 398 were delivered in 2001; 443 in 2002.

Chevrolet Camaro RS 2001-2002

PRODUCED: 841
ENGINE: 231-cubic-inch V-6
HORSEPOWER: 205
TORQUE: 225 lb-ft
¼-MILE TIME: 15.80 at 86 mph

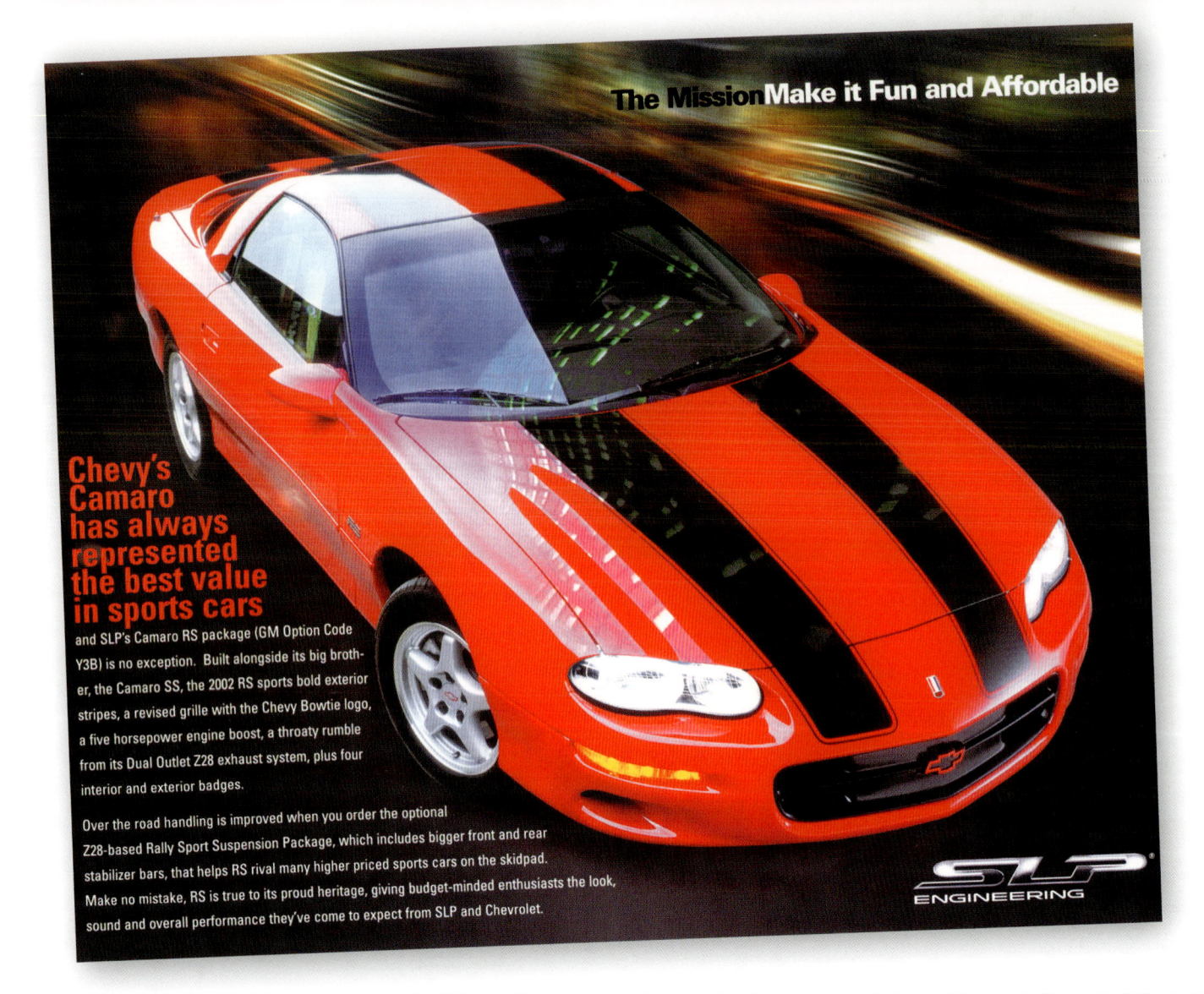

The Mission Make it Fun and Affordable

Chevy's Camaro has always represented the best value in sports cars

and SLP's Camaro RS package (GM Option Code Y3B) is no exception. Built alongside its big brother, the Camaro SS, the 2002 RS sports bold exterior stripes, a revised grille with the Chevy Bowtie logo, a five horsepower engine boost, a throaty rumble from its Dual Outlet Z28 exhaust system, plus four interior and exterior badges.

Over the road handling is improved when you order the optional Z28-based Rally Sport Suspension Package, which includes bigger front and rear stabilizer bars, that helps RS rival many higher priced sports cars on the skidpad. Make no mistake, RS is true to its proud heritage, giving budget-minded enthusiasts the look, sound and overall performance they've come to expect from SLP and Chevrolet.

SLP ENGINEERING

The 2001–2002 Camaro RS was an attempt by SLP and Chevrolet to make a semi-performance car that was "fun and affordable." The V-6–powered $849 Camaro RS option was just that, yet only 841 were sold over two model years. *SLP*

Chevrolet Camaro SS 1998–2002

"For those that can't get enough of a wild thing, there's Camaro SS," read Chevrolet's 1998 full-line brochure. "It's back . . . and it's hotter than ever."

Camaros got a nice facelift for 1998, with fixed composite headlights and an open, oval air intake. The biggest news was under the hood, where both F-bodies were now motivated by the aluminum 346-cubic-inch LS1 V-8 right out of the C5 Corvette, creating 305-horsepower. SLP again applied their mojo to the Z28 to create the SS, adding another 5 horsepower with the Performance Exhaust System. A total of 2,397 SSs were built in 1998, 1,485 six-speeds and 912 automatics.

The Camaro SS was hardly changed for 1999, but sales more than doubled to 4,829. The SS rolled into the new century more popular than ever, and sales nearly doubled again, with 8,913 delivered. Like the 2001 Firehawks, Camaro SS received the Corvette's LS6 intake manifold and revised cam profile and now produced 335 horsepower. Sales of the hotter '01 seemed soft, at 6,332, but that number is deceiving: Chevrolet stopped production of the 2001 Camaro two months early to begin producing a special model for the Camaro's swan song in 2002—the 35th Anniversary Camaro SS.

Features available only on the 35th Anniversary SS included:
- Bright Rally Red exterior with exterior stripe package
- Special black SS wheels with machined edges
- 35th Anniversary badging on exterior and dashboard
- 35th Anniversary emblem embroidered into front seats
- Anodized brake calipers
- Special Ebony/Pewter leather seating surfaces
- Special Trophy Mat in Ebony vinyl with embroidered 35th Anniversary emblem

Chevrolet issued a gorgeous twenty-one-page brochure for the final Camaro, with the SS featured on at least seven pages. Rick Baldick, Camaro brand manager, wrote on page three: "To everyone who has ever owned—or ever dreamed of owning—a Chevy Camaro, we dedicate the 35th anniversary of 'Performance—American Style.'"

"It's hard to believe the Mustang and Camaro have been butting heads, burning rubber, and racing for pinks for 35 years," commented Matt Stone in *Motor Trend*. "But since there's a 35th

SLP's Camaro SS 35th Anniversary model was striking in both Coupe and Convertible form. The 35th Anniversary was hugely popular, with 11,191 of the $32,780 Camaros sold. At the time, no one knew if the 2002 Camaro would be the last of the storied Camaro line. The SLP-built Camaro SS 35th Anniversary celebrated the Camaro's long and successful history in great style. *General Motors*

Anniversary Camaro, it must be so." Pitted against a 2001 SVT Cobra, he observed:

> Ford cranks impressive horsepower and lots of revs out of its handbuilt 4.6L DOHC V-8—but not enough to outgun the larger-cube overhead-valve LS1 in any straight-line contest. The Cobra's 5.38-sec 0–60 time hangs impressively with all the great muscle Mustangs of the '60s, but the Camaro's impressive low-end torque grunts it to a ²⁄₁₀ths advantage. That lead grows to ³⁄₁₀ths through the quarter, the SS also finishing the 1320 exactly 4 mph faster.

The 35th Anniversary Camaro SS was popular, with 11,191 of the special $32,780 Camaros sold.

And then the inevitable. The trade publication, *Wards Auto World*, on August 30, 2002, posted this news item:

> General Motors Corp.'s Ste.-Therese, Que., Canada, plant closed its doors for good Aug. 29 after 37 years in operation and 4 million units produced. The plant opened in 1965 with production of the '66 Chevrolet Biscayne. Most recently it produced GM's muscle cars, the Chevrolet Camaro and Pontiac Firebird, which are ending production due to falling demand. Ste.-Therese was running well below its 250,000-unit annual capacity, producing only 40,000 cars per year.

C'est la vie.

Within a few years, the Sainte-Thérèse plant was leveled and the land reclaimed. Terry Maxwell eventually left Zeke's Performance and went to work in vintage automobile restoration and sales in Montréal. SLP carried on with their aftermarket parts and conversion businesses in Michigan and New Jersey, until this story in the April 2009 issue of *Car and Driver*: "SLP's newest burning bird has four doors and outguns its Firebird-based forebears." That's right: SLP had created a Firehawk version of Pontiac's G8 four-door sedan, packing 500 supercharged horses. But in a strange twist of déjà vu,

the G8, and the Pontiac Division, would soon be history and, after producing thirty-four units, the Firehawk G8 was stillborn.

Ed Hamburger, with his son David, Canadian business partner Terry Maxwell, and a talented team of employees, had joined forces to create some amazing performance automobiles, combining fine engineering and great craftsmanship, along with a dose of international cooperation. In just nine years, SLP Automotive Canada produced over 55,000 performance vehicles for Pontiac and Chevrolet, far more than any other specialist had ever built for a US automaker. Sadly, the days of specialists like SLP, working hand in hand with manufacturers to create direct-to-dealer supercars with full factory warranties, was over.

The double curse of litigation and legislation made it impossible for specialists like SLP to continue. For Detroit to continue building performance supercars, all development and manufacturing would need to be done in-house—and the style, performance, workmanship, and exclusivity that only a low-volume specialist could deliver were gone.

Chevrolet Camaro SS 1998–2002

 # PRODUCED: 34,140
ENGINE: 346-cubic-inch V-8
HORSEPOWER: 305 (1998–2000); 335 (2001–2002)
TORQUE: 335 lb-ft (1998–2000); 350 lb-ft (2001–2002)
¼-MILE TIME: 13.80 at 106 mph (1998)

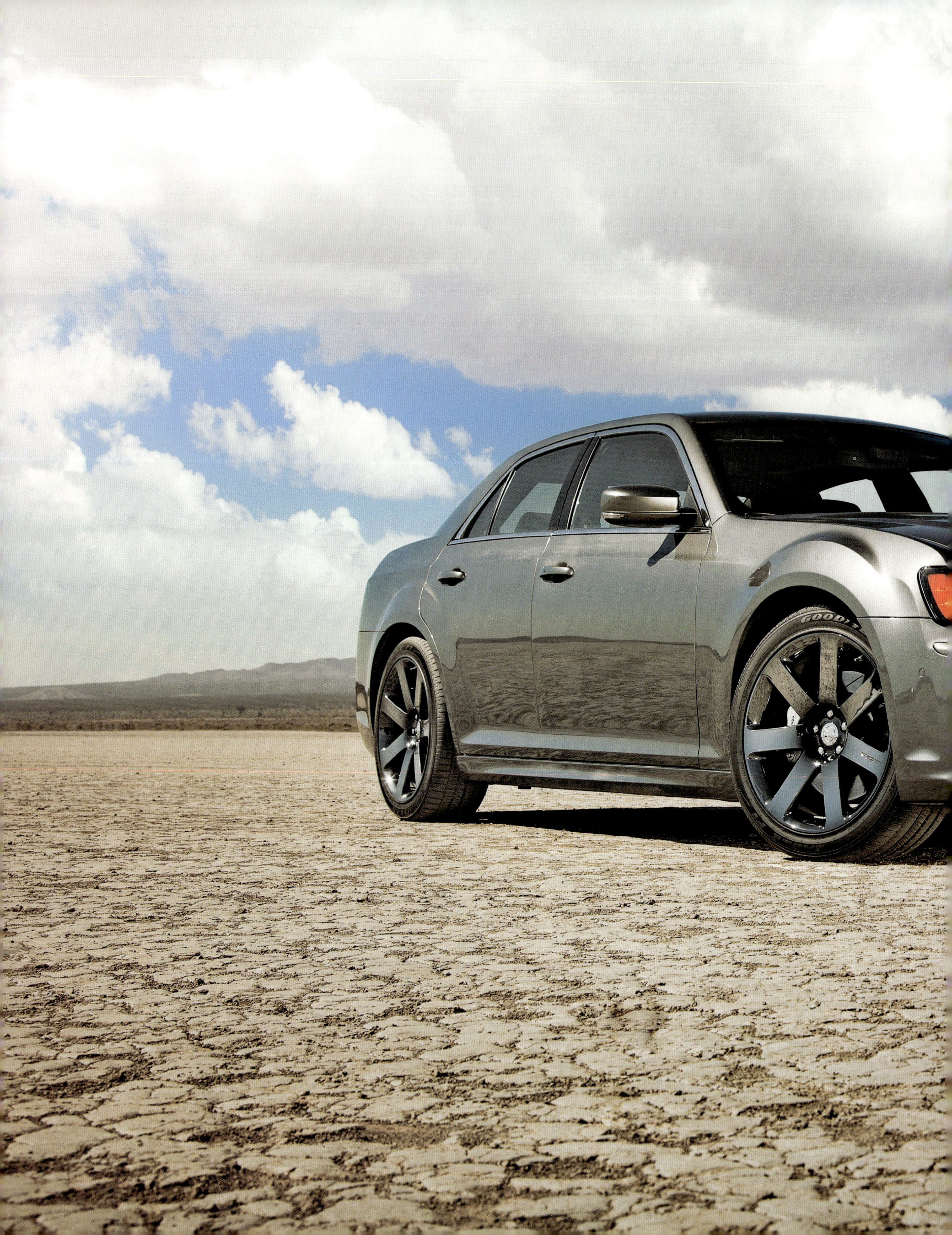

SECTION THREE

The Manufacturers

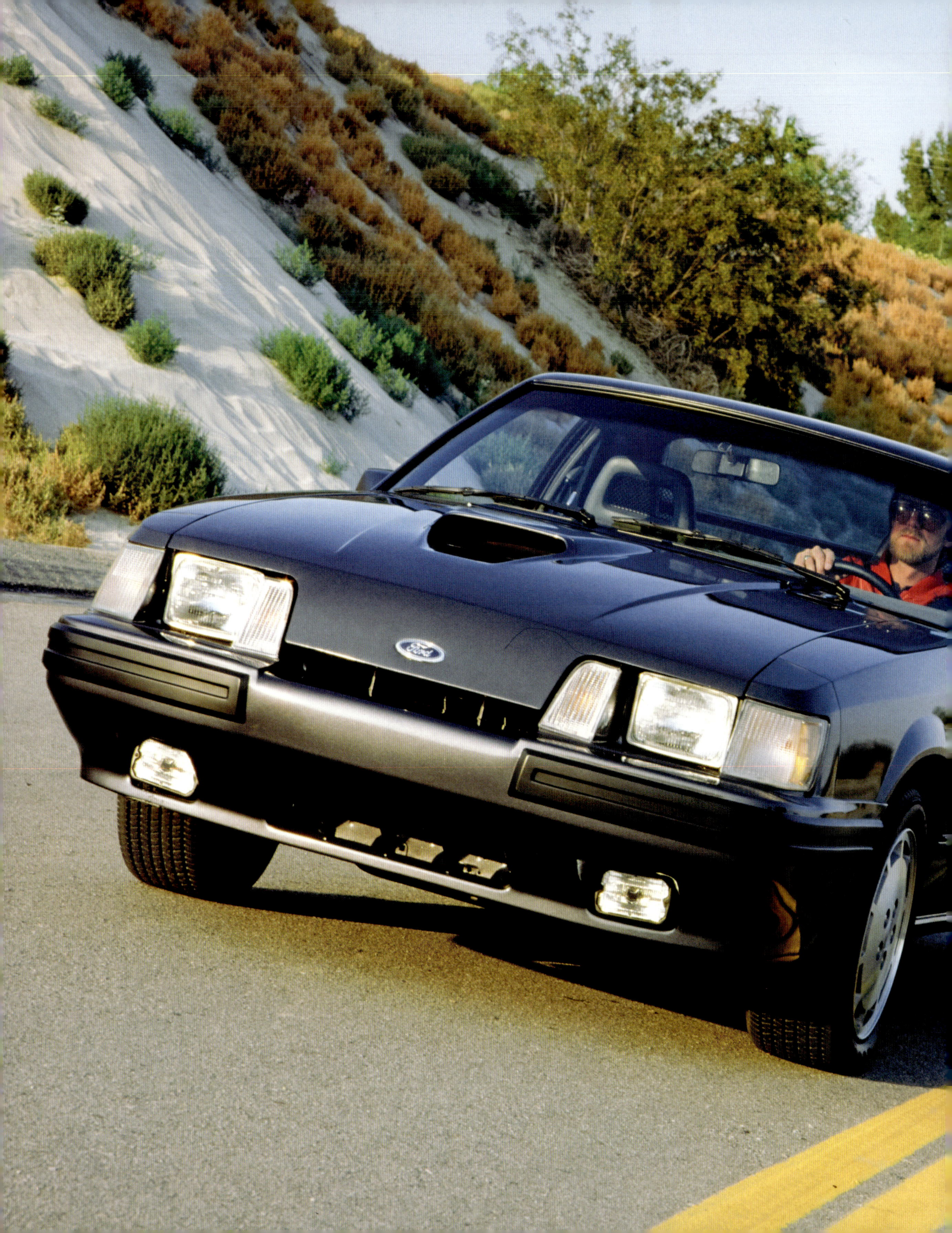

Chapter 12

SVO/ SVT
Unconventional Wisdom

President Jimmy Carter called it the "malaise," the general depression affecting the mood of the American people throughout the 1970s, and our cars reflected that feeling. Just look at some of the most popular automotive paint colors from that time: beige and brown. That decade created some of the most unmemorable cars we have ever seen.

Slowly, ever so slowly, the cloud of despair began to lift. You could see it in some of the new automobiles of 1982, like the aerodynamic third-generation Camaro and Firebird. There were rumors of an all-new Corvette, too. While Ford's third-generation Mustang was now four

LEFT: While the 1984 Mustang GT was a brute-force straight-line performer, the sophisticated SVO Mustang did everything very well. Power was by a 140-cubic-inch (2.3-liter) four-cylinder packing a AiResearch T3 turbocharger, electronic fuel-injection, and an air-to-air intercooler under the hood scoop. With an electronically-controlled 14 psi of boost on hand, the SVO four generated 176-horsepower at 4,400 revolutions per minute. Coupled with a quick-shifting, five-speed manual, upgraded suspension, four-wheel disc brakes, and driver-focused interior, the SVO delivered shockingly good performance—without a V-8. At $16,000 you could buy a new Mustang GT and a Ford Escort instead of one SVO Mustang, but the SVO developed a small but dedicated following, and pointed to the future—like the four-cylinder 2016 Shelby EcoBoost GT. *Archives/TEN: The Enthusiast Network Magazines, LLC*

PREVIOUS PAGES: In 2008, Dodge revamped the Charger and SRT8. *Archives/TEN: The Enthusiast Network Magazines, LLC*

years old, the performance Mustang GT was a comparably good car. Performance, however, was a relative term, with a rare vehicle that could achieve 0–60 times under 10 seconds.

It was about this time that Ford created the Special Vehicle Operations (SVO) group, led by Michael Kranefuss from Ford's European division. With just thirty-two people on the team, SVO attacked every aspect of Ford's US products, both for the street and on the racetrack.

SVO Mustang 1984–1986

Conventional wisdom dictated creating a muscle car that used a big V-8 engine in a small American car. That's just what Ford did when it introduced the Mustang GT in 1982, their initial attempt at resurrecting the muscle Mustangs of the past. Powered by a 302-cubic inch (5-liter) Cleveland V-8, it became the first of the legendary "5.0" Mustangs—even if that V-8 generated only 157 horsepower and did 0–60 in, perhaps, 8 seconds.

But SVO's first vehicle was very different. Released in 1984, the Mustang SVO had a modern look, with an aerodynamic front fascia, unique biplane rear wings, and a sleek monochrome paint scheme devoid of graphics. It rode on big 16x7 alloy wheels with 225/50VR-16 European Goodyear NCT tires. And under the hood, with its single offset duct, was a four-cylinder engine. Four cylinders? But this was no ordinary econo wheezer: the 140-cubic-inch (2.3-liter) four packed an AiResearch T3 turbocharger, electronic fuel injection, and an air-to-air intercooler under that hood scoop. With an electronically controlled 14 psi of boost on hand, the SVO four generated 176 horsepower at 4,400 rpm. Coupled with a quick-shifting five-speed manual, upgraded suspension, four-wheel disc brakes, and driver-focused interior, the SVO delivered shockingly good performance—without a V-8.

Ford's president, Donald Petersen, called the SVO "our most definitive effort on the American scene to put together the finest we have in the way of a smaller-displacement, higher-revving, turbocharged kind of touring car." In *Motor Trend*, Kevin Smith commented:

> The SVO's combination of advanced technology, spirited performance, distinctive appearance, and realistic price will surely intercept a few folks on their way to Supras and ZXs, and maybe pick off the odd Audi shopper. An American GT could do worse these days.

Over at *Hot Rod*, that bastion of traditional American performance, they called the SVO "the finest handling, most balanced Mustang ever sold, in our opinion." With a heritage of cars like the Shelby GT350 and Boss 302 in its past, that was a bold statement. The '84 SVO Mustang cost around $16,000, six grand more than the GT, but 4,506 buyers felt it was worth the extra money.

The SVO returned in mid-1985, now with 205 horsepower, aero headlights, Hurst-shifted five-speed, greater refinement, and a price $1,400 less than the '84. *Motor Trend* pitted the 1985½ SVO against the V-8-powered Camaro IROC-Z and found that "both cars lapped the racetrack at nearly identical speeds despite their wildly divergent personalities." After driving both cars, they found the IROC-Z's V-8 felt "dated" and concluded, "We like the '85½ Mustang SVO. We are mainly seduced by its high-revving, big-hearted little motor and its precise, tight-coupled controls." Just 1,951 of the midyear SVOs were sold, with another 3,378 of the nearly identical '86 models ordered. That, sadly was the end of the Mustang SVO.

SVT Cobra 1993

After the Mustang SVO, the team continued as the aftermarket performance parts group of Ford. Then, in 1991, SVO morphed into SVT—the Special Vehicle Team founded by Neil Ressler, vice president of Research & Vehicle Technology and chief technical officer, and Robert L. Rewey, group vice president for Marketing and Sales, Ford Automotive Operations. As Ford described it:

> The idea was to assemble talented driving enthusiasts at Ford and some of its key suppliers into a small, cross-functional group of engineers, product planners, and marketing professionals with a common mission: create vehicles to satisfy the unique desires of the knowledgeable driving enthusiast.

At the 1992 Chicago Auto Show, SVT introduced the first of their offerings: the 1993 SVT Cobra. The '93 Mustang would be the last year of the third-generation pony, which had lasted fourteen years, and SVO made sure the last was the best. At its heart, the SVT

Ford SVO Mustang 1984–1986

- **# PRODUCED:** 9,844
- **ENGINE:** 140-cubic-inch I-4 Turbo
- **HORSEPOWER:** 176 (1984); 205 (1985–86)
- **TORQUE:** 210 lb-ft (1984); 248 lb-ft (1985–86)
- **¼-MILE TIME:** 15.50 at 90 mph (1984)

Ford SVT Cobra 1993

- **# PRODUCED:** 4,993
- **ENGINE:** 302-cubic-inch V-8
- **HORSEPOWER:** 235
- **TORQUE:** 280 lb-ft
- **¼-MILE TIME:** 14.50 at 98.0 mph

The 1993 SVT Cobra pushed the 5.0 V-8 as far as it could go: GT40 heads, GT40 upper and lower intake, Crane cast aluminum 1.7 roller rockers, 24-pound injectors, a 70mm MAF, and a 65mm throttle body. That resulted in 30 more horsepower than the Mustang GT's 205 horsepower, and 5 more lb-ft of torque, giving 0–60 miles per hour times of 5.7 seconds. *Ford Archives*

Cobra took the famous 5.0 V-8 to its zenith: GT40 heads, GT40 upper and lower intake, Crane cast-aluminum 1.7 roller rockers, 24-lb injectors, a 70mm MAF, and a 65mm throttle body. That resulted in 30 more horses than the Mustang GT's 205 horsepower, and 5 more lb-ft of torque, giving 0–60 miles per hour times of 5.7 seconds.

The rest of the SVT Cobra was equally attractive, with unique body moldings and rear bumper, and a special grille with the return of the "running horse" emblem. In back was a unique spoiler and SVO-style taillights. The big 17x7.5 seven-spoke alloy wheels were specific to the Cobra, due to the special offset needed for the four-wheel disc brakes (the SVO was the only other "Fox" Mustang to have rear discs). The suspension was upgraded with Tokico shocks and struts, and the Cobra rode on Goodyear Gatorback P245/45ZR-17 shoes. Cobras were only available in Black Clearcoat, Vibrant Red, and a color unique to Cobras, Teal Metallic.

With a new Mustang on the way for '94, *Motor Trend* commented:

> A glimmer of hope for Ford fanciers is this year's vitamin-fortified Mustang Cobra. By raiding Ford's voluminous storehouse of parts, tossing away some old-car chaff, and shoveling in more horsepower, the familiar old steed has been given a new lease on life.

In a cage match against Chevy's all-new, Corvette-powered Z28 Camaro, the aging "Fox" had its hands full:

> The Z28 wins in acceleration, top speed, braking, and handling. The Cobra scores highest in passenger comfort and utility, and has improved its grip with the new 17-inch tires.... With a base price of $17,195 and an as-tested tally of $19,812, a loaded Z28 about equals what it'll cost to get into a base Mustang Cobra ($19,550). Keep in mind, though, the Cobra includes air conditioning and power equipment as standard. Benefits for Camaro buyers include dual airbags, the six-speed, standard ABS, and the fabulous LT1 engine.

Still, 4,993 buyers ponied up for the last, and best, of the "Fox" Mustangs.

Ford also built 107 SVT Cobra-R Mustangs that year. Weight is the enemy for any track-focused vehicle, and SVT removed the rear seat, radio, air conditioning, and sound-dampening material. Heavy-duty MacPherson struts, Koni shocks all around, and a front-strut tower brace aided handling. Larger brakes and unique three-spoke wheels completed the Cobra-R. Intended for serious racers only, and available only in Vibrant Red, the '93 Cobra-R became an instant collectible.

SVT Lightning 1993–1995

Imagine the unholy union of a SVT Cobra with an F-150. Ford dropped a bombshell like that on the 1992 Chicago Auto Show: the SVT F-150 Lightning. With its 1990–93 Chevrolet 454SS and '91 GMC Syclone sport trucks, General Motors served notice that pickups were not just for hauling stuff anymore. For 1993, SVT joined the party with the Lightning.

The Lightning packed a 351-cubic-inch (5.8-liter) Windsor V-8 with GT40 heads and manifolds and free-flowing exhaust, churning 240 horsepower through an E40D four-speed automatic and tall 4.10:1 rear axle geared for acceleration. The truck was lowered 1 inch in front, 2.5 inches in the rear, with beefy springs, Monroe Formula GP shocks, and big 1-inch stabilizer bars, riding on 7-inch

ABOVE: The SVT group created Ford's first performance truck, the 1994 Lightning. *Automotive History Preservation Society*

LEFT: Ford's literature for the 1994 SVT Lightning emphasized practicality as well as performance. It was one of those rare vehicles that could truly "haul" in more ways than one.

cast-aluminum five-spoke wheels, and Firestone Firehawk GTA P275/60HT-70 tires. A unique front air dam with foglights, and Lightning graphics all around, finished the package.

Motor Week called the Lightning a "Mustang GT with a cargo bed." They saw 0–60 in 7.2 seconds and 15.8 seconds at 86 miles per hour on the 'strip, and also claimed that "Lightning handles nearly as well as the Mustang GT, with excellent cornering grip and an amazing lack of body roll." Yet the hunkered-down Lightning could still haul 700 pounds in the bed and pull a 5,000-pound. trailer, something the high-tech GMC Syclone couldn't do. Available only in Performance Red or Black, Ford sold 5,276 Lightning trucks in 1993.

White became another optional color in 1994, and Ford sold 4,007 more that year, plus an additional 2,280 in its last year, 1995. As *Motor Week* concluded, "The Lightning certainly is a bolt of charged air for sport trucks, and it strikes us just right."

CHAPTER 12

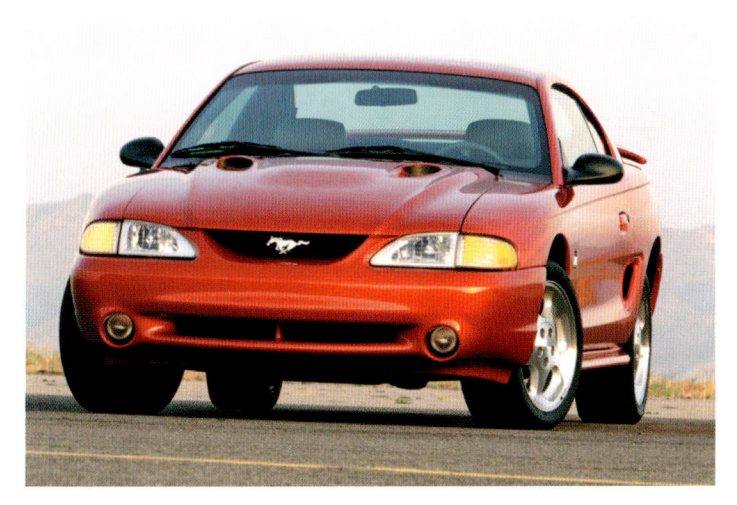

TOP: Stylists proposed three different versions of the SN-95 Mustang, including the most aggressive design, called "Rambo." *Ford Archives*

ABOVE, LEFT: Ford's all-new overhead-cam 4.6-liter (281-cubic-inch) "Modular" V-8 became the heart of the Mustang. Lesser Mustangs got the single-overhead-cam engine, but the SVT Cobra packed the new double-overhead-cam (DOHC) four-valve powerplant. Despite the small displacement, the Cobra produced 305 horsepower at 5,800 rpm, with 300 lb-ft of torque a 4,800 rpm, a huge improvement over the '95's 240 horsepower and 5 more than the '95 Cobra-R. *Ford Archives*

ABOVE RIGHT: Just a few years before, photographing a current Mustang with a '65 Shelby GT350R would have seem like heresy, but the 1995 SVT Cobra-R could actually perform at the legendary Shelby's level. Like the rare 1965 Shelby GT 350R, the 300-horsepower Cobra R was a track-only vehicle, with a 351-cubic-inch engine based on the F150 Lightning pickup's powerplant. The $30,000 Cobra R could turn .89 g on the skidpad while delivering 0–60 miles per hour in 5.4 seconds, and a 14.0 seconds at 99 miles per hour time slip. Just 250 were built. *Archives/TEN: The Enthusiast Network Magazines, LLC*

SVT Cobra 1994–1998

Ford celebrated the Mustang's 30th anniversary with the long-awaited replacement for the fifteen-year-old third-generation car. Codenamed SN-95, the newest Mustang was still based on a heavily updated "Fox" platform, and 80 percent was new. Design director Patrick Schiavone brought back some design elements from the original Mustang, with details like the side C-scallop, open grille with galloping pony emblem, tri-bar taillights, and a dual-cockpit interior. Stylists developed three possible themes for the new Mustang: athletic "Bruce Jenner," muscular "Arnold Schwarzenegger," and hyper-aggressive "Rambo." The final design contained mostly the "Bruce Jenner" theme, and, though modern, it still had that Mustang "reach."

The '94 Mustang was *Motor Trend*'s Car of the Year, and it won accolades around the world. Ford didn't forget the performance-minded buyer, and SVT brought back the Cobra. "The essential ingredients for a memorable driving experience are an engine that breathes deeply during a rush to the redline and a chassis that balances poise with predictability," stated the SVT Cobra's brochure. The drivetrain remained mostly carried over from the '93 Cobra,

Ford SVT Cobra 1994-1995

 # PRODUCED: 11,017

ENGINE: 302-cubic-inch V-8

HORSEPOWER: 240

TORQUE: 285 lb-ft

¼-MILE TIME: 14.70 at 97.4 mph

Ford SVT Cobra 1996-1998

 # PRODUCED: 28,760

ENGINE: 281-cubic-inch V-8

HORSEPOWER: 305

TORQUE: 300 lb-ft

¼-MILE TIME: 14.20 at 100.0 mph

The long-awaited engine upgrade came in '96. Conventional wisdom would suggest a modern update to the pushrod Windsor or Cleveland engines from the 1960s. Instead, Ford's all-new overhead-cam 4.6-liter (281-cubic-inch) "Modular" V-8 became the heart of the Mustang. Lesser Mustangs got the single-overhead-cam engine, but the SVT Cobra packed the new double-overhead-cam (DOHC) four-valve powerplant. Despite the small displacement, the Cobra produced 305 horsepower at 5,800 rpm, with 300 lb-ft of torque a 4,800 rpm, a huge improvement over the '95's 240 horsepower and 5 more than the '95 Cobra-R. It also just happened to be the same output as the Cobra's competition, the Firebird WS6 and Camaro SS. Cobra engines were hand-built at Ford's Romeo, Michigan, plant on the "Niche-Line" by two craftsmen, who signed the plaque located in the left valve cover.

How did the new engine perform? "Running through the five nicely spaced ratios of the new Cobra's excellent BorgWarner T50 transmission, it's the uncanny smoothness of this drivetrain that separates it from any previous pony car's," discovered *Motor Trend*.

> Though it will propel the 3,565-pound, $27,580 Cobra to 60 mph in just 5.6 seconds and cleave its path through the quarter mile in only 13.9 seconds with a 102.1 mph terminal velocity, it does the task with remarkable gentleness.

No wonder Ford sold 10,002 SVT Cobras in 1996, another 10,049 in 1997, and 8,654 in 1998—outselling the Firebird WS6 and Camaro SS combined.

SVT Lightning 1999–2004

As good at the first SVT Lightning was, it just never looked fast. The bricklike F-150 was replaced in 1997 with a new-generation F-150 pickup. The styling was more rounded and carlike, and, underneath, Ford's aged Twin I-Beam front suspension was finally replaced with conventional independent suspension. Ford also replaced the low-tech OHV V-8s with the cutting-edge Modular engines. This formed the basis of the next Lightning, introduced in 1999.

The SVT team started with the shortest, lightest F-150 available, the regular-cab Flairside, giving the Lightning a more sensual, yet aggressive look. They hunkered-down the suspension, giving the truck the four-wheel disc brakes from the big F-250, and 18x9.5 five-spoke alloy wheels and unidirectional Goodyear Eagle 295/45ZR-18 F1-GS tires at the corners.

The Lightning would have been just another show truck if it wasn't for the supercharged SOHC 5.4L Triton V-8 under the hood. An Eaton Generation IV blower pumped 8 psi through a water-to-air intercooler into the engine, producing 360 horsepower and 440 lb-ft of torque. That moved the 4,600-pound. Lightning to 6.2-second 0–60 times. But with the speed and handling that the Lighting featured, it was also practical. "It will launch with aggressive assurance at a drag strip," the Lightning brochure bragged, "then turn around and carry an 800-pound payload, tow a 5,000-pound trailer, and ride with remarkable aplomb."

but it was wrapped in the shell that added a little "Schwarzenegger" to the new car. Just three colors were offered: Rio Red, Crystal White, and Black Clearcoat. All Cobras now received four-wheel disc brakes and ran on beautiful 17x8 wheels and Goodyear Eagle GS-C, P255/45ZR-17 skins.

For the first time, the SVT Cobra was also available as a convertible, and the ragtop was selected to pace the 70th running of the Indianapolis 500. All convertibles were called "Indy 500 Pace Car Replicas," and included a rear deck lid badge, serialized dash plaque, and Official Indy 500 Pace Car graphics.

In their April 1994 issue, *Motor Trend* called the Cobra the "Wildest pony in the corral." Compared to the '93 Cobra, the newest Mustang weighed 110 lbs. more, and it showed: 0–60 in 6.2 seconds for the '93, 6.1 for the '94. In the quarter mile, the '93 ran 14.4 at 97.4 miles per hour, the '94 in 14.8 at 95.4 miles per hour. As *MT* noted, "The engine of our '94 Cobra produced noticeably more torque, but ran out of steam above 5,500 rpm," while the '93 "came on much stronger as the revs climbed, pulling viciously to its 6,000-rpm redline." It was a lot of Mustang for around $21,000, and Ford sold all of the planed Cobras that year, 5,009 coupes and 1,000 convertibles.

The SVT Cobra was mostly unchanged for 1995, but it gained 5 horsepower. SVT also created 250 Cobra-R variants, powered by a 300-horsepower 351 Windsor. Suspension upgrades included Eibach springs, Koni "Yellow" shocks, and bigger stabilizer bars. BF Goodrich supplied the Comp T/A ZR P255/45ZR-17 tires. Though street legal, the Cobra-R was geared toward the track in every way.

The 1999 SVT Lightning, powered by a supercharged SOHC 5.4-liter Triton V-8, turned 6.2-second 0–60 times. A press release dated August 13, 2002, proclaimed: "Today, the Ford SVT F-150 Lightning was certified as the 'World's Fastest Production Pickup Truck' by Guinness World Records, Ltd. after reaching 147 miles per hour at Ford's test track." *Ford Archives*

You could order the stylish Lightning in any color as long as it was Black Clearcoat, Bright Red Clearcoat, or Oxford White Clearcoat, all with a Medium Graphite cloth interior with leather accents. For 1999, Ford sold 2,000 Lightnings, with Bright Red the dominant color. Silver Metallic was added in 2000, with another 4,966 trucks sold.

Ford gave the Lightning some nice upgrades in 2001, including a new intake manifold that raised output to 380 horsepower. Monotube Bilstein shocks improved handling, while the passenger-side shock was repositioned in front of the axle to reduce axle wrap. That added up to 0–60 in 5.8 seconds!

Lightning received a nice style upgrade, too, with headlamps, corner lamps, fog lamps, and taillamps featuring clear lenses, and an LED third brake lamp. Upper and lower grille inserts also got a new design. No wonder 6,381 Lightnings were built. A new color, True Blue was added in 2002, and 4,726 were sold.

Sonic Blue replaced True Blue in 2003, and Dark Shadow Gray became an option. The real news for 2003, however, was reported in a press release dated August 13, 2002:

Today, the Ford SVT F-150 Lightning was certified as the "World's Fastest Production Pickup Truck" by Guinness World Records, Ltd. after reaching 147 miles per hour at Ford's test track. Since the truck's introduction in 1999, the supercharged SVT Lightning has been unofficially called the world's fastest pickup by numerous media outlets. Now it's a matter of official record. "We're proud to have certification from Guinness World Records," says Tom Scarpello, Ford SVT marketing and sales manager. "It is a well-deserved record for the engineering team, and overdue confirmation to all the SVT F-150 Lightning owners out there who have known for years that they drive the fastest truck on the planet!"

Ford built another 8,051 supertrucks in 2003 and 2004 before production ended. Ford introduced a new F-150 in 2005, but the Lightning was not brought back.

TOP: The updated 1999 SVT Cobra had more of the "Rambo" look. *Ford Archives*

ABOVE, LEFT: Due to the issues of the 1999 SVT Cobra, Ford suspended the Cobra for 2000. But SVT built 300 Cobra-R track racers that year, sporting a 385 horsepower monster under the domed hood. *Ford Archives*

ABOVE, RIGHT: The 2003–2004 SVT Cobra looked Terminator tough with a bit more Rambo style, including redesigned front and rear fascia, new heat-extraction hood, special rocker moldings, and side scoops. It was a fitting farewell for the final iteration of the Fox-family Mustangs. *Ford Archives*

RIGHT: *Car and Driver* reported, "More important to sporty drivers is the feel of the Cobra on twisty pavement. The IRS makes the car feel more supple and thus more readable in corners. The rear end is less susceptible to bump steer than before." *Automotive History Preservation Society*

172　CHAPTER 12

SVT Cobra 1999–2004

Introduced in 1994, the "Fox-4" Mustangs received their usual midlife styling update in 1999. The new design, called "New Edge," had more of the "Schwarzenegger" theme, while the SVT Cobra added a bit of the "Rambo" look. The real "Rambo," however, was under the Cobra's hood. The 4.6-liter DOHC engine got a new tumble-port cylinder-head design that improved combustion efficiency and increased output to 320 horsepower at 6,000 rpm, 15 more than the previous year. SVT also added independent rear suspension to the Cobra in an effort to make the ultra-Mustang more drivable on rough pavement.

As *Car and Driver* reported:

> More important to sporty drivers is the feel of the Cobra on twisty pavement. The IRS makes the car feel more supple and thus more readable in corners. The rear end is less susceptible to bump steer than before, and as the geometry has been set up for a touch of toe-out as the car begins to heel over, then for toe-in (and safe understeer at the rear axle) at full lean, its off-center steering response is better, and its handling is more neutral at the limit. Hence, 0.03 g better skid pad performance at 0.88 g.

One mystery was noted in the *Car and Driver* review:

> We expected to hit 60 mph in about five seconds flat, but 5.5 was the best we could do—0.1 second slower than the previous model. Top speed was also down, from 153 to just 149 mph in the slightly more aerodynamic car.

It wasn't an anomaly. Ford had to investigate these and other complaints and, on August 6, 1999, stopped selling the Cobra. The intake and exhaust systems had to be redeveloped, and Cobras already in owner's hands were recalled and retrofitted. Despite the setback, 4,040 Cobra coupes and 4,055 convertibles were sold.

Due to the issues of the 1999 SVT Cobra, Ford suspended the Cobra for 2000. But SVT built 300 Cobra-R track racers that year, sporting a 385-horsepower monster under the domed hood. To produce that power, Ford used cutting-edge tricks like Carillo connecting rods, forged pistons, higher-flow aluminum cylinder heads, Cobra 5.4-liter intake cams, tubular-steel exhaust headers, low-restriction two-piece intake manifold, a higher-flow single-bore 80mm throttle body, and a K&N air filter. Eibach springs lower the "R" 1.5 inches in front and 1.0 inch at the rear, plus Bilstein shocks and struts, and Brembo brakes. A V-6-style rear bumper covered the 20-gallon fuel cell, and the front bumper featured a removable splitter. Five-spoke 18x9.5 alloy wheels mounted BFGoodrich G-Force KD tires. The drivetrain featured a Tremec T-56 six-speed and Gerodisc hydromechanical differential with 3.55:1 gears. The ultimate Fox-4 Mustang, the ultra-light, street-legal (barely) 2000 Cobra-R topped out at 175.3 miles per hour and could pull 1.01 g on a skid pad.

The SVT Cobra returned in 2001, much the same as the '99, and now producing a true 320 horsepower at 6,000 rpm. Ford sold 3,867 coupes, 3,384 convertibles. Then, in 2002, Ford suspended Cobra production again, this time to create what SVT engineers named, in a Arnold Schwarzenegger-like twist, the legendary "Terminator."

What made the 2003 SVT Cobra special was its supercharged 4.6-liter DOHC heart. Putting a blower on this engine, and doing it right, was no easy task. John Coletti's SVT crew used a cast-iron block instead of the usual aluminum, which engineers deemed strong enough to contain the blast of an Eaton M112 roots-style supercharger pushing 8 psi. Stout-forged Zolner pistons and Manley H-beam connecting rods were also added. An aluminum flywheel drove a TREMEC T-56 six-speed transmission to a 3.55:1 rear axle. Stronger 31 spline half shafts and revised upper and lower control arms made the independent rear suspension strong enough for the Terminator's 390 horsepower at 6,000 rpm and 390 lb-ft of torque at 3,500 rpm. The 2003 SVT Cobra looked Terminator tough with a bit more Rambo style, including redesigned front and rear fascia, new heat-extraction hood, special rocker moldings, and side scoops. It was a fitting farewell to the final iteration of the Fox-family Mustangs.

Ford GT 2005–2006

One-hundredth anniversaries are certainly special occasions, and Ford celebrated its 100th year with a truly special automobile, the return of the Ford GT.

Part of Henry Ford II's "Total Performance" philosophy in the 1960s was to conquer motorsports not just in the United States,

---

Ford SVT Cobra 1999-2002

- **# PRODUCED:** 15,746
- **ENGINE:** 281-cubic-inch V-8
- **HORSEPOWER:** 320
- **TORQUE:** 317 lb-ft
- **¼-MILE TIME:** 14.10 at 101 mph

Ford SVT Cobra 2003-2004

- **# PRODUCED:** 19,140
- **ENGINE:** 281-cubic-inch V-8
- **HORSEPOWER:** 390
- **TORQUE:** 390 lb-ft
- **¼-MILE TIME:** 12.90 at 111 mph

Ford Returns to Le Mans

At the North American International Auto Show in 2015, Ford surprised the automotive world by unveiling a new Ford GT. "The GT is the ultimate execution of an enthusiast supercar," said Raj Nair, Ford group vice president, Global Product Development.

GT includes innovations and technologies that can be applied broadly across Ford's future product portfolio—another proof point that Ford continues raising the performance bar while ultimately improving vehicles for all of our customers.

Ford said the structure would be "aluminum front and rear subframes encapsulated in structural carbon fiber body panels" and, instead of brute force, it would be powered by "the next-generation twin-turbocharged 3.5-liter EcoBoost V-6" that features "a wide powerband with impressive time-to-torque characteristics."

"It's great to see that Ford has the ability to follow up with a vehicle that has been a pillar of their racing history," said Camilo Pardo, designer of the 2005–2006 Ford GT.

The new Ford GT has taken the vehicle's DNA and evolved from the 1966, to the 2005, and now into something very advanced. There's definitely an evolution of all the

TOP: The new Ford GT pays homage to the past while looking to the future. It is a technological wonder, inside and out. *Ford Archives*

ABOVE: "It's great to see that Ford has the ability to follow up with a vehicle that has been a pillar of their racing history," Camilo Pardo said, designer of the 2005—2006 Ford GT. "The new Ford GT has taken the vehicle's DNA and evolved from the 1966, to the 2005, and now into something very advanced. There's definitely an evolution of all the ingredients that make up a GT40/Ford GT integrated into a very complex, aerodynamically influenced configuration. It's very apparent that this design is geared towards racing development." *Ford Archives*

ingredients that make up a GT40/Ford GT integrated into a very complex, aerodynamically-influenced configuration. It's very apparent that this design is geared towards racing development. Although we hear that it's a street vehicle, it definitely looks like its assembly, engineering and design is out to win races. I would imagine, its target once again would be the same as Henry Ford II's, which is to outperform Ferrari in all categories.

Then, on June 12, 2015, Ford announced:

The Ford GT race car will compete in the 24 Hours of Le Mans—referred to by many as the Grand Prix of Endurance and Efficiency—starting next year. Revealed today at the famous circuit in Le Mans, France, Ford GT will compete in the Le Mans GT Endurance class for professional teams and drivers (LM GTE Pro). The new race car—a further proof point of Ford innovation—is based on the all-new Ford GT supercar unveiled in January. Both the production car and race car will arrive in 2016 to mark the 50th anniversary of Ford GT race cars placing 1-2-3 at the 1966 24 Hours of Le Mans."

"When the GT40 competed at Le Mans in the 1960s, Henry Ford II sought to prove Ford could beat endurance racing's most legendary manufacturers," said Bill Ford, executive chairman, Ford Motor Company. "We are still extremely proud of having won this iconic race four times in a row, and that same spirit that drove the innovation behind the first Ford GT still drives us today."

TOP: The new race car is based on the all-new Ford GT supercar unveiled in January. Both the production car and race car will arrive in 2016 to mark the 50th anniversary of Ford GT race cars placing 1-2-3 at the 1966 24 Hours of Le Mans. *Ford*

ABOVE: Carroll Shelby ran Ford's Le Mans program in 1966–1967. *Ford Archives*

TOP: The Ford GT revealed in 2003 was not intended for racing, but it would be an ultra-performance street machine that carried the spirit of the Le Mans GT Mark II. "We definitely had a target vehicle in mind when building the GT," said Neil Ressler, head of the project for Ford. "The Ferrari 360 Modena. We think we've got what it takes to beat Ferrari—again."

ABOVE: Designer Camilo Pardo based the Ford GT on the Mark II, but increased the dimensions a few inches all around for a more comfortable driving experience. The 1960s racers suffered from excessive "lift" and Ford's engineers worked hard to increase downforce without changing the basic Mark II look.

Ford GT 2005-2006

 # PRODUCED: 4,038

ENGINE: 330-cubic-inch V-8

HORSEPOWER: 550

TORQUE: 500 lb-ft

¼-MILE TIME: 11.70 at 127.69 mph

but also on the international stage. That included powering Formula 1 champions starting with Lotus in 1967, and winning the "Greatest Spectacle in Racing," the Indianapolis 500, beginning in 1965. Ford also spent millions to win the biggest race outside the United States, the 24 Hours of Le Mans. That culminated in the historic 1-2-3 finish of the Ford GT Mark II over perennial victor Ferrari in 1966 in the first-ever live satellite TV broadcast. Ford was victorious again in 1967 with the advanced GT Mark IV, and when a rule change eliminated the 427 engines Ford used, they prevailed again in 1968 and 1969 with the 305-cubic-inch GT40.

The Ford GT revealed in 2003 was not intended for racing, but it would be an ultra-performance street machine that carried the spirit of the Le Mans GT Mark II. "We definitely had a target vehicle in mind when building the GT," said Neil Ressler, head of the project for Ford. "The Ferrari 360 Modena. We think we've got what it takes to beat Ferrari—again."

Designer Pardo based the Ford GT on the Mark II, but increased the dimensions a few inches all around for a more comfortable driving experience. The 1960s racers suffered from excessive lift, and Ford's engineers worked hard to increase downforce without changing the basic Mark II look. Power for the Ford GT came from a supercharged 5.4-liter Modular engine that was based on the SVT Cobra and Lightning powerplants. Roush helped develop the 550-horsepower engine that was built at the Romeo plant. Ricardo Consulting Engineers supplied the six-speed transaxle.

In just eighteen months, the Ford GT was ready for production as a 2005 model. Mayflower Vehicle Systems in Norwalk, Ohio, did the primary assembly, while Saleen Special Vehicles in Troy, Michigan, painted the cars. Installation of the drivetrain, along with interior finishing, was completed at Ford's Wixom, Michigan, plant.

The great Dan Gurney, who co-drove the Mark II with A. J. Foyt to victory in 1966, got to drive one of the Ford GT prototypes. "The chassis feels very balanced and predictable out there. It's with you all the way," he told *Motor Trend*. Carroll Shelby, who had fielded the Mark II that Gurney drove in 1966, was a consultant on the Ford GT program.

When the Ford GT hit the showrooms in 2005, the suggested retail price of $139,995. Most buyers opted for the McIntosh sound system, racing stripes, painted brake calipers, and forged alloy wheels for an additional $13,500. For 2006, a Heritage Livery Package, duplicating the blue-and-orange Gulf Racing colors of the victorious 1968–1969 GT40, was added. "Long, low and lithe, the GT's endless collection of timeless, rollercoaster curves look as good now as they did at Le Mans in the 1960s," said *EVO* magazine.

Production ended on September 21, 2006, with 4,038 GTs built, short of the planned 4,500. But sometimes it takes a few years for a vehicle's importance to be felt. A 2006 Heritage GT, with just 6 miles on the odometer, sold for $415,250 in 2013. That's says a lot about the Ford GT's impact.

TOP, LEFT: New for 2006, the limited-edition Ford GT "Heritage" paint livery, one of the most memorable looks in Ford racing history, features a Heritage Blue with Epic Orange—striped exterior and four white "roundels," allowing customers to apply the number of their choice. *Ford Archives*

ABOVE, RIGHT: The first three production Ford GT supercars honored the company's 100th anniversary by looking back on historic vintage Ford GT moments at Le Mans, including a podium sweep in 1966. The cars also showed a path to the future with modern engineering and technology. *Ford Archives*

ABOVE, LEFT: Ford's Special Vehicles Team was charged with "Polishing the Blue Oval."

Ford Shelby GT500 2007–2014

Any time a next-generation Mustang arrives, it's big news. When Ford starts with the proverbial clean sheet of paper, even bigger. That was its generation five, codenamed S197. "When you're designing a new Mustang, you're the steward of 40 years of automotive history," said Chief Designer J. Mays. "If you don't get it right, you've got 8 million Mustang fans to answer to. We wanted to capture the essence of the car. We looked at what made the best Mustangs good and the lesser Mustangs not as good."

TOP: The 2007 Ford Shelby GT 500 saw the reunion of Ford and Carroll Shelby develop into the return of the Shelby Mustang. Shelby was involved in the development of the Ford-built Shelby GT500. "It's one thing to put 450 horsepower in an exotic supercar," he said at the time. "It's another to put that much power in something as affordable as a Mustang." The fact that they not only met their goal but pushed on to 475 horsepower is a remarkable achievement. *Ford Archives*

RIGHT: Two legends, famed race car driver and sports car manufacturer Carroll Shelby (at left) and Edsel Ford II, the father of Ford's modern racing initiatives, share a few words during Ford's 110th year in racing at the Ford display during the 2011 SEMA Show in Las Vegas. *Ford Archives*

LOWER RIGHT: The Ford Shelby GT500 Durability car was personally piloted by Shelby during testing at the historic Sebring International Raceway in 2012. *Ford Archives*

That hard work paid off—there is no mistaking the nature of the '05 model. On the top-of-the-line GT, the four-valve, four-cam Terminator was gone, replaced with an innovative three-valve SOHC 4.6-liter V-8. With less complexity and lower cost, the new engine produced 4.6-liter 3V SOHC V-8 300 horsepower. Not bad, but where was the Cobra?

More than a year passed before this bombshell headline: "Carroll Shelby and Ford Special Vehicle Team join forces to create a modern successor to the famous Shelby GT500 of the late 1960s." Is there a more magical name in American automobile lore than Shelby? The magic was more than just a name. "It's one thing to put 450 horsepower in an exotic supercar," Shelby said at the time. "It's another to put that much power in something as affordable as a Mustang. The fact that they not only met their goal but pushed on to 475 horsepower is a remarkable achievement."

The GT500 clearly was special. The vehicle represented much more than merely licensing the Shelby name. Like the original Shelby Mustangs, Mr. Shelby "spoke with their people in the design center and met with engineers at the track during testing and development," said Gary Patterson, Shelby American's vice president of International and Strategic Sales. "I also know that it was important to Ford that the cars be worthy of the Shelby name."

The bulging hood had heat extractors near the leading edge to pull hot air from the engine compartment while generating downforce. Up front were wide lower fascia openings with a functional air splitter. The upper intake features the famous Cobra logo floating off-center. On either side, slanting headlamp openings add to the dramatic front appearance. A rear spoiler helped reduce aerodynamic lift. Goodyear Eagle F1 Supercar tires-255/45WR-18 in front, 285/40WR-18 in back, mounted to 9.5-inch-wide, cast-aluminum wheels inspired by the Ford GT's optional forged rims, keep it all under control. You can see the four-piston Brembo calipers and 14-inch rotors through the front wheel spokes. And when the Shelby GT500 hit the showrooms, horsepower was listed at 500—25 more than announced.

"The restrained, performance-oriented SVT design theme has become instantly recognizable to enthusiasts without brash styling cues," said Doug Gaffka, design director, Ford SVT vehicles. "The GT500 takes a huge leap forward by combining the modern Mustang muscle car with the classic Shelby performance look."

"The classic tunes still rock when Carroll Shelby grooves the melody and Ford's SVT garage band hammers out the rhythm," wrote *Automobile*.

> The group's latest riff is a pair of Ford Shelby GT500s—one coupe, one convertible—capable of rattling root beer mugs on cruise night and spanking Chevrolet Corvettes on the drag strip. They're classic muscle cars from the 8-track era tuned up for another go: bragging rights to 500 horsepower, room for double-dating, and the security blanket of a full factory warranty. Crank up the big V-8, click the faithful Tremec six-speed into first—and one touch of the gas is all it takes to rock you back to 1968, when a Shelby GT500KR ("King

Ford Shelby GT500 2007-2010

PRODUCED: 21,214
ENGINE: 330-cubic-inch V-8
HORSEPOWER: 500
TORQUE: 317 lb-ft
¼-MILE TIME: 12.90 at 112 mph

of the Road") Mustang cost $4,473. Back then, the 7.0-liter Cobra Jet V-8 delivered a bazookalike torque hit without waiting for the tach needle to climb the dial. Today, an even more forceful smack is provided by a medium-size V-8 pressurized to 9.0 psi by the belt-driven blower.

The original muscle cars were one-trick ponies that ran out of options at the end of the quarter mile. This new one goes fast, stops well, corners hard enough to scare dates, and should be comfortable to live with on a daily basis. But best of all, the Ford Shelby GT500 makes Chevy and Dodge fans purple with envy.

Mustangs received their midmodel styling update in 2011, and Shelby's got an even bigger kick out of the supercharged 5.4-liter—550-horsepower at 6,000 rpm and 510 lb-ft of torque at 4,500 rpm. By 2014, the last year of the fifth-generation Mustang, the Shelby GT500 was motivated by the most powerful engine in America, a blown 5.8-liter generating 662 horsepower that was still handcrafted on the Romeo Niche-Line! GT500s also got SVT-designed Bilstein electronic dampers that allowed push-button adjustments, part of the optional Performance Package. At $54,800, the last GT500 provided more spank for those expensive Corvettes.

Ford F-150 SVT Raptor 2010–Today

How do you define "high performance"? Is it 0–60 and quarter-mile times? Is it slalom speeds and skid pad g-forces? Or is it the ability to traverse open desert at over 100 miles per hour?

The 2010 Ford SVT Raptor forever changed the conventions of performance. Other trucks may have looked the part, but the Raptor is the only factory high-speed, off-road truck—ever.

"We started doing another third-generation Lightning," Chief Engineer Jamal Hameedi told *Autoweek*.

> And we were really struggling, actually, to match the performance of the second-generation Lightning. We thought, "Why don't we try something different? Why don't we try to really amplify a truck's DNA versus putting kind of a sports car halo around a pickup truck?" That's when we started going down the super off-road avenue.

ABOVE: The 2010 Ford SVT Raptor forever changed the conventions of performance. Other trucks may have looked the part, but the Raptor is the only factory high-speed off-road truck ever. *Ford Archives*

LEFT: The 2014 F-150 SVT Raptor Special Edition, which adds unique new touches to the high-performing off-road pickup truck, including a unique new exterior color, Ruby Red Metallic, upgraded interior and custom exterior graphics. *Ford Archives*

LOWER LEFT: The 2011 Ford F-150 SVT Raptor added a SuperCrew option that outsold the two-door model by 30,000 units. *Motor Trend* found "the Raptor is very comfortable and stable in normal driving while offering woeful handling at the limit. It feels immense and powerful behind the wheel, and traffic seems less like something you're participating in than it does an annoyance scurrying at your feet." *Ford Archives*

180　**CHAPTER 12**

What resulted certainly looked the part. "What we wanted to do when we were developing this vehicle," Senior Exterior Designer Bruce Williams said, "we wanted to emphasize the width of the vehicle, as far as the forms of the vehicle go, really kind of soft and racy, harkening the whole idea of a pre-runner, the whole Baja feel of a vehicle." Williams and his team removed any traces of chrome, because "the suspension is the real jewelry of the vehicle, that's what we're showing off," he said.

The suspension featured an impressive 12.1 inches of travel, and sat 2.2 inches taller and 6.6 inches wider than a standard F-150. It rode on 35-inches tall LT315/70R17 tires and four-wheel disc brakes. Keeping it all under control are dual Fox Racing Shox with remote reservoir and internal fluid bypass on either side of the rear axle, and similar single Fox Shox up front. Powered by either the standard 5.4-liter V-8 (standard in 2010 only) or the 6.2-liter Boss V-8 (optional in 2010, standard beginning in 2011), the Raptor moved at speeds that would humble a 1980s muscle car, thanks to the 6.2's 411 horsepower at 5,500 rpm.

Off-road, Raptor's speed was electronically regulated to 100 miles per hour, but even that number is insane. Yet this is not some backyard tuner's project. In order to sell through dealers with a full warranty, Ford engineers had to make sure Raptor could deliver these speeds without breaking. That required regular testing on Ford's desert test area, with, said Ford, "a wide range of surfaces including fast sandy washes, deep-rutted silt beds, steep climbs in deep sand, and slow meticulous crawls through tight trenches."

For *Petersen's 4-Wheel and Off-Road* magazine, selecting the 2010 "4X4 of the Year" was easy:

> The Ford 150 Raptor doesn't even break a sweat as it muscles through tough, rocky, and pitted terrain—the kind that would tear up the body and shocks of any ordinary pickup. Accomplishing a smooth ride off-road is no easy feat for some, but the enthusiasm and pride that exudes through from Ford's multitalented engineers comes across in the quality of their craftsmanship that will fill you with pride as you drive down the road . . . or path. Displaying the type of truck they would design for themselves, the engineers definitely had fun designing and building this evolution of the Ford F-150! . . . . This is a truck that will leave you happy, with a feeling of satisfaction as you exit the cabin following any task you need accomplished, or by simply returning from a jaunt around town.

But *Motor Trend* also found that

> The Raptor is very comfortable and stable in normal driving while offering woeful handling at the limit. It feels immense and powerful behind the wheel, and traffic seems less like something you're participating in than it does an annoyance scurrying at your feet.

Well, it wasn't supposed to be another Lightning, was it? It didn't sell like the Lightning, either. In 2010, 10,437 were delivered, far exceeding expectations. Starting in 2011, both two-door (SuperCab) and four-door (CrewCab) versions were offered, and sales continued to climb, with 7,517 SuperCabs and 37,090 CrewCabs sold from 2011 to 2013. Ford has had to increase production of the Raptor just to meet demand for this unique vehicle. An even better Raptor is promised for 2017.

Ford Shelby GT350 2015–Today

The sixth-generation Mustang, S550, appeared in 2015—another clean-sheet design. That alone is big news. "We added a lot of content to the new Mustang in order to hit our performance targets and meet today's customer expectations," said Dave Pericak, Mustang chief engineer. "With a base curb weight of 3,524 pounds for Mustang EcoBoost fastback, and increases ranging from six pounds to 87 pounds for V-6 and GT fastbacks, Mustang is still substantially lighter than the competition."

Then Ford announced a new Shelby: "The GT350 is the most track-ready Mustang ever—a world-class sports car that is the byproduct of a world-class development team. This car being offered was used by that team to make this machine what it is: the next chapter in the legend."

Conventional wisdom would suggest carrying over the 662-horsepower engine from the '14 GT500. Instead, Ford revealed the GT350's engine, codenamed "Voodoo," as a "clean-sheet design unique to the Shelby cars," said Ford.

> The engine is Ford's first use of the race-derived flat-plane crank, and its 8,250 rpm redline is the highest of any Ford in history. At 526 horsepower, its V-8 is the most powerful naturally aspirated engine ever created by Ford. Its extremely wide torque curve puts 90 percent of its peak torque on hand between 3,450 rpm and 7,000 rpm.

Voodoo's 180-degree crankshaft creates a howling firing order that has to be heard.

It may seem like a downgrade compared to the GT500, but the light weight of the sixth-gen Mustang meant that less power was needed to deliver more. Plus, superchargers are heavy, adding up to 300 pounds where it's needed the least—over the front wheels. Less brute force was needed to push the GT350 through turns,

---

Ford Shelby GT350 2015–

 # PRODUCED: 100 (GT350); 37 (GT350R)

ENGINE: 315-cubic-inch V-8

HORSEPOWER: 526

TORQUE: 429 lb-ft

¼-MILE TIME: 12.50 at 117 mph (GT350); 12.20 at 119 mph (GT350R)

The 2013 Ford Shelby GT500 on track at Road Atlanta. The 662 horsepower Shelby GT500 was the world's most powerful production V-8 and was backed up by chassis, aerodynamic and braking performance that made the Shelby GT500 an outstanding all-around sports car. *Ford Archives*

since the latest Shelby features independent rear suspension and superior weight distribution.

The GT350 also worked the air better. "Everything we changed on GT350 is purely functional-driven design, with the goal of improving the overall performance of the car," said Chris Svensson, Ford design director for the Americas. "We optimized the aero shape of the car, and then finetuned what was left to increase downforce and cooling airflow." All bodywork from the windshield forward is unique to this high-performance model and up to 2 inches lower than Mustang GT.

"The outgoing Shelby GT500 was all about violent, face-flattening velocity, teaming 662 supercharged horses with a solid rear axle," wrote *Road & Track*.

> Ford's newest Shelby takes an entirely different approach. Based on the latest "S550" Mustang chassis, it wears a fully independent rear suspension and builds on that with magnetorheological dampers, unique, aero-über-alles bodywork, and a naturally aspirated 5.2-liter V-8 with the long-rumored flat-plane crankshaft. It's a thoroughly modern pony built for racetracks with apexes instead of those with burnout boxes. For the latter, the Dodge Boys have options if you're interested . . . . The Shelby GT350 is set to redefine everything we ever knew about not just the Mustang, but pony cars in general—Z28 be damned.

A few months later, at the North American International Auto Show in January 2015, Ford unveiled the Shelby GT350R. You know what "R" stands for. *Road & Track* then commented:

> The Camaro Z28 has a problem now, because this is the ultimate Mustang. Ever. Period . . . . If you leave all the other weight-reduction measures in place, the 350R tips the scales 130 pounds lighter than the standard GT350 Performance Pack model. In addition, the GT350R gets 19-inch carbon-fiber wheels. That change alone shaves 52 pounds of unsprung weight from the car. Those, incidentally, are wrapped in bespoke-compound Michelin Pilot Sport Cup 2s. The suspension is substantially revised from the standard GT350—lower ride height, and different, track-oriented settings across the board, right through to the MagneRide programming.

Only one hundred GT350 and thirty-seven GT350R models were built in 2015.

Carroll Shelby is no longer with us to witness the latest GT350 revolution, having passed away in 2012, but Gary Patterson, his long-time friend and employee, said:

> Carroll was certainly aware of the new GT350 project and had authorized it to be a Ford program before his passing. It is unfortunate that he could not see what a great car the 2015 GT350 and GT350R turned out to be. I am certain that he is proud.

TOP: The new GT350 builds on Carroll Shelby's original idea—transforming a great everyday car into a dominant road racer—by taking advantage of a dramatically improved sixth-generation Mustang to create a truly special driving experience. "When we started working on this car, we wanted to build the best possible Mustang for the places we most love to drive—challenging back roads with a variety of corners and elevation changes—and the track on weekends," said Raj Nair, Ford group vice president, Global Product Development. *Ford Archives*

ABOVE, LEFT: SVT and Shelby Mustang engines were produced at Ford's Romeo, Michigan, plant by two craftsmen. Like artists, they sign the plaque on the valve cover of each engine they build. *Ford Archives*

ABOVE, RIGHT: 2015 Mustang in production at the Flat Rock, Michigan, plant. *Ford Archives*

RIGHT: August 20, 2015—employees at Ford's Flat Rock, Michigan plant cheer the first production Shelby GT350R off the line. *Ford Archives*

SVO/SVT: UNCONVENTIONAL WISDOM

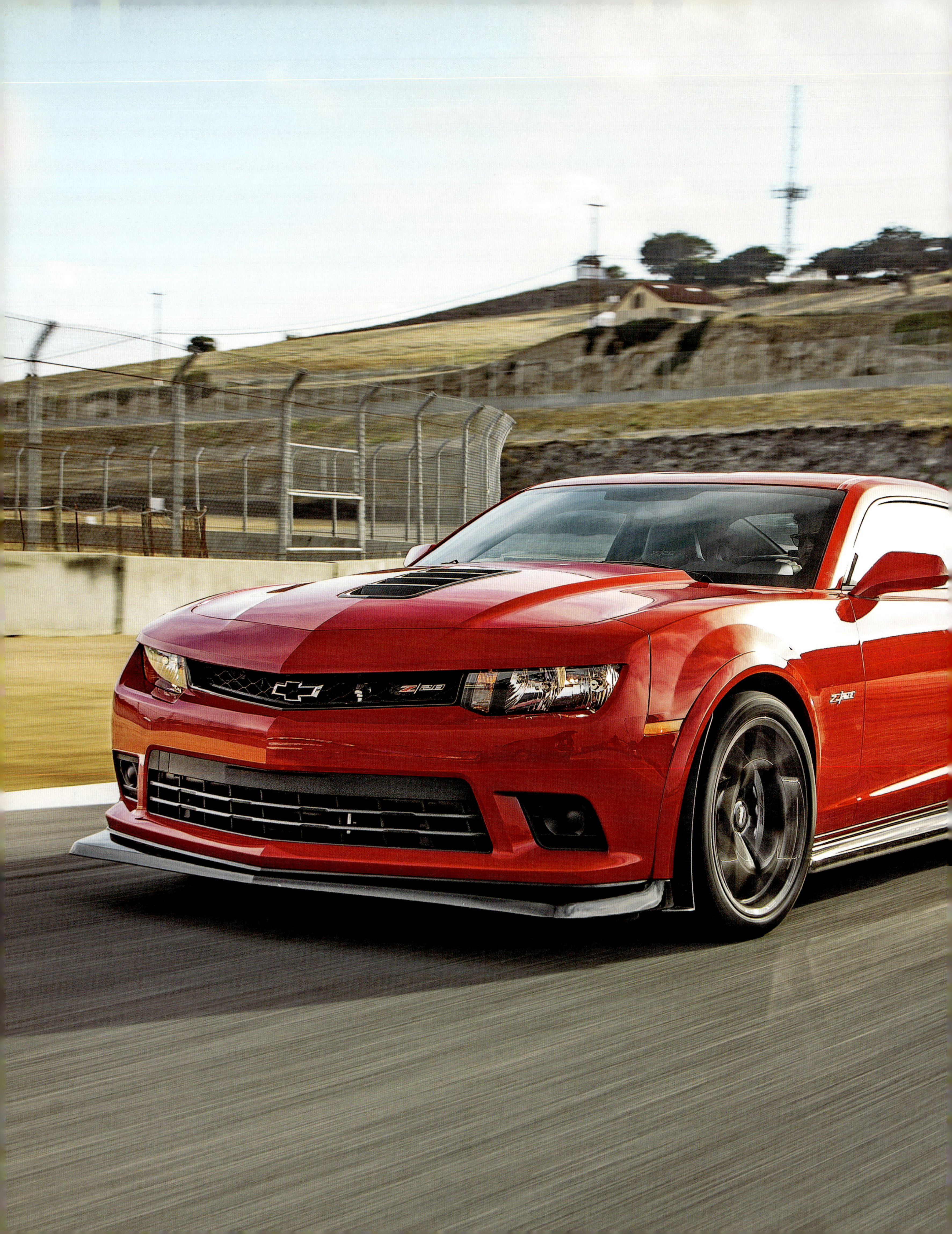

Chapter 13

Chevrolet

Conquering the Green Hell

Chevrolet may be as American as baseball and apple pie, but no manufacturer offers as worldwide an outlook as General Motors. GM has engineering offices in Europe, Australia, and South Korea, along with the famed GM Tech Center in Warren, Michigan. And, since 1997, no American manufacturer has developed their supercars at the famed Nürburgring in Germany as much as Chevrolet.

The 12.9-mile Nürburgring Nordschleife (North Course) undulates around Germany's Eifel Forest with a mix of long straightaways, tight turns, suspension-pounding *Flugplatz* ("flying place") jumps, and 1,000 feet of elevation changes. It's the longest permanent racetrack in the world; with seventy-three turns, it's the most demanding of both car and driver. Deemed decades ago to be too dangerous for Formula 1, F1 champion Jackie Stewart called the track the "Green Hell." Every aspect of automotive engineering—horsepower, braking, suspension, aerodynamics, and endurance—are tested to the extreme there.

All manufacturers have their own highly secretive test tracks, but the beauty of the Nürburgring is that it's a public place, and all manufacturers of high-performance automobiles use the demanding course to some degree, so you have a very public baseline of what other vehicles have

Back in the Sixties the Z/28 Camaro was designed to win Trans Am series championships, which it did—twice in three years. The Trans Am series is long gone, but the modern track-focused Z/28 still delivers world-class performance: it's 2014 lap of 7:37:47 at the Nürburgring placed it 39th among the "street legal" cars at the time. *Archives/TEN: The Enthusiast Network Magazines, LLC*

done—and great bragging rights and marketing fodder for those that do well. As *Popular Science* said, "Beating the 'ring, and making a YouTube video to prove it, is about the best marketing move a sports car company can make, even one that plans to roll only a double-digits' worth of cars out of its production facility."

C5 Corvette Z06 2001–2004

It should come as no surprise that Chevrolet's first attempt on the Nürburgring was 1997, the year the company launched its the fifth-generation Corvette. That car was a total transformation, including the engine, from the previous model. Development of the C5 took place around the world, from the extreme winter cold of northern Canada to the blazing heat of the Australian outback, and everyone agreed it was the most refined Corvette yet.

To see how the C5 performed on the world stage, David Hill, Corvette chief engineer, and his assistant, Tadge Juechter, took the new car to the Nürburgring. Utilizing a standing start (today's runs always begin after a "hot" warmup lap), the C5 toured the Nordschleife in 8:40:00. At the time, it was quite an acceptable performance for a mass-production vehicle, though today it barely puts it into the top 300 lap times. Four years later, Chevrolet rolled out a new high-performance Corvette, the Z06.

Chevrolet doesn't have a performance brand like Ford's SVT and Chrysler's SRT. What Chevy *does* have is racing in its DNA, going back to founder Louis Chevrolet competing in the 1905–1910 Vanderbilt Cup road races on Long Island. Chevy also has over six decades of experience building Corvettes, and Corvette's racing program since 1999, in partnership with Pratt and Miller, has been

The 1963 Corvette Z06 was built for sports car racing, with heavy-duty suspension and brakes, and fuel-injected 360-horsepower 327 V-8. *Chevrolet*

incredibly successful in addition to featuring technology developed by Corvette Racing and applied to street machines. The 2001 Z06 Corvette was a prime example.

"We've enhanced the Corvette's performance persona and broken new ground with the Z06," said David Hill at its launch. "With 0–60 times of four seconds flat and more than 1 g of cornering acceleration, the Z06 truly takes performance to the next level." Like supercar level.

Chevrolet began with the C5 Hardtop, a Corvette introduced in 1999. Stiffer, stronger, and about 100 pounds lighter than the coupe, the hardtop was conceived to be a lower cost entry-level

ABOVE, LEFT: The 2000 Corvette Z06 took its name from the 1963 Corvette option that turned the Sting Ray coupe into an SCCA Production—class racer, powered by the then state-of-the-art fuel-injected 327 V-8. The engine's moniker was also a nod to history, since the LS6 was the last great big-block Chevy engine, packing 454 cubic inches. *Chevrolet*

186 CHAPTER 13

ABOVE: The 2001 Z06 was stealthy, with the rear brake ductwork and unique wheels the only obvious tip-off—perfect for those surprise shock-and-awe attacks. *Chevrolet*

RIGHT: Commemorative Edition Corvettes in 2004 had chrome emblems front and rear reading "Commemorative 24:00 Heures Du Mans 2 GTS Wins." *Tom & Kelly Glatch*

Corvette with smaller wheels and tires and a cloth interior. That never happened, and the Hardtop came with the same equipment as the other Corvette models. But the Hardtop's strengths made it the obvious choice to take to Hill's "next level."

Most obvious was a boost in horsepower, from 350 horsepower in the stock LS1 engine to 385 in the Z06's new LS6 version. Torque also improved 10 lb-ft over the LS1. Redline jumped from 6,000 rpm to 6,500; one year later, horsepower leaped to 405. To get this power to the ground, the Z06 was an inch wider, with 17x9.5 alloy wheels in front, 18x10.5 out back, all wrapped in sticky Goodyear Eagle F1 SC tires. The Z06 got the exclusive FE4 suspension package, with stiffer, stronger everything. More powerful disc brakes plus front and rear cooling ducts quickly slowed things down when needed. It was available in just five colors: Speedway White, Quicksilver Metallic, Torch Red, Millennium Yellow, and Black. The Z06 was stealthy, with the rear brake ductwork and unique wheels offering the only obvious tip-off—perfect for those surprise shock-and-awe attacks.

The Z06 took its name from the 1963 Corvette option that turned the Sting Ray coupe into an SCCA Production—class racer, powered by the then-state-of-the-art fuel-injected 327 V-8. The engine's moniker was also a nod to history, since the LS6 was the last great big-block Chevy engine, packing 454 cubic inches. That's a lot of performance heritage to stuff into one car. "Nürburgring, at the extreme edge of the envelope, provides conditions that can't be easily duplicated anywhere else," said Hill, so they went back in 2002. How did the Z06 fare? It blasted over a minute off the standard C5's time, down to 7:56.00!

For the last year of C5 production, Chevrolet introduced a special Z06. "The great racing success of the C5-R is more than just symbolic, it's a real testament to the world-class technology and performance of the Corvette," Hill said. "We've created the 2004 Commemorative Edition to share our racing achievements with Corvette enthusiasts, while bringing real performance and technology upgrades to the Z06."

Those racing successes included attaining 1st and 2nd in class at the 24 Hours of Le Mans in 2001, 2002, and 2004, and 1st and 2nd overall at the 2002 24 Hours of Daytona. That's overall, not in class, meaning that Corvette Racing defeated not only their GTS-class competition, but the faster Prototype-class vehicles.

RPO 1SC wrapped the 2004 Corvette in LeMans Blue paint, and special commemorative wheel centers, and chrome emblems front and rear, reading, "Commemorative 24:00 Heures Du Mans 2 GTS Wins." This beautiful package was available on 2004 Corvette coupes and convertibles, as well as the Z06—but only the Z06 received a unique carbon-fiber hood. Similar to the piece used on the racing C5-R, the carbon-fiber hood represented a collaboration between Chevrolet, MacLean Systems, and Toray Composites; it weighed 20.5 pounds, removing 10.5 pounds from the front of the Z06. It was the largest painted, carbon-fiber component used on a production vehicle in North America at the time, but this hood also displayed true carbon-fiber craftsmanship, with the fibers arranged

CHEVROLET: CONQUERING THE GREEN HELL 187

TOP: The racing stripes of the C5-R distinguish it from its brethren. *Tom & Kelly Glatch*

ABOVE: Similar to the piece used on the racing C5-R, the carbon-fiber hood was a collaboration between Chevrolet, MacLean Systems, and Toray Composites, and weighed 20.5 pounds, removing 10.5 pounds from the front of the Z06. It was the largest painted carbon-fiber component used on a production vehicle in North America at that time, but this hood also displayed true carbon-fiber craftsmanship, with the fibers arranged in a single direction. *Tom & Kelly Glatch*

Chevrolet Corvette Z06 2001-2004

 # PRODUCED: 28,388

ENGINE: 346-cubic-inch V-8

HORSEPOWER: 385 (2001); 405 (2002–04)

TORQUE: 385 lb-ft (2001); 400 lb-ft (2002–04)

¼-MILE TIME: 12.40 at 116 mph

in a single direction. The Commemorative Z06 had a unique red-and-silver stripe, which matched the victorious 2001 Le Mans racer, and which let the beautiful carbon-fiber weave of the hood show through.

Regular 1SC Corvettes got a Shale interior, which was black on the Z06. All had crossed-flags embroidery on the headrests. The Z06 also got polished alloy wheels. Yet the beauty was more than skin deep, with all 2004 Z06 Corvettes receiving refined shock absorber valving, stiffer upper control arm bushings, and softer rear anti-roll bar bushings. Small details, but the lessons learned on the Nordschleife often result in small refinements—refinements that made the 2004 Commemorative Edition Z06 a fitting farewell to the fifth-generation Corvette.

C6 Corvette Z06 2006–2013

Like great artists, automotive engineers are never satisfied with their work, and the quest for advances in technology and materials improvement never end. As good as the fifth-generation Corvette was, a better one was already being developed, just three years after the C5's launch.

The C6 debuted at the North American International Auto Show in Detroit in January 2004. "The C6 represents a comprehensive upgrade to the Corvette," said Hill at the introduction. "Our goal is to create a Corvette that does more things well than any performance car."

Though it started with the same basic hydroformed structure as the C5, the new Corvette looked like it spent a lot of time in the gym, with a tighter, more muscular appearance. The drivetrain and LS-series engine also received a boost. Chevrolet estimated 70 percent of the C6's components were new, though industry experts thought the figure was closer to 30 percent. Nonetheless, this was a significant upgrade, as Hill explained:

> The C6 is more competition-influenced—given our championship experience with Corvette Racing—than any previous Corvette. Our

goal was a performance car at home in virtually any environment. That means more than just raw performance. It calls for improved ride comfort, a precisely built and technically sophisticated interior, and a sleek new body that is fresh and contemporary, while still instantly recognized as a new Corvette.

Though GM built a "mini-Nordschleife" at their Milford, Michigan, proving grounds in 2003, the C6 also spent time at the actual Nürburgring. The results were significant: a best time of 7:59.00, locking it into 97th place among the street vehicles (as of 2015), and very close to the previous Z06's mark.

Bringing a new car to production is a huge undertaking, and Chevrolet waited a year to get the C6 right before the return of the Z06. When it did, it became the first Chevrolet to break the 500 horsepower mark, with the new 427-cubic-inch (7-liter) LS7 engine rated at 505 horsepower at 6,300 rpm and torque of 470 lb-ft at 4,800 rpm, using the new Society of Automotive Engineers (SAE) J2723 standard. "In many ways, this is a racing engine in a street car," said Dave Muscaro, assistant chief engineer for the powerplant. "We've taken much of what we've learned over the years from the 7.0 liter C5-R racing program and instilled it here."

ABOVE: Tom Peters designed the 2005 C6 Corvette, with the Z06 version coming out in 2006. The ZO6's LS7 2006 7.0-liter V-was rated at 505 horsepower at 6,300 rpm. *Chevrolet*

ABOVE, LEFT: The 2008 Z06 Corvette toured the "Green Hell" in 7:42.90, cutting over 13 seconds from the previous Z06, and rocketing to 52nd among the world's supercars. *Chevrolet*

ABOVE, RIGHT: The 2008 Z06 Corvette toured the "Green Hell" in 7:42.90, cutting over 13 seconds from the previous Z06 time, and rocketing to 52nd among the world's supercars. *Chevrolet*

Chevrolet Corvette Z06 2006-2013

 # PRODUCED: 29,409

ENGINE: 427-cubic-inch V-8

HORSEPOWER: 505

TORQUE: 470 lb-ft

¼-MILE TIME: 11.50 at 127.1 mph

CHEVROLET: CONQUERING THE GREEN HELL

Chevrolet Corvette ZR1 2009-2013

 # PRODUCED: 4,684

ENGINE: 376-cubic-inch V-8

HORSEPOWER: 638

TORQUE: 604 lb-ft

¼-MILE TIME: 11.30 at 131 mph

The 2013 Corvette 427 Convertible commemorates the 60th anniversary of Corvette, and the last model year of the C6 Corvette. The 427 Convertible blends elements of the Z06 and ZR1, including the Z06's 427-cubic-inch (7.0-liter) LS7 engine. *Chevrolet*

The Z06 also received carbon-fiber composite fenders that were 3 inches wider than stock, which barely covered the huge 18x9.5 front- and 19x12 rear-wheels. The rakes were equally huge: 14-inch rotors with six-piston calipers in front, 13.4-inch rotors, and four-piston items out back. The Z06 also got an aluminum version of the hydroformed chassis structure, fabricated at a separate facility down the road from the Bowling Green plant. This made the Z06 a battle-ready 3,132-pounds, down 67-pounds from the standard coupe.

The new Z06 toured the "Green Hell" in 7:42.90, cutting over 13 seconds from the previous Z06, and rocketing to 52nd among the world's supercars. "Testing at the Nürburgring is one of the important methods we have to validate our car in the toughest track conditions," said Tadge Juechter, who was now Corvette vehicle line director and chief engineer after the retirement of David Hill. It also proved the 2006 Z06 was faster than the Porsche 911 GT3 RS, Pagani Zonda C12 S, and Lamborghini Gallardo Superleggera. At a price of $65,800, *Autoweek* called the Z06 "the best supercar buy of all time."

C6 Corvette ZR1 2009-2013

There will always be automotive snobbery, and there's only one cure for that kind of thinking—the rebirth of the "King of the Hill" Corvette, the ZR1. Instead of building a super-Corvette at a reasonable price, like the Z06, what if Chevy's engineers held nothing back? That was the challenge of General Motors CEO Rick Wagoner. Building on the remarkable work done on the Z06, the ZR1 was introduced to a stunned automotive press in the summer of 2008. It packed the explosive punch of the new supercharged 376-cubic-inch LS9 engine (codenamed the Blue Devil, after Wagoner's alma mater, Duke University).

The twin-rotor Eaton R2300 supercharger fit under the ZR1's carbon-fiber hood, yet it blew the LS9 to 638 horsepower. But unlike the supercharger kits you can buy and install yourself, every component of the ZR1 was evaluated against the kind of speeds the Blue Devil could generate, and upgrades were made where necessary. Most notable are the huge Michelin Pilot Sport 2 tires on unique 20-spoke alloy wheels, 19-inch up front, 20-inch in back. World-class Brembo carbon-ceramic disc brakes were added, and the ZR1's body was completely done in carbon-fiber material. That body feature many aerodynamic tweaks crafted in the wind tunnel, like the splitter added to the front fascia, along with widened fenders, roof panel, and rocker moldings. No need to just brag—the ZR1 actually shows the carbon-fiber weaving through the special paint, while the LS9 supercharger is displayed through a window in the hood for all to see.

History was repeating itself, as the ZR1 was named after the original "King," the 1990–1995 ZR1 powered by the Lotus-developed DOHC V-8. But as brutal as the LS9's horsepower could be, the new ZR1 actually drives wonderfully under normal street conditions. Its price was $106,000—staggering for a Corvette, but a fraction of what comparable supercars cost.

In 2012, both the Z06 and the ZR1 received the option of Michelin Pilot Sport Cup tires. Chevrolet warned: "They are competition-oriented tires, optimized for warm, dry conditions to increase cornering and handling capability." There was also new traction control for the "King."

As *Car and Driver* commented:

Carmakers make big claims about improved products all the time. For us, the proof of the pudding is in the eating (or driving), but a good stand-in is the Nürburgring lap video. While validating the upgrades it has made to the 2012 Chevrolet Corvette ZR1 and Z06—specifically the former's brake-based Performance Traction Management system and new Michelin Pilot Sport Cup run-flat tires—Corvette engineer Jim Mero turned in a stunning ZR1 lap time of 7 minutes 19.63 seconds on the 'Ring's famous Nordschleife, more than six seconds faster than the previous best of 7:26.4 set in a 2009 ZR1 also driven by Mero.

That, auto snobs, places the ZR1 in 12th and the Z06 14th on the Nürburgring's fastest times.

CHAPTER 13

Camaro ZL1 2012–2015

When the last of the fourth-generation Camaros rolled off the Sainte-Thérèse, Canada, assembly line on August 27, 2002, many thought it was the end of the line. No successor was announced, and nothing was under development. It was the end of a long, fabled road.

A Camaro concept car appeared at the 2006 North American International Auto Show in Detroit that put this early epitaph in doubt. Designed by Tom Peters, who also crafted the C6 Corvette, with assistance from Sangyup Lee, the show car was immediately recognizable as a Camaro, yet it was thoroughly modern. A convertible version was unveiled at the same show a year later. The reaction to these concepts was so great that GM decided to bring the new Camaro to production as a 2010 model.

The fifth-generation Camaro was based on the rear-drive "Zeta" platform, which it shared with the Australian Holden Commodore VE, the Chevy SS, and the short-lived Pontiac G8. V-6 power was standard, but the performance SS model featured the Corvette LS3 engine tuned for 422 horsepower, driving either a Tremec six-speed manual or a six-speed paddle-shifted automatic. Times to 0–60 were about 4.7 seconds for the automatic and 4.9 ticks for the manual.

True to form, Chevrolet waited two years as it perfected the Camaro before dropping the ZL1 bomb. "From the original Camaro to the current Corvette ZR1, Chevrolet has a long history of delivering world-class cars that outperformed competitors at several times the price," said Chris Perry, vice president, Global Chevrolet Marketing. "The ZL1 is no exception. There are very few cars at any price that can match the power, features, and track capability of the Camaro ZL1."

The original 1969 ZL1 was created by Chevy dealer Fred Gibb and Vince Piggins, Chevrolet's product promotions manager. They wanted to build the fastest NHRA Super Stock drag racer on the

TOP: The Chevrolet Camaro ZL1 coupe delivered exceptional, all-around performance at the drag strip, the road course and as a daily driver. The ZL1 Convertible was added in 2013. These are 2015 models. *Chevrolet*

ABOVE, RIGHT: The heart of the 2012 ZL1 was called the LSA, a variant of the LS7 Corvette engine with a slightly smaller supercharger, producing an insane 580 horsepower with 556 lb-ft of torque. *Chevrolet*

Chevrolet Camaro ZL1 2012-2015

 # PRODUCED: 13,550 (approx.)
ENGINE: 376-cubic-inch V-8
HORSEPOWER: 580
TORQUE: 556 lb-ft
¼-MILE TIME: 12.40 at 117 mph

CHEVROLET: CONQUERING THE GREEN HELL

The 2012-2015 Camaro ZL1 was named after the 1969 ZL1 that was created by Chevy dealer Fred Gibb and Chevrolet's Product Promotions Manager, Vince Piggins. They wanted to build the fastest NHRA Super Stock drag racer on the planet by stuffing Chevrolet's new all-aluminum Can-Am 427 engine in a Camaro. The rules required at least fifty factory-built cars to qualify for competition. A total of sixty-nine cars were ultimately ordered, priced at a staggering $7,400 each. *Tom Glatch*

planet by stuffing Chevrolet's new all-aluminum Can Am 427 engine in a Camaro. The rules required a minimum fifty factory-built cars to qualify for competition. The first of the special COPO Camaros arrived at Gibb Chevrolet on Christmas Eve 1968 with a price of over $7,290—twice the cost of a '69 Z28 and almost twice what Gibb expected. A total of sixty-nine cars were ultimately ordered, though at that price few were sold, and many were sent back to Chevrolet and converted to less-expensive iron-block cars just to move them. But the ZL1 Camaros were fast—so fast they're the stuff of legends.

The heart of the 2012 ZL1 was the LSA, a variant of the LS7 Corvette engine with a slightly smaller supercharger, producing an insane 580 horsepower with 556 lb-ft of torque. Transmissions were a beefed-up Tremec TR6060 "MG9" six-speed manual or a paddle-shifted six-speed Hydramatic 6L90 automatic. The ZR1-inspired suspension included Magnetic Ride Control and Performance Traction Management. "With Magnetic Ride Control, we can offer customers the best of both worlds: A comfortable ride that makes the ZL1 appropriate as a daily driver and the incredibly precise body control that makes the ZL1 so enjoyable on the track," said Al Oppenheiser, Camaro chief engineer.

Aerodynamics were also given serious development. The new front fascia and splitter weren't just for show: they were part of a total package that took the Camaro from 200 pounds of lift at 150 miles per hour to 65 pounds of downforce. "From the driver's seat, the added downforce makes a huge change in the feel, and responsiveness of the ZL1 at high speeds," said Oppenheiser.

One of the best examples of how aerodynamics improved the performance of the ZL1 is the "*Fuchsröhre*," or Foxhole at the Nürburgring. In the ZL1, you can take that sweeping left-hand corner flat-out in fifth gear—nearly 160 mph. That's a great testament to the confidence-inspiring stability and control the aerodynamic design helps give the Camaro ZL1.

With 0 to 60 taking less than four seconds, and a top speed in excess of 180 mph, the power and acceleration of the Camaro ZL1 rivals many supercars. And, horsepower is only half of the story, as the most significant measurement of the ZL1's potential is lapping the Nürburgring in 7:41.27. That is a great testament to the power, braking, grip, and balance of the Camaro ZL1, and to the well-rounded performance of the ZL1 that sets the bar for the sport-car segment.

And it placed Chevy's hottest Camaro 48th on the 'Ring's top-100 list.

Wrote *Car and Driver*:

Aided by GM's third-generation Magnetic Ride Control adaptive shocks, our 4,118-pound ZL1 danced far better than it had a right to. A few circles around our 300-foot skid pad revealed 0.99 g of grip, the beefy 20-inch Goodyear Eagle F1 Supercar G:2 radials (285/35 front, 305/35 rear) hanging tight. Considering the amount of physics-defying grip on tap, it's surprising how true the ZL1 tracks on uneven broken pavement. Living with this superpony on a day-to-day basis is definitely an option.

Like all of Chevrolet's "track-capable" supercars, the ZL1 can take a day of pounding at the racetrack and not come home on a flatbed. Validation for any model intended for the track includes the "24Hour Test." "Passing the 24Hour Test is a requirement for all cars we call 'track capable,'" said Wayne McConnell, director of global vehicle performance.

The test pushes the car at 10/10ths on the track for a total of 24 hours. During the test the only mechanical changes allowed are replacing the brakes and tires. Today's test pushes the car harder than the vast majority of customers ever will. As a result, when we call a car "track capable," we are confident that it will perform reliably and consistently for our customers.

It might be named after a famed drag racer, but the newest ZL1 is a true all-around supercar—one with four-seats.

Camaro Z28 2014–2015

In 1967, Camaro option RPO Z28 was designed around the SCCA Trans-Am series rules. To compete in that popular series, the cars had to be nearly factory stock, with only the addition of safety equipment and racing tires and wheels. The rules mandated a

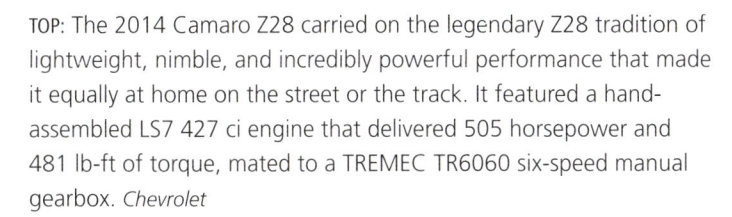

TOP: The 2014 Camaro Z28 carried on the legendary Z28 tradition of lightweight, nimble, and incredibly powerful performance that made it equally at home on the street or the track. It featured a hand-assembled LS7 427 ci engine that delivered 505 horsepower and 481 lb-ft of torque, mated to a TREMEC TR6060 six-speed manual gearbox. *Chevrolet*

ABOVE, LEFT: The 2014 Camaro Z28 was chosen as Official Pace Car for the 2014 Indianapolis 500. *Chevrolet*

ABOVE: The Z28 Camaro can achieve 1.5 g deceleration and 1.06 g lateral acceleration. There's no computer-controlled AWD, clutchless transmission, or other technology that masked the driver's ability, yet in the hands of a skilled pilot the Z28 was incredibly fast—its 2014 lap of 7:37:47 at the Nürburgring placed it 39th among the "street legal" cars at the time. *Chevrolet*

5-liter (305-cubic-inch) production engine, which is why Chevrolet developed the high-winding 302 small-block especially for the car. It also had the heavy-duty suspension, fast-ratio steering, and aerodynamic aids to make it nearly ready for the track.

Few people understood the concept of the stripped-down, battle-bred Camaro, and only 602 Z28s were sold that first year. Yet, in the hands of driver/engineer Mark Donohue, Roger Penske's Sunoco-sponsored Z28s won the Trans-Am championship in 1968 and 1969, and the legend was born. After 1970, the Z28 diminished into a mildly upgraded Camaro for most years—but the legend lives on.

Chevrolet Camaro Z28 2014-2015

 # PRODUCED: 1,700 (approx.)

ENGINE: 427-cubic-inch V-8

HORSEPOWER: 505

TORQUE: 481 lb-ft

¼-MILE TIME: 12.70 at 116 mph

CHEVROLET: CONQUERING THE GREEN HELL

In 2014, Chevrolet went back to the Z28's roots, developing a supercar that could deliver all aspects of the driving experience, then take that experience to another level. Mark Reuss, GM president in North America, challenged the Camaro group to develop a Z28 that was worthy of the legend. "He gave us two requirements," said Oppenheiser. "One is, you gotta put it on a diet. And two, you gotta beat anything, anything, that Ford puts out on the street." The result is a purposeful track racer that could still be driven on the street with reasonable comfort.

"The ZL1, originally, was going to be called the Z28," admitted Oppenheiser.

> As it got closer to launching, and introducing the car in Chicago, it just didn't sit well with me. I'm a purist, and Z28 is an iconic name, and we promised we wouldn't bring that out until the car that deserved it came out . . . . I didn't think this was the right marriage with the name and the car. We came up with the ZL1 name, which fits perfectly with the tie to the '69 high-horsepower, aluminum-block car.

The ZL1 handled very well, but with track time the primary purpose of the Z28, Chevrolet took the suspension even further, adding stiffer control arm bushings, increased spring rates, and specifically tuned anti-roll bars. The ZL1 was also the first and only mass-production automobile to apply Dynamic Suspension Spool Valve (DSSV) dampers taken directly from Formula 1 racing, with five different settings to meet different performance and pavement conditions. Then there are the huge Formula 1–style Brembo brakes, with Carbon Ceramic-Matrix™ rotors and fixed monobloc calipers, just like those used in the ZL1 Corvette. Wrap those brakes with unique 19-inch alloy wheels and Pirelli PZERO™ Trofeo R tires, and the Z28 can achieve 1.5 g deceleration and 1.06 g lateral acceleration.

Chevrolet does not have a performance brand, like Ford's SVT and Chrysler's SRT. What Chevy does have is racing in its DNA, going back to founder Louis Chevrolet competing in the 1905–1910 Vanderbilt Cup road races on Long Island. *Chevrolet*

The Z28 features a normally aspirated 427-cubic-inch (7-liter) 505 horsepower LS7 engine derived from the Z06 Corvette. That's 75 horsepower less than the supercharged ZL1, but the lack of a blower shaves some critical weight off the front of the Z28. The LS7's dry sump system prevents oil starvation at the extreme lateral g's that this Camaro was capable of hitting. The only transmission is the Tremec TR6060 close-ratio six-speed manual, driving a 3.91:1 helical limited-slip differential. Weight was further reduced by using light, form-fitting Recaro front seats with manual adjustments; thin, non-folding rear seats; minimal sound deadening; and ultra-light rear glass. The Z28 is 300 pounds lighter than the ZL1, and 100 less than the Camaro SS with the performance 1LE handling package. As part of the Z28's diet, air conditioning is optional, only a basic radio is available, and the sole speaker is for the door chimes. Then again, what better music is there than the growl of the LS7 engine?

The Z28 was an old-school driver's car built to quickly separate the men from the boys. There's no computer-controlled AWD, clutchless transmission, or other technology that masked the driver's ability, but in the hands of a skilled pilot the Z28 was incredibly fast—its 2014 lap of 7:37:47 at the Nürburgring placed it 39th among the street-legal cars at the time. That amazing lap was also set on a day when part of the course experienced precipitation.

According to Oppenheiser:

> One of the challenges of testing at the 'Ring is that the track is so long that conditions can change radically in a single lap . . . . Adam Dean, the development driver for Z28, did a heroic job driving in deteriorating conditions. Based on telemetry data from our test sessions, we know the Z28 can be as much as six seconds faster on a dry track.

But the Z28 isn't one of those unobtainable exotics that produce similar times at the 'Ring. In 2014, 500 were built; another 2,500 were planned for 2015, to be available at any Chevy dealer for $72,305.

C7 Corvette Z06 2014–Today

When *Automobile* magazine proclaimed the 2014 Corvette "Automobile of the Year" and named Tadge Juechter "Man of the Year," Chevrolet scored an unprecedented award grand slam. "Only the fifth chief engineer in the Corvette's sixty-one-year history, he's likely to go down in the books as the one who got it right. For that he is *Automobile*'s 2014 Man of the Year," the magazine proclaimed.

> Juechter's team did far more than finally bolt in decent seats: the C7 is a top-to-bottom reimagining of what the Corvette could and should be. The car is full of thoughtful engineering, from the seven-speed manual with rev matching that is engaged by using paddles to sensors that know when the tires are properly heated.

The object of such acclaim is the reborn Stingray. Tom Peters was again responsible for the new Corvette's shape, this time with primary design by Kirk Bennion. Sleek yet edgy, the team drew

TOP: Tom Peters was responsible for the C7 Corvette's shape, this time with primary design by Kirk Bennion. Sleek yet edgy, the team drew inspiration from the current F-22 and F-35 fighter aircraft. But they also applied many aerodynamic lessons learned from Corvette Racing. "Ferrari can leverage F1 technology and components; we leverage our ALMS Corvette race car, which has been a huge benefit," Bennion told *Motor Trend*. *Chevrolet*

ABOVE, LEFT: The comfortable cockpit of the Z06 is driver focused. "We put the interior designers on the track so they could understand what it's like to live in a 1 g environment, to have skin pushing on hard objects," designer Kirk Bennion told *Motor Trend*. *Chevrolet*

ABOVE, RIGHT: The 2014 Chevrolet Corvette Stingray's frame makes its way down the composite line in the brand-new $52 million Body Shop at General Motors' Bowling Green Assembly. On the composite line, twenty-one robots and two production teams work together to bond the composite panels to the frame. *Chevrolet*

LEFT: The 625-horsepower LT4 engine has a dry-sump oiling system in common with C7-R racers. *Chevrolet*

inspiration from contemporary F-22 and F-35 fighter aircraft. But they also applied many aerodynamic lessons learned from Corvette Racing. As Bennion told *Motor Trend*:

> Ferrari can leverage F1 technology and components; we leverage our ALMS Corvette racecar, which has been a huge benefit. One of the areas where we did a lot of work was in CFD [Computational Flow Dynamics]. We spent a lot of time on the radiator positioning, and the outlet on the hood. I tell people those blades on the hood are each at their own specific angle which is dictated by its aero-path efficiency.

Underneath is the familiar hydroformed space frame, but now all Corvettes receive the aluminum chassis previously reserved for the Z06 and ZR1 and a carbon-fiber hood; coupes get a carbon-fiber roof insert. And all are powered by a fifth-generation small-block, with the standard engine reviving the LT1 name. Small, lighter, and more fuel efficient, the LT1 was loaded with Variable Valve Timing and cylinder deactivation to achieve these goals, yet it packs 455 horsepower at 6000 rpm and 460 lb-ft of torque.

The stunning interior was now crafted with the best of materials, but the design was also highly purposeful. "We put the interior

LEFT: The 2016 Corvette Z06 C7.R Edition pays homage to the Corvette Racing race cars. Offered in coupe and convertible models, only 500 will be built; each will have a unique, sequential VIN. *Chevrolet*

designers on the track so they could understand what it's like to live in a 1 g environment, to have skin pushing on hard objects," designer Bennion told *Motor Trend*.

Technically, it's the seventh-generation Corvette, but everyone involved made it clear that this is the legendary Stingray, reborn. According to Bennion:

> We did that very late and it wasn't until the car was really done, where we knew what we were going to have, we knew it was going to look like this, and have this technology, that we named it that.

We asked ourselves, "Is the design compelling enough? Is it worthy enough of the Stingray name?" Which we felt was giving a Corvette a special name. We felt making the car special enough to call it a Stingray, but also giving the starting point for the C7 Corvette a really good name was very key to the car.

On the road, the Stingray really is special, as *Automobile* discovered:

With 460 lb-ft of torque (add 5 with the performance exhaust), the ability to fry the Michelin Pilot Super Sport rubber is always there, just a push of the traction control button away. When you're more interested in go than in show, the Corvette gets down and boogies. We clocked an 11.9-second quarter mile at 118 mph; 60 mph ticks by in less than four seconds. Launch control is available should you want to clock yourself, and there's a function that will record your time so you can amaze your friends. Full-throttle blasts are accompanied by a race-car-worthy soundtrack trumpeting from the quad exhaust pipes, but under mellower circumstances the engine emits a muted yet purposeful rumble.

That brought the Stingray to supercar levels of performance. But never fear: one year after the Stingray's triumphant return, the Z06 was again unleashed—this time in both coupe and convertible versions. According to Juechter:

> Simply put, until recently it was not possible to create an open-roof structure strong enough to meet Corvette's highest performance levels. It required advancements in computer-aided engineering, metallurgy, and manufacturing—many of which did not exist five years ago—to make a frame strong enough for a Z06 Convertible.

The new structure is 20 percent stronger than the previous Z06 frame, and there is hardly a weight penalty for choosing a ragtop over the coupe.

This latest Z06 was now supercharged, utilizing the all-new LT4 powerplant. The new, more efficient 1.7-liter supercharger spun faster to make more power at lower rpm, and was only 1 inch taller than the standard LT1. Horsepower was now 650 at 6,400 rpm, torque 650 lb-ft at 3,600 rpm. The special Performance Build Center, which handcrafted each Z06 and ZR1 engine for the C6, moved from Wixom, Michigan, to the Bowling Green plant in 2014.

Chevrolet Corvette Z06 2015–

 # PRODUCED: 8,653

ENGINE: 376-cubic-inch V-8

HORSEPOWER: 650

TORQUE: 650 lb-ft

¼-MILE TIME: 11.40 at 127 mph

Z06 buyers could now help build their own engine, then return to Bowling Green a few weeks later to see their work installed on the assembly line into the Z06 they ordered.

Transmissions are a seven-speed manual, but the fastest option is the GM-developed eight-speed paddle-shift automatic transmission. Forget what you know about the slushboxes of the past: with lockup clutches, this transmission delivers the same kind of power as the manual, yet shifts faster than the dual-clutch boxes certain German manufacturers tout, and faster than any human with a stick shift.

Tires play a big part in the Z06's performance, and the standard Michelin Pilot Super Sport P285/30ZR19 front tires are 1.5 inches wider than the tires on the Stingray, while the 335/25ZR20 rear tires are 2 inches wider.

As potent as the Z06 is, the available Z07 package adds adjustable front and rear aero components for unprecedented aerodynamic downforce; Michelin Pilot Super Sport Cup tires for enhanced grip; and Brembo carbon ceramic-matrix brake rotors that improve braking performance and contribute to greater handling through reduced, unsprung weight. And now there's no need to tell "fish stories"—the unique Performance Data Recorder (PDR) enables users to record high-definition video of their driving experiences on and off the track, complete with telemetry overlays.

If the Z06/Z07 sounds like the closest thing you can get to a Corvette Racing C7-R for the street, you're right. While rumors persisted that an ultra-fast ZR1 was in the works, it's hard to imagine anything better that the Z06. We're waiting for the numbers to come from the Nürburgring to prove it.

Camaro SS 2016

At a glance, the 2016 Camaro looks like an upgraded fifth-gen car. But unlike certain Japanese automakers that roll out a few minor trim changes and call the car "all-new," the sixth-generation Camaro truly is an all-new specimen.

If the Gen5 Camaro had a fault, it was a bit too large and heavy. The "Six" cures that by building off the "Alpha" platform shared with the Cadillac ATS and CTS sedans. When Cadillac began developing the ATS, they targeted weight reduction as a major goal, with world-class results. Leveraging that development for the new Camaro made total sense, and "Six" comes in hundreds of pounds lighter than before. But the new Camaro is hardly a dressed-up Caddy, as over 70 percent of the components are unique to the Gen6.

The new Camaro was introduced on May 16, 2015, at Detroit's Belle Isle racetrack. The base model is powered by a 2.0L turbo inline four, with a 335 horsepower DOHC V-6 available. The SS model returns as the only performance model, powered by a new 376 ci (6.2L) LT1 small-block built off the LS series of engines. Preliminary numbers are 445 horsepower at 6,000 rpm with a matching 445 lb-ft of torque.

While no slouch at 445 horsepower, the SS is not quite supercar material. Will a ZL1 or Z28 return? No one is saying, but if Chevrolet follows their usual *modus operandi*, the new Camaro will undergo revisions to reach perfection before a high-performance version is launched a year or two from now. No doubt the Nürburgring will be involved at some point in the development. Then Chevrolet will again be able to conquer the "Green Hell"—with either two or four seats!

The first performance fifth-generation Camaro was the SS. Producing 426 horsepower through a six-speed manual (400 horsepower with automatic), *Motor Trend* reported the "Camaro SS is more powerful than its rivals, although excessive weight hampers performance." They recorded "a 13.1-second quarter-mile at 110.8 miles per hour. Its 25.2 seconds at 0.73 g average on the MT Figure-8 is equally impressive."
Archives/TEN: The Enthusiast Network Magazines, LLC

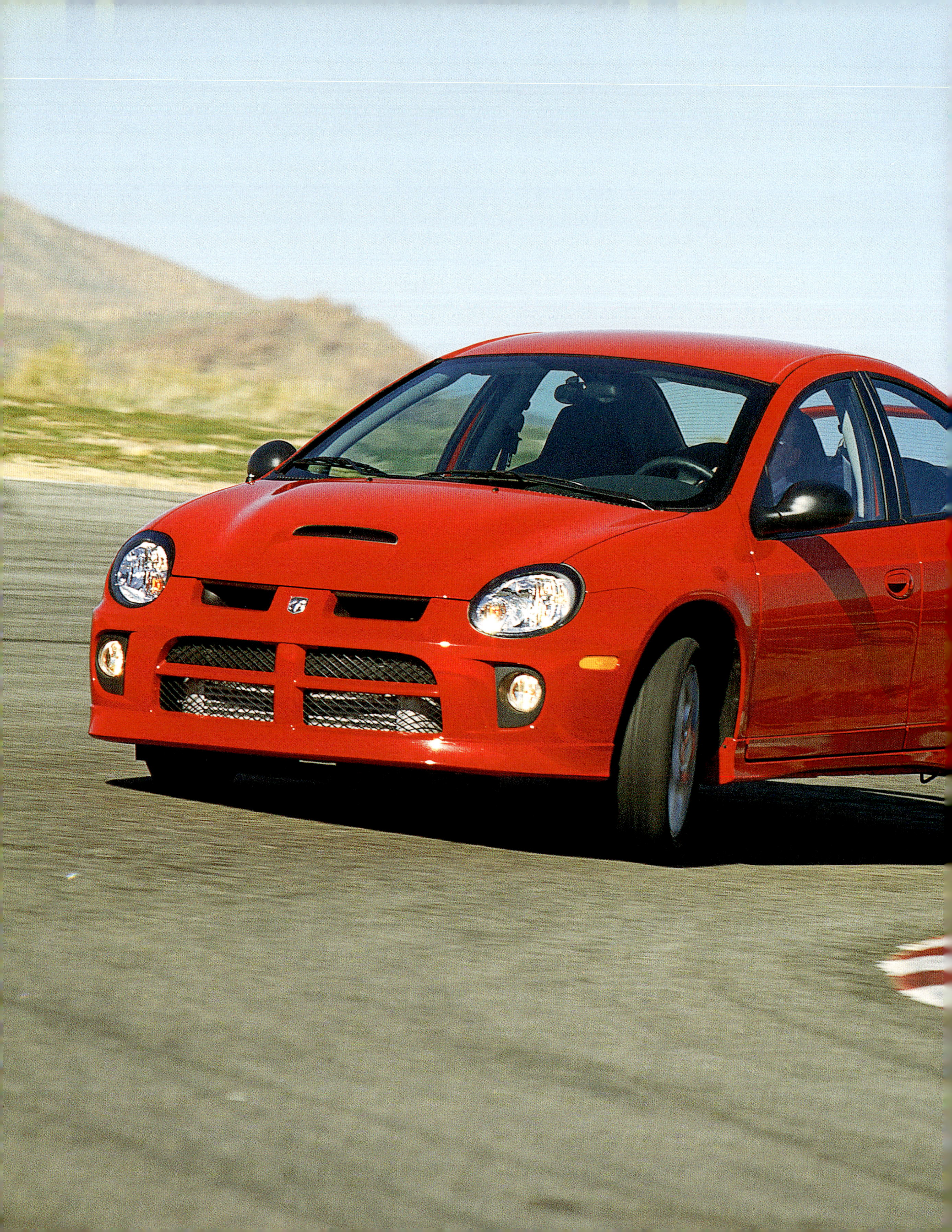

Chapter 14

SRT: Right-Brain Thinking

Just a few years after Chrysler's near-death experience with bankruptcy, they uncoiled the Viper show car at the North American International Auto Show in January 1989. It was an improbable revelation from a company best known for boring minivans and frumpy K-Cars.

General Motors has had their "halo" car, Corvette, since 1953. Over at Ford, the Mustang has been the symbol of the best Dearborn has to offer, going back to 1964. But since the wild days of the Hemi 'Cuda and Charger Daytona, Chrysler had no such flagship vehicle. Can just one vehicle change a company's fortunes?

Dodge Viper RT/10 1992–2002 and Viper GTS 1996–2002

I started with a discussion on a cold February day in 1988. The legendary Bob Lutz, Chrysler's president and vice chairman, paid a visit to Tom Gale, the company's vice president of Design. Lutz described how he arrived at the meeting in his book, *Guts: The Seven Laws of Business That Made Chrysler the World's Hottest Car Company*:

When the son of Chrysler designer Tom Gale brought home a Japanese compact to tune, Gale went to work, convincing management to build the Neon SRT-4. *Car and Driver* discovered: "The Neon SRT-4 rips to 60 miles per hour in 5.6 seconds, to 100 in 13.8, covers a quarter-mile in 14.2 seconds at 102 miles per hour, and keeps on huffin' all the way to 153 miles per hour. Clearly, this is no ordinary Neon." *Archives/TEN: The Enthusiast Network Magazines, LLC*

No one had seen anything like the Viper when it was revealed in 1989. It revolutionized the American sports car industry and invigorated the Dodge brand. *FCNA*

Dodge Viper RT/10 1992-2002/ Viper GTS 1996-2002

 # PRODUCED: 10,013 RT/10; 7,332 GTS

ENGINE: 488-cubic-inch V-8

HORSEPOWER: 400 (1992); 450 (1996)

TORQUE: 450 lb-ft (1992); 490 (1996)

¼-MILE TIME: 13.90 at 109 mph (1992); 12.4-second at 117.3 mph (1996)

Dodge Viper SRT-10 2003-2010/Viper GTS 2006-2010

 # PRODUCED: 9,522

ENGINE: 505-cubic-inch V-8

HORSEPOWER: 500

TORQUE: 525 lb-ft

¼-MILE TIME: 12.20 at 118.0 mph

I was blasting my 1985 Autokraft MK IV Cobra [a splendid recreation of the Shelby Cobra of the 1960s] around some of southeastern Michigan's more interesting roads one day in the warm weather months of 1988, pondering Chrysler's situation and reflecting on how the original Cobra, with its lightweight, two-seat aluminum body and its outrageously powerful Ford V-8 engine had become the single most imitated sports car in history.

That visit between Lutz and Gale resulted in some sketches and clay models, which resulted in the decision to create the Viper show car.

A former Marine, Lutz had held managerial positions at BMW Motorrad (Motorcycle) and Ford of Europe before following Lee Iacocca to Chrysler. Along with the Autokraft Cobra, he owned a 1978 Dodge Lil' Red Wagon while at Chrysler. "Maximum Bob," as he's known in the industry, gets it.

Some big names helped create the first Viper. Right from the start, they knew they wanted to use a variant of the V-10 engine Chrysler was developing for its 1994 Dodge Ram Heavy Duty trucks. That engine was based on Chrysler's 360-cubic-inch V-8, and Roush Engineering created a V-10 for the show car out of two 360s. Boyd Coddington fabricated the tube chassis and supplied the wheels, while the craftsmen at Metalcrafters handformed the mostly steel body. The Cobra's creator himself, Carroll Shelby, was already a consultant for Chrysler after following his friend Iacocca from Ford, and he advised the team during Viper's creation. "When we unveiled the car in January 1989 at the Detroit auto show, it blew the roof off," Lutz wrote. "Nothing remotely like it had ever been displayed by an American or foreign volume producer." But the Viper, for its shock and awe, was still a show car.

TOP: In 1996, a spiritual successor to Carroll Shelby's Cobra Daytona Coupe racer, the Viper GTS, arrived in showrooms. It looked like a RT/10 with a roof tacked on, but 90 percent of the components on the GTS were new. *FCNA*

ABOVE: The Viper GTS became the basis for the GTS-R Competition Coupe. The factory-backed Oreca team won the GTS class at the 24 Hours of Le Mans three straight years with it, along with two American Le Mans Series championships and five FIA GT crowns. *FCNA*

Chrysler received letters from people begging the company to build the Viper. Some sent deposits, a few others sent blank checks. Chrysler really had no choice but to develop the Viper for production.

Team Viper worked under Chrysler's first iteration of Lutz's "Platform Team" concept, comprising eighty-five engineers who'd left their regular jobs to bring the beast to showrooms. Two development mules were created. After Chrysler Chairman Iacocca drove one of those cars, he gave the team thirty-six months and a $50 million budget. They did it, on budget, in thirty-three months.

This was Chrysler's first tubular space frame, their first all-aluminum engine, and their first use of plastic-molding technology for the body. Their creation, the 400-horsepower, 488-cubic-inch, six-speed 1992 Viper roadster, was shown at the North American International Auto Show. "Pure and simple, we had to turn a fairy tale into real life. Every aspect of the Dodge Viper lives up to the

SRT: RIGHT-BRAIN THINKING 201

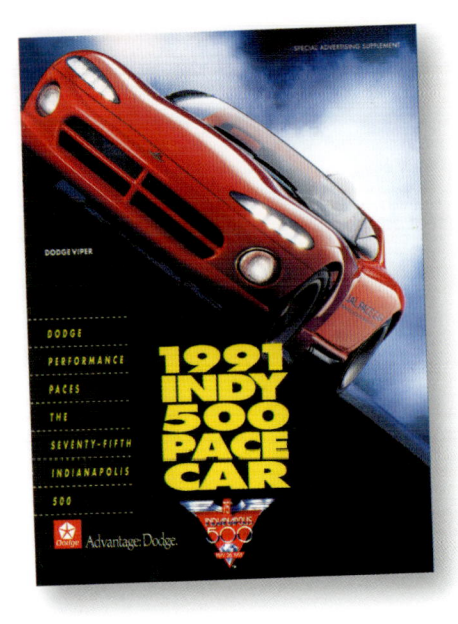

LEFT: The Viper was chosen as the 1991 Indianapolis 500 Pace Car with Carroll Shelby at the wheel. *Author's Collection*

promises made by the original car," said Herb Helbig, senior manager for Team Viper.

The results were stunning. "It has been two days since I first keyed the Viper to life," wrote Ron Sessions in the October 1992 issue of *Road & Track*.

It elicits whoops and hollers of approval. A pair of Young Turks in a Toyota MR2 let loose with a lusty catcall of the sort usually reserved for the L.A. Lakers cheerleaders. A middle-aged couple in a Bronco with Indiana plates pull up alongside and flash the thumbs-up sign. A biker who could pass for one of the Grateful Dead chugs his Harley even with the Viper to cut a gap-toothed smile and a nod of recognition. "Dig it man; the Harley Hog of sports cars." When is the last time an American car, let alone one from Chrysler, has caused such a stir?

This limited-production automobile did far more for Chrysler than anyone expected. No longer was Chrysler "the minivan company" or the "K-Car company." Now, the image around the world was "the Viper company."

Viper was the perfect expression of what Lutz calls "right-brain cars." "Left-brain" cars are completely utilitarian, practical in every aspect—and totally boring. Think "Prius." "Right-brain" cars, of course, are just the opposite. Think "Viper."

Now, a large manufacturer like Chrysler can't survive building only "right-brain" cars, but if every product has some of that "right-brain" excitement and passion, success is assured, Lutz believed. And, as history has shown, the first-generation Viper was the catalyst at Chrysler for many more vehicles built with a dose of Viper DNA.

Three years later, the Viper GTS—a spiritual successor of Shelby's Cobra Daytona Coupe racer—arrived in showrooms. It looked like an RT/10 with a roof tacked on, but 90 percent of the components on the GTS were new. Weight was reduced, yet the GTS was much easier to live with, including standard air conditioning, power windows, power door locks, and air bags. Many of those improvements also found their way on to the RT/10 a year later, and horsepower on both versions jumped to 450.

The GTS the first enclosed Viper, and it became the basis for the GTS-R Competition Coupe. The factory-backed Oreca team won the GTS class at the 24 Hours of Le Mans three straight years with it, along with two American Le Mans Series championships and five FIA GT crowns.

Team Viper also created a new variant of the GTS beginning in 1999, the American Club Racer (ACR). Enough said. What did it take to turn a street machine into a vicious street-legal track machine? When it's a Viper, not much.

Starting with the race-tested Viper GTS, 10 extra horses were added using a K&N air filter and polished intake hoses. Gutting the Viper of air conditioning, sound system, and foglights reduced 60 pounds of weight. Suspension components derived from the GTS-R racers, Michelin Pilot Sport high-performance radials (P275/35ZR18 front, P335/30ZR18 rear), and one-piece 18-inch BBS wheels finished the package. In their first year, 215 of these super snakes were sold (out of 1,314 Vipers total), and another 218 sold in 2000—any wonder what Viper owners like to do in their spare time? The ACR was a fitting exclamation point to the story of the first Viper models.

During the 1990s, Chrysler released not only the Viper on the automotive world, but the only mass-produced hot rod, the Prowler. Team Viper and the Prowler's creator, the Specialty Vehicles Engineering group, eventually were merged, becoming first the Performance Vehicles Operation (PVO), then, in 2004, Street & Racing Technology (SRT).

Dodge Neon SRT-4 2003–2005

SRT's first automobile was hardly a supercar in the strictest sense, but the Neon SRT-4 smacked the marketplace upside its head, all the same. Stephan Zweidler was an engineering student working on Team Viper in 1998. He recalled the event that inspired the SRT4:

> Tom Gale, then head of design at Chrysler, was less than pleased that his son was modifying an import with a body kit and performance parts, so he challenged some younger product planning group staffers to develop a competitive sport compact variant of the popular Neon. That's how the "built for enthusiasts, by enthusiasts" high-performance SRT-4 came to be.

That group of young gearheads dropped the turbo 2.4-liter four from the PT Cruiser GT into the compact Neon, and teamed it with a New Venture Gear T-850 manual five-speed transaxle used on the European diesel minivan. They added five-position shocks, upgraded springs, and special steering gear. A critical development was creating equal-length half-shafts to minimize the torque-steer of the powerful front-drive Neon. Even the front seats were adopted from the Viper.

As *Car and Driver* discovered:

> One look reveals the probable character of the beast, so let's just cut right to the quick. The Neon SRT-4 rips to 60 mph in 5.6 seconds, to 100 in 13.8, covers a quarter mile in 14.2 seconds at 102 mph, and keeps on huffin' all the way to 153 mph. Clearly, this is no ordinary Neon.

Dodge hoped to sell 3,000 SRT-4 Neons, but produced over 25,000 between 2003 and 2005. Lutz may have retired in 1999 after the merger of Chrysler and Daimler-Benz, but his "right-brain" thinking was still selling cars.

The Neon SRT-4 was powered by the turbo 2.4-liter four from the PT Cruiser GT teamed with a New Venture Gear T-850 manual five-speed transaxle Car and Driver discovered: "The Neon SRT-4 rips to 60 miles per hour in 5.6 seconds, to 100 in 13.8, covers a quarter-mile in 14.2 seconds at 102 miles per hour, and keeps on huffin' all the way to 153 miles per hour. Clearly, this is no ordinary Neon." *FCNA*

Dodge Viper SRT-10 2003–2006

"The Dodge Viper wrote the book on the ultimate American sports car," said Gale in 1991.

The 1992 RT/10 Roadster represented Chapter One, with the foreword written by the 1989 Viper concept car. The story progressed page by page, year by year, until 1996, when we started a new chapter titled "the GTS Coupe." The new Viper convertible represents the third chapter in the Dodge Viper's storied history.

Don't worry, the 2003 Viper was hardly a kinder and gentler bedtime story: it featured 500 horsepower, 525 lb-ft of torque, and now 505 cubic inches of displacement.

Executive Engineer John Fernandez stated:

The new Dodge Viper is the only production car in the world that will be able to claim 500 horsepower, 500 pound-feet of torque and 500 cubic inches displacement. Five hundred has always been a magic number. It's been a performance target for Viper and the Specialty Vehicles Engineering team for years. But we knew it would require architectural changes to reach. The new car gives us the platform we needed to raise the bar for what a sports car should be.

It also had a new look, with a true convertible top and a sharper, even more aggressive stance. What started simply as a project to add a folding top to the existing RT/10 turned into a full-blown redesign when it was discovered 90 percent of the body panels would need to be replaced. Tasked with designing the new Viper convertible was Osamu Shikado, a Japanese-born designer who had been with Chrysler since 1994.

Osamu Shikado was tasked with designing the new Viper convertible. A Japanese-born designer who had been with Chrysler since 1994, Shikado said, "To enhance the new Viper's muscular form, we gave the body a strong profile with higher beltline, dramatic side gill and a 'bump-up' rear fender shape." *FCNA*

"When I look at the original Viper, the most important design cues are the two massive elements which interlocked at the middle of the body," Shikado said.

The original Viper has distinctive characteristics, but from some angles it looks cartoonish. I added some crease lines on the body surface. It is the strongest departure from the very rounded original one. My intention was to make it appear to have been sculpted out

The Ram SRT-10 was intended to be the fastest production pickup ever. *FCNA*

of solid metal, representing strength and power. To enhance the new Viper's muscular form, we gave the body a strong profile with higher belt line, dramatic side gill and a "bump-up" rear fender shape. A lower hood incorporates a larger grille opening—boasting an even bolder version of the Dodge-signature cross-hair design—and adds integrated engine louvers for effective airflow in the engine compartment. The rear wheels were moved back 2.6 inches and the A-pillar was pulled three inches forward to allow for bigger doors and for improved ingress and egress. I like the rear three-quarter view. It looks like some kind of predator set to capture the prey.

Along with the exterior redesign, another young designer, Ralph Gilles, freshened the Viper's interior. Remember that name. "The interior is all about the driver—a performance environment," Gilles said.

> There is a huge emphasis on knowing what the machine is doing, focusing on the tachometer. The other gauges are secondary. And we found space for a dead pedal. For me personally, simplicity was another point. I didn't want the interior to be too gimmicky. Just straightforward, with basic shapes. The overall impression when someone gets in the car is every bit as good as any of the other supercars in fit and finish. In addition, the interior is very authentic, very honest.

"Omnipotent is too tame a word for this 505-cube beast," wrote *Motor Trend* of their first drive.

> Despite having significantly more venom (+50 horsepower/ +35 lb-ft), the power curve is much smoother and wider, which produces a less-violent-feeling engine than before . . . . A redesigned cockpit delivers more passenger space, better ergonomics, and good control of wind buffeting—but it's still a bit tight. The press kit mentions a seven-speaker, 310-watt AM/FM/CD stereo system, but the raspy rumble emanating from the sidepipes is all the music we need . . . . Dodge's SRT-10 remains a world-class sports car that'll gladly ram horns with all competitors.

In 2005, SRT added another benefit: the SRT Track Experience. All owners of SRT vehicles are eligible for a day at the track, with professional driver instruction, and it's free. Participants get to drive vehicles supplied by SRT, so their own car is safe from driver error. It's a one-time perk built into the cost of any SRT vehicle, and it's available at twenty-five tracks around the US. Returning participants pay $500, which is still a bargain.

The Viper GTS returned in 2006, this time based on the 2003 Viper's updated underpinnings. As in the past, the coupe quickly outsold the roadster by a good margin.

Dodge Ram SRT10 2004–2006

The November 19, 2003, press release from DaimlerChrysler headquarters said it all: "Dodge Unleashes the Fastest and Most Powerful Production Pickup Ever, the 150 MPH Viper-Powered 2004 Dodge Ram SRT10."

It made perfect sense, in a twisted sort of gearhead way. The Viper's engine was derived from Dodge's V-10 truck engine, so why not drop the Viper's powerplant into a Ram supertruck?

For 2005, DaimlerChrysler announced: "Dodge Ram SRT10 Quad Cab—Performance for the Whole Family." Without a load on the hitch, the Ram SRT10 Quad Cab could be provoked to 0–60 in 5.3 seconds, ¼-mile in 13.7 seconds at 103.0 miles per hour. *FCNA*

"With the Ram SRT10, the PVO team set out to create the fastest, most powerful production pickup ever—the ultimate Dodge Ram," said Wolfgang Bernhard, chief operating officer, Chrysler Group, at the announcement. "The goal at PVO is to out-muscle everything in our class through superior engineering and by drawing on our engineers' vast motorsports experience."

Make no mistake, this is not a truck engine dressed to look like a Viper—it's the same aluminum engine hand-assembled at Viper's Conner Avenue plant in Detroit. Bernhard added:

The Ram SRT10 represents a cohesive design that blends brute power with the engineering refinement usually reserved for the world's best sports cars . . . . This is not a bolt-on kit for a Ram. PVO has created a new vehicle that blends a race-inspired interior, functional aerodynamics for high-speed driving, and a modified suspension to maximize handling without sacrificing ride. The Ram SRT10 has been refined and perfected into a sports truck that is luxurious, fast, and represents the ultimate in its class. No one has ever experienced anything like the Ram SRT10.

Automobile opined:

By dropping the Viper's 500-horsepower V-10 and six-speed manual transmission into the Ram, DaimlerChrysler's [PVO] team has not only trumped the Ford Lightning, but it's created the most powerful production pickup truck in the entire history of the universe—which is a fine thing to do if you've got some spare Viper powertrains kicking around . . . . While the Ram SRT-10 charges to 60 mph in a scant 5.3 seconds, the truck is intended to be more than a straight-line dragster, and the basic Ram chassis has been extensively modified to provide the turning and stopping capabilities appropriate to a 155 mph vehicle. Those extroverted brake calipers grip fifteen-inch front and fourteen-inch rear rotors, the suspension is lowered one inch in the front and two-and-a-half inches at the rear, and stiffer springs and Bilstein monotube dampers are used all around.

A 155 miles per hour pickup? The Ram SRT10 press release duly notes:

On Feb. 2, 2004, an unmodified Dodge Ram SRT10 earned a spot in the Guinness Book of World Records as the world's fastest production pickup truck, with a measured top speed of 154.587 mph (248.783 kph) sustained over a "flying kilometer." That's what a 505 cu.in. (8.3L) V-10 pumping out 500 horsepower and 525 lb-ft torque can do, especially when routed through Viper's T-56 six-speed manual gearbox and a 4.56:1 rear axle.

Dodge Ram SRT10 2004-2006

 # PRODUCED: 9,527
ENGINE: 505-cubic-inch V-8
HORSEPOWER: 500
TORQUE: 525 lb-ft

SRT: RIGHT-BRAIN THINKING

Sold from 1955 to 1965, the original Chrysler 300 cars were legendary for their style and performance. The 1955 Chrysler C-300 was the most powerful automobile in America. They held that distinction in 1956 and 1957, too. *FCNA*

For 2005, DaimlerChrysler announced: "Dodge Ram SRT10 Quad Cab—Performance for the Whole Family." While the two-door SRT10 may have been the ultimate adult toy this side of the "Naughty or Nice Shop," it wasn't the most practical truck around. The new four-door variant addressed that flaw.

A Dodge press release explained the update:

> One distinction is an automatic transmission—a super-duty four-speed that is specially tweaked to provide optimum performance with the capability of towing 8,150 pounds. The Dodge Ram SRT10 Quad Cab has several other unique features supporting its towing capability, including a special transmission cooler, heavy-duty torque converter, special front and rear strut and spring assemblies, and all-Ram season tires.

The regular SRT10 rode on 305/40R22 Pirelli Scorpion tires, while the Quad Cab substituted Pirelli Scorpion all-season tires.

Still, without a load on the hitch, the Ram SRT10 Quad Cab could be provoked to 0–60 in 5.3 seconds, ¼-mile in 13.7 at 103 miles per hour—just 4 miles per hour and 0.4 seconds slower than the two-door SRT10. Neither was cheap—$47,605 for the two-door and $51,810 for the Quad Cab in 2006—but what do you expect for a *Guinness Book of World Records* holder?

Chrysler 300C SRT-8 2005–2010

When Chrysler and Daimler-Benz joined forces in May 1998, it was the largest merger in world history at that time. Chrysler was the most profitable automaker in the world, Mercedes one of the most technically proficient. Through a basic stock swap, the two became one, and Daimler-Benz Chairman Jürgen Schrempp called it a "marriage made in heaven" and a "merger of equals."

Chrysler management and employees soon found how equal the "merger of equals" was. Due to the value of Daimler-Benz stock, Chrysler owned 43 percent of the German company, Daimler-Benz 57 percent of Chrysler. For the most part, Stuttgart, not Auburn Hills, now called the shots. By the early 2000s, both companies were bleeding red ink.

When Daimler-Benz sold Chrysler in 2006, the *New York Times* wrote:

> Daimler-Benz was an eager bidder for Chrysler nine years ago, attracted by its highly profitable lineup of Jeep and minivans.... The merger never resulted in the savings or market power that the creators envisioned, however, as the company struggled to put a mass market brand, Chrysler, together with Mercedes-Benz, a luxury company, while keeping both prosperous.

But one of the few benefits Chrysler got from the marriage was the LX platform and the WA580 transmission, both shared development between Chrysler and Mercedes.

Burke Brown was LX platform lead for the project. "The rear-wheel drive cars had gotten started quite a bit before the Mercedes stuff happened," he told *Allpar.com*.

> But that really put a fire under that because of Dieter [Zetsche, DaimlerChrysler Chairman] and his heritage of Mercedes, which is very much rear-wheel drive, and now our parts bin was twice as big, and we had a whole bunch of rear-wheel drive parts that would've cost us a lot more to get our hands on, with tooling and all that stuff. That put the rear-wheel drive stuff in high gear, because we had the 580 transmission. We had their rear end, which was a nice, lightweight, high-torque rear axle with independent suspension.

The result was the stunning 2005 Chrysler 300. Available in rear-wheel-drive or all-wheel-drive, with V-6 or the all-new 5.8-liter Hemi, the reborn Chrysler 300 was a smashing success, especially after the Gilles and Freeman team wrapped the LX with that distinctive, muscular body. Interestingly, before joining DaimlerChrysler, Freeman helped design the new Beetle and Audi TT for VW. *Motor Trend* named the new 300 "2005 Car of the Year," while *Car and Driver* listed it on their Top 10 in 2005 and 2006. The original Chrysler 300 cars, sold from 1955 to 1965, were legendary for their style and performance. Powered by the first-generation Hemi engine, the 1955–1956 300 had dominated NASCAR and USAC stock car racing those years. A new legend was about to be born.

Of course, as great as the new 300 was, that Hemi power just begged for an SRT upgrade. Thus, the 300C-SRT8 was created. Under the hood was an upgraded 6.1-liter SRT Hemi delivering 425 horsepower and 420 lb-ft of torque. That's a magic number, since the original 426 Street Hemi offered from 1966 to 1971 was also rated at 425-horsepower. The only transmission was the stout five-speed automatic. Other mods included a chin spoiler, 20-inch SRT-branded wheels, a trunk spoiler, 3.5-inch exhaust tips, and a half-inch less ground clearance.

Car and Driver commented:

> Chrysler's 300C SRT8 is the car we thought the American auto industry would not build again. After the muscle-car era, US automakers relinquished the high-performance family-sedan

Available in rear-wheel-drive or all-wheel-drive, with V-6 or the all-new 5.8-liter Hemi, the reborn Chrysler 300 was a smashing success, especially after the Ralph Gilles and Thomas Freeman team wrapped the LX with that distinctive, muscular body. The real news was the 300C SRT8 version. *Car and Driver* commented: "Chrysler's 300C SRT8 is the car we thought the American auto industry would not build again. *Motor Trend* named the new 300 "2005 Car of the Year," while *Car and Driver* listed it on their Top 10 in 2005 and 2006.

formula to the Germans (who added refinement but charged elitist prices) and Japanese (who charged a little less than the Germans but somehow sterilized the whole thing). What makes the SRT8 version of Chrysler's 300C exceptional is that it's the first sedan from anyone, anywhere, to combine the refinement and performance of the pricey supersedans with a sticker of $42,095, no incentive necessary. It's something the US auto industry should have done long ago, but it was worth the wait. Chrysler has built a true four-door American muscle car here—for pity's sake, it's a 4,212-pound brick that can hit 173 miles per hour! Perhaps more impressive is that from 70 to 0, it halts those two-plus tons in a fade-free 162 feet.

As Brown told *Allpar.com*:

I have often thought that if it wouldn't have been for the Mercedes thing, we probably wouldn't have had the 300, the rear-wheel drive cars. If they would've come they would've come a lot later and probably wouldn't have hit that sweet spot in the market where people really grabbed onto it.

Dodge Magnum SRT-8 2005–2008

A Dodge Magnum brochure depicted a bikini-clad surfer loading a board into the back of one. That's the Magnum, kind of a fun-loving, modern-day '57 Chevy Nomad wagon.

The Magnum was the second part of the LX platform launch, and it shared many of the Chrysler 300's components. Like the 300, the Magnum featured components derived from the W211 Mercedes-Benz E-Class, including the rear suspension, front seat frames, wiring harnesses, steering column, and the five-speed automatic transmission's design. The LX also used the double wishbone front suspension derived from the W220 Mercedes-Benz S-Class. And, like the new 300, Magnum was available in two- or all-wheel-drive.

The same SRT-8 package available on the 300 was offered on the Magnum, with the same results. The Magnum SRT-8 was again rear-drive only, with the same 425-horsepower Hemi, high-performance four-wheel antilock brakes with vented 14-inch front and 13.8-inch rear discs, and Brembo Performance four-piston calipers.

Wrote *Motor Trend*:

The Magnum SRT8 launches well at around 2,500 rpm (over 1 g in initial acceleration) with just a wisp of wheelspin. Go wide open too soon, and those monster Goodyears cook in an instant. The 20-inch Eagle F1 Supercar tires are standard with the SRT8 model (it needs the added grip), with four-season RS-As optional for those who'd dare drive an SRT8 in all seasons. Any vehicle that reaches 30 mph in less than two gut-flattening seconds is destined for a good run to 60: The Magnum SRT8 sets the bar at 5.1 seconds and nails the quarter mile in 13.1 at 108.2 mph.

Comparing it to the Magnum's German cousin, the supercharged Mercedes-Benz E55 performance wagon, *MT* discovered that:

On the skid pad, the Magnum is again checking its orbit with periodic front-brake applications but comes through with a 0.90

ABOVE: The SRT-8 got a nice facelift for 2008, but the Magnum was abruptly discontinued in the US by the end of the calendar year. *FCNA*

LEFT: A Dodge Magnum brochure depicted a bikini-clad surfer loading a board into the back of one. That's the Magnum: kind of a fun-loving, modern-day '57 Chevy Nomad wagon. *Author's Collection*

average g to the E55's 0.84 g. Put it all together in our figure-eight, and the Magnum SRT8 combines its go/slow/turn abilities better with a 26.1-second lap at 0.70 g average to the E55's 26.3 at 0.70 g average. This shows that, while the E55 may be more powerful, it can't make up for the tenacious grip of the Magnum.

Their conclusion? "The Magnum SRT8 is an astonishing performance value; a car with the power and the handling to match the macho menace of its slammed sportwagon styling."

The SRT-8 got a nice facelift for 2008, then the Magnum was abruptly discontinued in the United States around the end of the calendar year, apparently so that Chrysler's new owners, Cerberus Capital Management, could squeeze a bit more profit out of the Brampton, Ontario, plant by cancelling a shift. Oddly enough, the Magnum was still sold in Europe until 2012, with a Chrysler 300 front clip and marketed as the "300C Touring." Thanks to its sporty, yet utilitarian nature, the Magnum is still a favorite of people that have to haul gear but still want to look good or go fast doing it. Musicians love them, since there's plenty of room for a Marshall stack and a couple of Fender Strats. And when it's a Magnum SRT-8, well, that's just life "cranked to 11"!

Dodge Charger SRT8 2006–2010

"You can talk and make all the excuses, but front-drive vehicles don't have the image, don't have the same handling; and they don't have the ability to sell the upscale that drives the value people see," Tom Gale told *Motor Trend*.

> We did research and found we could add $5,000 to $6,000 in perceived value to a vehicle by going rear-drive. I said, "If I can prove to you that I can generate value in the eyes of the customer faster than I'm adding cost, why wouldn't we do this? Why would you pass on $6,000 worth of image to stay with front-drive?"

Along with the Chrysler 300 and Dodge Magnum introduced in 2005, a third variant of the LX came along the next year with another storied name from the past: Charger. Unlike the two-door Chargers built from 1966 through 1974, the new Charger was a four-door. It didn't have any real styling cues from the 1960s cars either, but it had an aggressively sporty look that made it clear: Charger was back. And under the hood was another blast from the past, an optional Hemi, this time the all-new third-generation engine. Like the other LX cars, a 3.8-liter V-6 was standard, and all-wheel-drive was an option, except on the top-of-the-line SRT8 model.

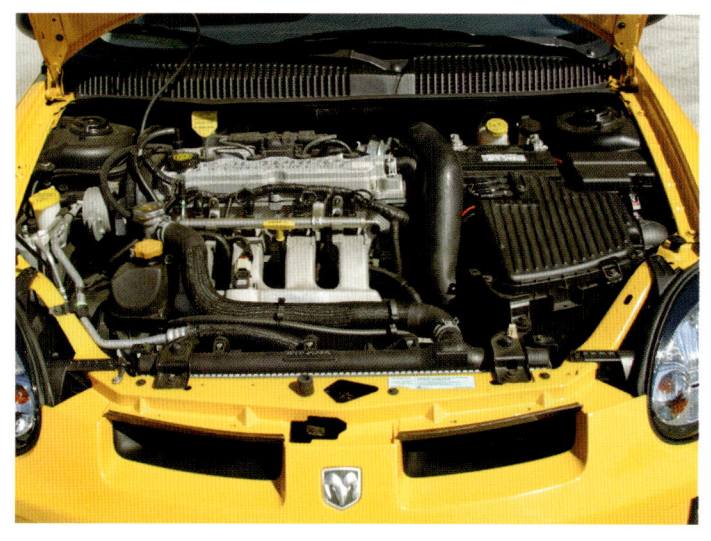

Those SRT8 Chargers were blessed with large-diameter anti-sway bars, specially tailored spring rates, Bilstein shocks, Brembo four-piston disc brakes all around, and 20-inch forged aluminum wheels covered with Goodyear F1 Supercar three-season tires. Inside, the car came with deeply sculpted and aggressively bolstered front seats trimmed with suede inserts, faux "carbon-fiber" leather trim on the steering wheel, and special satin silver finish on the center stack. Full instrumentation includes a 180 miles per hour speedometer, tachometer, and temperature gauges. The interior was finished in Dark/Light Slate Gray.

"The 2006 Dodge Charger SRT8 is the car that a lot of long time Mopar fans have been waiting for," said *Motor Week*'s TV report.

TOP: A third variant of the LX came along in 2006 with another storied name from the past: Charger. Unlike the two-door Chargers built from 1966 through 1974, the new Charger was a four-door. *FCNA*

ABOVE, LEFT: The Super Bee model returned in 2007. "Finally, a car with the muscle to do real justice to one of Chrysler's most famous muscle car nameplates," said *MotorWeek TV*. *FCNA*

ABOVE, RIGHT: SRT's first automobile was hardly a supercar in the strictest sense, but the Neon SRT4 made a splash in the marketplace all the same. *FCNA*

SRT8 2006-2010 Dodge Charger

 # PRODUCED: 5,829
ENGINE: 370-cubic-inch V-8
HORSEPOWER: 425
TORQUE: 420 lb-ft
¼-MILE TIME: 13.20 at 109 mph

The Dodge Challenger R/T fits in between the base V-6 cars and the ultra-performance SRT8 and Hellcat Challengers. *Motor Trend* discovered "half of the Challenger's appeal is that it's so politically incorrect. The thing's almost subversive. . . . But hey, when life gives you a snarling 372 horsepower, 400 pound-feet of torque, six-speed manual muscle car with a fully defeatable traction control system, you gotta make the most of it. That, and lots of black tire marks." *Archives/TEN: The Enthusiast Network Magazines, LLC*

Hot Rod magazine said it bluntly: "If You Can't Run 11-second Times In A Hellcat Challenger, You Can't Drive." Dodge engineer Jim Wilder gave the formula: transmission in Track mode, suspension in Street mode, traction control in Sport, and, of course, use the red key for 707 horsepower. He should know—he's the driver who made the official NHRA-sanctioned times of 11.20-seconds on street tires and 10.80-seconds on drag radials. *Archives/TEN: The Enthusiast Network Magazines, LLC*

Finally, a car with the muscle to do real justice to one of Chrysler's most famous muscle car nameplates. And at Dodge, muscle naturally means a Hemi V-8. In this case, it's Chrysler's biggest Hemi, the SRT-tuned 6.1-liter. With 425 horsepower and 420 pound-feet of torque on tap, it's the kind of punch that made the original Charger a legend. Yet even with the modest EPA fuel economy ratings of 14 city/20 highway, it's actually a lot more efficient than its predecessor.

Motor Week recorded 0–60 in 5 seconds, and stopped from 60 miles per hour in just 128 feet. They also blasted 1,320 feet in 3.4 seconds at 104 miles per hour. Dodge Public Relations noted the SRT8 had a "horsepower-per-liter rating that exceeds even that of the legendary 1966 Street Hemi."

Dodge Challenger SRT8 2008–2010

A fourth variation of the LX platform was introduced for 2008, the reborn Dodge Challenger. Created by shortening the LX by 4 inches, the new LC platform was clothed in a body faithfully based on the 2006 Challenger show car designed by Michael Castiglone. And that body won't strike knowledgeable onlookers as anything less than a modern interpretation of the classic 1970–1974 Dodge Challenger pony car.

Challenger was a late addition to the 2008 lineup, and only SRT8 Challengers were built that year. Those '08 Challengers were available in black, silver, or Hemi Orange only, with dual hood stripes in carbon fiber. Each Challenger in the 2008 run had a numbered dash plaque.

"Thanks to that monster motor and a short first gear, the Challenger does earn a dollop of street cred, hitting 60 mph in 4.8 seconds, charging through the quarter mile in 13.3 at 108 mph, and running to a drag-limited top speed of 168 mph," wrote *Car and Driver* of its first road test.

But the Challenger SRT8 is more than just a drag-strip junkie. Its LX platform, for all its heft, does bring with it a sophisticated suspension that made easy work for Chrysler's Street and Racing Technology team to engineer a combination of decent ride quality and tenacious grip, neither of which is a strong suit of muscle cars from bygone years (or, for that matter, of the current Ford

Mustang). So, like any SRT8 product, it may be inescapably a family car in many ways, but it's a fast and capable performance car, too. The multilink front and rear suspension is tuned for amazingly flat cornering, something vividly apparent on Angeles Crest Highway, where we flogged it left and right but watched the horizon that was the big, long hood stay level with the ground. Coupled with the sticky optional Goodyear F1 Supercar summer tires, the suspension imparted the Challenger with some pretty astonishing grip in corners. On the skid pad in Michigan, which admittedly was described as "really slippery" that day, the Challenger pulled a respectable 0.86 g with moderate understeer that can be corrected by the pedal on the right.

They recorded 0–60 in 4.8 seconds, 0–100 mph in 11.4, and the quarter in 13.3 at 108 miles per hour. That was lot of punch for $40,208.

The SRT8 returned for 2009, as did lesser V-6 and Hemi models. But the Hemi Orange paint and carbon-fiber stripes were gone. Considering that Chrysler was now privately owned by Cerberus Capital Management, it's a minor miracle the new Challenger existed at all—and a major miracle the SRT team was able to create a truly great competitor for the Mustang.

Dodge Viper SRT10 ACR 2008–2010

In 1998, Lutz wrote in his book, *Guts*, "The Viper, in brief, was becoming profitable in ways impossible to quantify." A decade later, *Car and Driver* reported in its August 2008 issue that:

> Chrysler has no timetable to sell its Viper operations, but the sportscar assets have attracted interest from third parties in North America as well as abroad, says Jim Press, Chrysler vice chairman and president. That's right, snake lovers, if you come up with enough cash—piles of it—you could have all the tire-smokin', gas-suckin', hooligan-style fun you could dream of with your very own Viper-making operation.

And Viper, Cerberus Capital Management hoped, would soon be gone. Hello, left-brain thinking.

Remarkably, SRT was able to forge ahead with the Viper while also building roadsters and coupes for faithful customers. No Vipers were built in 2007, but production at Conner Avenue began again for the 2008 model run, and, thankfully, Viper was better than ever.

With engineering support from McLaren Automotive and Ricardo Consulting Engineers, the Viper's V-10 featured new cylinder heads equipped with computer numerically controlled (CNC)—shaped combustion chambers, larger valves, and variable valve timing. The beast now displaced 510 cubic inches (8.4 liters), generated 600 horsepower, and shook the ground with 560 lb-ft of torque. The venerable T56 gearbox was replaced with a slick-shifting Tremec TR6060 six-speed, while the Dana M44-4 rear end gained a GKN Visco differential. There was also a new hood with a larger, more efficient hood scoop for air induction and larger, functional hood louvers. Dodge claimed a top speed of 202 miles per hour for the coupe and 197 miles per hour for the convertible—with the top down! *Car and Driver* saw a 0–60 in 3.7 seconds, 0–100 in 7.6 seconds, and the quarter mile 11.6 seconds at 126 miles per hour.

Viper engines are assembled at the same plant the Viper itself is built, the Connor Avenue Assembly Plant in Detroit. FCNA

With lessons learned from the previous generation's GTS-R racers, SRT built a street-legal machine with all the goodies for the track, heralding the return of the Viper ACR. While other manufacturers brag about their times around the daunting Nürburgring Nordschleife, a 2008 Viper ACR laid down this fact: its 7:22:10 time by driver Tom Coronel on August 18, 2008, makes it the fastest rear-drive production automobile at that track. Almost seven years after the record run, no one has surpassed it.

Dodge Charger SRT8 2011–Today

The 2006–2010 Dodge Charger was the triumphant return of a classic muscle car. But the new Charger never looked quite right, a design compromise made by designers who were forced to employ as many Chrysler 300 components as possible. That changed with the updated 2011 Charger.

Gilles was now the head of Design for Chrysler, and the head of SRT. His team also had the support of Chrysler's new owners, Fiat. Charger would now look like a Charger. Moving the top of the A-pillars back 3.5 inches, and the C-pillars back a similar amount, gave the new roofline a sleeker look. The bold, C-shaped recess along the side was a modern take on the 1970 Charger. And the new full-width taillights—called the "raceway"—were also inspired by the 1969–1970 Chargers. A great deal of attention was given to the new car's interior, too, addressing many of the complaints of cheap-looking materials.

The 2011 and newer Charger would now look like a Charger. Moving the top of the "A" pillars back 3.5 inches—and the "C" pillars back a similar amount—gave the new roofline a sleeker look. The bold C-shaped recess along the side was a modern take on the 1970 Charger. The Super Bee returned in 2012. "If a 392 cubic-inch V-8, Hemispherical combustion chambers, 470 horsepower, 175 miles per hour top speed and RWD don't get you excited, then the 2012 Dodge Charger SRT8 is definitely not the car for you," wrote *Popular Mechanics*. FCNA

V-6 models (SXT, SXT Plus) and V-8 models (R/T, R/T Plus, R/T Max) returned, again available in rear-drive or all-wheel-drive. Of course, an SRT8 version returned, too, now powered by a 470 horsepower 6.4-liter Hemi. "This is not an appearance package that's been influenced by anything superficial," said Dodge.

Charger SRT8 stands out with a proprietary fascia with an aggressive air intake and culminates with a rear spoiler sworn to keep this vehicle firmly planted. Unique rear styling, side sill trim, and new 20-inch split-spoke forged aluminum SRT design wheels complete a package that's built to perform. Hinting at the power lurking beneath is a standard air exhauster in the hood for improved engine cooling, and enormous twin four-inch round dual exhaust outlets. The interior is equally fierce. A new leather-wrapped, heated, flat-bottom, SRT-logo three-spoke steering wheel with contoured palm rests eagerly waits for hands to grip it. Other SRT features include: heated and ventilated high performance-bolstered front seats with suede inserts; special bolstering on door panels; dark engine turn aluminum IP cluster and shifter bezel accents; die-cast steering wheel-mounted paddle shifters; customer-selectable "Sport" mode.

"If a 392 cubic-inch V-8, Hemispherical combustion chambers, 470 horsepower, 175 mph top speed and RWD don't get you excited, then the 2012 Dodge Charger SRT8 is definitely not the car for you," commented *Popular Mechanics* a year later.

On the road, the SRT8's adaptive shocks provide a livable ride but automatically stiffen up when sensors signal the need for tighter handling. At Willow Springs Raceway near Rosamond, Calif., we manually set the suspension to Sport, toggled off the electronic stability control, and let the Dodge do its thing. For a car that weighs 4,400 pounds, the Charger SRT8 knows how to hustle. Surprisingly tossable, your grandmother could pull a solid g in several of the Willow's corners. If you botch an apex, the forgiving chassis saves you. The big, slotted Brembo brakes reassuringly burn off the big Hemi's speed corner after corner.

It went like a Charger, and now the 2012 Charger looked like one, too.

Chrysler 300C SRT8 2012–2014

"They fixed it!" So wrote *Road & Track* about the rejuvenated Chrysler 300C SRT8. "Not that there was anything truly wrong with the previous 425-horsepower Chrysler 300 SRT8 introduced in 2005, but this new one, oh boy, does it take a much-needed tall step to the next level."

Gilles's team gave the 300C an updated look without losing the big sedan's appeal, and focused on bringing the interior up to world-class standards, as *R&T* discovered:

Dodge revamped the Charger, and the performance SRT8, in 2012. Testing the SRT8, *Car and Driver* reported, "The Charger's extra-strength Hemi rumbles to life with authority and always feels ready to overwhelm the rear Goodyears with its 470 pound-feet of torque. Our best runs happened without the car's launch-control software and required a careful throttle foot to optimize wheelspin. Get it right and 60 miles per hour passes in 4.2 seconds . . ." Not bad for a 4,400-pound four-door sedan. *Archives/TEN: The Enthusiast Network Magazines, LLC*

Unlike its predecessor that sacrificed civility for bludgeoning performance—with 0–60-mph times of just under 5 seconds and a quarter-mile time of 13.3 sec. trumping a Nissan 370Z of today—this revised model offers civility. With the flick of a touchscreen button, the standard ADS [Adaptive Damping Suspension] Bilstein shock absorbers can transform the SRT8 ride quality from decently snubbed to a feel-every-crack taut. Its more potent 6.4-liter Hemi V-8 can switch between 4- and 8-cylinder operation, resulting in considerably better highway cruising fuel efficiency. Output, though, has been raised to an even 470 for both horsepower and torque. There's enough thrust here to challenge a Porsche Cayman S across an intersection with a 0–60 time of 4.5 sec. or gap it slightly at the drag strip with a 12.9-sec. run.

In May 2014, though, the same publication reported:

Get one while you can. The Chrysler 300 SRT is an endangered species, due to die in 2015, and there's not going to be a replacement. You see, in the new constellation of Fiat Chrysler Automobiles, Dodge wears the horsepower pants. Chrysler-branded SRT products are a casualty of the new world order.

The newly updated Charger was a great machine, but there's something about a luxury sedan, with 522 watts of Beats by Dr. Dre sound, that can go 175 miles per hour.

Ralph Gilles's team gave the 2012 300C SRT8 an updated look without losing the big sedan's appeal, and focused on bringing the interior up to world-class standards, as *R&T* discovered: "unlike its predecessor that sacrificed civility for bludgeoning performance—with 0–60-miles per hour times of just under 5 seconds and a quarter-mile time of 13.3 sec. trumping a Nissan 370Z of today—this revised model offers civility." *FCNA*

SRT: RIGHT-BRAIN THINKING

A luxury car with 470 horsepower and 470 lb-ft of torque? That was the 2013 Chrysler 300 SRT8. *Motor Trend* declared, "Nowadays, most performance cars—even sedans—draw attention to themselves with look-at-me spoilers, gaping hood scoops, and shouty exhaust notes. The 2013 Chrysler 300 SRT8 doesn't follow any of those conventions. This 470-horsepower sleeper is not only easily overlooked as a run-of-the-mill 300, but also packs performance that would embarrass quite a few modern sports cars." Sadly, 2013 would be the last year for the SRT8 in Chrysler 300 form. *Archives/TEN: The Enthusiast Network Magazines, LLC*

SRT Viper 2013–2014/Dodge Viper & Viper ACR 2015–Today

Some feared it would never happen. But, by 2010, Chrysler had a new owner, Fiat, and a new CEO, Sergio Marchionne. Marchionne's background is finance, but his love of automobiles matches his knowledge of business, and he made that very clear: on September 14, 2010, at a dealer conference in Orlando, Florida, Marchionne reportedly concluded his remarks to dealers by unveiling a 2012 Dodge Viper prototype. Gilles then announced in the fall of 2011 that the fifth-generation Viper would debut at the New York Auto Show in April 2012.

True to their word, the Viper returned, beginning as a 2013 model. But Viper was no longer a Dodge. SRT was spun off as a separate performance brand, much like Ram trucks were also spun from Dodge.

"Beyond being the flagship for the new SRT Brand, the launch of the 2013 Viper proves that we simply would not let the performance icon of the Chrysler Group die," Gilles said. "Willed to live on by a very special group of performance enthusiasts inside the company and across Viper Nation, this SRT team under our new leadership was challenged to not just continue the legendary Viper, but to create a world-class supercar that would showcase the very best we have to offer."

Despite rumors to the contrary, the chassis was a completely updated version of the original Viper's, lighter and more ridged than ever. The venerable V-10 returned, too, now packing a 640 horsepower punch, 40 more than in 2010. It also generates 600 lb-ft of torque, the most torque of any naturally aspirated engine in the world.

The latest Viper also had new skin. Made out of carbon fiber and aluminum, this time it had more of the voluptuous curves of the original. Though convertible prototypes have been spied, only the coupe has been offered so far.

But the real news was inside. The new Viper featured gorgeous leather seats made by Sabelt. These feature a lightweight Kevlar/fiberglass shell created by resin-transfer molding technology. Sabelt also makes seats for Ferrari, another company in the Fiat family. On the upscale GTS model, all interior surfaces are covered in handcrafted leather, and both the base Viper and the GTS feature Harman Kardon sound.

Car and Driver was the first to drive the new Viper, and they were impressed:

> Always during the process, the development team was looking to save weight, and they did—a startling 150 pounds, which is indeed noticeable as you stuff the 2010 model, then a 2013, into a tight corner on the track. That original, topless 1992 Viper with virtually no equipment weighed 3,272 lbs. This new one, with all the creature comforts and electronic safety features you'd ever want, starts at a svelte 3,297 pounds, for a base Viper with the SRT Track Package.

Another version was introduced in 2014, the Viper TA (Time Attack). Limited to just thirty-three units, this ultra-snake featured Pirelli P Zero Corsa tires, matte-black Sidewinder II wheels, and specially calibrated two-mode Bilstein Damptronic suspension. Under the hood, the aluminum structural X-brace was replaced by a lighter carbon-fiber brace. Only one color was available, Crusher Orange, along with a black interior with Crusher Orange stitching. And crush the competition it did. On March 18, 2013, *Motor Trend* tested the TA at Mazda Raceway Laguna Seca to see how it fared

TOP: When the Viper returned in 2013, Chrysler's head of design, Ralph Gilles, brought back many of the curves that graced the first-generation Viper. Underneath, the venerable V-10 now packed a 640-horsepower punch, 40 more than in 2010. It also generated 600 lb-ft of torque, the most torque of any naturally aspirated engine in the world. *Archives/TEN: The Enthusiast Network Magazines, LLC*

ABOVE, LEFT: No other supercar, with the possible exception of the Porsche 911, has advanced so far while retaining its original character. Handcrafted by sixty-four UAW artisans at the Connor Avenue plant, Viper is truly unique among the world's supercars. *FCNA*

ABOVE RIGHT: The Connor Avenue plant has been the home of the Viper since 1996. *FCNA*

RIGHT: The new Viper GTC model, with a starting price of $94,995, allowed customers to create their own one-of-a-kind Viper. "With 8,000 exterior color options, 24,000 custom stripe colors, 10 wheel options, 16 interior trims and 6 aero packages, there are more than 25 million ways for buyers to customize their one-of-a-kind Dodge Viper," said Chrysler. *FCNA*

LOWER RIGHT: Ralph Gilles had worked his way up from designing the 2003 Viper interior, to head of design, Fiat Chrysler Automobiles N.V.; before this promotion he was president and CEO—Motorsports, and President and CEO of the SRT Brand. Gilles joined Chrysler right out of Detroit's College for Creative Studies in 1992. He witnessed firsthand the dramatic boost the first Viper gave the company's image and products. Today he's the creative force behind all Fiat-Chrysler vehicles, and a Viper fanatic. *FCNA*

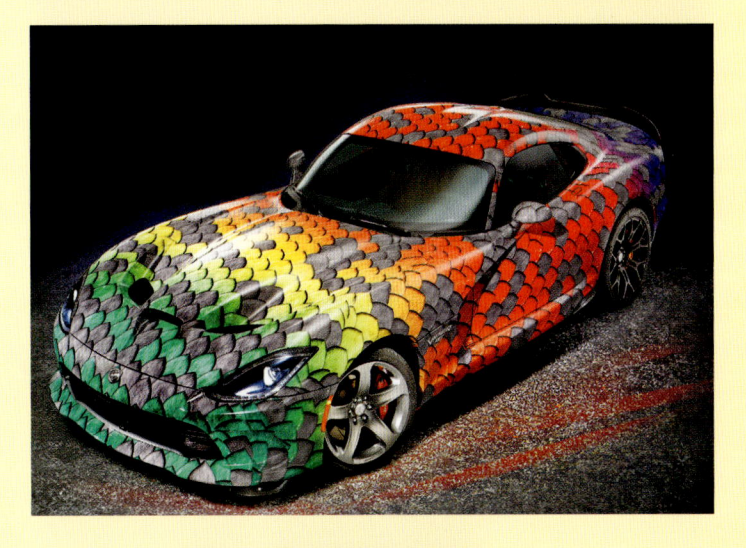

SRT: RIGHT-BRAIN THINKING

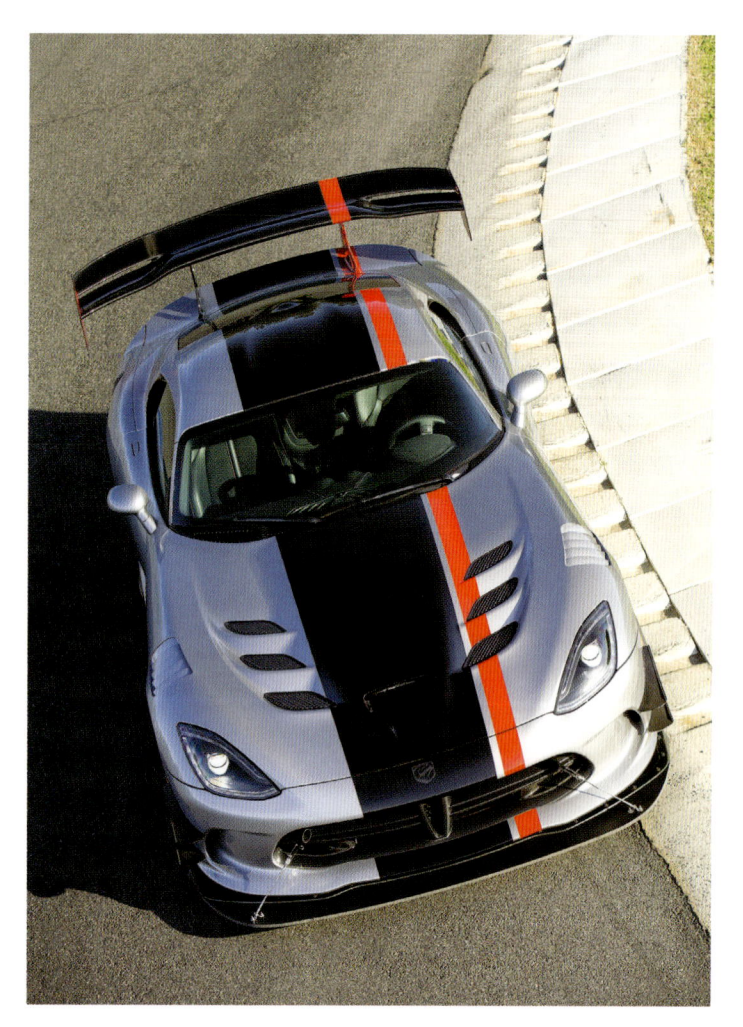

ABOVE, LEFT: "The ACR holds more track records than any other car," said Dodge boss Tim Kuniskis, "and it's been certified by the SCCA, which is how it should be." The ACR's records include a staggering 1.28.65 minute circuit of one of America's most famous tracks, Laguna Seca, in California. *FCNA*

ABOVE, RIGHT: The Viper ACR's subtle curves and prominent spoiler are more than enough to make racing fans go "schwing!" *FCNA*

against the 1:33.70 lap record held by the Chevrolet Corvette ZR1. The Viper TA turned a 1:33.62 lap using stock Corsa tires, then blasted a 1:30.78 time using slicks.

By 2015, the Viper was again a Dodge, with SRT becoming Dodge's high-performance brand. It featured an increase of 5 horsepower with a 1 mpg improved mileage rating. Dodge also lowered the pricing on the new Vipers by as much as $15,000 to stimulate sales. Other changes included a new Viper GT model, slotted between the base car and the loaded GTS. GT buyers got the two-mode, driver-adjustable suspension and five-mode electronic stability control system from the GTS, along with Nappa leather seats with Alcantara accents and contrast stitching. The Viper TA returned as the improved TA 2.0, with an updated aero package featuring a bigger rear wing, new front dive planes, and a new carbon-fiber front splitter. The TA 2.0 was limited to just ninety-six cars annually.

Finally, for 2016, the Nürburgring-beating Viper ACR returned. Upgrades included Brembo Carbon Ceramic Matrix 15-inch two-piece rotors and six-piston front calipers, and its unique track suspension features 10-setting, double-adjustable, Bilstein coil-over racing, which delivers up to 3 inches of suspension height adjustment, and massive Kumho Ecsta V720 high-performance tires (295/25/19 front, 355/30/19 rear), designed and developed specifically for the ACR, that Dodge claimed "delivers lap times that are 1.5 seconds faster than off-road-only race tires." As fast as the 2010 ACR was, the 2016 edition was certainly the fastest street-legal Viper track car ever.

SRT/Dodge Viper 2013–

 # PRODUCED: 2,427 (thru 2015)

ENGINE: 512-cubic-inch V-8

HORSEPOWER: 640

TORQUE: 600 lb-ft

¼-MILE TIME: 11.5 at 127.3 mph

Handling the Hellcat

Nick Kurczewski, writing in the July 22, 2014, issue of the *New York Daily News*, spoke for everyone who's driven one with the red key:

> If I didn't think I'd severely burn my lips, I'd kiss this howling Hemi engine right about now. I've just parked the "world's most powerful muscle car" alongside a row of tanker trucks, parked in a gritty industrial corner on the north side of Portland, Oregon.
>
> Despite being over 90 degrees outside, I've been driving with the windows down for the entire afternoon. You would too when the car you're piloting packs a whopping 707-horsepower, 650 lb-ft of torque, and the capability to scrape against the 200 mph top speed barrier.
>
> The way the Challenger bellows its way down public roads, or around the flowing curves of Portland International Raceway, is also pretty hair-raising. Imagine driving a high horsepower muscle car and, suddenly, someone presses the fast-forward button. In the Challenger Hellcat, that happens every time you roll your right foot into the gas pedal.
>
> Careful with that thing, good sir, because punching the gas will summon up nothing but smoky and static burnouts (not that those can't be loads of fun!). Get it right, and the five-link independent rear suspension hunkers down to slingshot the Hellcat down the road. A launch control system helps to master the ultimate 0–60 mph run—call me old-fashioned, but I prefer those messier, tire-burning trips down the drag strip.
>
> Surprisingly, I found myself enjoying the Hellcat more on public roads, where bursts of speed are taken in bite-sized morsels, versus the do-or-die, warp-speed-all-the-flipping-time feel of the car on the racetrack. You can't ease up and afford not to give the Hellcat anything but 100 percent of your attention on the track. It's so fast, I ended up turning on the ventilated seats to help keep my own cool.
>
> Dial things back and, believe it or not, the Hellcat is as docile as a sofa-loving tabby. The suspension is still very pliant over bumps and rough roads, and the hollow stabilizer bars (32 mm front, 18 mm rear) keep the Challenger nice and level.
>
> Now here comes the really good part and, possibly, the biggest surprise about the Hellcat. Over the past few months, many have speculated (including this guy) that Dodge's muscle car masterpiece car would ring in somewhere around $80 grand, or thereabouts. That would pit the Hellcat directly against the 505 horsepower Chevrolet Camaro Z28.
>
> Lo and behold, the Hellcat carries a starting price of $59,995 (excluding destination charge and gas guzzler tax). With those factored in, along with a smattering of options—like a power sunroof ($1,195) and Uconnect infotainment system ($695)—you can still easily keep the Hellcat below $65,000.
>
> Is it worth that kind of financial outlay? Hellcat yes, it is!

The fearsome Dodge Hellcat.

ABOVE: On July 11, 2014, Dodge dripped this press release bomb: "The new Challenger SRT Hellcat captured the title the 'FASTEST MUSCLE CAR EVER' with a National Hot Rod Association-certified quarter-mile elapsed time of 11.2 seconds at 125 miles per hour (miles per hour) with stock Pirelli P275/40ZR20 P Zero tires. With drag radials, the run dropped to just 10.8 seconds at 126 miles per hour." *FCNA*

RIGHT: Beware the red key. With great power came great responsibility and, for the first time in Dodge's hundred-year history, a car came with two keys. The black key only allowed 500 horsepower to be generated, while the red key unleashed the entire 707 horsepower Hellcat beast. *FCNA*

Perhaps the most significant offering beginning in 2015 was the "one-of-one" program. According to Tim Kuniskis, president and CEO, Dodge and SRT:

Because every Viper is handcrafted with such an extreme level of detail, we have the unique opportunity to make each one even more special by giving buyers the opportunity to customize each vehicle to their exact specifications. Now, Viper owners will be able to say their Viper is truly one of a kind."

Finally, Chrysler was leveraging the handcrafted nature of the Viper. The new Viper GTC model, with a starting price of $94,995, allowed customers to create their own one-of-a-kind Viper.

The press release declared:

With 8,000 exterior color options, 24,000 custom stripe colors, 10 wheel options, 16 interior trims, and 6 aero packages, there are more than 25 million ways for buyers to customize their one-of-a-kind Dodge Viper . . . . To help buyers confirm their color choice,

218 CHAPTER 14

Dodge will provide a complimentary Viper speed form replica so they can confirm their color selections before their Viper is built.

An online tool allows buyers to design their own Viper—or let the rest of us just dream a little. And exclusivity is one of the keys to the Viper's appeal. In 2014 alone, Chevrolet made over 40,000 Corvettes. Since 1992, around a total of 33,000 Vipers have been built. Now you can order one that's totally unique.

With 240 more horsepower than the original Viper RT/10, and the huge strides made in tire, suspension, and braking technology, Viper is alive and better than ever. Yet Viper retains the visceral appeal of the first prototype. No other supercar, with the possible exception of the Porsche 911, has advanced so far while retaining its original character. Handcrafted by sixty-four UAW artisans at the Connor Avenue plant, Viper is truly unique among the world's supercars.

Dodge Challenger SRT Hellcat 2015–Today

The terms "corporate officer" and "epic burnout" might seem to be polar opposites, like oil and water or fire and ice. But when the corporate officer is Ralph Gilles, the venue is the 2014 Mopar Nationals, and the car is the 2015 Dodge Challenger SRT Hellcat, well, the Pirellis were frying!

Gilles had worked his way up from designing the 2003 Viper interior, to head of design, Fiat Chrysler Automobiles N.V. Before this promotion he was president and CEO—Motorsports, and president and CEO of the SRT Brands. Gilles joined Chrysler right out of Detroit's College for Creative Studies in 1992, witnessing firsthand the dramatic boost that the first Viper gave the company's image and products. Now everything was coming together in

ABOVE: It's subtle, but the Hellcat spent 35 percent more time in the wind tunnel, which is why the aluminum hood featured a power bulge with a Viper-like cold-air intake. The hood also included dual air extractors to remove heat and cut air turbulence in the engine bay. The top of the front fascia came down lower over the headlights and grille, and a new splitter added downforce. *FCNA*

Dodge Challenger SRT Hellcat 2015-

 # PRODUCED: 7,168

ENGINE: 376-cubic-inch V-8

HORSEPOWER: 707

TORQUE: 650 lb-ft

¼-MILE TIME: 11.9 at 124 mph

another iconic supercar, the 707-horsepower SRT Hellcat—the most powerful production American automobile ever.

Those sound like fighting words, but on July 11, 2014, Dodge dripped this press release bomb:

> The new Challenger SRT Hellcat captured the title "FASTEST MUSCLE CAR EVER" with a National Hot Rod Association-certified quarter-mile elapsed time of 11.2 seconds at 125 mph with stock Pirelli P275/40ZR20 P Zero tires. With drag radials, the run dropped to just 10.8 seconds at 126 mph.

Like Ford's 2016 Shelby GT350 and Chevy's 2014–15 Z28 Camaro, the Challenger SRT Hellcat was a complete performance machine, with the kind of engineering no bolt-on tuner kit can provide. One look tells you something is different. It's subtle, but the Hellcat spent 35 percent more time in the wind tunnel, which is why the aluminum hood featured a power bulge with a Viper-like cold-air intake. The hood also included dual air extractors to remove heat and cut air turbulence in the engine bay. The top of the front fascia came down lower over the headlights and grille, and a new splitter added downforce. The fog lamps were relocated down low, and the Air Catcher inlet port rams air directly into the engine airbox through the driver-side parking lamp. Side sill molding and a larger rear spoiler completed the Hellcat's aero package. The changes are many, but they were necessary to create a legitimate 199 miles per hour street automobile.

With great power came great responsibility, and, for the first time in Dodge's one hundred-year history, a car came with two keys. The black key only allowed 500 horsepower to be generated, while the red key unleashed the entire 707-horsepower Hellcat beast.

Dodge Charger SRT Hellcat 2015–Today

> Due to unprecedented demand for the 2015 Dodge Charger and Challenger SRT Hellcats, we are temporarily restricting orders while we validate current orders that are in the system. Fiat Chrysler Automobiles has stopped taking orders for the Dodge Challenger and Charger SRT Hellcats so it can work through a lengthy backlog.

That's a good problem to have. Tim Kuniskis, president and CEO of the Dodge and SRT Brands, commented:

> For the last eight years, a large part of the Dodge Charger's successful formula has been its many personalities. It's a muscle car, a performance sedan, a family-capable sedan; its success is that it can be any or all of those things, depending on how the customer chooses to equip their car.

That is just what *Car Craft* discovered.

Is it a street car? Yes. To drill the point home, the press car had baby seats, leather, navigation goodies, a comfortable seating position, and a good sound system that didn't have to fight the exhaust note. In the default street mode, it's just like driving a nice sedan. Click it into Track mode, and you get abrupt 160-millisecond shifts. Near the redline, the interrupter creates a shotgun blast from the exhaust as you upshift, all the while the computers keep the car glued to the ground and going straight. Does it handle? With 275s on 20s all the way around, we couldn't push it far enough to over or understeer on the street, there simply wasn't enough room. We didn't care because for us, a Dodge like this is for the quarter mile . . . this car runs 11-flat on street tires, makes 707 horsepower and 650 lb-ft with factory longevity, has onboard drag electronics so you can text your fastest timeslip to your friends, has a intercooled supercharger, and on top of it all, can get you, your kid, and three of your friends to the dragstrip and back without your wife having any idea what is in the driveway. Unless you tell her, that is..

"We've sold 88,000 muscle cars [this calendar year], Challengers and Chargers, and 4,000 of those have been Hellcats," Kuniskis told *Automotive News*. "It's a small sliver of what we sell, but it really creates a halo for the rest of the lineup. For example, the next highest car, the Scat Pack Challenger, I have essentially a zero-day supply. It's sold out."

The same way the original Viper transformed the image of Chrysler in the 1990s, the Hellcat Challenger and Charger are renovating today's Fiat Chrysler North America. More than fifteen years after Bob Lutz retired from Chrysler for a stint at GM, his "right-brain" thinking is still ingrained in the company—and the muscle car world is a better place for it!

Dodge Charger SRT Hellcat 2015-

 # PRODUCED: 1,334

ENGINE: 376-cubic-inch V-8

HORSEPOWER: 707

TORQUE: 650 lb-ft

¼-MILE TIME: 11.4 at 128 mph

RIGHT: August 13, 2014—The day Tim Kuniskis, president and CEO, Dodge and SRT brands, unveiled the 2015 Dodge Charger SRT Hellcat. The Charger's supercharged 6.2 liter HEMI Hellcat engine produces 707 horsepower and delivers unrivaled four-door performance with a quarter mile elapsed time of 11.0 seconds on production tires and a top speed of 204 miles per hour. *FCNA*

BELOW: August 13, 2014—Mark Rudisueli, head of SRT Engineering, unveiled the 2015 Dodge Charger SRT Hellcat today. The Charger's supercharged 6.2-liter HEMI Hellcat engine produces 707 horsepower and delivers unrivaled four-door performance with a quarter mile elapsed time of 11.0 seconds on production tires. Hellcat is the most powerful V-8 engine Chrysler has ever produced. *FCNA*

Conclusion

From Royal Bobcat to SRT Hellcat, it's been a wild ride! No question, the 1960s were great. The late 1980s and 1990s were pretty special, too. But today? We can pick up a car capable of 500 to 750 horsepower or more. Cornering at 1 g. Top speeds over 200 mph with the brakes to stop it. Air conditioning, leather, sound systems, and 30 mpg.

Carly Simon had it right: "These are the good old days!"

Index

A. C. Cars Ltd., 73, 74, 82, 83, 90
A. O. Smith Inland, 85
Ace, 73
ACS/McLaren, 141
Adams, Herb, 19
Addison, Jimmy, 18
AeroWagon, Callaway, 135
Alfa Romeo GTV6, 124, 125
Allard, Sidney, 73
Allard J2, 73
Allegheny International, 107
Allen, Tim, 114, 117–118
AMC, 101–104, 106–107
American Club Racer (ACR), 202
American Le Mans Series, 201, 202
American Rogue, 102, 103
AMX, 102
Arning, Klaus, 82
Aston Martin, 73
Astro, 141
ATCO Dragway, 53
Atlantic Road Racing Championship, 124
Austin Healey 3000, 79
Avanti, 42

B&M Automotive, 107
Baker, Buck, 98
Baldick, Rick, 160
Baldwin Motion, 46–57
Baldwin Motion Phase III, 50–51
Ballish, Brian, 19
Barracuda, 83, 98
　　AAR 'Cuda, 42
　　'Cuda Super Stock, 40
　　GSS King 'Cuda, 45
Barrett-Jackson, 57
BASF, 116, 118
Bean, Dave, 48
Beitzel, Jeff, 137, 138, 139, 140, 143
Bel Air, 39
Belair, Keith, 95
Belle Isle racetrack, 197
Beltz, John, 99, 100, 101
Bennion, Kirk, 195–196
Berger, Matt, 65
Berger, R. Dale, Jr., 65
Berger, William, 65
Berger Chevrolet, 31, 65
Bernhard, Wolfgang, 205
Beswick, Arnie "The Farmer," 16
Bimbi, Stefano, 66
Biscayne, 48, 61
Blackbird, 18–19
Blocker, Dan, 60
BMW 320i, 124
Bob Bondurant's School of High Performance Driving, 124
Bob Tasca Ford, 64–65
Bondurant, Bob, 76–77

Boser, Jerry, 144–145
Boser, Tom, 156
Brabham, Jack, 79
Bravada, 143
Brock, Peter, 74, 77, 81
Brown, Burke, 206, 207
Bucher, Jim, 65
Busby, Jim, 124

Cadillac, 73
Callaway, Reeves, 122–135
Callaway Cars, 122–135
Camaro, 48–49, 57, 58–59, 65, 83, 120–121
　　Baldwin Motion Phase III, 8–9, 52, 53, 54
　　C8, 131
　　Callaway, 133–134
　　Callaway SuperNatural, 129
　　Callaway Z28 SC652, 134
　　Nickey 427, 61–62
　　Nickey 454, 66
　　RS, 159
　　SS, 151, 153–155, 160–161, 170, 197
　　Super, 28
　　Turbo Z, 35
　　Yenko, 29–31, 33
　　Yenko Super, 26–29
　　Z28, 32, 35, 64, 167, 182, 184–185, 192–194
　　ZL1, 189, 191–192
Campbell, Bill, 96
Campbell, Sir Malcolm, 78
Campisano, Jim, 147
Can-Am racing, 64
Cannon, John, 60
Carpenter, Susan, 134
Carr, Joe, 111
Carroll Shelby Engine Company, 90
Carrozzeria Gransport, 77
Carrozzeria Scaglietti, 73
Cartwright, Hoss, 60
Castiglone, Michael, 210
Catalina
　　Hardtop Coupe, 12
　　Royal Bobcat, 12–16
　　Super Duty, 10–11, 12, 98
Cerberus Capital Management, 208, 211
Challenger, 120–121, 145, 146
　　Hellcat, 217, 218
　　SRT Hellcat, 219–220, 221
　　SRT-8, 210–211
　　T/A, 42
Chaparral Can-Am, 138
Charger
　　Shelby, 89
　　SRT Hellcat, 220–221
　　SRT-8, 208–210, 211–212
Cheetah, 61
Chessnoe, Chris, 134
Chevelle, 22–23, 48, 49, 62, 101
　　Nickey 427, 62–63

　　Yenko, 32, 33
　　Z16, 60
Chevrolet, 184–197
Chevrolet, Louis, 186, 194
Chevy II, 34
Chevy SS, 191
Chicago Auto Show, 141, 167
Chrysler, 89–90, 98, 102, 198–221
　　300C SRT-8, 206–207, 212–214
Chrysler Shelby Performance Center (CSPC), 89
Cicale, Tony, 127
Circuit de Reims-Gueux, 76
Clean Air Act (1970), 56
Cobra, 25
　　Daytona Coupe, 76–77
　　"Dragonsnake" Shelby, 31
　　Shelby, 31, 61, 72, 74–77, 82–83, 90
　　SVT, 166–167, 169–170, 172–173
Coddington, Boyd, 200
Coe, Dave, 25
Coletti, John, 119, 173
Collins, Bill, 12, 19
Collins, Jim, 16
Commando, Super, 40
Conway, Joe, 94
Coronel, Tom, 211
Coronet, 32, 42
　　Hemi, 18
Corvair, 16, 25, 26, 61
　　Corsa Sport Coupe, 25
　　Monza, 124
Corvette, 24, 25, 28, 32, 42, 46–47, 48, 49, 51, 57, 58, 60, 61, 62, 64, 67, 73, 78, 81, 219
　　427, 190
　　Baldwin Motion Phase III GT, 50, 51, 53
　　C5 Z06, 186–188
　　C6 Z06, 188–190
　　C6 ZR1, 190
　　C7 Z06, 194–197
　　Callaway, 134–135
　　Callaway C7, 128–129
　　Callaway C12, 130
　　Callaway C16, 131–132
　　Callaway Speedster, 127–128
　　Callaway Supercharged, 132–133
　　Callaway SuperNatural, 128
　　Callaway Twin-Turbo, 122, 124–128
　　FIA GT3 Z06.R, 130–131
　　LT1, 32, 34
　　Mako Shark, 48–49, 53, 55
　　Motion Can-Am Spyder, 56–57
　　Motion Manta Ray, 55
　　SS-427, 48
　　Z06, 74, 82
　　ZR1, 127, 216
Cramer, Payton, 64, 82, 85
Craw, Nick, 124
CS-1 concept car, 91
Csere, Csaba, 140

222

Cuthbert, Kevin, 151
Cutlass, 98, 101, 104, 106
Cypress Gardens Corvette Show, 128

Daimler-Benz, 206
DaimlerChrysler, 204–206
Dana Chevrolet, 31, 64
D'Antonio, Tom, 90
Dart, 40–41, 101
    Hemi, 40
Davis, David E., 17
Daytona 500, 14, 16, 39
Daytona American Challenge, 60
Daytona Continental, 77
De Soto, 39
Dean, Adam, 194
    DeLorean, John Zachary, 11, 12, 16, 17, 20, 21, 98–99, 119
DeLorenzo, Tony, 25
Demmer Tool and Die, 100, 101, 102, 103, 104, 105, 106
Demon, 36–37, 42–45
Denison, Jeff, 150
Dent, Larry, 149
Dernoshek, Warren, 28
Detroit Auto Show, 201
Detroit Dragway, 12
Deuce, Yenko, 32, 34
Deuce Nova, Yenko, 42, 107
Deutschman, Paul, 125, 126, 127, 128–129, 135
Dick Harrell Speed Shop, 26, 27, 28
DiScipio, Vinnie, 122–135
Dombroski, Paul, 64
Donohue, Mark, 25, 193
Duntov, Zora, 32, 51, 138
Duster, 42, 145, 146

Earnhardt, Dale, 147
Earnhardt, Dale, Jr., 130
Ehrenpreis, Joel, 57
Eighty Eight, 101
Estes, Elliot M. "Pete," 12, 100
Explorer, 121

F85, 124
F-150, 121
    SVT Raptor, 179–181
Feher, Akos J., 94
Fernandez, John, 203
Ferrara, Dennis, 51, 53
Ferrari, 17, 73, 76–77, 142, 176, 195
    Enzo, 119
    FF, 135
Fiat, 214
Fiat Chrysler Automobiles N.V., 215
Firebird, 18–19, 83, 98–99, 106, 139
    Comp T/A, 149–150, 153
    Firehawk, 147–149, 152–153, 156–159
    WS-6, 144–145, 149–152, 158, 170
Fittipaldi, Emerson, 122
Focus, 121
Force, John, 147
Ford, Bill, 175
Ford, Edsel, II, 178
Ford, Henry, II, 79, 175, 176
Ford SVO/SVJ, 164–183
Formula Atlantic open wheel series, 109
Formula Vee, 122
426 Hemi, 39
Fox, Herb, 64
Foyt, A. J., 60, 177
Frank, Phil, 112–114, 116, 117
Fred Gibb Chevrolet, 64
Freeman, Thomas, 206, 207
Frey, Donald, 74

G8, 191
Gaffka, Doug, 179
Gale, Tom, 199–200, 202, 208
Garrad, Ian, 79
Gee, Russ, 12, 16, 19
Gibb, Fred, 64, 191, 192
Gibb, Helen, 64, 65
Gilles, Ralph, 204, 206, 211, 213, 214, 215, 219–220
Glory Days (Wangers), 12, 20
GNX, 140
Goldsmith, Paul, 25
Good, Tim, 126

Goodwood Revival, 77
Granatelli, Andy, 82
Granatelli, Joe, 82
Granatelli brothers, 42, 44
Grand National, 57
Grand Prix
    Hurst SSJ, 96–97, 107
    Royal Bobcat, 15, 16
Grant, Jerry, 25
Greater Los Angeles Auto Show, 127
Greenwald, Larry, 106
Greenwood, John, 56–57
GT, 174–175, 176–177
    "Heritage," 177
    Mark II, 176
    Mark IV, 176
GT40, 138, 176
GTO, 16–17, 20–21, 42, 62, 98, 106
    Royal Bobcat, 17, 20–21
    Royal Bobcat Judge, 21
GTX, Saleen, 121
Guldstrand, Dick, 64
Gurney, Dan, 120, 177

Haga, Henry, 53
Hale Products, 107
Hall, Jim, 73, 138, 143
Hamburger, Dave, 161
Hamburger, Ed, 144–161
Hameedi, Jamal, 179, 181
Hancock Park Associates, 120
Harrell, Dick, 26, 28, 29, 60–61, 62, 64
Hayner, Stu, 148
Haywood, Hurley, 148
Hedrick, Ed, 30, 31
Helbig, Herb, 201–202
Hendrick Motorsports 25th Anniversary Camaro, 133
Hertz Sports Car Club, 82, 85, 87
Hill, David, 186, 187, 188–189, 190
Hirschbeck, Denny, 40, 41
Hobbs, David, 124
Holden Commodore VE, 191
Holman & Moody, 12
Hoover, Tom, 11, 18–19
Howard, Benny, 77
Hugus Ed, 73
Huntington, Roger, 14, 16
Hurst, George, 20, 96–107
Hurst GSS Supercat Hellcat, 45
Hurst Performance, 20, 40, 96–107
Hurst-Campbell, 96, 98
Hurst/Olds, 98–101, 104–106
Hutton, Paul, 101

Iacocca, Lee, 79, 89, 200, 201
Impala, 49
    Callaway SS, 129–130
IMSA Bridgestone Potenza Supercar Championship, 148
IMSA series, 56
Indianapolis 500, 79, 138, 139, 140, 170, 176, 193, 202
IROC Camaro, 57

Jaguar, 70, 81
Javelin, 102
Jaworske, Larry, 57
Jaws of Life, 107
Jeffords, Jim, 60
Jenkins, Bill "Grumpy," 51, 55
Johnson, Tony, 115, 119
Jones, Parnelli, 112, 120
Juechter, Tadge, 186, 190, 194, 196

Kamm, Wunibald, 76
Kaplan, David, 125–126
Kaplan, Ronnie, 60
Kar Kraft, 138
Keebler, Jack, 150
Kelly, Scott, 138, 139, 140, 141, 142, 143
Kim, Calvin, 133–134
Knieper, Tony, 19
Knudsen, Semon "Bunkie," 12, 98
Kosak Dodge, 45
Koss, John, 141
Kranefuss, Michael, 166
Kraus, Harvey, 39
Kraus, Len, 39
Kraus, Norm, 36–45

Kuniskis, Tim, 216, 218, 220–221
Kupfer, Gary, 49, 51, 55, 57
Kurczewski, Nick, 217

Laguna Seca, 216
Lamborghini Gallardo Superleggera, 190
Lancer, Shelby, 90
Landreth, Dave, 102
LaSalle, Dan, 151
Latimer, Kay, 126
Laughlin, Gary, 73
LaViolette, Vince, 94
Lawton, Bill, 65
Lee, Sangyup, 191
Liberman, "Jungle Jim," 65
Lightning, SVT, 167–168, 170–171
Lincoln, 73
Lindemann, Bud, 101
Lingenfelter, John, 125, 126–127
Link, Aaron, 189
Lord, Jack, 35
Los Angeles International Auto Show, 80
Lotus, 176
Lucas, Ted, 100
Luft, John, 70
Luikens, Jim, 65
Lutz, Bob, 102, 199–201, 202, 211, 221

Magnum SRT-8, 207–208
Mahler, John, 25, 48
March, Lord, 77
Marchionne, Sergio, 214
Marion, Doug, 60
Markus, Frank, 90
Maserati, 70–71, 73, 84
Mattison, Jim, 149–150
Mattola, Tommy, 130
Maxwell, Terry "Zeke," 148, 151, 156, 161
Mayflower Vehicle Systems, 177
Mays, J., 177
Mazda Raceway Laguna Seca, 216
McClellan, Dave, 124, 125
McConnell, Wayne, 192
McCurry, Bob, 40
McDuffie, J. D., 65
McGonegal, Ro, 32
McHose, Chuck, 83, 116, 117
McKeller, Malcolm "Mac," 12
McLaren Automotive, 211
Mead Motors, 61
Mears, Rick, 122, 124
Mecum, Dana, 77
Mercedes-Benz, 26
    E55, 207–208
Mercury Cougar, 83
Mero, Jim, 190
Miles, Ken, 72, 77, 79, 83, 84
Milford Proving Grounds, 16, 189
Mims, Donna Mae, 25
Mini, 79
Mitchell, Bill, 51
MJ Acquisitions, 120, 121
Monte Carlo, 57
Monte Carlo Rally, 79
Monterey Historic Races, 118
Moon, Dean, 73
Mopar Nationals, 219
Morgan, Dave, 25
Motion Performance, 47, 48–49
Mountain, Chuck, 136–137, 138, 143
Mr. Norm's Grand Spaulding Dodge, 36–45, 65, 101
Mulsanne Straight, 76
Muscaro, Dave, 189
Mustang, 40, 65
    Black Label, 110, 121
    Boss 302, 117, 120
    Boss 429, 138
    GT, 164–165, 166
    GT350, 25, 42, 68–69
    Saleen, 110, 111, 115–118, 120
    Saleen RRR, 114, 117–118
    Shelby, 42, 51, 178
    Shelby 1000, 93–94
    Shelby Ecoboost GT, 165
    Shelby GT350, 79–82, 83–89, 181–183
    Shelby GT350R, 109, 169, 182, 183
    Shelby GT500, 83–89, 177–179, 182
    Shelby GT500 Super Snake, 92–93

INDEX   223

Shelby GT500KR, 179
Shelby GT-H, 90–91
Shelby GTS, 93
SN-95, 169
Super Cobra Jet, 65
SVO, 164–165, 166
SVT Cobra-R, 167

Nader, Ralph, 20, 26
Nair, Raj, 174, 183
Nassau Trophy Race, 60
National Advisory Committee for Aeronautics (NACA), 87, 154
National Hot Rod Association (NHRA), 12
Nell, Tom, 19
Neon SRT-4, 198–199, 202–203
New England Dragway, 53
New Smyrna Beach Airport, 24, 25
New York Auto Show, 90, 94, 214
New York International Auto Show, 50, 51
New York Rod and Custom Show, 57
NHRA Division One Super Stock Eliminator Championship, 31
NHRA Manufacturer's Championship, 31
NHRA National Open, 53
NHRA Pro Stock, 55
NHRA Super Stock racing, 145, 146
NHRA Winternationals, 14, 16
NHRA World Championships, 106
Nichols, Ray, 12
Nickey Chevrolet, 51, 58–67
Nickey Performance, 66
North American International Auto Show, 174, 182, 188, 191, 199, 201
Nova, 34, 48, 49, 64
    Nickey 454, 62, 66
    Yenko, 32, 35
Nürburgring, 185–186, 187, 189, 190, 211

Oldsmobile, 98–101
Omni GLH, 89
Oppenheiser, Al, 192, 194
Owen, Bill, 138

Pagani Zonda C12 S, 190
Palitz, Louis, 106
Palm, Gregg, 140
Panch, Martin, 25
Pardo, Camilo, 174–175, 176
PAS, Inc. (Production Automotive Services, Inc.), 136–143
Patterson, Gary, 93, 179, 182
Paxton Products, 82
Penske, Roger, 124, 193
Pericak, Dave, 181
Perry, Chris, 191
Peters, Tom, 189, 191, 195
Petersen, Donald, 166
Petty, Lee, 98
Phase III GT, 46–47
Pickett, William, 106
Piggins, Vince, 25, 26, 31, 191
Pocobello, Mike, 136–137, 138, 143
Politzer, John "Cheater," 19
Porsche
    356, 109
    911 GT3 RS, 190
Portland International Raceway, 217
Posey, Sam, 124
Press, Jim, 211
Proffitt, Hayden, 14
Prototype Automotive Services, 136–137
"Purple People Eater," 60

Rager, Greg, 25, 33, 35
Rallye 250, 107
Ram SRT-10, 204–206
Ranger, 121
Raptor/Baja, Shelby, 94
Rebel Machine, 106–107
Rediker, Frank, 12
Redline Motorsports, 57
Remington, Phil, 77, 79
Ressler, Neil, 166, 176
Reuss, Lloyd, 138
Reuss, Mark, 194
Reventlow, Lance, 60
Rewey, Robert L., 166

Ricardo Consulting Engineers, 176, 211
Rivera, Paula, 91
Riverside Raceway, 74, 77, 79
Road Runner, 42, 106
Roadrunner, Hemi, 32
Roberts, Glenn "Fireball," 14
Robinson, Aaron, 159
Roe, Doug, 28
Rolex 24 Hours of Daytona, 129
Rootes Group, 78–79
Rosen, Joel, 46–51, 53, 55, 56
Roush, 176, 200
Royal Pontiac, 11–21
Rudisueli, Mark, 221
Rutherford, Dick, 25

Saleen, Steve, 108–121
Saleen Automotive, 108–121
    S7, 112–113, 114, 118–120
    S281, 116, 118
    S302, 121
    S320H Parnelli Jones editions, 112–113, 114
    S351, 114, 118
    SSC, 108–109, 115
Salvadori, Roy, 73
Scalzo, Joe, 87
Scarab, 60
Scarpello, Tom, 171
SCCA racing, 60, 79, 81, 84, 192, 216
    Drivers' Championship, 118
    Escort Showroom Stock Endurance Series, 111, 115
    Manufacturers' Championship, 118
    World Challenge series, 115, 117
Schiavone, Patrick, 169
Schiffer, Eric, 19
Schlesser, Jo, 76–77
Schornack, Milt, 19, 20
Schorr, Marty, 48, 49, 51, 55–56
Schrempp, Jürgen, 206
Schridde, Charles, 141
Schroeder, Don, 142
SC/Rambler, 101–104
Seaman, Walt, 91
Sears Point Raceway, 110, 111
Sebring 12 Hours of Endurance, 25
Sebring International Raceway, 178
Seelig, Al, 60, 66
SEMA, 57, 133, 178
Sessions, Ron, 202
Shane, Bob, 82
Sharp, Hap, 25
Sheikh Khalid, 135
Shelby, Carroll Hall, 25, 32, 42, 64, 70–95, 175, 177, 178, 179, 182, 200, 202
Shelby American, 70–95
Shelby Automobiles, Inc., 90
Shelby Continuation Daytona Coupe, 95
Shelby Daytona, 89, 91
Shelby Series I, 90
Sherman, Don, 124
Shields, Mike, 120
Shikado, Osamu, 203–204
Shinoda, Larry, 53
Silva, John, 48, 53
Silverado, 134
Simonin, August "Gus," 48
Simonin, Ed, 48
Sledgehammer, 125, 126–127
Smith, Carroll, 127
Smith, Dale, 100
Smith, Kevin, 166
SMS Supercars, 120–121
Sonoma, 141
Sonoma GT, 142
Spehar, Ted, 18
Sports Car Club of America (SCCA), 25, 79
SportTruck, Callaway, 134
Stacey, Pete, 83, 116, 117
Stempel, Bob, 100, 101
Stepani, Edward, 58
Stepani, Jack, 58, 60
Stewart, Jackie, 185
Stewart, Lance, 148
Stickles, Don, 25
Sting Ray, 53, 82
Stinger
    Yenko, 25, 28
    Yenko II, 35

Stingray, 196
Stone, Matt, 160–161
Street-Legal Performance, 144–161
Stroppe, Bill, 12
Studebaker, 42
Suburban, 134
Sullivan, John, 151
Sunbeam Alpine, 78–79
Sunbeam Electric Corporation, 106–107
Sunbeam Tiger, 78–79
Super-Z, 35
Svensson, Chris, 182
Swiatek, Don, 60, 66

T & G Enterprises, 149
Tahoe, 134
Tanner, Howard, 57
Tasca, Bob, 64–65
Teague, Dick, 11
Tempest, 16
Tempest Le Mans, 16
Thomas, Bill, 61, 62
Thompson, Jerry, 25
Thompson, Mickey, 14, 16, 82
Thunderbird, 85
    "Battlebird," 25
"Tirebird," 149–150
Trans Am, 147
    Pontiac 20th Anniversary Turbo, 136–137, 138–140
Trans Am series, 120, 185, 192–193
Triad Services, 136–137
12 Hours of Reims, 76
12 Hours of Sebring, 73, 119
24 Hours of Daytona, 25, 149, 187
24 Hours of Le Mans, 73, 128, 129, 130, 174–175, 176, 177, 187, 201, 202
Typhoon, 143

Unsafe at Any Speed (Nader), 26

Van Den Doorn, Jean-Pierre, 75
Vanderbilt Cup, 186, 194
Vega, 35
    Motion Super, 55–56
    Turbo, 35
Venture Corporation, 90
Villeneuve, Jacques, 109
Vinegroon, 60
Viper, 90
    ACR, 214–216, 218–219
    GT, 216
    GTC, 215, 218
    GTS, 199–202
    RT/10, 199–202
    SRT, 214–216, 218–219, 221
    SRT-10, 203–204
    SRT-10 ACR, 211

Wagoner, Rick, 190
Wangers, Jim, 12, 14, 16, 17, 20, 21, 96–97, 98–99, 102
Warner, Stewart, 28, 30
Watson, Jack "Doc," 98, 99, 101
Wawee, Mike, 65
WCS Grand Finale, 53
Welfringer, Lynn, 101
Wildcat Concept, 136–137
Wilder, Jim, 210
Wilkins, Ed, 70
Williams, Bruce, 181
Willow Springs Raceway, 84, 212
Wilson, Asa "Ace," Jr., 12, 20
Woehr, Ernst, 130
World Manufacturer's Championship, 76–77, 95
Wyer, John, 73
Wyss, Wallace, 77

Yenko, Don, 22–34, 42, 51, 107
Yenko, Frank, 24, 25
Yenko Chevrolet, 22–35
Yenko Sports Cars, 25
Young, Bruce, 61
Yunick, Smokey, 12, 14

Zazarrine, Paul, 33
Zweidler, Stephan, 202

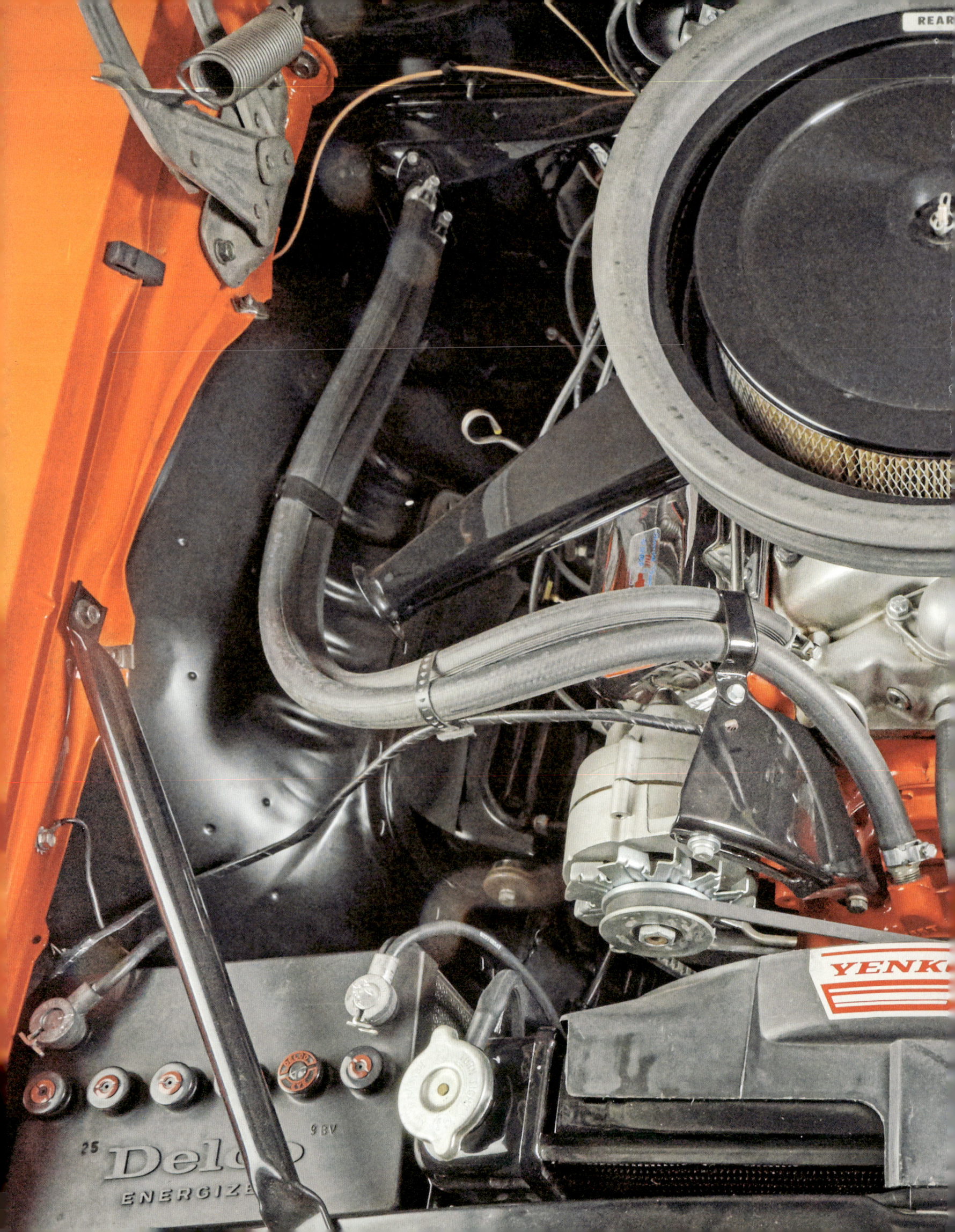